*South Africa and the Logic of
Regional Cooperation*

South Africa and the Logic of Regional Cooperation

James J. Hentz

INDIANA UNIVERSITY PRESS

BLOOMINGTON AND INDIANAPOLIS

This book is a publication of

Indiana University Press
601 North Morton Street
Bloomington, IN 47404-3797 USA
http://iupress.indiana.edu

Telephone orders   800-842-6796
Fax orders   812-855-7931
Orders by e-mail   iuporder@indiana.edu

© 2005 by James J. Hentz

MANUFACTURED IN THE UNITED STATES OF AMERICA

Library of Congress Cataloging-in-Publication Data

Hentz, James J.
South Africa and the logic of regional cooperation / James J. Hentz.
p. cm.
Includes bibliographical references and index.
ISBN 0-253-34464-6 (cloth : alk. paper) — ISBN 0-253-21721-0 (pbk. : alk. paper)
1. South Africa—Foreign relations—1994– 2. South Africa—Foreign relations—1989–
1994. 3. South Africa—Foreign economic relations. 4. South Africa—Economic
conditions—1991– 5. Regionalism—Africa, Southern. 6. Africa, Southern—Economic
integration. 7. African cooperation. I. Title.
DT1971.H46 2005
337.1′6—dc22   2004028794

1 2 3 4 5   10 09 08 07 06 05

To Michele, Julia, and Kate

Contents

Contents

Acknowledgments

The strengths of this book reflect the influence of many scholars and friends; the weaknesses are my own. My debts begin with my graduate studies at the University of Pennsylvania. Two of my professors had the greatest impact on my thinking, Thomas Callaghy and Fritz Kratochwil. Their standards of scholarship continue to be my marker. Two friends from graduate school provided invaluable critiques of the early part of my work, Devin Hagerty and Rey Koslowski. Penn provided a research grant for my first extensive field research in South Africa, where I was a visitor at Rand Afrikaans University (RAU). My debts to RAU are too numerous to list, but two stand out. Professor Piet Liebenberg was my official host. We met while he was a visiting fellow at the Foreign Policy Research Institute in Philadelphia. Although there is a wide philosophical divide between us, Piet indefatigably supported my research while I was in South Africa. The second debt goes to my roommate while living in Yoeville (Johannesburg), Ned Breslin. He had lectured at Witswatersrand University, and when I left he was director of Operation Hunger. I learned a lot about South Africa from him. The writing, and continuing research, was supported by many institutions and scholars. While I was a visiting assistant professor at Dartmouth College, Nelson Kasfir was an informal mentor. The bulk of this manuscript was written while an assistant professor at the Virginia Military Institute (VMI). VMI has funded numerous research trips to Africa and to conferences around the world where I presented my research. Indiana University Press was the good shepherd of this book. In particular I would like to thank Dee Mortensen and Richard Higgins for their support. A special thanks goes to Kate Babbitt, my editor. We did not always agree on specifics, but the book is a much better read due to her labors.

Jan Vansina concluded *Paths in the Rainforests: Toward a History of Political Tradition in Equatorial Africa* by saying, "But then scholarship is a collective endeavor and the goal after all is the central issue of a whole discipline." My final debt of gratitude goes to the family of Africanists around the world who share the same goal, but particularly to those living in South Africa. From the former group, the scholars of Research Council #40 of the International Political Science Association stand out, particularly Morten Bøås, Kevin Dunn, Sandra Mclean, Tim Shaw, Fred Söderbaum, and Ian Taylor. They have helped me understand regionalism and Africa. South African scholars have always been very welcoming and indulgent of an outsider claiming to have something to say about their country. I hope I have added a little to our collective understanding of Africa.

I dedicate this book to my wife, Michele, and daughters, Julia and Kate, who always expect me to bring a little bit of Africa home with me and who never leave my thoughts when I'm away.

Abbreviations

ABSA   Amalgamated Banks of South Africa
ACP   Africa, Caribbean, Pacific countries
AHI   Die Afrikaans Handelsinstituut
ANC   African National Congress
BLS   Botswana, Lesotho, Swaziland
BLSN   Botswana, Lesotho, Swaziland, Namibia
BTI   Board of Trade and Industry
CBI   Cross-Border Initiative
CIC   Cabinet Investment Cluster
CTCA   Commission for Technical Cooperation in Africa South of the Sahara
CODESA   Convention for a Democratic South Africa
COMESA   Common Market for Eastern and Southern Africa
CONSAS   Constellation of Southern African States
COSAB   Council of Southern African Bankers
COSATU   Congress of South African Trade Unions
CSA   Commission for Scientific Cooperation in Africa South of the Sahara
DBSA   Development Bank of Southern Africa
DTI   Department of Trade and Industry
EAC   East Africa Community
ECA   Economic Commission for Africa
ECSC   European Coal and Steel Community
EEC   European Economic Community
EMS   Export Marketing Scheme
EOI   export-oriented industrialization
EU   European Union
FEDSAL   Federation of South African Labor Unions
FOB   free on board
FTA   free trade area
GATT   General Agreement on Tariffs and Trade
GEAR   Growth, Employment and Redistribution
GEIS   General Export Incentive Scheme
GSP   generalized system of preferences
HCTs   High Commission Territories
IDC   Industrial Development Corporation
IFIs   international financial institutions
IMF   International Monetary Fund
IPF   Industrial Policy Forum
ISCOR   Iron and Steel Corporation
ISI   import substitution industrialization
ISP   Industrial Strategy Project
LDCs   less-developed countries

LHWP	Lesotho Highlands Water Project
LLDCs	least-developed countries
MDC	Maputo Development Corridor
MERG	Macroeconomic Research Group
MFN	most-favored-nation
MK	Umkhonto weSizwe (Sword of the Nation)
MMA	Multilateral Monetary Agreement
NACTU	National Council of Trade Unions
NAFCOC	National African Chamber of Commerce
NEDLAC	National Economic Development and Labour Council
NEF	National Economic Forum
NEM	Normative Economic Model
NSMS	National Security Management System
NP	National Party
OAU	Organization of African Unity
OECD	Organization for Economic Cooperation and Development
OSDICC	Overall SDI Coordinating Committee
PAC	Pan Africanist Congress
PTA	Preferential Trade Area
QRs	quantitative restrictions
RDP	Reconstruction and Development Programme
RENAMO	Resistëncia Nacional Moçambicana
SACOB	South Africa Chamber of Business
SACP	South African Communist Party
SACU	Southern African Customs Union
SADC	Southern African Development Community
SADCC	Southern African Development Coordination Conference
SAFTO	South African Foreign Trade Organisation
SAIIA	South African Institute for International Affairs
SAIRR	South African Institute of Race Relations
SANNC	South African Native National Council
SAPs	structural adjustment programs
SAPP	South Africa Power Pool
SASOL	South Africa Coal, Oil and Gas Corporation
SATUCC	Southern African Trade Union Co-ordination Council
SDIs	spatial developmental initiatives
SWAPO	South West Africa Peoples Organization
TEC	Transitional Executive Council
TPRM	Trade Policy Review Mechanism
UDF	United Democratic Front
ZANU	Zimbabwe African Nationalist Union
ZAPU	Zimbabwe African People's Union

South Africa and the Logic of
Regional Cooperation

Map of Southern Africa.

1

Introduction:
Defining the Future—South Africa's
Foreign Economic Policy and Regional
Cooperation in Southern Africa

Nelson Mandela was freed from Robben Island Prison by F. W. de Klerk on February 11, 1990, after twenty-seven years of incarceration. Nine days prior to his release, all opposition groups, including the African National Congress (ANC), were unbanned. Apartheid was in full retreat, and South Africa entered a transition period that led to full democratic freedom four years later. South Africa's emergence from the dark ages of apartheid signaled more than a new purpose for its people; it represented a new hope for the entire subcontinent of Southern Africa. What role post-apartheid South Africa would play in the region was anxiously anticipated and debated within the region by leading world powers, international institutions such as the International Monetary Fund (IMF) and the World Bank, and, most important, within South Africa.

Two things were certain. First, South Africa was the dominant regional economy: its GDP in 1990 was nearly four times that of the rest of the region, its trade was about three times the rest of the region's total, and it purchased 7 percent of the products of the region and produced 30 percent of the goods the region imported.[1] Its neighbors were dependent on South

Africa's transportation infrastructure for their own exports, and the country accounted for about 90 percent of the electricity generated in the region.[2] South Africa's economy was far more sophisticated and diverse than even the relatively economically advanced Zimbabwe, although it was still dependent on the mineral sector. The future of the region would depend on choices made in the new South Africa. The second certainty was that there would indeed be a new South Africa to play a new regional role. The decade prior to South Africa's transition was the worst for the post-independence countries of Southern Africa. Apartheid South Africa shoulders some of the blame. South Africa's rearguard action against anti-apartheid forces that camped in neighboring countries cost the region approximately 60.5 billion dollars and an estimated 1.5 million lives between 1980 and 1988.[3] Apartheid South Africa's economic penetration of the region and military forays were fueled by the militarization of its society.[4]

With the end of the Cold War, the period of destabilization came to a close and the ANC and other opposition groups that had lived in South Africa's neighboring countries had an apparent debt of gratitude to pay to their erstwhile hosts.[5] From the perspective of the ruling National Party (NP), the end of the Cold War also meant they would no longer be able to play the anticommunist card to defend their aggressive regional policies. And as the ANC gathered political power in South Africa, first informally and, after the 1994 election, formally as the governing party, it would remember the sacrifices that neighboring countries made for its cause. As one leading South African scholar who was active in the policy debates stated, "[I]rrespective of the political orientation of a future South African government, all aspects of regional interaction are bound to undergo far-reaching change."[6]

It was less certain exactly how the new South Africa would formally recast its regional relations. The United States and the international financial institutions (the IMF and World Bank) took a rather Pollyannaish view. In Bill Clinton's words, "South Africa can be a beacon of economic development and prosperity for all southern Africa."[7] South Africa's neighbors were more wary, concerned that Pretoria would become the new *bambazonke,* or "grab-all." They worried that, freed from the restraints imposed by international sanctions, South Africa as the regional superpower would get only richer as the rest of the subcontinent got poorer. This concern was particularly strong regarding the distinct possibility that South Africa would attract most of the foreign investment to the region. A 1994 headline in South Africa's *The Star* represented the concerns of South Africa's neighbors: "'Big Brother' [Is] Causing Angst."[8] The reality this book chronicles proves to lie somewhere between the optimism of the international community and the pessimism of some of South Africa's neighboring countries.

South Africa's regional economic relations have been recast, albeit with powerful residues of its past. Its current leadership openly, even pleadingly, ties its future to the economic development and stability of the entire subcontinent of Southern Africa. It does so, however, while walking a tightrope between the political demands of a newly enfranchised majority and the demands of an entrenched economic elite. It must somehow meet the rising expectations of the once disenfranchised and dispossessed in a country that is still struggling to balance the scales of economic wealth and economic opportunity. And it must do so in a radically different international environment. These demands delimit and define what South Africa can do for the region. Thus, as post-apartheid South Africa works to define a new image and purpose for itself, it is committed to cooperating with its neighbors.

For ideological reasons and to protect labor-intensive industry in South Africa, the new ANC government would attempt to promote South African development within a framework that would also help its neighbors. However, as this book reveals, the dynamics of South Africa's political economy, and in particular the enduring power of the business sector, pushed the new ANC government in a different direction. The new ANC government that came to power with the election of Nelson Mandela in April 1994, in fact, had to balance the demands of those who had been disenfranchised by apartheid with the demands of a powerful economic elite who had been enriched by apartheid. The new Mandela government, as well, would also have to contend with powerful international influences. The new government steered a middle course between the demands of those who lost under apartheid and those who had been the winners.

This book examines transitional South Africa's debate over the future of economic cooperation in post-apartheid Southern Africa. Transitional South Africa is defined as the years between F. W. de Klerk's unbanning of the ANC in 1990 and the second post-apartheid South African election on June 2, 1999. The transition has two distinct periods: from 1990 until 1996 and after 1996. The break between these two periods is the adoption of the new ANC economic plan under President Mandela and Vice President Thabo Mbeki in 1996 called Growth, Employment and Redistribution (GEAR) that at the very least represented the ANC government's political balancing act—how to represent the interest of disparate segments of South Africa's political economy.

As South Africa realized that the days of apartheid were coming to an end and that the opportunity to recast regional relations in a more positive manner was possible, how would it organize its regional relations? In fact, there were different ways to do this—what were the choices? Finally, who in South Africa, with support from outside players such as the international financial institutions (IFIs), the European Union (EU), and GATT (General Agreement on Tariffs and Trade—World Trade Organization), supported which of those choices? The question that South Africa faced at the cusp of the post–Cold War era and its rejection of apartheid was not whether or not it should or should not now cooperate with its neighbors but what would be the fundamental architectural design of a new framework of cooperation among the states of Southern Africa.

Cooperation among States

Historic conjunctures are opportune moments to examine institutional change.[9] As it began to shed its past as an international pariah, South Africa hotly debated the future of regional economic cooperation in Southern Africa. But the potential of cooperation or, more accurately, of *how* to cooperate, in Africa has been limited by its consideration within the international relations literature on cooperation among states, which typically wants to know why states do or do not cooperate.[10] The history of failed regional economic integration schemes in Sub-Saharan Africa, in fact, attests to the inadequacy of international relations theory.[11] For instance, much of international relations theory dealing with economic integration theory builds on the experience of Europe. Thus, schemes in Africa such as the Economic Community of West African States and the East Africa Community (EAC) adopted a blueprint from a very different place and time, and, like other such schemes in Sub-Saharan Africa, they failed.

Steve Weber cautions that "[t]he question about the origins of institutions comprises not only why they happen but also why one institution and not another comes into being when an excess of alternatives exists."[12] But these theories are more interested in *why* rather than *how* states cooperate.[13] We are interested in the how, and this means a short theoretical digression on the logic of regional economic integration.

This book argues that South Africa was not debating whether or not to cooperate with its neighbors. The different constituencies that make up the South African polity had already decided that regional economic integration/cooperation would be an integral part of its foreign policy. The question was how South Africa would formally reintegrate into the region. Within South Africa, three approaches to regional economic integration were debated: developmental regional economic integration/cooperation, market regional economic integration/cooperation, and ad hoc economic cooperation. These three approaches to formalizing regional economic integration/cooperation also represented tighter or looser ties to South Africa's neighbors. Developmental regional economic integration envisioned post-apartheid South Africa as closely tied to its neighbors through a web of cooperative endeavors across multiple areas, such as water, electricity, trade, and production, anchored by a strong regional organization such as the Southern African Development Community. At the other end of the spectrum, ad hoc economic cooperation envisioned South Africa cooperating with its neighbors via a series of bilateral deals with almost no institutional anchor.

Developmental regional economic integration promotes greater regional interdependence and argues that for regional economic integration to work it must first and foremost focus on equitable regional development. In the Southern African context, this means that South Africa cannot be allowed to develop ahead of its poorer neighbors. Interdependence, which simply means that national economies are dependent on one another for economic development, is one way to promote regional equality. The other way is through a central role of the state—almost dirigisme at the regional level. This would entail, for instance, making sure that industries and investment are fairly distributed among the members of the regional economic integration scheme. In short, developmental regional economic integration is very much a state-led process. There are very few examples of this approach in Africa, largely because of past reliance on the European experience to model regional economic integration in Sub-Saharan Africa. Nonetheless, as will be discussed below, the Southern African Development Coordination Conference (SADCC) came closest to the developmental model of regional economic integration.

Regional economic market integration/cooperation also promotes regional interdependence but does so by progressively removing the barriers to economic activity among states in the region. This typically starts by reducing barriers to intraregional trade such as tariffs, but later can include dismantling barriers to other factors of production, such as the movement of people. In its later stages it will usually allow for the free flow of capital and possibly, as in the case of Europe, a single uniting currency. The important difference between the developmental approach and the market approach to regional economic integration is that in the latter case the market drives the process. Rather than the states, the market is the engine for closer economic integration in the region. The Southern African Customs Union (SACU) is a good example of this approach in Sub-Saharan Africa.

Ad hoc regional economic cooperation is the least formalized of the three approaches. This approach relies heavily on bilateral agreements between states within a region. This has often been labeled *project* or *functional cooperation.* Here two states may agree to promote a project, such as a new road or railway connecting the two states, a way to produce and share energy or water resources, or even co-development of a specific industrial project. It is considered ad hoc because it is not part of a larger plan to induce regional interdependence or even part of a regional scheme. Nonetheless, it is a form of regional economic integration/cooperation, and by connecting countries, albeit in an ad hoc manner, it does create a more integrated region. Apartheid South Africa's approach to the region, often called the hub-and-spoke approach, is an example of ad hoc cooperation. The idea of a Constellation of Southern African States (CONSAS), as discussed below, was meant to promote this approach.

Each of these three models was promoted during the transition period in South Africa and each by a different constituency. Regional developmental cooperation/integration was the stated plan of the ANC. It had strong support from labor, particularly the Congress of South African Trade Unions (COSATU) and from Afrikaner small business. Essentially, labor-intensive industries and small businesses needed an active state to export their products to the region (or protect them from regional competition). Left to market forces alone, regional economic integration would most likely do more harm than good to the economic welfare of these sectors. Regional market integration/cooperation was favored by the old Afrikaner bureaucracy that ran SACU. To some extent, it was also supported by South African business interests that had done so well under SACU. Ad hoc cooperation was favored by South Africa's conglomerates. Largely for ideological reasons, but also because they did not need much institutional support to protect and promote their interests in a region they already dominated, they did not want to encourage regional interdependence (mutual dependence). This sector is dominated by South Africa's capital-intensive industries, usually with ties to large South African financial institutions. A bilateral deal with weaker neighbors would not only promote their economic interests but would also promise continuing regional dominance for their industries.

Neofunctionalism

Neofunctionalism explains the process of regional economic integration by movement along a linear path from a customs union to an economic union and argues that development is propelled by demands inherent in the relationship between the desire to cooperate and the original institutional arrangement in pursuit of that goal. In a customs union, intragroup trade faces no common barriers and members maintain a common external tariff on trade with nonmembers. SACU is an example. An economic union goes beyond merely removing barriers and allows, as well, for the free movement of capital, labor, and all goods and services. It entails the harmonization of almost all economic activity between or among the partners. The EU is the best example. The EU has progressively removed economic barriers among its members and now pushes for a "convergence" in macroeconomic policies, such as inflation rates and levels of government debt. Under GATT (and now World Trade Organization) rules, this is essentially considered both legal and orthodox. However, as will be related below, such a process does not work among developing states because it exacerbates economic inequality between the rich and the poor—South Africa and its neighbors. This is particularly true when one state, such as South Africa, is far more economically advanced than the rest in the region. Andrew Hurrell notes that the early theorists of European integration were obsessed by a particular end goal.[14] That is, the original plan to cooperate pushes the participants to deepen and broaden their cooperation. This has been used to explain how Europe progressed from the European Coal and Steel Community (ECSC) under the Shuman plan to a European Economic Community to the European Union. An analysis of domestic politics is missing; neofunctionalism, because it is embedded in the literature on European regional economic integration, focused on state elites and international (regional) organizations. There was little exploration of who would benefit, or why, within the participating states.

The linear process described in neofunctionalism's explanation of economic integration in Western Europe was difficult to replicate in Africa. When they achieved independence, African states inherited underdeveloped, poorly articulated economies and rising populist expectations. African economies had two dominant characteristics, both of which were predicated on the state's role as the source of patronage resources: African states had short political time horizons and they emphasized import/export sources of revenue.[15] (African leaders are under pressure to deliver goods and services to their constituency in a very short time and to fund their programs through collecting import and export taxes.) Revenues from indirect taxes, primarily import and export taxes, coincided with the interests of elite in Africa because they used these resources to fund their patron-client networks.[16] African political systems were typically built on personal relationships between rulers and ruled. The tie that bound these two groups together was the flow of money and services (patronage) by the ruler to the ruled. Therefore, the elite did not stand to benefit from regional economic integration based on a linear model because that strategy would immediately reduce the flow of indirect taxes, thereby reducing patronage resources. In addition, the cost in terms of the losses in customs revenue would occur before the potential benefits of such a move would be realized.[17] Since by definition, a customs union reduces the amount a state collects in indirect taxes, it reduces the revenue available (patronage resources) for building and supporting patron-client networks. As Rod Falvey and Cha Dong Kim state:

> Trade liberalization [the progressive elimination of barriers to interstate trade, such as tariffs and quotas], which ultimately will involve deep cuts in both import and export taxes, can be expected to have a negative impact on a government budget that is already unbalanced. Restructuring the tax system to give it a broader base will take time, and government revenue will need to be maintained in the interim.[18]

Finally, in general, the state was at the center of the industrialization process in Africa, and therefore, as a World Bank study argued, trade liberalization in Africa would be inhibited because it would accelerate the necessary, but politically difficult, restructuring of a large number of nonviable businesses, the bulk of which are in the public sector.[19] In the case of South and Southern Africa, South Africa's powerful conglomerates would be competitive while its neighbors would have a more difficult time. The history of SACU, discussed below, demonstrates this point.

Developmental Integration/Cooperation

Developmental integration/cooperation addresses the apparent weaknesses in market integration theory (movement along a linear path from a cus-

toms union to an economic union), which ignores the market failures endemic to customs unions and common markets. There was a tendency for
industry to cluster in the more developed areas of the region. Thus, for
example, South African business dominated the SACU market. The most
advanced of the developing countries benefited disproportionately from
participation in an integration scheme based on the market approach.[20]
Also, customs unions, one of the stops on the way to an economic union,
retarded the economic development of the less economically advanced
partners. Developmental integration is more concerned with promoting
industrialization and economic development than with market efficiencies.
It also rejects the basic antistatist premise of neoliberal orthodoxy, which
argues for a much smaller role for the state in the national economy.[21]
James Mittelman states:

> Not only does [developmental integration] assign priority to the coordi-
> nation of production and the improvement of infrastructure, but it also
> calls for a higher degree of state intervention than does the market
> model, as well as redistributive measures such as transfer taxes or com-
> pensatory schemes administered by regional funds or specialized banks.
> Trade integration is to be accompanied by attempts to promote coordi-
> nated regional industrial development.[22]

In practice, regional economic integration/cooperation in the developing world, no matter what form it takes, is a response to the perceived
inequities of the international economic order. Because developing countries believe that they cannot compete on equal terms with industrially
developed nations, they form regional economic integration schemes (of
various types) that they hope will improve their position in the global
economy. But while developmental integration outlines how to overcome
the inequalities endemic to market integration/cooperation, it cannot explain how, or why, such Pareto optimality—that is, the best that can be
achieved without causing damage to any social group—can be obtained.
For instance, the Organization of African Unity's 1980 Lagos Plan of Action[23] to encourage regional economic integration argued that the economic malaise ravishing Africa was:

> a legacy of integration into the world economic system on unequal
> terms, colonial exploitation, and the structure of the international sys-
> tem which ensured continuing unequal terms of exchange with the in-
> dustrialized world.[24]

But, as John Ravenhill states: "The predominance of crude dependency and world systems approaches in the study of Africa's international economic relations has led to the international system being accorded an over-deterministic role at the expense of internal factors."[25] To understand regional economic integration/cooperation in Sub-Saharan Africa, one must understand that it is largely a response to what is perceived as a hostile international economic order. But the devil is in the details, and domestic politics and institutions provide those details.

While there is a growing appreciation for the importance of understanding how preferences are formed, there is still a tendency to frame the problem of cooperation among states as a choice between cooperation and noncooperation.[26] That is, cooperation theory may explain why institutions are important, but does not explain how cooperation is institutionalized or why particular institutional arrangements evolve. Like its neofunctionalist and dependency antecedents, cooperation theory largely ignores the domestic dimension of cooperation among states. It is important to link international cooperation to state preferences, but it is also important to understand that states have preferences concerning both whether or not to cooperate and how to cooperate. Preference formation in transitional South Africa for how to institutionalize regional cooperation was based on a structure of relations grounded in regional interdependence, how countries are dependent on each other.[27] These regional interdependencies are shaped by how domestic political dynamics interact with international subsystems, such as the World Trade Organization, within an international political economy.

Interdependence and Cooperation: South and Southern Africa in the Post-Apartheid Era

As apartheid approached the end of its almost 50-year run, old ways and new ways for how to structure regional economic relations were debated. As economist Tony Hawkins stated: "The issue has become not whether the region should integrate economically but the logistics—who, how and when."[28] The "how" was debated inside and outside South Africa. During South Africa's transition, the three existing patterns of institutional cooperation in Southern Africa were regional developmental cooperation/integration, regional market cooperation/integration, and regional ad hoc cooperation. Each of these was reflected in existing organizations (in the case of ad hoc cooperation, the organization was theoretical).[29] They are, respectively, the SADCC, SACU, and an organization for Southern African cooperation. Each will be discussed below.

The debate in transitional South Africa over regional economic integration/cooperation centered on a disagreement over which of the three above patterns should provide the guiding principles for regional economic relations. But in practice the lines are not so clearly drawn. The different types are not necessarily mutually exclusive,[30] and the classification of the different approaches and the theories associated with those approaches are not always clear. For instance, the metamorphosis of the Southern African Development Coordination Conference into the Southern African Development Community (SADC) has been described in different ways. The original SADCC pursued developmental cooperation through project coordination and sectoral cooperation.[31] The new SADC, at least in the beginning, embraced a laissez-faire process but still supported a strategy (model) based on "developmental cooperation."[32] Thus, the new SADC has been labeled "developmental" and "market" regional integration.

The challenge is to understand that the process of cooperation among states can be institutionalized in different ways and that institutions can be expected to serve particular interests. The typology I use is based on how cooperation is institutionalized and what interests it will serve. Simply put, interests (and by interests I mean who inside the country, in this case study South Africa, benefits most by the choices the states makes among the three models that were debated: regional economic developmental integration/cooperation, regional economic market integration/ cooperation, ad hoc regionalism) will promote processes that allow them to thrive, often, if not always, at the expense of competing interests.

The two main regional institutions ostensibly promoting regional cooperation/integration in Southern Africa during the transitional period were the Southern African Customs Union, originally formed in 1910 and renegotiated in 1969, and the Southern African Development Community, originally created as the Southern African Development Coordination Conference in 1980 and changed to the Southern African Development Community in 1992.[33] Alongside these two organizations there was a third path—informal ad hoc cooperation. Each of these three approaches to cooperation adhered to distinct architectural principles for the institutionalization of regional economic relations in post-apartheid Southern Africa and each promoted particular interests within South Africa.

SACU includes the BLSN states (*Botswana, Lesotho, Swaziland,* and *Namibia*) and South Africa.[34] It is primarily concerned with trade and possible monetary cooperation and represents market cooperation/integration where "the integrating force of the market is released through the removal of restrictions and barriers to regional trade, rather than through positive government interventions."[35] This process favors the deepening of cooperation by stages from a common market to an economic union. Thus, SACU was based on the classic process of market cooperation by which cooperation/integration proceeds along a linear path with four stops: a free trade area, a customs union, a common market, and finally an economic union. SACU also has a built-in compensation mechanism to account for the effects a customs union can have on its less developed members. In the case of SACU, South Africa compensated for the fact that it gathered more economic gains due to the SACU arrangement than its partners by distributing a disproportionate amount of SACU tax revenues to Botswana, Lesotho, and Swaziland (and later Namibia). The renegotiation of SACU in 1969 was actually done to adjust revenue-sharing among SACU members to be even more in favor of South Africa's partners.[36]

But SACU could not fully mitigate the negative effects of polarization and trade diversion typically engendered by market integration. Polarization is when the most advanced state attracts most of the investment and continues to develop exponentially faster than its partners; trade diversion is when the less developed countries pay higher prices for goods they import from the dominant regional economy, which can hide behind regional tariff walls. South Africa's SACU partners suffered from both. The compensation mechanism built into SACU to redress the growing advantages it gave to South Africa was augmented in 1976 to account for the lack of industrialization in the BLS states.[37] (The BLS states refer to Botswana, Lesotho, and Swaziland. The term changed to the BLSN states when Namibia joined SACU.) Nonetheless, these countries reportedly lost between $20 and $30 million per year in revenue because of their participation in SACU.[38] The Southern African states had been importing overpriced South African goods and paying for them with hard currency.[39] In 1992 alone, South Africa's trade surplus with the SACU countries was 8 billion rand, accounting for more than 40 percent of its total manufactured exports.[40] South Africa had trade-diverting gains and the BLS states had trade-diverting costs.[41] That is to say, South Africa's neighbors imported products from there that it once imported from outside the region and therefore South Africa increased its exports, but at a cost to its neighbors who paid more for those imports. In fact, the SACU compensation mechanism was primarily political, and within South Africa there was active resistance to BLSN industrial development, particularly during apartheid but to some extent afterward as well.[42] There is no clear evidence that the compensation funds have had any positive effect on economic diversification and development in Southern Africa.[43]

SACU is complemented by the Common Monetary Area. All SACU members except Botswana are members.[44] The Common Monetary Area works under the Multilateral Monetary Agreement (MMA) of 1992 that brought Namibia into the agreement.[45] It follows the linear model of regional integration because monetary integration is one of the defining elements of an economic union.[46]

The SADC counts all ten regional states as members: Botswana, Lesotho, Malawi, Mozambique, Namibia, Swaziland, Tanzania, Zambia, Zimbabwe, and, as of 1994, South Africa.[47] The SADC's immediate precursor, the Southern African Development Coordination Conference, was the Front-Line States' response to P. W. Botha's Total National Strategy, which included his call for a Constellation of Southern African States.[48] By expanding the common market (SACU), CONSAS would have tied South Africa's neighbors tightly to itself as the subcontinent's hub of transportation and trade. When South Africa's neighbors rejected CONSAS, forming the SADCC instead, Pretoria undertook to destabilize the region, which included military forays as far north as Zambia. The SADCC was reconstituted as the SADC in 1990 in anticipation of apartheid's demise and South Africa's future membership.

The SADCC's members had had previous experiences with the inequalities of market cooperation: the BLSN states with SACU; Malawi, Zambia, and Zimbabwe with the Central African Federation; and Tanzania with the East African Community (Kenya, Tanzania, and Uganda). The SADCC, therefore, originally rejected the market model.[49] Instead, cooperation under SADCC would include a wide range of issue areas beyond trade, including production and transportation, and would build on the interdependencies among its members. It would be predicated on multilateral negotiations in "baskets" of issues that would facilitate trade-offs in such areas as trade, labor mobility, industrialization, and water and energy.[50] Each of these areas was characterized by strong regional interdependencies. This approach comes under the general rubric of developmental cooperation and was expected to ameliorate the natural inequities that accompany market integration. In James Mittelman's words:

The *developmental integration* model was introduced as an alternative to a one-sided emphasis on efficiency maximization of existing capacity—not surprising, in the context of a low level of productive capacity.[51]

Developmental regional economic integration/cooperation would not merely rely on a state's comparative advantage, what it could most profitably trade, but, given the limited economic development (capacity) of these states, this approach seeks to develop a stronger, more diversified economy, then focus on trade. It would also call for a strong role for the state. In Balefi Tsie's words:

> The pre-occupation with cutting, squeezing and downsizing the state is incompatible with the broad fundamental assumptions of the strategy of development integration. In its broader meaning . . . developmental integration requires strong state intervention.[52]

In fact, as Fred Söderbaum notes, the debate over developmental regionalism overlaps with the classical debate on the role of the state in economic development.[53] One prominent approach to addressing the natural inequalities of market cooperation through strong state management is to encourage multisectoral linkages such as linking agreements in trade to agreements in energy or transportation; this is the approach the SADC adopted.[54]

Ad hoc cooperation refers to bilateral cooperation via trade or infrastructure projects (in the case of South Africa's transition, ad hoc cooperation is sometimes called *functional cooperation*). Andrew Hurrell characterizes it this way: "Regional cooperation may involve the creation of formal institutions, but it can often be based on a much looser structure, involving patterns of regular meetings with some rules attached."[55] Ad hoc cooperation resembles apartheid South Africa's drive for CONSAS.[56] Dr. Simba Makoni, the former executive secretary of the SADCC, argued that there were people in South Africa who still favored a constellation of Southern African states with South Africa at the center,[57] and Carol Thompson notes that the idea of CONSAS "continues to re-emerge under new guises."[58] A "South African Briefing Paper" produced by the South African Consulate General in New York in 1990, at the cusp of the transition, emphasized bilateral cooperation, one way to promote ad hoc regionalism. Even in the early years of the transition, the apartheid elite were trying to shape a post-apartheid policy for the region that would protect their interests. The examples it used to describe increasing regional cooperation in Southern Africa were South Africa's Veterinary Research Institute at Onderstepoort, rail transport, Cahora Bassa Dam (Mozambique), the Lesotho Highlands Water Project (LHWP), Maputo Harbor, and the Sua Pan Soda Ash Project in Botswana.[59] The idea of a new CONSAS was dubbed a neo-apartheid policy by anti-apartheid groups because it would use a series of bilateral agreements to reinforce the status quo in Southern Africa[60] and strengthen the hub-and-spoke configuration of the subcontinent.

To understand preference formation in transitional South Africa, we must ask, What are the driving forces of the regionalization process?[61] As Michael Schulz, Fredrik Söderbaum, and Joakim Ojendal posit:

> To a large extent regionalism can be seen as a *political phenomenon,* shaped by political actors (state and non-state) that may use regionalism for a variety of not necessarily compatible purposes . . . what kind of actors [are] driving the project, with what means, and for what purposes.[62]

South Africa's Regional Relations: A "Bottom-Up" Approach

The debate in transitional South Africa was precisely over how to cooperate. Recognizing that domestic politics defines the parameters of the possible cooperative arrangements in Southern Africa is the first step toward expanding and complementing cooperation theory.[63] According to Andrew Moravcsik's formulation of a "positive liberal international relations theory," "[L]iberal theory rests on a 'bottom-up' view of politics in which the demand of individuals and societal groups are treated as analytically prior to politics."[64] Moravcsik also delineates three main variants of liberal theory linking social preferences to state behavior—ideational, commercial, and republican.[65] Finally, Moravcsik argues that liberal theory is strongest when combining its three variants.[66]

This book is organized around these three variants of liberal theory. I argue that to understand the debate in transitional South Africa over how to institutionalize its regional economic relations, we must understand the interaction of ideology and material factors that are embedded in economic interdependence and how they are filtered through the state. This does not, however, complete the story of preference formation in transitional South Africa.

Global systems of international relations and regional arenas or subsystems are interpenetrated.[67] Events and choices made at the local level, say inside South Africa, are influenced by events and choices made outside the state. For instance, decisions made by the IFIs both constrain and shape decisions made in South Africa. On the other hand, since states are a constituent element of the international system, decisions made by states affect how the international system operates. Andrew Axline argued that in the case of the Third World, "[T]he trade and investment policies of [industrial nations] play a large role in defining the alternative to regional integration and the cost of participation of the member governments."[68] Obviously, large developing states such as South Africa have more choices than smaller states; this was certainly the case in transitional South Africa. Richard Higgott posited that "the existing vertical linkages with Europe are likely to prove, in the short run at least, more significant for the pursuit of export oriented industrialization . . . in Africa's semi-industrialized states than its horizontal linkages with regional neighbors."[69] An interesting historical illustration of this point is the trade agreement South Africa signed with Germany in 1929 that led to a revision of the South Africa–Southern Rhodesian tariff agreement. South Africa was willing to manipulate regional relations in the pursuit of ties to the North that would advance its industrialization.[70] Transitional South Africa faced similar choices, but they were embedded in domestic political struggles.

The problem of trade diversion discussed above that informs much of the debate on the benefits of regional economic integration in the developing world also assumes linkages between system and subsystem. Trade diversion, a negative by-product of regional economic integration, occurs if participants in a customs union are at different levels of development and/or have different levels of trade with external powers. The result is that relative gains benefit the more advanced state. It is an irony that the problem of relative gains, which developmental integration was meant to correct, occurs within an integrating region precisely because these economies have such extensive ties to trading partners outside the region.[71]

While politics begins at home, important international opportunities and constraints affect the ideological and material dimensions of economic foreign policy in South Africa. To demonstrate this, I adopt an "open polity approach," which is to say that the political system is open to or influenced by specific interests, such as labor or business, and that this influence can come from the outside or the inside.[72] The international political economy, through its ideological and material influences, impacts domestic competition (both commercial and ideological) among powerful actors within South Africa who seek to influence government policy. That is, the international political economy aids or supports specific domestic interests in South Africa. It has also subtly influenced the development of the post-apartheid South African state. International factors are integral to ideological, commercial, and republican explanations of South Africa's preferences concerning regional cooperation.

This book does not focus on intergovernmental bargaining among the states of Southern Africa. As Björn Hettne posits, regional politics must be understood as "an aggregation of and 'concertation' of national interests."[73] This book focuses on how and why power brokers in transitional South Africa decided which form of regional economic cooperation to pursue. I deal with the antecedent conditions for South Africa's formal reintegration into the region and not with the subsequent bargaining among Southern African states.

The structure of the book is diachronic. Chapter 2 presents a historical sketch of apartheid South Africa's regional relations. It serves three purposes: it places post-apartheid South Africa's regional foreign policy in historical context; it introduces the prevailing themes threading their way through the apartheid and post-apartheid eras and connects the two time periods; and it describes the importance of an analytical framework that includes both domestic determinants of regional relations and the impact of international influences. Chapter 3 outlines the preferences of social groups in transitional South Africa for how to institutionalize cooperation in post-apartheid Southern Africa. Chapters 4 through 6 describe and explain transitional South Africa's preferences for the underlying architectural principles of regional economic cooperation in post-apartheid Southern Africa. These chapters combine two variants of liberal theory, ideational and commercial. The ideological explanation, Chapter 4, comes first, because it was the basis for subsequent policy debates. The next two chapters examine the commercial bases of group preferences for the institutionalization of regional economic cooperation in post-apartheid Southern Africa. They examine, respectively, the development of South Africa's industrial/trade policy and the development of its macroeconomic/finance policy. Although they are separate chapters, industrial and finance capital are typically closely linked in developing countries, and in South Africa the ties were particularly strong.[74] Both chapters take a bottom-up approach by focusing on domestic determinants of transitional South Africa's regional economic policy. Chapter 7 then examines ideological and commercial influences on preference formation in transitional South Africa as they were filtered through and influenced by international institutions, specifically GATT, the EU, and the IFIs.

Chapter 8 examines how preferences at the societal level are aggregated at the state level; that is, different elements of society, labor versus business, for example, push for their preferred policies. But what the state decides as these interests are vetted through the institutions of the state, with their own preferences, will not likely exactly resemble any one set of preferences. It is a "republican" explanation. This chapter covers the period immediately after the April 1994 election up to the second election campaign in 1999. The form of the new South African state and South Africa's regional foreign policy, while hardly set in stone, had taken shape by the end of this period. The concluding chapter looks at post-apartheid South Africa's regional foreign policy. Although the political processes this book traces had hardly reached a conclusion, South Africa's regional relations, and the institutionalization and political implications of those relations, had taken a discernible turn.

These chapters are organized in the order in which ideational, economic, and republican influences created the mosaic of South Africa's evolving regional relations. As analytical categories, ideational, commercial, and republican explanations of policy choices are, furthermore, an abstraction. For instance, the ideological debate over South Africa's domestic economic policy and the debate over its trade policy overlapped. Nonetheless, the ideological debate preceded and foreshadowed subsequent policy debates. And the South African state was shaped within the crucible of these policy debates.

Michael Bratton and Nicolas van de Walle define a regime transition as a "shift from one set of political procedures to another, from an old pattern or rule to a new one."[75] But more important for the analysis in this book, "[I]t is an interval of intense political uncertainty during which the shape of the new institutional dispensation is up for grabs by incumbent and opposition contenders."[76] This was the state of transitional South Africa as it tried to carve out a new regional role.

2

Setting the Stage:
South and Southern Africa, 1948–1989

In order to understand a state, one must understand its history.[1] The post-apartheid South African government, while emphatically rejecting apartheid, has found use for the centralized state that it inherited, and its post-apartheid regional relations contain residues of its past. South Africa's policies regarding regional relations both have included domestic imperatives, including those of state-building and internal pressure from social groups, and relate to and are refined by international pressure. For example, F. W. de Klerk has admitted that the decision to unban the liberation movement was the result of a combination of national and extranational conditions.[2]

Although the National Party (NP) came to power in South Africa in 1948 by reaching an electoral pact with the Afrikaner Party, the 1953 election marked the birth of the modern South African state that the NP would dominate until 1990. In those thirty-five years, the NP built a strong state. South Africa became the dominant power in Southern Africa, even as it became a pariah in the international community.[3]

The apartheid era can be divided into roughly five periods. Although such constructs are always artificial, these periods mark important watersheds in South African history. For each period, I examine the interplay of domestic, regional, and international forces at work. The first period,

1948–1958, includes the administrations of D. F. Malan (1948–1954) and Johannes Strijdom (1954–1958). The second period tracks the premiership of Hendrik Verwoerd (1958–1966), and the third period tracks the reign of Prime Minister John Vorster (1966–1978). The fourth period begins with P. K. Botha as prime minister and ends with his resignation as state president in 1989. The subsequent rise of F. W. de Klerk marks apartheid's denouement and the first act in South Africa's transition.

The events that constitute this periodization of apartheid South Africa's regional relations foreshadow four major themes of post-apartheid South Africa's regional relations. First, although South Africa's regional relations changed from period to period, the country always had a strong interest in its neighbors. The 1909 South Africa Act, which created the modern South African state by joining two British self-governing colonies (Natal and the Cape Colony) with two defeated Boer republics (Free State and the Transvaal), included a clause that envisioned that Bechuanaland (Botswana), Basutoland (Lesotho), Swaziland, and Southern Rhodesia (later Zimbabwe) would later join the Union of South Africa.[4] As early as World War II, Prime Minister General Jan Smuts of South Africa lobbied Great Britain, unsuccessfully, to transfer the High Commission Territories (HCTs) of Botswana, Lesotho, and Swaziland to South Africa. Smuts, a pro-British South African, expressed both the importance of the HCTs to South Africa and his frustration with British policy when he said, "Thus it shall be from the Zambezi to Simons Bay: Africa for the Afrikaners." Peter Vale notes that until his death Smuts transposed the idea of South and Southern Africa.[5] Second, South Africa always pursued regional and continental ties with an eye toward its tenuous ties to the West. Third, domestic political calculations drove South Africa's regional and international relations. Finally, the ANC inherited the strong, albeit no longer exclusive, state, which its predecessor, the NP, had created to insulate itself from domestic and international pressures for reform.

1948–1958: D. F. Malan and Johannes Strijdom

The Domestic Dimension

Merle Lipton characterized the 1948–1960 period as the "the consolidation of apartheid."[6] Malan and Strijdom focused on consolidating Afrikaner rule, but because South Africa's domestic and foreign affairs were intertwined, each also addressed foreign-policy issues.[7]

Three developments defined this period: the evolution of a strong Afrikaner state, the NP's hegemony over the major institutions of South Africa's political economy, and the creation of an Afrikaner business class.[8] The strong Afrikaner state was a response to the increasingly threatening domestic and international environment. The 1953 elections marked the beginning of the NP's dominance of Parliament and, for all practical purposes, the end of parliamentary power. Over the next decade, the NP consolidated its power by thoroughly penetrating state institutions, such as the Department of Trade and Industry and the Department of Foreign Affairs, and state corporations, such as the Iron and Steel Corporation (ISCOR), in order to promote the development of an Afrikaner business class. By 1992, 46 percent of all White middle-class employment outside the primary sectors was in the state sector.[9] However, the success of Afrikaner consolidation planted the seeds for its demise. As Stephen John Stedman states, "The very success of apartheid in lifting Afrikaners into affluence induced divisions within their ranks concerning the need for political change and created an opening for the National Party in the early 1980s to attempt basic reforms."[10] The creation of a strong Afrikaner business class would later come to haunt the NP, as the logic of capitalism was revealed to be incompatible with that of apartheid.[11]

Two central debates punctuated the process of consolidating Afrikaner rule during this period: the controversy over the government's decision to disenfranchise the Cape Coloureds and the controversy over the NP's push to consolidate state power by changing its immigration policy. The United Party, the official opposition party in Parliament, lost its fight against disenfranchising the Cape Coloureds.[12] Strijdom believed that the United Party planned to "plough under" the Afrikaners through a more liberal immigration policy that would encourage the influx of British immigrants.[13] His government pushed through a new citizenship act stipulating that British subjects had to wait five years to apply for the right to vote, replacing the old rule that the right to vote was automatic after two years. One of the most important tasks on the NP's agenda was to promote the interests of its core constituency—White workers, Afrikaner *petite bourgeoisie,* and small farmers—and erode the influence of English-speaking Whites who commanded the heights of South Africa's economy.

The NP's consolidation of state power was most clearly illustrated by its policy of reserving jobs for Whites. In the late 1950s, many businesses, most of which were run by English speakers, preferred to hire cheap Black labor. The government responded by crafting the Job Reservation Determination No. 3 of 1958, which reserved fifteen different operations, such as who could use certain machinery, for Whites. In 1959, when The Industrial Council, which represented workers in favor of the job reservation and employers opposed to job reservation, vetoed the Determination, the government amended the Industrial Council Act, which allowed it to overrule the decisions of the Industrial Councils.[14] The government strengthened its hand against both British businesses and Black labor, protecting its Afrikaner constituency against competition from above and below.

Finally, the inchoate institutionalization of apartheid during these years was represented by such legislation as the Prohibition of Mixed Marriages Act (1949), the Population Registration Act (1951), and the Bantu Education Act (1955). Apartheid and the apartheid state gained strength. What domestic resistance there was during this period was barely active and came from Black political groups through civil protest and peaceful actions.

The International Dimension

Malan and Strijdom forged an Afrikaner state embedded in apartheid rule. They also ushered in an era of international isolation. Four underlying themes defining South Africa's regional relations for the next half-century were shaped in the process: South Africa repeatedly displayed intense interest in the High Commission Territories, which during this period were still British protectorates; its regional foreign policy was tied to its pursuit of international legitimacy; it focused on closer ties with Africa in general and Southern Africa in particular; and when government-to-government relations between it and African states frayed, South Africa kept the weakened lines of communication open by functional cooperation in areas such as technology and science.

Malan and then Strijdom advanced Afrikaner dominance of South Africa while the colonial (White) dominance of the rest of Africa was in full retreat. Shielding South Africa from what they saw as the contagion of decolonization and the advance of majority rule was the priority of their foreign policy. Malan, acting as his own foreign minister, outlined his Africa policy in a document entitled "The African Charter," which was imbued with the notion of an African continent safe for "Western European Christian Civilization."[15] He planned to ally with the Western powers by offering South Africa as a bulwark against the spread of communism and as an outpost of White domination. He failed.

The United Nations led the world in disapproval of apartheid South Africa during this period. In 1946, Jan Smuts had already suffered the humiliation of being shunned by the very institution that he had helped to create, foreshadowing South Africa's isolation. Early UN hostility to South Africa revolved around South Africa's control over South West Africa (Namibia), the status of Indians within its borders, and apartheid. Frustrated by growing international isolation from what it considered its Western cousins, South Africa, as it would again and again, turned its attention to Africa. Malan forcefully pushed for the incorporation of the HCTs into South Africa, but Great Britain resisted what would have amounted to South Africa's colonization of the HCTs.

South Africa's growing isolation and its failure to annex the HCTs led Malan to promote functional cooperation as a way to maintain its tenuous ties to the rest of Africa. It was also an attempt to gain a modicum of international legitimacy. In 1950, South Africa helped create the Commission for Technical Cooperation in Africa South of the Sahara (CTCA). It hoped to preempt the creation of a similar UN agency that Pretoria suspected would interfere in South Africa's internal affairs.[16] South Africa subsequently participated in several CTCA conferences and the following year was instrumental in launching the Commission for Scientific Cooperation in Africa South of the Sahara (CSA).[17] These commissions enabled South Africa to mitigate the effects of its growing isolation by communicating with African states outside of official political channels and by acting as lifelines to the West.

Malan's foreign policy was notable for its stubborn denial of the changes sweeping across Africa. His successor Johannes Strijdom took a more pragmatic path. He and his forceful foreign minister, Eric Louw, did not ignore the winds of change, but they continued the pursuit of regional hegemony. Like his predecessors, Strijdom failed to incorporate the HCTs, and this failure was reinforced by a second regional setback. For decades South Africa had anticipated the incorporation of Southern Rhodesia,[18] but in 1953, Southern Rhodesia, Northern Rhodesia, and Nyasaland, under the auspices of British rule, formed the Central African Federation, Great Britain and Southern Rhodesia's response to South Africa's regional ambitions.

Although buffeted by repeated foreign-policy setbacks, South Africa became more convinced that its path to better relations with the West lay in closer ties with the rest of Africa. The growing importance of Africa to South Africa's foreign policy was reflected by the creation in 1959 of South Africa's Africa Division in the Department of Foreign Affairs, its first geographical division. Finally, like Malan before them, Strijdom and Louw, in light of failed initiatives to improve South Africa's international and regional image, turned to functional cooperation. South Africa increased its participation in the CTCA and CSA, and Louw created a Roving Trade Commission for Africa.

The enduring themes of apartheid South Africa's foreign policy between 1948 and 1958 intertwined to create a strong hold on its future. Its foreign policy can be depicted as a series of concentric interests. At the center was the dominant domestic imperative of the survival of the Afrikaner state. Regional, continental, and international relations were crafted to promote and protect Afrikaner interests at home. But growing isolation internationally limited the apartheid state's ability to use foreign policy to influence its neighbors.

1958–1966: Hendrik Verwoerd

Verwoerd's premiership continued and strengthened the prevailing themes of the prior era. Because the Afrikaner state became stronger and the South African economy entered its golden period, a new matrix of opportunities and constraints matured even in the wake of domestic turbulence. South Africa had more resources to pursue its regional strategy, but its international position continued to deteriorate.

The Domestic Dimension

The defining domestic moment of Verwoerd's premiership was Sharpeville. Each successive administration would experience a similar punctuation mark in domestic discord, and each would be a more serious threat to the Afrikaner state. In March 1960, the South African police fired on a group of demonstrators whom the Pan Africanist Congress (PAC) had called upon to protest the South African pass laws. Sixty-seven Africans were killed and 126 wounded. Sharpeville marked an important change in the character of the anti-apartheid struggle in South Africa. Prior to World War II, the anti-apartheid struggle was fundamentally a reform movement led by Black elites, and from the end of the war until 1960 it had largely been based on nonviolent civil action. After Sharpeville, this all changed. In 1961, Umkhonto weSizwe (MK; Sword of the Nation), which was made up of ANC and SACP (South African Communist Party) cadres,[19] was formed as the armed wing of the ANC, and Poqo ("pure" or "only") was formed as the armed wing of the PAC. The anti-apartheid movement moved beyond South Africa's borders as neighboring countries became rear guards for the anti-apartheid struggle.

Even while domestic and international opposition to apartheid inten-
sified, Verwoerd advanced Afrikaner dominance at home and deepened
apartheid. His reign marked the beginning of a strong South African state
that aggressively asserted its interests domestically and regionally. On the
domestic front, the South African state successfully suppressed the anti-
apartheid struggle; Nelson Mandela was arrested in 1962, and seventeen
of the MK high command were arrested at Rivonia the following year.
Verwoerd also oversaw the hardening and deepening of the NP's African
labor policies. In the early 1960s, most of the African unions were outlawed, and in 1962 he refused a request by the gold mines in the Orange
Free State for more permanent housing for African workers.

Because South Africa was in the middle of the "Great Boom" of 1961
to 1970,[20] the NP could consolidate its power, it had greater economic
resources to maintain the apartheid edifice at home, and it was able to
protect Afrikaners from the Black majority rule that existed in the rest of
Africa. Between 1960 and 1970, the GNP of South Africa went from
about 5,200 million rand to 12,400 million rand. The main period of real
economic growth during this decade was between mid-1962 and mid-
1964, during which real gross domestic product rose by 5.6 percent in
1962, 8.1 percent in 1963, and 6.7 percent in 1964. The growing economic strength of South Africa and the political dominance of the NP
enabled Verwoerd to pursue a more aggressive regional foreign policy, even
as South Africa's pariah status hardened.

The International Dimension

As Verwoerd strengthened the Afrikaner grip on the state, South Africa
sank deeper into international isolation. Sharpeville occurred shortly after
Great Britain's Prime Minister Harold Macmillan's February 1960 "Winds
of Change" speech, given in front of the combined houses of South Africa's
Parliament. Macmillan spoke of inevitable anticolonial nationalism in Africa and against the notion of racial superiority. Verwoerd responded by
blaming Sharpeville on external influences; he seemed to relish turning
South Africa into a laager.[21] More confident than contrite, Verwoerd argued that seeking international popularity would only lead to the destruction of the White nation in South Africa.

South Africa's growing pariah status, accelerated by Sharpeville, was
reflected in its standing with international organizations. The year 1960
was the "Year of Africa"; sixteen countries became independent in that
year. Africa's influence in international organizations subsequently grew

significantly. Africa's success at further isolating South Africa was mirrored by South Africa's lack of success in its attempts to use its tenuous ties to the rest of Africa to achieve rapprochement with the West. In the face of uncompromising hostility to apartheid, Verwoerd withdrew South Africa's application for membership renewal in the Commonwealth of Nations at the 1961 Prime Minister's Commonwealth Conference. In 1962, the UN formed the Special Committee on Anti-Apartheid. As Ibrahim Gambari notes, "[B]y the 1960s, apartheid united the UN in a way that few issues had ever done."[22]

As the outside world became increasing hostile, Verwoerd followed the established pattern of shrinking the laager. His first foreign-policy goal was to reduce the possible threat from his neighbors by incorporating the HCTs. Verwoerd, however, added a new twist; incorporation would occur under the rubric of his homeland policy, which relegated the African population to so-called ethnic homelands.[23] This would directly link South Africa's domestic agenda to its regional policy. The homelands made up approximately 15 percent of the land, and the Africans 85 percent of the population; incorporating Botswana, Lesotho, and Swaziland would create the illusion of a much more equitable arrangement by altering those proportions. The numbers would be reversed. Great Britain, again, rejected South Africa's petition.

South Africa's ambitious linking of domestic and regional policy objectives was possible because of its booming economy and relative stability in its bordering countries. Angola and Mozambique were still under friendly Portuguese control; Ian Smith's White-settler-controlled Rhodesia Front declared independence (via a Unilateral Declaration of Independence) from Great Britain in 1965 to preempt independence and majority rule, as had already happened in Zambia and Malawi; and South West Africa (Namibia) was still controlled by South Africa. This cordon sanitaire, along with an economic boom, protected South Africa from the "contagion" of majority rule and opened the door to new instruments of economic statecraft.

Verwoerd propagated the establishment of a common market together with a "consultative political body of free Black and White states" in Southern Africa.[24] It is important to point out, however, that Verwoerd purposefully deemphasized any political aspect of regional integration,[25] foreshadowing the position taken by conservative elements during the transition. The combination of the growing strength and diversity of South Africa's economy and concomitant domestic pressures created the opportunity for regional cooperation. In 1965, South Africa's minister for planning called for intraregional marketing arrangements, and a 1965 article published by the Anglo-American Corporation of South Africa argued for closer economic cooperation among South Africa, South West Africa, the BLS states, Rhodesia, and the Portuguese colonies of Angola and Mozambique. The article argued that because South Africa had already attained a considerable measure of economic maturity, it could offer to the region capital, technical skills, and managerial expertise through its familiarity with Africa.[26] These themes would be revived during the transition period.

1966–1978: John Vorster

John Vorster's premiership, which followed Verwoerd's assassination, actually encompasses two periods. He rode to office on the tailwinds of Verwoerd's strong state, South Africa's economic boom, and mature apartheid. But he left office with the apartheid system under siege and South Africa in accelerating economic decline. The break came in the early 1970s as South Africa's economy declined and its African workers responded by challenging the labor relations system. Hein Marais feels that the series of strikes centered in Durban "announced the end of apartheid's 'golden age'—with class struggle, for the first time in almost 25 years, reaching an organized pitch that could unsettle the rhythms of capital accumulation."[27] Under Vorster, South Africa's apartheid capitalism was threatened at home from both ends of the ideological spectrum. Business began to challenge its inefficiencies, and labor began to challenge its inequities.[28] International isolation became more proactive and its regional neighbors more threatening.

The Domestic Dimension

It is ironic that the economic boom of the 1960s became a political liability for Vorster. As D. Hobart Houghton stated in 1980:

> It is becoming increasingly clear to all industrialists that as long as traditional and legal restraints are placed upon the employment of coloured people, Asians and Africans in more skilled and responsible jobs, scarcity of workers in these categories is bound to be a major factor inhibiting growth. South Africa has been forced to face the economic reality that

the maintenance of the industrial colour bar is incompatible with rapid
growth, and all sections of the nation have become increasingly aware of
this during the boom.[29]

The 1960s economic boom was largely driven by the exponential
growth of the manufacturing sector; between 1960 and 1970, manufacturing grew by 158 percent.[30] By 1970, industry (manufacturing, construction, electricity, water, and gas) was already accounting for 30 percent of
GDP, while mining had declined to 10 percent.[31] South Africa's growing
business interests had four major concerns: increasing exports, importing
capital technology, maintaining political stability, and increasing labor
mobility. The most immediate and sensitive of these issues was the supply
of labor.

The government responded by restricting the supply of labor. First, it
made it more difficult for Blacks to stay or settle in urban areas by chip-
ping away at Section 10 rights, which restricted the movement of Blacks.
Vorster said, "[W]e must face economic realities, but we must also face
political realities."[32] In addition, the 1968 Bantu Labour Regulations Act
promoted new migrant labor while tightening the pass laws. Second, if the
economy was to continue to grow, industry would have to continue to
expand. Since the government was not in favor of bringing more Black
workers to the urban areas (White areas), the answer seemed to be to bring
the industries to Black areas (homelands). The government thus decentralized manufacturing through the creation of "growth points" along the
Bantustan borders. This policy went through two phases. In the first, the
government attempted to accomplish decentralization through incentives
for businesses, such as loans, subsidies, tax relief, and compensation for the
use of Black labor. However, when business did not respond as expected,
the government used the Environment Act to control the expansion of
industry into White areas. The gap widened between the government and
the business community it had nurtured.

Nonetheless, while the state was strengthened by the apartheid system, business became virtually the only group with influence over state
policy.[33] Vorster was more amenable to the concerns of the business community than Verwoerd had been, but his halfway measures on behalf of
business eroded the NP's traditional support base—working-class Afrikaners, who felt that the government's priorities were shifting toward the
needs of business.[34] Vorster walked a tightrope between the more conservative elements of the NP, who did not want any departure from strict
Verwoerdian apartheid, and the more liberal elements of the NP, who ad-

vocated the reform of apartheid. Even the large Afrikaner monopolies began to loosen their links to the NP.[35] Hein Marais notes that "[t]he traditional core of the NP (White workers, Afrikaner *petite bourgeoisie* and small farmers)—the rightwing of the party—became marginalized and the party came to pivot on the organizations of a maturing Afrikaner capital."[36]

Vorster promised to reform apartheid. Government policy stressed reform in certain socioeconomic areas by ending prohibition on White investment in the homelands, and increasing flexibility on job restrictions, thereby opening up more jobs to Blacks, while still maintaining strict adherence to political apartheid. But the reforms antagonized the conservatives and did not go far enough to satisfy business. The growing tension within the NP was punctuated by Dr. Albert Hertzog's break from the NP in 1969 to form the conservative Herstigte Nasionale Party.

Following the 1970 elections, the government tried to strengthen its political position through ad hoc measures such as commissions of inquiry. But more important, it became authoritarian. In 1969, the Bureau of State Security replaced Republican Intelligence (the state intelligence agency). During the 1970s, its head, General H. J. van den Bergh, used his strong ties to Vorster to all but control the government. Vorster reigned over a strong state and a strong economy that was nonetheless developing deep fissures. Economic decline in the latter 1970s shook the political fault lines created by a quarter-century of NP rule. In a curious coincidence of interests, business was disenchanted with the antinomies of apartheid capitalism, and labor was disenchanted with playing Cinderella to the princes of capital. This strange combination would make apartheid capitalism impossible, and it would lay the groundwork for new interest-group dynamics during the transition.

The second period of Vorster's premiership presented him with a new set of economic and political dynamics. Vorster came to power during robust economic growth. But the economic boom created new challenges that the ensuing bust exacerbated. By 1975, the economy was in serious decline; the growth rate had dropped to 2.2 percent for the year.[37] Vorster's government also faced the inchoate Black union movement, which was symbolized by the Durban strikes of 1973 and led to the Bantu Labour Relations Regulation Amendment Act, which gave Africans a limited right to strike. The impact of South Africa's economic downturn was felt mainly in the townships. For instance, 53 percent of the formerly employed population had lost their jobs.[38]

Sharpeville left an indelible mark on Verwoerd's era; Soweto did the same for Vorster's latter period. On June 16, 1976, 15,000 schoolchildren

gathered to protest the government's insistence that Afrikaans be the official language in Black schools. The subsequent confrontation with police
triggered a month-long revolt, caused 1,000 deaths, and had long-term
reverberations. The government reacted to Soweto by becoming yet more
repressive, while business responded by calling for more reform. Both
agreed that the central problem was stability. Sir Albert Robinson, chairman of a large Johannesburg industrial firm, stated:

> We are entering a decisive phase in the history of South Africa. . . . The
> business community must play its part in applying pressure to encour-
> age peaceful change, more particularly in the field of race relations and
> the breaking down of discrimination.[39]

The business community responded to Soweto by forming the Urban
Foundation to lobby the government for change, especially concerning
housing for Blacks. But the division between Vorster and business remained. At the national convention of the Associated Chambers of Commerce in October 1976, Vorster stated:

> Efforts to use business organizations to bring about basic change in gov-
> ernment policy will fail and cause unnecessary and harmful friction be-
> tween the Government and the private sector. You cannot ask me to
> implement policies rejected by the electorate and in which I do not
> believe.[40]

South Africa's slow political and economic burn during Vorster's latter
years ignited a domestic fire fueled by labor and business discontent.

The International Dimension

During Vorster's administration, South Africa increasingly focused on
Southern Africa. However, as South Africa's domestic and international
environments became more threatening, its regional policy became more
aggressive. Vorster's general Africa policy was broadly known as the outward policy.[41] It differed from South Africa's earlier Africa policies in a
number of ways. It accepted the irreversibility of the transfer of political
power from the European metropoles to the African centers, ending a long
period of denial. South Africa could accept the reality of a steady transfer
of power to African centers because in the first half of the 1970s, South
Africa's cordon sanitaire was still intact and its economy was booming.
Rhodesia posed some threat because of the insurgency against Ian Smith's

government, but South Africa had already sent police there as early as 1965. South Africa had also strengthened its hold on the BLS states by renegotiating the South African Customs Union in 1969. It also attempted to establish bilateral and direct contacts between itself and specific African states and establish a niche for itself as a broker in Southern African conflicts. Finally, the outward policy emphasized collaboration between the government and the private sector and parastatals (state-owned corporations).

Four goals defined the outward policy during the early years of Vorster's administration: secure the White state, promote exports and technological links, reduce dependence on the West, and gain acceptance as a continental power. The emphasis during the first years was on the first two goals. Vorster's government pursued the final two goals by what became known respectively as the dialogue movement and détente. When South Africa failed to play a role on the continent, it retreated to the safe haven of its regional laager.

The dialogue movement was Vorster's attempt to reach across Africa for the recognition and legitimacy that the West increasingly denied South Africa. Improving relations with Africa would improve South Africa's relations with the West.[42] In fact, dialogue enjoyed some early success. On November 7, 1969, Dr. K. A. Busia, the prime minister of Ghana, stated that he was in favor of dialogue with South Africa. President Felix Houphouet-Boigny of the Ivory Coast announced on November 4, 1970, that he intended to arrange a gathering of African leaders to meet with South Africa, a move supported by leaders from Madagascar, Gabon, Senegal, and the Central African Republic.

But there also was a growing movement in Africa to condemn South Africa's domestic and regional policy. In September 1969, the Organization of African Unity (OAU) adopted the Lusaka Manifesto, which had earlier been issued by the Conference of East and Central African States, calling for an end to colonialism in Mozambique, Angola, Rhodesia, and South West Africa. It also included South Africa within its anticolonialism mandate.[43] In 1971, the Mogadishu Declaration, which was adopted by the Conference of East and Central African States, reiterated the Lusaka Manifesto, stating that "the only alternative left to Africa is to use all means available to them to change the abominable and hateful policies of apartheid, colonialism, and racialism."[44] In January 1973, at its meeting in Accra, the OAU wrote its Charter of African Liberation, explicitly accepting the tenets of the Mogadishu Declaration. In January 1975, the OAU Liberation Committee announced the Dar es Salaam Declaration, stating its "unflinching determination to realize the freedom and independence of Rhodesia and Namibia and the total destruction of apartheid and racial discrimination in South Africa."[45] Thus, while South Africa more assiduously explored contacts with the rest of Africa in the 1970s, the tide of African opinion flowed in the opposite direction. Events in Southern Africa would soon make the dialogue movement moot.

The matrix of threat and opportunity facing South Africa unalterably changed on April 24, 1974, when Portugal's president António Salazar was overthrown.[46] The cordon sanitaire was broken. Northern Namibia was now open to attacks by the anti–South African guerilla force called South West Africa Peoples Organization (SWAPO) from southern Angola. Mozambique became a base for forces fighting the Ian Smith regime in Rhodesia, and South Africa was now directly vulnerable to ANC and PAC penetration from Mozambique.

The new regional equation led to the second manifestation of Vorster's outward policy—détente. As Barber and Barratt wrote: "This policy (détente) differed from dialogue in two important respects: it was directed at more specific policy goals, and it was confined to southern Africa."[47] Once again, South Africa's foreign policy shrank to its inner concentric circles. Vorster enunciated the theme of his détente policy in a speech in front of the South Africa Senate on October 23, 1974:

> I believe that southern Africa has come to the crossroads. I believe that southern Africa has to make a choice. I think that choice lies between peace on one hand and an escalation of strife on the other. The consequences of escalation are easily foreseeable. The toll of a major confrontation will be too high for southern Africa to pay. . . . But there is an alternative way. That way is the way of peace. The way of normalizing relations, the way of sound understanding and normal association. I believe that southern Africa can take that way. I have reason to believe that it is prepared to take that way. And I believe that it will do so in the end.[48]

Vorster was successful in improving relations with the BLS states. He had met with Chief Leabua Jonathan soon after he became prime minister of Lesotho, followed by the renegotiation of SACU. South Africa also approached Mozambique. Vorster, supported by his foreign minister, Hilgard Muller, stressed the importance of economic cooperation and existing mutual links, such as the power plant at Cahora Bassa Dam. Most important, the early success of détente played well in the West.

The gem in Vorster's détente crown was to be a joint effort by Presi-

dent Kaunda of Zambia and Prime Minister Vorster to broker a peaceful
settlement of the civil war in Rhodesia. This arrangement alone indicated
a level of success for détente. Kaunda was to encourage the Rhodesian
nationalist parties, ZAPU (Zimbabwe African People's Union) and ZANU
(Zimbabwe African Nationalist Union), to move to the negotiating table,
while Vorster was to use his influence with Ian Smith to get the ruling
Rhodesian Front government to the table. The culmination of this process
was the August 1975 Victoria Falls meeting between the Black national-
ists and the Rhodesian Front. But the détente initiative in Rhodesia ultimately failed. The immediate cause for the failure was Rhodesian and
South African domestic politics. Ian Smith did not want the negotiations
to succeed because he was not yet convinced that his minority White regime would have to eventually bow to the pressure of the nationalist
struggle. The nationalist movement, furthermore, had its own problems.
Robert Mugabe, who was in the process of gaining control of ZANU,
remained in Mozambique during the conference. The relationship between Mugabe and Kaunda was strained because of Kaunda's support for
Mugabe's rival nationalist leader, Joshua Nkomo.

Vorster's Rhodesia policy also faced strong internal opposition. The
conservatives in South Africa believed that pressuring Ian Smith to compromise with Blacks was the first step down the slippery slope of capitu-
lation to the Black majority at home. The *verkrampte* element in South
Africa (the conservative element of the NP) opposed any expanded relations with Africa; the laager mentality of the *verkramptes* meant that "the
outward policy would have profound and negative effects on South Africa's
domestic structures, they opposed extended relations with neighboring
black states."[49] Those opposed to a more active South African policy in
Africa were in the minority, but they nonetheless complicated Vorster's
domestic calculations and indirectly provided Ian Smith with leverage to
resist Vorster's initiatives.

The third reason for the failure of détente was the combination of the
Angolan time bomb and SWAPO in Southwest Africa. In 1975, South
Africa invaded Angola, ending in a single stroke its stated adherence to
the Lusaka Manifesto. South Africa was accused of "tough military action
against SWAPO and of wrecking any prospect of an early settlement in
Namibia on terms acceptable to the OAU."[50] In Mozambique in February
1976, Kenneth Kaunda, Samora Machel (Mozambique), Julius Nyerere
(Tanzania), and Seretse Khama (Botswana) agreed that armed struggle was
necessary to free Southern Africa from the remnants of colonial rule. These
venerable leaders of the anticolonial struggle initiated the formation of the

Front-Line States to confront the political and security aspects of South African regional dominance.

The outward policy had an important economic dimension. South Africa had to maintain the system of labor migration that facilitated the recruitment of cheap labor for its mines, and it had to find new markets for its industrial products. Because its products were not competitive internationally, the region became an important export market. South Africa used foreign exchange earned from regional exports to pay for the growing level of high-tech imports necessary to expand its industrial capacity. Between 1964 and 1969, South Africa's percentage of Malawi's imports went from 6 percent to 15 percent, and in 1967 a trade agreement was reached between the two countries. Rhodesia's Unilateral Declaration of Independence and the international economic boom that followed created tremendous opportunities for South Africa. Between 1964 and 1969, South Africa's share of Rhodesia's imports went from 24 percent to 80 percent.[51] Zambia, because it responded to the Unilateral Declaration of Independence by closing its borders with Rhodesia, also became more dependent on South Africa.

South Africa's economic machinations were a central component of the détente policy. In February 1974, Vorster spoke of a "power bloc" of sovereign independent states in the region.[52] He used the language of interdependence, but he was pursuing regional hegemony.[53] By the later stages of Vorster's premiership, relations with the West, Africa in general, and Southern Africa in particular had almost reached their nadir. In November 1977, the South African Institute for International Affairs (SAIIA) and the South African Institute of Race Relations (SAIRR) held a symposium entitled Where in the World Is South Africa?[54] The title of Peter Vale's paper provided the answer to this rhetorical question: "South Africa as a Pariah International State."

The growing hostilities toward South Africa led to the promotion of secret ventures initiated by Dr. C. P. Mulder, minister of information, and Eschel Rhodie, secretary of the South African Department of Information, to shore up South Africa's international image. The Department of Information's budget for covert activity went from 3.2 million in 1966 to 10.7 million rand in 1974. Barber and Barratt give a good compendium of its activities: "Among its many, sometimes bizarre, activities were secret funding of British and American politicians; financing research institutions; buying or attempting to buy control of Western newspapers; organizing campaigns against hostile politicians; and secret African contacts."[55] The Bureau of State Security, under the control of General

Hendrik van den Bergh, complied with the Department of Information's schemes. The exposure of the Department of Information's activities, which became known as Infogate, led to the fall of Vorster. Although the role of Defense Minister P. W. Botha in Infogate was questioned, the 1978 Erasmus Commission Report exonerated him, and he became the next South African leader. Vorster had come to power in the wake of growing South African confidence. Botha came to office with South Africa buffeted by domestic, regional, and international pressures to end apartheid.

1978–1989: P. W. Botha

Botha came to power on September 28, 1978, in the wake of a power struggle within the National Party. He promised to accelerate the reform process begun by Vorster. Instead, he instituted a near-totalitarian state.

The Domestic Dimension

Unlike his predecessor, Botha did not ride to office on an economic boom. Robert Price has called the 1980s "a period of stagnation and decline for the South African economy."[56] South Africa's real economic growth rate since World War II had averaged over 5 percent annually; it declined in every five-year period after 1979. From 1975 to 1980, the real growth rate was 2.8 percent; from 1980 to 1985, it was 1.1 percent. While the entire population of South Africa was affected by the recession of the 1980s, the Blacks and the homelands bore the burden of adjustment. By 1988, Blacks accounted for at least 95 percent of the unemployed, and their general quality of life was far below that of Whites.[57] This would be the legacy left to the ANC government a decade later.

Botha's response to the political and economic crises was three-pronged: reform, more repression, and hegemony over the region. Although these policies were interconnected and overlapped, they can be considered separately. Botha came to office promising the wide-ranging reform of apartheid. He accepted the Bantustan policy of his predecessors but recognized the permanence of urban Africans and therefore stopped the erosion of Section 10 rights.[58] He allowed the erosion of petty apartheid.[59] But his most radical and important reform was the Constitution of 1983. It was meant to placate international public opinion by replacing the Whites-only franchise with a multiracial franchise. However, the new franchise and its two new chambers included only Indians and Coloureds; the goal was to limit the participation of these two groups in the anti-apartheid movement by co-opting them into the political system. His strategy did not work; the first election in 1984 under the new constitution witnessed only a 29.6 percent turnout by Coloureds and a 20.2 percent turnout by Indians.[60]

The new constitutional dispensation triggered the formation in August 1983 of the United Democratic Front (UDF). The UDF was not a political party but rather an umbrella organization for many groups that had accepted the ANC's 1955 Freedom Charter, a manifesto by the ANC that called for full political rights for all South Africans. By March 1984, the UDF had over 600 affiliated organizations with a combined membership of over 2 million.[61] The ANC, meanwhile, had stepped up its activities in South Africa during the 1980s. Although it may have had relatively little effect on the ground, it affected the psychological mood of the country.

Economic decline, the disproportionate burden felt by the Black population, and a new constitutional dispensation that still excluded Blacks created a highly volatile political environment. The spark came in the form of the 1984 rent increases by the local councils, long considered instruments of the apartheid government. On September 3, 1984, 60 percent of the workers, as well as most students, staged a stayaway. The following November, the largest stayaway in South African history was organized in the Vaal triangle (the southern part of the Pretoria-Witwatersrand-Vereeniging region) by trade unions, student groups, and the UDF and it spread across the entire area.

The 1984 disturbances were to the Botha administration what Soweto had been to Vorster and Sharpeville to Verwoerd. Just as Soweto was a greater threat to apartheid than was Sharpeville, the 1984–1986 disturbances were a qualitatively different phenomenon than its precursors. The trade unions, the UDF, and the ANC were better organized and had deeper support both within and outside the country. Robert Price aptly captures the impact of the 1984–1986 insurrection:

> In rendering the townships ungovernable, the insurrection of 1984–86 operated not just at the level of physical control (fighting the police and army, eliminating informers, disrupting community council administration, and the like), but also on the level of political psychology.[62]

While the township insurrections of 1984–1986 demonstrated the depth and breadth of Black opposition to apartheid, portions of the White population were becoming increasingly critical of the government. Rising emigration and a growing reluctance to serve in the armed forces were symptoms of the weakening confidence in the state. The most persistent and potentially debilitating criticism of the state came from the business community. The chairman of Gencor, South Africa's second-largest mining-finance house, stated, "We should be opening more mines, putting up more plants. . . . That we haven't . . . is because uncertainty has produced a lack of confidence."[63] Wealthy White South Africans increasingly supported the UDF, forming the Friends of the UDF and even fundraising for the opposition movement.

Botha recognized the importance of government-business relations and in 1979 attempted to bridge the gap between the two in his watershed speech at the Carlton Conference. He promised to reduce state controls over economic affairs and to reform the apartheid system. The immediate response to the speech was positive, but two years later at the follow-up conference in Good Hope, the business community remained skeptical. South African business was concerned with the accelerating domestic instability as symbolized by the Trek to Lusaka, which was initiated in September 1985 when a group of South African executives met with senior members of the ANC's National Executive Committee in Lusaka, Zambia. The meetings with the ANC soon spread to other segments of South African society.

The 1984–1986 disturbances marked a new dimension in the liberation struggle.[64] The opposition to apartheid had widened and deepened; the formal opposition to Pretoria had become more militant with rear bases in the Front-Line States, and informal opposition grew within the White community, particularly in the business community. The response to the new constitutional dispensation went well beyond the protests of those to whom it would deny the franchise. Finally, the discussion of a new constitution led to a split in the National Party. In 1982, Dr. Andries Treuernicht, NP leader for the Transvaal, and twenty-one other NP members refused to support Botha's reforms and were expelled from the party. Treuernicht subsequently formed the Conservative Party.

The International Dimension

South Africa's foreign policy under Botha, which was run out of the State Security Council, was part of South Africa's Total National Strategy, a reaction to what was labeled the "total onslaught" of communism. It was the final shrinking of the Afrikaner laager. Colin Vale, a well-known Afrikaner academic, explained the perceived threat thus:

[It] can be assumed that the Soviet Union will cling to any territory over which it acquires control in Africa, and will only surrender it if the centre collapses or if overall strategy favours such a move. In black Africa, the Soviets have already selected and effectively controlled at least three states and are preparing the ground for three more: Zimbabwe, Namibia, and South Africa.[65]

Vale painted parallels between the nineteenth-century "scramble for Africa" and the Soviet Union's 1970s machinations in Africa. He argued that the Soviets would use African proxies—the ANC in South Africa, SWAPO in Namibia, and ZAPU in Zimbabwe—in their attempt to gain control of South Africa.[66]

To combat the total onslaught, the South African state would need to commit all its resources to the task. Deon Geldenhuys reported that "one obvious strategy that the government is adopting to weather the storm is to prepare South Africa for a siege. . . . It is also possible to discern an aggressive new style in South African diplomacy."[67] South Africa's 1974–1975 military budget was 1½ times the 1973–1974 budget, and the 1977–1978 military budget was 3½ times that of 1973–1974.[68] But even more significant was the metamorphosis of the South African state. Recommendations made by Justice Potgeiter in 1972 led to the Security Intelligence and State Security Council Act No. 64 and the birth of the State Security Council. The restructuring of the state, of course, was resisted, and Botha had to first rein in the Bureau of State Security and the South African bureaucracy. Nonetheless, South Africa became a garrison state.

Botha reduced the number of cabinet committees from twenty to four, and the secretary of the State Security Council sat as a member of the working group of the other three committees. Furthermore, many of the civil servants that served on the committees were seconded military officers. As Robert Rotberg observed, "Indeed, the National Defense [*sic*] Management System has superseded the cabinet, the party, and the electorate in many areas."[69] The National Security Management System was created to provide the policy-making State Security Council with implementation capability. In 1987, *Africa Confidential* reported that:

[t]he National Security Management System . . . is an elaborate shadow state charged with combating the revolutionary forces ranged against the state. Under cover of a year-old national State of Emergency, it has usurped the functions of local councils and downgraded the role of parliament government, whose existence is unknown, even to many whites. President Botha and his security chiefs control it.[70]

Botha's Total National Strategy was shaped by his 12 Point Plan, first enunciated at the Natal National Party Congress in August 1974, while he was still defense minister.[71] Points 8, 9, and 10 were concerned with foreign relations and illustrated South Africa's shrinking sphere of influence. Point 8 dealt with Botha's idea of a Constellation of Southern African States (CONSAS) in the region, point 9 argued that South Africa must defend itself, and point 10 floated the idea that South Africa might have to adopt a neutral position in the East-West conflict.[72]

CONSAS was rooted in Verwoerd's call for a "commonwealth" and in Vorster's call for a constellation of states. As Peter Vale opined, it was essentially "atavistic."[73] However, Botha's CONSAS had a more coercive character than had its precursors, and it sought to institutionalize South Africa's regional hegemony. Unlike earlier efforts at regional cooperation, it stressed the security aspect of cooperation. In fact, Geldenhuys and Venter, two South African academics specializing in foreign affairs, equated the CONSAS idea with an alliance.[74] Geldenhuys argued that CONSAS was built on three assumptions: that the moderate states of the area faced a common communist threat, that CONSAS could be built on the existing level of cooperation, and that the centripetal force of South Africa's regional dominance would certainly keep the neighboring countries within its economic orbit but politically independent as well.[75]

CONSAS was officially launched during Botha's address before business leaders at the Carlton Conference in Johannesburg on November 22, 1979. Botha hoped to gain the cooperation of the business community and at the same time placate conservatives by leaving the exact nature of CONSAS ambiguous (recall that elements in South Africa had long been wary of closer ties to its neighbors). On the security side, nonaggression pacts would be signed. On the economic side, CONSAS would provide an enlarged common market, technological links, transport links, and the exchange of knowledge and capital to develop the region. It was a largely functionalist approach to cooperation.[76]

Botha's CONSAS initiative was a response to the imminent independence of Zimbabwe-Rhodesia. But he had counted on the moderate Bishop Abel Muzorewa winning the first Zimbabwean election. The victor was Robert Mugabe, an avowed Marxist. The states of Southern Africa did not respond to the CONSAS initiative as expected. Instead, fortified by an independent Zimbabwe, the Front-Line States met in Arusha, leading to the formation of the SADCC. Botswana's President Khama's opening address at the founding meeting in Arusha, in fact, referred directly to CONSAS as motivation for the SADCC.[77]

What Davies and O'Meara called the second stage of Botha's Total National Strategy, the "policy of destabilization," followed South Africa's failure to draw its neighbors into CONSAS.[78] The period of destabilization has been characterized in two ways: as a centrally planned and orchestrated policy and as a fractious response to external events. From the first perspective, Joseph Hanlon reasoned that "[t]hese actions are part of a coherent South Africa strategy to use the neighboring states in defense of apartheid."[79] Other scholars argued that there was a high level of bureaucratic infighting, that the left hand did not always know what the right hand was doing, and that there was in fact no destabilization policy per se.[80] Regardless of which characterization is correct, South Africa used the full range of resources at its disposal to destabilize the region, including cross-border raids to destroy the rear bases of the ANC.

South Africa also applied economic pressure, such as cutting off gasoline and delaying rail service to Zimbabwe, decreasing the number of migrant workers in South Africa's mines, reducing the use of Mozambique's railways and ports, and delaying custom-union payments to the BLS states. As Hanlon stated, "The military attacks catch press headlines, but outside Angola and Mozambique, South Africa's economic power in the region is in some ways more critical."[81]

It is curious that even as South Africa pursued a more aggressive regional policy, it saw regionalism as its only way out of an externally imposed isolationism. As Robert Price argued, Pretoria's regional strategy of hegemony contained an inherent tension because it used an unacceptable method, destabilization, to demonstrate regional hegemony.[82] By mid-1985, South Africa's foreign relations had reached their nadir. Botha remained defiant, stating that the top priority was to restore domestic order and that he would not give in to international pressure.[83]

Botha was aware of potential international pressure, such as economic sanctions, that could be used against South Africa.[84] On August 15, 1985, he gave his much-anticipated "Rubicon Speech" at the Annual National Party's Province Congress in Durban. South Africa's foreign minister, Pik Botha, had briefed Western leaders in advance, and the speech was in fact broadcast to the United States, Great Britain, and Germany. However, what P. W. Botha delivered was not a radical departure from apartheid but rather a continuation of his incremental reforms and the maintenance of grand apartheid. The international community was shocked. The rand, which had been falling since 1983, fell to a low of 0.35 to the American dollar in August of 1985; the Johannesburg stock exchange was closed for the first time since Sharpeville; Chase Manhattan Bank in New York decided not to roll over maturing short-term loans to South Africa; and other banks followed suit.[85] South Africa had sunk to the depths of its pariah status.

South Africa did get a short reprieve from international pressure. In fact, some would argue that South Africa's aggressive regional foreign policy was due to the more permissive policy environment created by Ronald Reagan and, to a somewhat lesser extent, Margaret Thatcher. Rotberg, for instance, argued that it was only after Reagan came to office in 1981 that destabilization became South Africa's first line of defense,[86] and Gilbert M. Khadiagala feels that the Reagan administration strengthened Pretoria's regional agenda.[87] There certainly was a coincidence of interest between South Africa and the United States during Reagan's presidency concerning Moscow's influence in Southern Africa. However, by 1983, Washington had also begun to question Pretoria's destabilization of the region.[88] A year later, Pretoria reached an agreement with Mozambique, the Nkomati Accords, which was to end South African support for RENAMO, the rebel force fighting the Mozambican government, in return for an end to Mozambique's support for the ANC. The Nkomati Accords were as much a signal to the West as they were a sincere effort to improve regional relations. Botha followed this success with an eight-nation tour of Europe.

Ill health would soon end Botha's reign, and an internecine struggle within the National Party ensued. The next president, F. W. de Klerk, would ease South Africa into its transition, if not actually direct it. The transition was certainly hastened by the end of the Cold War. But the process itself foreshadowed the pluralistic character of post-apartheid South Africa. On December 20, 1991, delegations from eighteen organizations and the government gathered at the World Trade Center outside Johannesburg to convene the first session of the Convention for a Democratic South Africa (CODESA). CODESA I ended in a deadlock, but CODESA II, which included twenty-one negotiating parties, picked up where it left off in May 1992. Although it too ended in deadlock, it led to an agreement on September 7, 1993, to create the Transitional Executive Council (TEC).[89] The TEC was composed of representatives of political parties that had settled upon a draft constitution in December 1993. It became operational in January 1994, was granted some autonomous power vis-à-vis the de Klerk government, and operated in practice as a parallel or partner body to the government. Black South Africans thereby shared a governing role with the apartheid government in the TEC, which included a subcommittee on regional economic integration.

The CODESA process is often characterized as elitist. The two dominant actors, the National Party and the African National Congress, did at the time seem to lose touch with their grassroots constituencies. But the mass movements that followed CODESA II were encouraged by labor, a key element of the ANC-led alliance, and brought the transition back to earth. This period was also witness to one of apartheid South Africa's episodic horrors. On the night of June 17th, a day after the June 16th rallies commemorating Soweto, shack dwellers in Boipatong Township in the Vaal triangle were killed by organized raiders. This energized the ANC alliance and forced the South African government to face yet another crisis of domestic stability. But "Boipatong's most direct political impact was felt not in the streets, but in the offices of foreign politicians and diplomats."[90]

The CODESA talks, the bilateral talks between the ANC and NP that followed them, and the March 1993 negotiations, which have been described as the most inclusive array of negotiation partners yet,[91] are an interesting and revealing story but will not be covered here. They revealed, nonetheless, the wide range of domestic and international interests concerned with the future of South Africa. The South African debate over its future role in the region was a reflection of these complex dynamics.

3

Debating the Future:
Regional Relations in the Post-Apartheid Era

The end of apartheid marked the end of the captured state. South Africa's domestic and regional policy could no longer be held prisoner by the preferences of the Afrikaner state or apartheid capitalism. Demands for change had focused on domestic politics, but they spilled over into foreign policy. The transition opened up a Pandora's box of competing policy preferences in both domestic and international politics. This chapter chronicles the debate over regional foreign policy.

Regional integration and cooperation was actively discussed and debated in transitional South Africa. In March 1991, South African business groups met with the SADCC and the Preferential Trade Area (PTA) in Swaziland for a conference entitled Scenario for a Sub-Continent. Three South African business groups organized it—the South African Chamber of Business (SACOB), the South African Foreign Trade Organisation (SAFTO), and the National African Chamber of Commerce (NAFCOC).[1] In late May 1993, bankers and finance ministers met in Somerset West, South Africa, to sketch a regional integration plan, although it did not result in a formal agreement.[2] The evolving new regional dispensation was a prominent theme in the 1992 ANC document "Ready to Govern."[3] South Africa's top civil servants, who were almost all loyal to the NP, were concerned about South Africa's future regional role.[4] In the first half of

1994, a working committee of the Transitional Executive Council (TEC) for regional integration was formed.[5] The TEC working committee consisted of two members of the ANC, two representatives of the Development Bank of Southern Africa (DBSA), the former director-general of the Department of Trade and Industry, and an economics professor from the University of Stellenbosch.

Interests and Articulated Preferences in South Africa: Institutionalizing Regional Cooperation

South Africa's regional relations and, most importantly, how those relations should be institutionalized or not formally institutionalized were actively debated during the transition period, and interested groups actively promoted clearly defined preferences. As Robert Davies stated:

> significantly different perspectives have, in fact, emerged between different forces in South African policy on the terms, principles, and approaches to govern a programme of closer regional economic cooperation and integration after apartheid. Future South African policy on this issue can thus be expected to depend to a considerable extent on the balance of forces established in the negotiation process now under way.[6]

A year later, in a study he co-wrote, Davies elaborated:

> A host of external agencies, as well as domestic and regional "interested parties" of all sorts, are in the process of preparing various proposals, and it is thus becoming increasingly urgent for the democratic movement to develop its own perspective on this critical issue.[7]

The proposals for how post-apartheid South Africa could become involved in regional cooperation can be categorized as developmental cooperation, market cooperation, and ad hoc cooperation. These categories are ideal types, and preferences about cooperation may cross analytical lines. This proves true by the end of the ANC's first term in power. Each proposal, nonetheless, had political and societal support. The following sections locate and examine the preferences for these three forms of regional cooperation.

The TEC working committee is symbolic of the debate in transitional South Africa over how to shape regional relations, and, in particular, how regional economic integration/cooperation would be promoted. There were different viewpoints, but as the conclusion to this book will argue, the approach the new ANC government eventually took reflected political compromises, and these compromises are foreshadowed in the makeup of the TEC Committee. For now, nonetheless, we turn to the positions of the relevant actors concerning how regional economic integration/cooperation in post-apartheid South Africa should be structured.

These three ideal types represent a progression from very limited formal arrangements (ad hoc cooperation) to highly institutionalized cooperation (developmental cooperation).[8] Within South Africa, the institutionalization of regional cooperation was often defined as a choice between cooperation and integration.[9] For the important constituencies within transitional South Africa, integration and cooperation had different meanings, although they were both about regional economic integration/cooperation. Big business, for instance, feared that integration meant external influence in South African affairs. It also meant being too closely tied to South Africa's poor neighbors. Business strongly resisted, even resented, a strong centralized regional organization that would promote regional integration. The ANC, on the other hand, seemed to embrace the notion of greater interdependence.

Integration is associated with a high degree of interdependence and ad hoc cooperation with limited interdependence. The institutionalization of cooperation, therefore, not only indicates the level of cooperation but also reflects how actors perceived the advantages and disadvantages of interdependence. Finally, the three ideal types, as policy proposals in transitional South Africa, also had spatial dimensions; that is, they disagreed about whether to follow the developmental, market, or ad hoc model and about what countries might be included in a regional economic integration/cooperation program. Thus, one position may encourage integration but only between South Africa and a few select countries, while another position may favor ad hoc cooperation but within a wider continental context.

Developmental Cooperation: The African National Congress, Labor, and Small Business

The ANC and what is often referred to as the democratic movement predictably moved the farthest away from apartheid South Africa's regional policy and advocated strong institutional ties to the region that would encourage greater interdependence. The ANC was an amalgamation of groups, and it was not at all clear at first what position the group would take regarding regional cooperation. The ANC's discussion document on foreign policy that was released in early 1994 covered "both poles of the current debate: co-operation versus integration"[10] in South Africa. Arne Tostensen posited that an ANC-dominated government would not deviate all that much from the former government's policy toward the region because "a rather narrowly perceived 'national interest,' however defined, is likely to carry the day."[11] Chris Alden, a well-respected South African political scientist, on the other hand, posited that "[p]erhaps the most obvious remaining concession to the ANC's history as a liberation movement is the stated commitment to ordering regional relations on a more equitable basis."[12]

ANC statements during the early transition period could be used to support either position. The argument that the status quo would survive the transition is given credence by the ANC's announcement that foreign policy would be subjected to domestic constraints and not to some sort of debt of gratitude to the Front-Line States. The 1992 ANC policy guidelines asserted that "[t]he foreign policy of a democratic South Africa will be primarily shaped by the nature of its domestic policies and objectives directed at serving the needs and interests of our people."[13] Trevor Manuel, the ANC head of economic affairs, was on record as cautioning that the ANC would need to work with business leaders on regional economic matters.[14] As the transition progressed through the first election and the administration of Nelson Mandela, the ANC drew closer to business. As will be argued in the following chapter, it is only natural for a party to expand its core when it goes from a resistance movement with an emphasis on overthrowing the state to a government with the responsibility to govern a country. Quite literally, as the former it exclusively represented one group, the disenfranchised, and as the other it represents the full spectrum of South Africa's political society.

However, the weight of ANC opinion as revealed in its position papers and statements pointed toward a new regional foreign policy. As Manuel cautioned at the SADC Annual Consultative Conference in 1993:

> A regional programme will not gain the legitimacy and support it needs to take off unless key stakeholders effectively participate in the process of formulating and executing the programme. The business community is clearly one such stakeholder, but there are also others including the trade unions, women's organizations, peasants' associations, and many other representative bodies.[15]

The ANC was formed by what could be considered a Black elite. Many of its early leaders were lawyers. Nonetheless, its constituency was mainly made up of the Black lower classes and labor. As successful as the rapprochement between business and the ANC may have been,[16] the "needs and interests of our people" means something different to an ANC government than it would to an NP-led government.[17]

The ANC and the democratic movement consistently argued for developmental cooperation and deeper regional interdependence. What institutional form that cooperation would take was less clear. However, there was agreement that bilateral relations should be rejected in favor of multilateral processes of cooperation in the region. The SADC, although it was itself in transition, was the vehicle the ANC chose for driving regional cooperation forward. As Trevor Manuel stated:

> Our longer-term objective is regional integration in an environment of non-exploitative, mutually beneficial relations. However, the short-term advantage sought in present relations with South Africa could relegate the principle of non-exploitative and mutually beneficial relations to a mere pipe dream. I am reminded of a slogan on a T-shirt being sold outside this door that reads, "United we bargain, divided we beg." I would like to appeal that, even in the short-term, relations with SA be guided by those six simple words.[18]

Manuel was warning SADC members that an equitable regional arrangement is more likely to be found in a multilateral rather than bilateral mode of cooperation. Post-apartheid South Africa would caution the SADC along the same line five years later when the SADC embraced the idea of a regional free trade area for Southern Africa. By eliminating most tariffs between countries within the SADC, a free trade area would be the first step in market cooperation/integration.

The most thorough analysis of South Africa's regional role by the democratic movement was the report of the Macroeconomic Research Group (MERG) entitled *Reconstructing Economic Relations with the Southern African Region: Issues and Options for a Democratic South Africa*. MERG was established in 1992 with Canadian and other foreign financing and involved top South African academics. The coordinator of MERG was Vella Pillay, who spent thirty-five years in exile as a leader of Great Britain's anti-apartheid movement. The group was left-leaning and supported by labor. Two of the study's authors would play central roles in the crafting of post-apartheid South Africa's regional trade policy: Mfundo Nkuhlu, future head of the African sector of the Department of Trade and Industry, and Rob Davies, future MP and chairperson of the Portfolio Committee on Trade. The report concluded that there were three possible avenues

South Africa's regional policy could take—neomercantilism, hegemonic bilateralism, and cooperative regionalism. Their choice was the third, the "path most consistent with principles already espoused by the ANC," which called for active participation in an organization established by the region that espoused the goals of cooperation and integration. Most important:

> [We recognise] that any such programme would, in the Southern African context, necessarily have to include significant counter-polarisation measures of various sorts, have a strong development focus and seek to involve in the process of formulation and execution a range of key constituencies. This option would also require the development of an approach that places all aspects of national economic policy within the parameters of a regional perspective.[19]

The ANC's prodevelopment policy was also embedded in its general foreign-policy goals and was consistent with the three cornerstones of the ANC's stated regional foreign policy. The first cornerstone was the ANC's emphasis on regionalism. Thabo Mbeki, head of the ANC's Department of International Affairs (later South Africa's first vice president and its second president), noted that the South African economy was linked to the economies of its neighbors in many ways and that economic growth in South Africa depended on its ability to export capital, goods, and services to those countries. If the South African economy was to grow, it also needed to maintain communication and transportation links with neighboring states and to import labor from those nations. He later argued for a regional system of "agreed relations," not a laissez-faire situation.[20] Nelson Mandela agreed: "Southern Africa commands a special priority in our foreign policy. We are inextricably part of southern Africa and our destiny is linked to that of a region, which is much more than a geographic concept."[21]

The second cornerstone of the ANC's regional foreign policy was equitable regional relations—a central component of the prodevelopment approach. At the 1991 SADC Annual Consultative Conference, Nelson Mandela stated that "a liberated South Africa will come into SADC on the basis of an agreed regional plan that would ensure balanced regional development and beneficial cooperation among various countries."[22] The ANC's blueprint for economic development for post-apartheid South Africa, the Reconstruction and Development Programme (RDP), took the position that "[i]f South Africa attempts to dominate its neighbors, it will restrict their growth, reducing their potential as markets, worsening their unemployment, and causing increased migration to South Africa."[23] Clearly, the ANC's foreign policy was a departure from the laager mentality of apartheid South Africa and the NP.

The third cornerstone of the ANC's regional policy was promoting regional interdependence. The link between advancing regional interdependence and supporting cooperation through sectoral bargaining was explained in the MERG study: "It has further been suggested that a mutually beneficial and sustainable new arrangement will best be arrived at through a process of negotiation and bargaining allowing for trade-off in various areas as well as the development of areas of cooperation."[24] ANC General Secretary Alfred Nzo (who was later the ANC's first foreign minister) noted that "[t]hat dialogue will have to address many concrete and complex issues—trade and investment policy, agricultural and industrial cooperation, tourism, transport, water, electricity, and the thorny issue of migrant labor."[25] By expanding the scope of integration/cooperation, the ANC would not only tighten the bonds of cooperation within the region but also introduce areas where South Africa could not dominate. By ceding some leverage to its neighbors, South Africa would indirectly reinforce the first goal of equitable regional integration/cooperation.

The ANC's regional foreign policy indicated a preference for cooperation to achieve economic development, and for the SADC as the vehicle for getting there. There was a close relationship between the two organizations; the SADC's 1993 "Regional Relations and Cooperation: Post-Apartheid Southern Africa—A Macro Framework Study Report" (by Chinyamata Chipeta and Robert Davies) shared contributors with the MERG study on regional cooperation.

The ANC's support for prodevelopment cooperation was congruent with the interests of South African labor for a number of reasons. Laissez-faire economic integration had the potential to destabilize the labor market in South Africa. Muzi Buthelezi, general secretary of the Chemical Workers' Industrial Union, argued that it was important to create opportunities for economic development and employment in all Southern African countries. The National Union of Metalworkers of South Africa concurred; its regional education officer stated that "we need a job creation strategy not only in South Africa but for the whole region."[26]

The cost to South Africa of ignoring the labor needs of its neighbors was clear. By one estimate, free regional labor mobility that would include labor would mean that South Africa would have to absorb 500,000 to 750,000 low-income people.[27] But South Africa had been reducing its level of migrant labor. The National Union of Mineworkers, the powerful

Black mineworkers' union, was ending its policy of supporting the migration of single men; because it is prohibitively expensive for whole families to move, this effectively inhibited labor migration. The Employment Bureau of Africa, the recruiting arm of the Chamber of Mines, had closed most of its distant offices. The effects of this policy were reflected in the reduction of the number of foreign workers in South Africa. For instance, the number of migrant employees in the gold and coal mines in South Africa peaked at 316,825 in 1987; it was 224,345 in 1991. The ANC has also registered concern about regional labor mobility: "The entire period since the mid-1970s . . . has seen a major reduction of 'foreign' migrant workers."[28] The ANC had also registered concern about regional labor mobility. The RDP stated: "If we seek mutual cooperation, we can develop a large, stable market offering stable employment and common labour standards in all areas, and thus reduce the pressure for migration from our neighbors."[29] The second reason South African labor did not support a laissez-faire approach to regional economic cooperation was that jobs would be lost if labor-intensive industries such as textiles and clothing, footwear, food, and paper were to move to cheaper labor markets in neighboring countries.[30] It was clear that efforts to address this by creating uniform wage structures across the region would likely fail. For instance, the Zimbabwe Congress of Trade Unions' textile affiliate accepted the idea of standardization in basic working conditions but not in wages, where it had a competitive advantage with South Africa.[31] Because the membership of the labor movement was tied to labor-intensive industry, it could not afford a market approach to regional integration.

In 1991, South African labor had already begun to cooperate with the SADC. First, the SADC created the Southern African Trade Union Coordination Council (SATUCC), which South Africa's two main labor federations, the Congress of South African Trade Unions (COSATU) and the National Council of Trade Unions (NACTU), had joined.[32] In 1991, SATUCC published the Draft Social Charter of Fundamental Rights of Workers in Southern Africa. COSATU played a major role in creating the document.[33] The Draft Social Charter focused on the "freedom of movement, residence and employment throughout the region." It also stated that workers must be guaranteed certain rights throughout the region to prevent "social dumping," or the practice of moving operations in pursuit of cheap labor.[34] As did the SADC, SATUCC envisioned regional cooperation/integration as a negotiated process; free market strategies were contrary to the regulatory thrust of SATUCC's approach.[35] Finally, as South African labor identified with the idea that small- and medium-size

enterprises were the best bet for creating employment, it would be expected to support the ANC's position.[36]

One source of unexpected support for the ANC's position was small-
and medium-sized Afrikaner businesses.[37] This sector supported strong regional ties because of their dependence on regional markets.[38] Explicit
support for the ANC was evident in statements by the director of Die
Afrikaans Handelsinstituut (AHI), which represents predominantly Afrikaner small- and medium-sized businesses, that South Africa should look
both politically and economically to its neighbors.[39] The AHI had developed a good relationship with the ANC; it is ironic that the Afrikaner *petit
bourgeoisie* had more in common with the ANC's vision for the region than
it did with the vision of Afrikaner-run big business.

Market Cooperation: The Bureaucracy

The position of the outgoing National Party government changed between
the early transition period and the months just before the 1994 elections.
Earlier, it had favored the creation of a regional common market that
would allow for both free trade and free movement of capital.[40] By 1992,
the desire for a common market had cooled. In 1992, the governor of the
Reserve Bank, for instance, warned against "vast new common markets in
Africa."[41] The approach favored by the ex-government was labeled the
"minimalist" scenario,[42] although it would ultimately include elements of
a common market.

Although bureaucrats, and in the case of South Africa this means
mostly Afrikaner government employees, can be considered a cohesive social segment of society,[43] treating the government as a distinct interest
group can be problematic. Within the apartheid South African government there was traditionally a disagreement between the Departments of
Finance and Foreign Affairs over the status of the Southern African Customs Union. In 1992, the Department of Finance considered SACU a
financial drain and went as far as proposing that it be dissolved. It also
demanded that South Africa's partners agree to a cut in their compensation.[44] The Department of Foreign Affairs, on the other hand, saw SACU
as valuable for improving South Africa's international image because it
created the appearance of "very cordial" economic relations between it and
some of its neighbors.[45] It vetoed Finance's suggestion.

But during the transition, the bureaucracy cohered on a common
policy proposal, what I refer to below as the Maasdorp Report, and thus
wielded considerable influence in the transition government. A *New York*

Times article put it this way: "Like a new groom who has agreed to take in his bride's difficult relatives, Nelson Mandela has found himself wedded to an extended family of some two million state employees, dominated by white, Afrikaans-speaking men."[46] A recurring theme in my discussions with South African government and business leaders was the enduring influence of the South African civil service, at least early in the transition. The bureaucracy was entrenched, powerful, and quite capable of influencing or shaping the policy agenda.[47] South African political economist Hermann Giliomee relates that the Afrikaners saw the state as an Afrikaner state: "[T]hey had come to value power not for purely instrumental reasons, but as an end in itself."[48] The ANC was aware of strength and influence of the civil service. The MERG group, for instance, supported the creation of a new fiscal and financial commission because it did not trust the civil service.[49] The South African newspaper *Business Day* described the situation thus: "The list of powerful interest groups outside the ANC's sphere goes on and on: the 1.2 million strong civil service is dominated by Afrikaners, who are scarcely natural allies of the ANC."[50] This interest group understood power and sought to protect its privileged place in South Africa's regional foreign policymaking.

On January 21, 1994, there was an interdepartmental meeting on South Africa's regional role in the post-apartheid era. Participants included the Department of Finance, the Department of Foreign Affairs, the Department of Trade and Industry, the Central Economic Advisory Center, the Development Bank of Southern Africa, and the Industrial Development Corporation. SACOB originally participated but later dropped out.[51] Each of these government agencies would play an important role in South Africa's regional relations. During apartheid, the Department of Foreign Affairs took the lead in promoting regional cooperation. This is largely because regional cooperation was primarily seen as a political tool. As argued in Chapter 2, better regional relations were seen as a way to soften South Africa's international image. Because the Department of Finance ran SACU, it also played a central role. However, its mandate did not include regional diplomacy and it was often at odds with the Department of Foreign Affairs over the benefits of participation in SACU because, while Foreign Affairs saw the political benefit of regional cooperation, the Department of Finance saw SACU as a drain on the state treasury. In the post-apartheid era, the Department of Finance plays a central role in regional integration/cooperation because it is in charge of South Africa's position as head of the finance sector of the SADC. The Department of Trade and Industry (roughly the same as the U.S. Department of Commerce) was handcuffed by sanctions during apartheid. It formulates and coordinates trade policies. During the transition, it played a key role in defining South Africa's regional relations and has largely superseded the role of Foreign Affairs in the formation of post-apartheid South Africa's regional relations and, in particular, concerning regional economic integration/cooperation. The Central Economic Advisory Service is a government-funded think thank. Among other things, during the transition it produced studies on how South Africa should promote regional economic integration/cooperation. The DBSA is a state development bank whose original mission was to help develop the homelands. During apartheid, these homelands were nominally independent states, thus the "southern" in its title. The international community did not accept this apartheid sleight of hand. During the transition, the DBSA's mandate expanded to include all of Southern Africa. It is a central player in developing South Africa's regional relations. The Industrial Development Corporation is a South African parastatal (state corporation). It provides capital for industrial projects, export and import financing, and small business development. As will be discussed in Chapter 5, it played a central role in defining transitional South Africa's manufacturing and trade policy. During that time it was aligned with the National Party. In the post-apartheid era it has made the adjustment to a more objective advocate of South Africa's (and the region's) economic development.

Subsequent meetings led to a report prepared by Professor Gavin Maasdorp entitled "A Vision for Economic Integration and Cooperation in Southern Africa" (hereafter the Maasdorp Report), which articulated a common position among the participating departments on how to institutionalize regional cooperation in post-apartheid Southern Africa.

The position of the Maasdorp Report was superficially similar to the ANC's position but had both obvious and subtle differences. The commonalities included a stated belief that the region was important, that equitable regional development was necessary, and that interdependence should be encouraged. However, the Maasdorp Report promulgated a linear process of regional economic cooperation. It called for an incremental or step-by-step approach that included trade and monetary integration where feasible, and economic cooperation along sectoral and policy lines to the fullest extent possible.[52] This approach would build on institutional strengths (for example, SACU), concentrate on commonalities, and adopt a "variable geometry," or multispeed, approach (that is, it would let a country join a grouping as and when it was ready instead of setting unrealistic timetables).

The institutionalization of cooperation under the Maasdorp plan was fundamentally different from that articulated by the ANC. First, it adopted the linear mode of market integration while rejecting linkages between issues and prodevelopment cooperation. Second, it was an explicit and implicit rejection of the SADC. One participant at the January 21st meeting stated that the SADC talked about economic integration but really wanted political union, an exaggeration of the SADC's intentions.[53] The ex-government's coolness toward the SADC, which was obvious early in the transition period, was partially a response to its close relationship with the ANC. For instance, although the SADC invited the government to the opening of its new Johannesburg office in the spring of 1993, which was marked by SADC Executive Secretary Simba Makoni's address to about thirty political, business, and labor organizations, it did not attend.[54] The Maasdorp Report represents the NP government's explicit rejection of SADC. First, it adopted SACU as the institutional anchor for regional economic integration/cooperation. This meant it supported the market approach. Second, SACU was run by the Afrikaner bureaucracy.

The SADC emphasized sectoral bargaining within a regional context. The Maasdorp Report was based on the institutional foundation of SACU, and, as political scientist Umesh Kumar stated: "Among all the economic integration arrangements, SACU is perhaps the only one in which the members have surrendered part of their economic sovereignty not to a supra-national body, but to one of their own members, South Africa."[55] SACU had buttressed South Africa's power and wealth in the region for close to a century.[56] The consensus in the Afrikaner bureaucracy was that the building blocks of a new regional dispensation would be SACU and the Common Monetary Area.

The SADC emphasized regional bargaining across many sectors, including trade, migration, water, transport, electricity. Its headquarters is in Gaborone. While not overtly pursuing political union, the SADC's form of regional economic integration/cooperation went well beyond the idea of moving from a free trade area to an economic union. In South Africa, SACU had been under reconsideration since 1981, and in 1993 a Joint Technical Task Group was set up to examine the SACU agreement. In particular, a controversy over the formula for revenue-sharing was central to the negotiations on changes to the SACU agreement. Prominent businessman David Brink felt at the time that it would be sensible to expand SACU.[57] The first issue in the reconsideration was whether SACU should in fact be expanded and what countries should be invited to join.

As the Maasdorp Report states, South Africa already had bilateral agreements with Malawi, Mozambique, and Zimbabwe. However, the report argued that no movement should be made along bilateral lines regarding renegotiations (i.e. with Zimbabwe, because the bilateral agreement was up for renewal) or new treaties:

> It would serve no purpose to tamper with such agreements before establishing a comprehensive multilateral economic cooperation strategy, after which the question of bilateral agreements can be addressed. Each of these agreements is a reflection of the particular circumstances pertaining at the time it was concluded.[58]

This stance is interesting for two reasons. First, it gives preference to a multilateral framework. Second, it implicitly acknowledges that the bilateral agreements already in place were negotiated in a different political climate, one where the goal was to gain legitimacy, not to obtain new markets. The bilateral agreement with Malawi, for instance, was considered pure political expediency.

Of the three countries in bilateral agreements with South Africa, Zimbabwe was considered the best candidate for inclusion in SACU; however, if Zimbabwe were to be included, SACU's compensation formula would have to be rewritten.[59] The Maasdorp Report argued that SACU could be expanded by merging with the Common Monetary Area, which would bring in Botswana, the only SACU member outside the Area. The report also noted that "[g]iven the high degree of *de facto* labor mobility, an agreement on immigration would then be all that would be required to convert SACU into a Southern African Common Market."[60] SACU would, therefore, be the organizational anchor of a process of market cooperation/integration, much as the European Coal and Steel Community and then the European Economic Community had been for Europe.

The final part of the Maasdorp Report proposed an association between the "new" SACU and the rest of the region along the lines of the European Free Trade Area and the European Union.[61] The report suggested phased tariff reductions between the core, the BLSN states and South Africa, and the rest; monetary agreements (for example, an exchange-rate union); and sectoral and technical cooperation.[62] It argued that the present Preferential Trade Area was particularly unwieldy and therefore envisioned an association between the SACU group and the rest of the SADC. The result of this differentiated cooperation dispensation would be:

- an economic union between South Africa and Lesotho
- a common market between the economic union, Swaziland, and Namibia
- a free trade area between the SACU and Zimbabwe
- a preferential trade area with the rest of SADC(C)[63]

The Maasdorp Report scenario followed the classic linear model of market integration.

The old-guard bureaucracy supported market cooperation, but it also acknowledged the importance of Southern Africa to economic development in South Africa. However, it focused on trade and monetary issues and paid little attention to regional development. In some ways, it mirrored the classic marriage between neofunctionalism and regional economic integration in Europe. The Maasdorp Report and the notion of SACU as the institutional core of economic regional integration in Southern Africa never gained traction. First, it represented the status-quo position of the bureaucrats (mostly Afrikaner). The rapid displacement of this group when the ANC came to power marginalized them. As will be discussed in Chapter 8, a new breed of bureaucrats came to dominate; in particular, the Department of Trade and Industry personified this change. SACU was never really abolished, but it was not at the center of debate or ANC policy after the 1994 election. In some cases, such as the DBSA, the change was driven not so much by a turnover in personnel as it was by an organization adopting to the policy preferences of the ANC.

Ad Hoc Cooperation: South Africa's Parastatals and Conglomerates

Ad hoc cooperation includes bilateral trade agreements and bilateral functional cooperation. Both were well established by the time of South Africa's transition. These were areas that some analysts inside and outside of government argued would be the most propitious avenues for cooperation between South Africa and the region.[64] Because bilateral relations would reinforce the status quo in Southern Africa, some (particularly opponents of apartheid) saw ad hoc cooperation as CONSAS redux and called it a neo-apartheid policy. Free of the trade constraints imposed by international economic sanctions, South Africa could continue to expand its influence in the region without necessarily joining a regional group. As Fantu Cheru, a political scientist and expert on Southern African foreign relations, noted, "The vulnerability of the neighboring countries is well understood by the [South African] business community and this explains partly why they favor bilateral relations over a formal regional integration."[65]

Professor P. Smit felt in September 1989 that before the end of apartheid, an informal but fairly effective regional system functioned in Southern Africa, centered on South Africa. This system was fairly effective from South Africa's perspective.[66] The system was characterized by a series of bilateral deals between South Africa and specific regional states. Some academics argued that there was nothing wrong with bilateral agreements. Dr. Paul J. Vorster, an Afrikaner academic and supporter of ad hoc cooperation, argued in 1989 that "the Republic does not seek to dominate, but rather to enter into pacts and agreements whereby mutual dependence and trust is created."[67] Vorster pointed to the Lesotho Highlands Water Project and the Maputo Port improvements in Mozambique as examples of positive bilateral cooperation.

But South Africa's economic dominance meant that it dominated bilateral agreements. It is curious that neighboring countries pursued bilateral deals right up to the 1994 elections, leading Robert Davies to comment:

> The second trend born of desperation on the part of neighboring countries and/or expectations, partly fueled by the present South African government's "new diplomacy," is towards bi-lateral deals based on a "pragmatic extension" of existing relations. This approach essentially involves prioritizing short-term advantage above long-term considerations of transformation.[68]

A 1993 SADC study on how to formally integrate South Africa into the region cautioned against continuing bilateral relations. It argued that the prevailing bilateralism was due to the perception that South Africa could be a "locomotive of growth" and that South Africa's limited resources put a premium on closing deals as soon as possible.[69]

This ad hoc position was favored by South Africa's conglomerate and parastatal sector. It was most forcefully propagated by the 1993 SACOB document on regional cooperation in post-apartheid Southern Africa, "South Africa's Options for Future Relations with Southern Africa and the European Community."[70] SACOB's economic policy director, Ben van Rensburg, echoing the theme of the study, argued in 1994 that South Africa should be cautious about which regional trade organization it joined and that it should look outside the continent for trading partners.[71] There were three main points in the SACOB document: extraregional trade should be emphasized, regional interdependence should be resisted, and regional cooperation should have a limited organizational superstructure.

The SACOB document's introduction states: "Commercial relations with the region are likely to rank lower in priority and may be fashioned more by political predilections than by a sober assessment of the national interest."[72] This was an implicit caution against joining the SADC. The underlining rationale of the SACOB approach was the opposite of that of the ANC. Whereas the MERG study, and ANC policy in general, emphasized the importance of the African market and of Southern Africa in particular, SACOB discounted the importance of Africa. The SACOB document clearly broke with ANC policy:

> Economic policy will be pursued in the knowledge that the country's economic welfare depends far more on its ability to compete on overseas markets than on penetration of African markets. . . . South Africa will not compensate neighboring countries for real or alleged damage inflicted by past South African policies; nor will it readily cede sovereignty or resources to any supranational body.[73]

In other words, South Africa should emphasize that it belonged to the First World and discourage the perception of itself as a Third World country.

It was because this view situated South Africa in the First World, and the rest of the region in the Third World, that SACOB ignored the question of equitable regional development. Instead, the problem was framed as SADC countries attempting to entrap South Africa in an arrangement meant to benefit the relatively underdeveloped. As one prominent South African business leader stated, "South Africa would have to be subject to all sorts of imposed and self-imposed restraints and limitations in order to maintain balance and any sort of harmony within the organization."[74] The SACOB document stated:

> SADCC members—and especially Zimbabwe, the most industrially advanced—are apprehensive of being overwhelmed economically and dominated politically by South Africa. Conscious of the great disparity between that country and its present members, SADCC planners propose to create a dense net of rules and obligations to neutralize the Republic's competitive strength while ensuring that at the same time it provides the financial wherewithal for the development of the other member countries.[75]

SACOB's view was grounded in its disdain for regional interdependence. As do the MERG and Maasdorp Reports, the SACOB document frames the question of regional economic relations by distinguishing between cooperation and integration. It defined regional integration as "a state of affairs or a process involving the combination of separate economies into larger economic regions"; it defined cooperation as "formalized co-operation between countries without impairing the participants' national decision-making."[76] SACOB accepted only a limited form of the latter:

> While sound in principle, therefore, the striving for close integration in Southern Africa must proceed with caution and sensitivity. The unpleasantness that preceded the disintegration of the East African Community and the many disputes within SADCC and the PTA illustrate the tensions apt to result when barriers to trade and labour movements between countries are dismantled.[77]

Instead, South Africa should confine its regional cooperation to "functional cooperation," such as cooperation around transport, power, and water.[78]

Edward Osborn, chief economist for Standard Bank and a leader of the business community, wrote to Trevor Manuel, then head of the ANC's Economic Research Division, counseling against South Africa joining either the SADCC or the Preferential Trade Area (COMESA, the Common Market for Eastern and Southern Africa). Osborn argued that "whatever progress is to be made with respect to intra-regional trade is going to happen on a natural bilateral basis."[79] He pointed out that the SACOB document said that the SADCC's transport projects had not yet restored pre-1975 capacities and that successful regional schemes such as the Lesotho Highlands Water Project, the north-south railway through Swaziland, Botswana's Sua Pan Soda Ash Project, and the hydroelectric projects at Kariba, Cahora Bassa, and Ruacana were accomplished via bilateral arrangements outside the ambit of the SADCC.[80] Osborn felt that the SADCC had had only limited success in the past and that the newly envisioned SADC would expect South Africa to be the regional engine for growth. Like Osborn, SACOB concluded that the best institutional arrangement to promote regional cooperation, as its members defined it, would be based on the OECD: "It could serve as the platform for the discussion and recommendations concerning the region's needs and future institutional arrangements."[81]

The second type of ad hoc cooperation is bilateral functional cooperation, which SACOB subscribed to. Gavin Reilly, executive director of the Anglo-American Corporation, outlined the pro–functional cooperation stance:

Political reform in South Africa has opened up further opportunities for cooperation in [Southern Africa] in the fields of tourism, transport, electricity supply, and the development and use of scarce water resources. These are the sinews that bind together the region. . . . We need substantive progress on the ground towards an enabling environment for business, rather than what may be, at the present time, castles in the air.[82]

Bilateral infrastructure cooperation was well established, and South Africa's firms were poised to continue their regional dominance. Prior to the April 1994 elections, there was already concrete evidence of increased interest in South Africa in regional project aid. SAFTO, with the support of the Department of Finance, was examining ways for South African companies to profit from development projects.[83] A number of South Africa's building contractors, equipment suppliers, and parastatals had increased their involvement in projects in Angola, Mozambique, and Zambia—for instance, the 1989 World Bank–financed project to upgrade Maputo's coal-fired power station.[84] Ironically, the quintessential example of multilateralism, the UN, may help South Africa avoid multilateralism at the regional level through project lending. In May 1994, a UN mission was in South Africa to explain procurement needs and procedures for its supplies, services, and projects in Africa.[85] Three functional areas in particular appeared optimal for this form of regional cooperation: water, electricity, and transportation. The beneficiaries would be South Africa's giant parastatals such as Pornet (ports), Eskom (power), Transnet (transportation), and, indirectly, the Development Bank of Southern Africa.

Developmental and infrastructure projects, indeed, did have the potential to stimulate both South Africa's domestic economy and its participation in the regional economy. Robert Davies noted that advice on how to get aid contracts from international donor agencies for such projects had become a growth industry in South Africa.[86] The manager of the South African Trade Organization, Andrew Maggs, stated:

South Africans are well poised to win World Bank tenders for projects north of our borders. They can offer shorter lead times than Europeans and the Japanese, cheaper prices because of the weak rand, close proximity to the countries, and technology consistent with the requirements of Africa.[87]

This approach was echoed by the head of the Economic Division of the Steel and Engineering Industries Federation of South Africa, who was also the convener of the Trade and Industry Working Group of the National

Economic Forum (NEF). He stated that building infrastructure for the rest of Africa had great potential and that South African engineers were already getting contracts.[88]

The ad hoc position, therefore, rejected even the more limited institutionalization of cooperation/integration promoted by the Maasdorp Report. It was, as well, an explicit rejection of regional interdependence and the clearest counterpole to the ANC's position.

During South Africa's transition, various groups presented clear preferences on how to institutionalize its future regional economic relations; CODESA II included twenty-one negotiating parties. Transitional South Africa was almost preternaturally pluralistic. Although the NP and the ANC dominated the discussions, the debate over cooperation in post-apartheid Southern Africa reflected divergent views. As with the apartheid era, South Africa had a strong interest in its region. And as with the apartheid era, regional relations were forged in the cauldron of domestic politics. It was, of course, no longer simply a matter of promoting NP interests. Post-apartheid South Africa's preferences for how to pursue regional relations were grounded in the ideological and material (commercial) foundations of self-interested domestic actors. The following chapters explore in more detail the source of those preferences.

The end of apartheid opened up new possibilities for South Africa in Southern Africa. This is best symbolized by South Africa's invitation to join the SADC, which was originally formed as an anti–South Africa alliance. But within South Africa there was a debate on exactly how to formalize regional relations and how to approach regional economic integration/cooperation in the region. The debate broke down into three positions: developmental regional economic integration/cooperation, market regional economic integration/cooperation, or ad hoc cooperation. Each had domestic support, respectively, by the ANC, Afrikaner bureaucracy, and big business.

Now that we have identified the competing preferences we need to explain where they came from. This is done in the next three chapters by looking at the competing economic ideologies, the competing manufacturing and trade polices, and the competing macroeconomic and finance policies in transitional South Africa. In short, the political economy of South Africa explains the preferences for how to formalize regional relations. But of course, policy in South Africa is not made in a vacuum—international factors matter.

External influences such as GATT (World Trade Organization), the IFIs, and the EU affected the development of South Africa's economy and, in particular, its trade policy. They directly and indirectly affect South Africa's regional economic relations. The post-apartheid South African state has certainly been pressured from the outside. How the South African state and its institutions actually make foreign policy is the subject of Chapter 7.

Both the local (domestic) and international politics of regional economic integration in South Africa are filtered through the state. The state itself, through the personal predilections of bureaucrats and the particular patterns of decision making concerning foreign affairs, has the final say on how South Africa will formalize regional relations. The state (republican explanation) may be the last piece of the analytical puzzle, but it is also where the ANC could institute the most change.

South Africa's journey from an international pariah state to a full and welcomed member of the international community and an acknowledged leader of the SADC is best understood by looking at its domestic dynamics and at how external actors affect those dynamics. A simple reading of the ANC prior to its election in 1994 would lead one to expect radical changes in South Africa's political economy and subsequently its regional policy once they were in power. This did not happen. However, certainly there was change. South Africa is now a member of the SADC and it actively seeks to cooperate with its neighbors. Nonetheless, the story of this book is not about the choice to cooperate but about *how* to cooperate—what the regional design and logic was behind choosing among three regional designs.

The new government, however, has not committed to a clear path among these three. It has, I argue, chosen to follow developmental integration/cooperation but in such a way that at the very least does not threaten the status quo—South Africa's large conglomerates remain powerful and influential. The following chapters will explain why this is the case. Almost a half-century of apartheid shaped South Africa's political economy. International forces have also inhibited the radical makeover some had expected. Nonetheless, the ANC's ideological proclivities, even in the face of material pressures, promise change. And the ANC does have a firm hold on the state. South Africa's regional relations have changed, and this means that neither regional market economic integration/cooperation nor regional ad hoc cooperation have been adopted. South Africa has taken a rather crooked path to developmental regional economic integration/cooperation. The ANC government has sought to placate business interests and international interests even as it seeks to represent a newly enfranchised Black majority and to reconstitute its regional relations.

4

Ideology and the Political Economy of Transitional South Africa

As Steven Krasner argued, "ideology coordinates expectations and delineates legitimate models of interaction between state institutions and societal actors, and may also serve as a basic source of identity."[1] In Emanuel Adler's words, ideologies "are powerful because they tell actors, including institutions, what to do."[2] What these two well-respected political scientists are saying is that both individuals and state institutions have ideological beliefs or predilections that influence the choices they make. Of course, rarely is ideology a perfect predictor of actual behavior. For instance, a senator from Pennsylvania may be ideologically in favor of a free market and free trade. But the senator might nonetheless vote for steel tariffs to protect an industry vital to the state (and his/her reelection): material interests matter. In the case of transitional South Africa, an ideological debate both preceded and helped define the debate over economic policy, including issues of manufacturing, trade, and regional economic foreign policy. It comes first in the series of chapters that explain the preferences outlined in the previous chapter because ideological leanings typically form the foundation of individual and institutional preferences concerning economic policy. Although such a debate never really ends, this chapter traces the ideological debate up until the eve of the first election in April 1994. Finally, one might conclude that the NP had little influence at this point. This would be a mistake. As the party in power, it still had the ability to shape the agenda and the debate in South Africa. Also, as it often spoke for big business, it represented a constituency even the ANC could not ignore. Indeed, one of the subplots of this chapter is that the ANC's policy moved more toward the NP's policy than vice versa. Michael Bratton and Nicholas van de Walle note that ideology is important for pro-democracy groups pushing for a transition.[3]

The ends pursued by the outgoing government and the ANC were fundamentally different. The outgoing apartheid government promoted consolidation of their constituents' dominant position in the national economy;[4] the ANC hoped to replace the old economy with a new one that would propel its disadvantaged core constituency up the economic ladder. Nonetheless, the newly elected ANC soon embraced neoliberal economic policies such as privatization of parastatals, low inflation, low deficits, and tight monetary policies. The neoliberal turn in post-apartheid South Africa was caused by a confluence of domestic and international currents embedded in the process of globalization.

The new ANC government argued that it was not rejecting the Reconstruction Development Programme but taking a middle road necessary to implement the program. For instance, Trevor Manuel, the ANC's first trade minister, argued in the fall of 1995:

> We are unambiguous about the fact that protection on demand has gone the way of the dodo. Furthermore, we have sufficient experience of bureaucratic failure to vest discretion in the state. This is the South Africa policy conundrum. We must, therefore, seek a middle route. Such middle route must be through a coalition of forces.[5]

Manuel is making two statements here. First, neither laissez-faire capitalism nor Keynesian economics will guide South Africa's economic and trade policy. Second, and more subtle and more telling, a "coalition of forces," or political bargain between supporters of those two economic philosophies, will be needed.

While the ANC and the NP had different ideological traditions, their ideologies were evolving in response to the vicissitudes of political power within South Africa and in response to external pressures. As early as 1990, the ANC and the NP government were acutely aware that external actors influenced South Africa's prospect for economic growth, particularly the World Bank and International Monetary Fund (IMF).[6] With their financial, intellectual, and political capital to draw on, the international financial institutions (IFIs) were a powerful force in transitional South Africa.[7]

The ideological debate underlying South Africa's foreign economic policy choices was evidenced in ANC/labor, NP, and IFI documents, and the discourse centered on those documents. Leading up to the April 1994 election in South Africa, the National Party and the African National Congress each produced, or adopted, blueprints for South Africa's post-apartheid economic development. The IFIs, as well, weighed in with their own advice.

The South African apartheid state had been strongly interventionist. The NP, after the watershed election of 1948, used the state to promote the interests of Afrikaners. The result was that 25 percent of the White labor force was employed in the civil service and another 50 percent in public corporations (parastatals).[8] The NP's industrial policy during this period aggressively pursued import-substitution industrialization (ISI).[9] However, the limitations of ISI had been known from the early 1970s (as a result of the Reynders Commission), and export-led growth, albeit with import protection, gained favor.

The NP's success in promoting its constituency's interests had the dialectical effect of challenging the apartheid system that had created an Afrikaner business class. During the 1980s, the NP began to move away from its strong statist position and use free market ideology to fill the ideological gap left by the increasingly discredited apartheid policy.[10] During the transition of the 1990s, both of South Africa's leading contenders for political power were in a state of ideological disarray,[11] and the NP was not alone in its growing acceptance of market principles. The ANC had also moved closer to market capitalism. There were different views within the ANC on economic policy and an evolution in its policy prescriptions that is typically traced back to a conference in Harare in April/May 1990. At this conference, the state was given a leading role in the post-apartheid economy.[12] As early as 1991, nonetheless, there were reports that the ANC and the business community had converged on a new economic policy for South Africa.[13] While the ANC's economic plan, entitled "The Reconstruction and Development Programme," remained ostensibly loyal to the ANC's philosophy, the new ANC government's 1994 white paper detailing how to implement the Reconstruction Development Programme outlined a more neoliberal program.[14] In fact, the ANC had long contained factions that were oriented toward the free market. Nonetheless, while the two major protagonists veered toward the ideological center, during the transition period they articulated different core beliefs, largely because of their different core constituencies.

The opposition movement in apartheid South Africa went through three stages.[15] The first phase was the Black Consciousness Movement as the center of opposition, which included the defiance campaign launched by the Nelson Mandela–led Youth League in 1952. The Charterist movement replaced the Black Consciousness Movement in the 1980s, though the latter remained central among fragments of the opposition movement. The focus of the Charterist movement was less on ideology and identity and more on concrete grievances. Civic organizations that constituted the core of the Charterist movement flourished because the apartheid economy was flourishing, among other reasons. The formal organizational arm of the Charterist movement was the UDF, which, in Anthony Marx's words, "avoided any explicit and detailed description of their ideology and thereby succeeded in forming a broad and active coalition."[16] The UDF's broad umbrella included key business interests in South Africa that were suffering from the fallout of apartheid. At first the UDF was less successful at getting the unions on board.[17] It was not until August 1987 that the UDF officially adopted the Freedom Charter and its anticapitalist rhetoric. As the 1980s came to an end, the UDF began to combine the anti-apartheid struggle with the anticapitalist struggle.

The third stage in the opposition struggle brings us to the transition period. After the UDF was banned in 1988, the South African union movement took center stage through its leadership of what became known as the mass democratic movement.[18] It combined the ideological coherence of the Black Consciousness Movement, through a focus on class issues, with the organizational coherence of the UDF. COSATU formally aligned with the ANC at a March 1986 meeting with the ANC in exile. This coalition, along with the South African Communist Party (SACP), would be the NP's opponent in the April 1994 election. In the process, COSATU was forced to water down its socialist rhetoric.

The apartheid opposition led by the ANC-COSATU coalition entered the transition period with an ethos of pragmatism but imbued with a strong ideological posture, partly because the economic downturn had radicalized labor's demands. By the end of the 1980s, the elites in the opposition movement had begun to respond to the pressures of a coalition led by the unionized workers.[19] In the waning days of apartheid, the ideological battle lines were clearly drawn. Although the ANC obviously contained remnants of its Charterist past, in particular Charterism's problem-solving orientation, it contested the first free election as a coalition that believed in a central role for the state in the post-apartheid economy. The incumbent NP government, on the other hand, distanced itself from in own quasi-socialist inheritance and distinguished itself from the ANC by embracing market capitalism. An NP election poster captured (if exaggerated) the ideological divide: "Sê vir die ANC en Kommunisme" (Tell it to the ANC and Communists). The positions of the competing groups were captured in their respective economic platforms. We now take a closer look at their respective ideologies.

In March 1993, the Central Economic Advisory Service, in consultation with the South African Reserve Bank, government departments, and the special economic advisor to the minister of finance (who acted as coordinator) published a document called "The Restructuring of the South African Economy: A Normative Model Approach" (referred to as the Normative Economic Model, or NEM). Although the authors had not intended it to become the NP platform, the NP adopted it as such.[20] The South African finance minister, Derek Keys, claimed at the time that South Africa had only one model for economic growth on the table—the NEM, which promoted a free market economy.[21]

The ANC's position in the debate over future economic policy in South Africa just prior to the April 1994 election was outlined in two documents: the "Reconstruction and Development Programme" (hereafter RDP) and *Making Democracy Work: A Framework for Macroeconomic Policy in South Africa* (hereafter MERG Report). The former was a policy document that went through several drafts and was official ANC policy. The latter was drafted by officials from MERG who were aligned with the ANC. MERG was left-leaning and seemed to have little leverage in the immediate ANC post-apartheid administration,[22] but many of its key members were important ANC officials and would obtain high-level positions in the first ANC government, and many of its ideas found their way into the RDP.[23] The RDP was the product of broad-based cooperation by the ANC, COSATU, the SACP, the South African Council of Churches, and the South African National Civic Organization. It was clearly consistent with a Keynesian developmental framework and represented the aspirations of the previously disenfranchised.[24] The RDP should, in fact, be read as a political manifesto, a descendant of the Freedom Charter. Patrick Bond called it "a state of mind—a philosophy—rather than an actual programme."[25] The second document, MERG's *Making Democracy Work: A Framework for Macroeconomic Policy in South Africa,* was a more detailed blueprint and a specific counterstrategy to the NP/ex-government's economic program. The MERG Report was addressed "to the Members of the Democratic Movement of South Africa," and it explicitly used the NP government's NEM economic development plan as a straw man.

Both the IMF and the World Bank were active, as well, in the debate over how to structure the post-apartheid economy. The preface to one IMF study stated: "Within this context [democratic South Africa], a debate has begun on the appropriate economic policies to be pursued in a new South Africa to address the country's acute socioeconomic backlogs. This study aims at making a contribution to that debate."[26] Hein Marais states that the "ideological barrage was incessant."

> Lavishly promoted (in the form of books, videos, multi-media presenta-
> tions, newspaper supplements), their impact was ensured by a bewilder-
> ing assortment of seminars, conferences, workshops, briefings, interna-
> tional "fact-finding" trips and high profile visits by carefully chosen
> "experts"—financed by business and foreign development agencies. The
> international financial institutions were in the center of this barrage.
> ANC leaders were fêted with private "orientation" sessions and confabs
> at exclusive game resorts.[27]

The purpose of the pressure from the IFIs was to convince the ANC that their quasi-socialist proposals would not work in South Africa. They hoped to get the ANC to join the Washington Consensus: the macroeco-nomic stabilization policies of the IMF, the adoption of market deregulation by the World Bank, supply-side economics, and a push for privatization.

The international influence on the domestic debate over future eco-nomic policy reveals in sharp relief the ideological divide separating the ANC and the incumbent government. It also reveals transnational alli-ances that would continue to influence and shape post-apartheid South Africa's political economy. In post-apartheid South Africa, these alliances would begin to crisscross the ANC-NP divide.

The Role of the State in Post-Apartheid South Africa

The ANC and the Role of the State

The economic policy propagated by the RDP and MERG Report lay some-where between undiluted statism and Keynesianism. The key COSATU planners who participated in drafting the RDP were Alec Erwin, Jay Naidoo, and Bernie Fanaroff.[28] The program called for unbundling and deracializing corporate ownership, a strategic role for the public sector (i.e., in providing housing, electricity, and water), a living wage, training for workers, land reform, and the more conservative policy of fiscal restraint. This will be elaborated below. The MERG Report made similar arguments, but with an even stronger leaning toward the left, such as the idea that the South African Reserve Bank be taken under the public wing.

As the NP's obvious successor, the ANC anticipated inheriting the levers of the state power that had been so arduously expanded by over forty years of Afrikaner rule. The ANC could naturally be expected to show less enthusiasm for a smaller state. But the ANC also had a strong socialist tradition. In South African political scientists Lipton and Simkins's words, the ANC:

> was also influenced by its own statist tradition and its beliefs, with origins in both Fabian and communist thinking, in the virtues of interventionist and even commandist economic planning and management, reinforced by its long-standing hostility to capitalism and its alleged symbiotic relationship with apartheid.[29]

The 1955 Freedom Charter that for close to four decades had stood as the anti-apartheid struggle's manifesto most prominently portrayed this tradition. Marina Ottaway described it thus:

> The Freedom Charter, the 1955 manifesto to which all ANC members subscribed, carried the strong imprint of ideas prevalent in the early period of Africa's anticolonial struggle, later formalized in some countries as doctrines of African socialism—an ideal of justice, equality, and economic development brought about through the intervention of a benevolent state in the best interest of the entire population.[30]

As Jeffrey Herbst argued, "the extremely vague Freedom Charter written in 1955—which seemed to demand the nationalization of the mines, banks, and monopolies—was still considered the last word on the ANC's economic doctrine when it was legalized in 1990."[31] As South Africa began its transition, the Freedom Charter, which was written in 1955, was still considered ANC doctrine.

Although the RDP represented a subtle move away from the strong statist position of the 1955 Freedom Charter,[32] it also responded to what the ANC considered to be the NP's ideologically cloaked dismantling of the state. The MERG Report stated that "the starting point for the calculations is the principle that in order to overcome a major failure of policy in the recent past, the relative size of public sector investment needs to be increased."[33] The long list of government-funded projects found in both the RDP and the MERG Report illustrated the demand-led philosophy of the ANC.

The RDP's statism was fueled by its perception that the NP was consciously eviscerating the state that it knew the ANC would soon control: "in recent years, under the cloak of secrecy, the apartheid state privatised or commercialized many agencies in the public sector (such as Transnet, Eskom, Telkom, Iscor, Forskor, SAA, the Post Office, Forestry, and others). Often this policy, unilaterally imposed for ideological reasons, harmed basic services."[34] The NP's rediscovery of the private realm was hardly surprising. The South African government was determined to shape the domestic, regional, and international environments under which any post-apartheid government would have to operate.[35] Nonetheless, supporters of privatization argued that the notion that South Africa's large parastatals, the backbone of Afrikaner economic privilege, should be privatized was consistent with the policy of "unbundling," or breaking up the overcentralized conglomerates that dominated the South African economy.

A draft chapter of the MERG Report written in part by Tito Mboweni (labor minister in the first ANC government) cautioned against rapid antitrust moves by the government and argued against forced unbundling.[36] The MERG Report added that "it is possible to assess the apparent shifts in government policy in which privatization, trade liberalization, and the abandonment of separate development have been to the fore."[37]

The MERG Report offered evidence for its conclusion by tracing the demise of the Board of Trade and Industry (BTI).[38] In the late 1980s, the BTI pushed for structural adjustment programs that would not rely purely on market forces, in effect relying on South Africa's traditional state-managed approach to economic development. In 1990, the Department of Trade and Industry crippled the BTI by withdrawing ninety personnel seconded there. The BTI Bill of 1992 further eviscerated the BTI,[39] and its role in planning economic development was displaced by the Industrial Development Corporation, which promoted reliance on private markets for economic development.[40]

The democratic movement countered that the parastatals could be used for Black empowerment.[41] The ANC hoped to inherit the extensive network of state corporations that the NP had used to promote Afrikaner employment. For the NP, privatization was one way to keep this valuable resource out of the hands of their rival.

Although the ANC's political tradition and its role as heir apparent to the state machinery seemed to reinforce a socialist ideology, the RDP claimed that the ANC favored a mixed economy. The RDP averred, "Neither a commandist central planning system nor an unfettered free market system will work."[42] The MERG Report added that "a strong but slim state is necessary in order to meet the two economic goals of the democratic movement,"[43] defined as a program where the state "has a strong role, leading and shaping the economic development, while the state machinery itself is reshaped to ensure that it does not, as in the past, absorb resources wastefully."[44] The very title of the plan, "Reconstruction and Development," reflected the Janus-faced character of the ANC's post-apartheid economic paradigm. The ANC would pursue economic growth with redistribution. But although the private sector had a crucial role to play in the economic development of post-apartheid South Africa, the ANC gave the leading role to the state. This was necessary, the RDP argued, because the integration of reconstruction and development demanded an active public sector; the market could not expect to make such a structural transformation on its own. Therefore, "there must be a significant role for public-sector investment to complement the role of the private sector." This assumption led the ANC to conclude that "the democratic government must therefore consider: increasing the public sector in strategic areas through, for example, nationalization, purchasing a shareholding in companies, establishing new public corporations or joint ventures with the private sector." And, the ANC reiterated, "The democratic government will reverse privatisation programmes that are contrary to the public interest."[45]

The ANC had certainly moderated its polarizing ideological position originally outlined in the Freedom Charter. Nonetheless, at least during the transition, it was ideologically committed to an essentially Keynesian economic policy of demand-led growth. While no longer socialist, and surely not monolithic, the ANC nonetheless propagated a demand-driven economic model with strong socialist undertones. This blend was deemed necessary if the ANC was to correct the social imbalances left by apartheid—its core "consensual belief."

The NP Government and the Role of the State

The NP's blueprint for the post-apartheid South African economy was fundamentally different from the ANC's plan. Rather than a Keynesian approach, the NEM promoted a supply-side monetarist approach. The foreword to the NEM document stated:

The low economic growth rate has not solely been the result of cyclical or other short-term factors, but has largely been due to deeper underlying problems in the economy that require more fundamental measures
than merely the stimulation of demand for goods and services.[46]

The NEM called for measures beyond simple Keynesian remedies for
downturns in the business cycle. Commenting on the apparent room for
increased production in the South African economy, the NEM observed:

> As far as capacity utilization is concerned, there are those who, appar-
> ently taking the point of view that the economy has large quantities of
> idle production capacity and/or that demand creates its own supply, see
> the solution to South Africa's economic growth problems in a strong
> stimulation of the domestic demand for goods and services—the so-
> called "kick-start" approach.[47]

The NEM apparently accepted that there was surplus capacity in the
nation's infrastructure, for instance in electricity, but its monetarist philosophy led to a fundamentally different conclusion than did the ANC's
Keynesian beliefs.

> As a matter of fact, the available electricity and transport facilities are
> sufficient to sustain an average real growth rate of at least 3 per cent per
> annum until the end of the decade, without necessitating any significant
> expansion of existing capacity. In the medium term, this represents a
> considerable economic advantage for the country since its financial re-
> sources need not be tapped for building infrastructure, leaving more
> room for income and employment-creating investment in the private
> sector.[48]

This was in line with the NEM's central argument that government
spending would crowd out private investment. For instance, the document
stated that the actual average real economic growth rate between 1973 and
1978 had been only 2.9 percent. Public fixed investment as a percentage
of total real GDP was 13 percent, as compared to only 9.3 percent during
the 1973–1978 economic boom.[49] The document concluded:

> Taking into account the demands the government is already making on
> the country's limited production resources, there is no scope for a further
> increase in the government's share in the economy: in fact this share
> should decrease.[50]

If the government spent less, then the ambitious program outlined by
the ANC would have to be severely curtailed, if not abandoned. The NEM

directly addressed this point in its statements concerning what it labeled "upliftment programmes." It argued that such programs should not be implemented at the expense of development in the "modern sector"; instead, they should be funded through a broadening of the tax base that would follow economic growth through investment in the private sector. The entire NEM plan hung on a reduction in government consumption— simple supply-side economics. It called for a reduction of 2.5 percent per annum in real terms over the first three years of the plan; anything less, it argued, would significantly reduce the real economic growth rate. Its conclusion was clear: "The strategy for higher economic growth and greater stability is based on more market-oriented policy making, with the private sector playing a more important role."[51]

The IFIs and the Role of the State in Post-Apartheid South Africa

The IMF's and World Bank's policy prescriptions for South Africa are not identical;[52] their distinct traditional missions have engendered differences.[53] The IMF's focus is more pointedly monetarist, while the World Bank does support a strong role for the state. But in the 1990s, both the IMF and World Bank propagated a free market–based restructuring of South Africa's post-apartheid economy. The World Bank's traditional emphasis on project lending gave it a Keynesian patina, but a close examination of its underlying principles reveals economic liberalism and a reliance on free market economics coursing through its system. The IMF and the World Bank were in broad ideological agreement and were both aligned with the NEM.

Before outlining the consensus among the IFIs, we must briefly discuss the World Bank's apparent affinity for demand-led growth. The MERG Report, for instance, noted that "there appears to be a wide consensus (from the World Bank to democratic movements economists) that the two major stimulants to private sector economic activity are higher levels of economic activity and the 'crowding in' effect of public sector investment spending, particularly on physical infrastructure."[54] But the claim that the World Bank supported a demand-driven economic model for South Africa was exaggerated. The World Bank did claim that South Africa's economic decline was largely due to the decline in parastatal investment.[55] It did not argue, however, for reinvestment in parastatals. In fact, it stated that "the productivity of capital (that is, the output-to-capital ratio) is higher in the private sector than in parastatals."[56] According to the World Bank, higher investment in sectors with lower productivity depresses the level and the rate of growth in GDP. The NEM followed in lockstep with this conclusion.[57]

Nonetheless, the World Bank acknowledged that the private sector responds positively to growth generated by the public sector and concluded that government investment should be at the level of the 1970s[58] and that it should focus on infrastructure projects. However, even in its support for government investment in infrastructure, which seemed to agree with the conclusions of the MERG Report, there were differences in the two plans. The MERG Report called for an across-the-board increase in infrastructural investment. The World Bank's suggestions were much more limited; it called for little new investment in transport, communication, or electricity generation.[59] The World Bank's focus was on reviving the private sector and greatly reducing recurrent spending by the government.

The IMF also argued for a reduction in the growth of government spending.[60] The IMF specifically supported supply-side measures; it concluded that "supply-side factors are more important determinants of growth than are demand conditions."[61] The World Bank, although less purely supply-side oriented, pointed out that distortions in South Africa's factor markets (labor and capital) reflected underlying structural weaknesses in the South African economy.[62] This was consistent with the NEM's position that low economic growth in South Africa was due to underlying problems, not to cyclical or short-term factors that can more readily be corrected by Keynesian manipulation of the economy.

Both the IMF and the World Bank cautioned against high inflation, which has often been linked to Keynesian pump-priming. For the IMF, it was a working assumption: "[I]t is assumed that monetary policy will continue to be used to bring inflation under control." The World Bank study argued that significant increases in inflation "would be destabilizing and foster greater social discontent." The NEM also had a strong anti-inflation stance, which the MERG Report argued was misdirected. The IMF, like the NEM, argued that South Africa's corporate taxes were high by world standards; the MERG Report directly challenged the IMF/NEM position.[63]

South Africa's Industrial Policy: The Manufacturing Sector

The ANC's Industrial Policy

The core objective of the ANC's industrial policy was to rejuvenate the manufacturing sector. Not only was this sector the engine of South Africa's rapid economic development before the recessionary 1980s but the excess capacity in this sector made it a natural candidate for the ANC's demand-led growth policy. The MERG Report emphasized the production of manufactured goods for domestic and export markets.[64] The RDP stated, "The key goals of our industrial strategy are a substantial increase in net national investment, especially in manufacturing, job creation and the meeting of basic needs."[65] The ANC emphasized the potential of the manufacturing sector for exporting.[66]

The ANC's focus on state-led growth was seen as a necessary corrective to apartheid South Africa's legacy of supporting capital-intensive industry. Furthermore, the highly concentrated ownership structure of South Africa's economy, in particular its mining sector, had led to collusion rather than increased competition.[67] Therefore, for the RDP, the most important area where the state should become more active was the mining industry. It recommended that South Africa "seek the return of private mineral rights to the democratic government, in line with the rest of the world. This must be done in full consultation with all stakeholders."[68]

The MERG Report also underlined the importance of what it called the manufacturing-agricultural complex. Some argued that the agricultural sector was increasingly insignificant, because by 1991 the agricultural sector was only accounting for approximately 10 percent of formal employment in South Africa and only 5 percent of South Africa's total exports.[69] But others felt that the importance of the agricultural sector was underappreciated: they noted that in 1988, only 34 percent of South Africa's agricultural output was directly consumed. They felt that there was great potential to use the other 66 percent to develop the economy using "downstream or forward linkages."[70] That is, agricultural products could be used in the production of other products, such as canned goods. Also, the agricultural sector is labor intensive. In 1988, it accounted for 28 percent of recorded employment in manufacturing.[71] Since the MERG analysis had a strong focus on job creation, the agricultural sector thereby took on more importance.

Creating new jobs was an integral part of the ANC's designs for the manufacturing sector and distinguished it from the NEM. The MERG Report stated:

Reliance on trickle-down cannot achieve the expansion on the supply side or the skills-base necessary for an internationally successful manufacturing economy; nor will it raise the levels of wages of the poorest employees at a rate sufficient to ensure a large domestic market for manufacturing as a secure platform for export growth.[72]

The ANC's industrial strategy shared the NP government's emphasis on manufacturing and exports. Unlike the NP, however, it favored an activist state that would reduce the influence of capital-intensive industries and focus state resources on creating employment, particularly within the mineral-industrial complex.

The NP's Industrial Strategy

The NEM also actively promoted the manufacturing sector. It argued that certain goods and services must be imported because South Africa could not produce them efficiently and that in order to protect the current account of the balance of payments, South Africa would have to earn foreign exchange from the production and export of goods and services for which it had a comparative advantage. It argued that exporting merchandise, excluding gold, was the major source of foreign-exchange earnings. From 1985 to 1991, exported merchandise averaged 19.1 percent of GDP. However, to finance the economy's foreign-exchange requirements, the export of merchandise as a percentage of GDP would have to average 23.4 percent of GDP.[73] And this would have to be driven by the private sector.

The NEM also argued that because of depreciation in existing assets over the past seven years, fixed investment in the private manufacturing sector had not even been sufficient to maintain existing assets; the manufacturing sector, in fact, suffered disinvestment.[74] The NEM argued:

> The decline in the investment ratio of private business enterprises, especially in the manufacturing sector, poses more serious implications for the country's growth capacity. The long-term growth rate of the total capital stock is determined to a large extent by the trend in private fixed investment, because in a market-oriented economy such as South Africa's public investment should function mainly in support of private investment.[75]

The decline of investment in the manufacturing sector was not just because private investment was being crowded out by public investment. Average profit rates in the manufacturing sector had been declining since 1981, and the NEM blamed the high cost of labor because it inhibited the creation of competitive export industries. However, as the NEM acknowledged, the most highly protected industries in South Africa were also the most labor-intensive ones. Therefore, large-scale trade liberalization could lead to higher unemployment.[76] Nonetheless, the NEM called for economic liberalization.

Thus, the NP's industrialization policy differed from the ANC's in two important ways: its focus was on the private sector and it would gladly sacrifice employment creation on the altar of free market liberalism.

The IFIs, Manufacturing, and Labor in South Africa

The IFIs agreed that South Africa needed to reinvigorate its manufacturing base to focus on exports. The World Bank report argued that South Africa would have to establish a transparent and credible incentive environment. The RDP, the MERG Report, and the NEM all acknowledged the importance of promoting a strong export sector, but they did not agree on how to accomplish this. The central issue of disagreement was labor's place in South Africa's political economy. The IFIs, along with the NEM as an ideological ally, in fact blamed high labor costs for South Africa's poor export performance.

One IMF report, for instance, argued that real wage growth had to be contained; a 1 percent drop in average wage increases in real terms, it argued, would increase employment by 1.5 percent.[77] A World Bank report made a similar argument:

> The natural growth path in a country such as South Africa is one in which the surplus resource (unskilled black labor) is absorbed quickly into productive employment. Such a path is hampered, however, if the real wage of unskilled labor rises before the labor surplus is exhausted or if the cost of capital is artificially low.[78]

This World Bank report also commented on the high incidence of strikes in South Africa, which in 1990 alone resulted in the loss of 2.8 million person-days.[79]

While high labor costs (and even labor power) was the whipping boy of the IFIs, the labor-aligned ANC had a different perspective. The MERG Report directly refuted the IMF's contention:

> The policy conclusions of the IMF are virtually identical to the NEM ones, and open to the same criticisms. . . . The IMF argues that, "if employment growth is to rise enough to begin alleviating the existing severe underemployment problem, real wage growth must be contained." . . . The IMF ignores the fact that there has never been a stable inverse relationship between real wages and the level of employment in South Africa.[80]

As with their contrary positions on the role of the state, the NP's and the ANC's industrial development strategies reveal different positions vis-à-vis IFIs' policy prescriptions. The ANC's position supported labor interests while the NP's position leaned toward the entrenched capital-intensive industries. And again, the NP found ideological support in the IFIs.

Labor and Economic Development in South Africa

Labor was an essential element of the ANC alliance, and both the RDP and the MERG Report emphasized the importance of labor issues. The MERG Report, for instance, drew heavily on the Industrial Strategy Project (ISP), which was initiated by COSATU, for its chapter on industrial, corporate, and trade policy.[81] Because the ANC's economic development strategy was demand-driven, it felt that low wages were part of the problem. The MERG Report went so far as to state that the NEM's conclusion that real wages should be limited to the rate of growth of productivity amounted to "abandoning government responsibility for achieving an adequate rate of growth of employment." The MERG Report blamed the NEM's antilabor bias on basic ideological differences that start at the theoretical level. It also saw the NP, IMF, and World Bank conclusions as analytically incoherent, colored by an antiworker bias, and unsupported by the available empirical evidence.[82]

The second element of the ANC's pro-labor platform was enhancing labor's role in policymaking. The RDP, for instance, stated that "negotiations and participative structures at national, industry and the workplace levels must be created to ensure that labor plays an effective role in the reconstruction and development of our country."[83] To this end, the MERG Report made detailed recommendations that would institutionalize labor influence. It favored strong centralized union bodies and more industry-level bargaining to strengthen labor power in South Africa.[84]

The NP, Labor, and Economic Development

The NEM's observations on the role of labor in the post-apartheid economy dovetailed nicely with its supply-side philosophy. The NEM argued that a focus on redistribution of the country's wealth would only decrease the domestic savings rate and lower economic growth and that that would inhibit more equal income distribution.[85]

Large-scale upliftment programmes in a stagnating economy, which are not aimed at promoting sustainable economic growth and result in an extensive redistribution of income, will, in turn, have a negative impact on savings, and will inevitably restrict economic growth. In contrast to this, measures such as training and more efficient production techniques will allow the benefits of growth to reach a larger proportion of the labour force in a growing economy and will furthermore promote employment-creating economic growth.[86]

The NEM concurred with the MERG Report's conclusion that South Africa's economy was too capital intensive but did not support the MERG Report's push for increased employment in the formal sector by promoting more labor-intensive industry. The NEM argued that the high capital-labor ratio in South Africa was the product of high labor costs, particularly the increase in nominal wages. It concluded that the average real increase in real wages should be limited to 0.9 percent per annum.[87]

The NEM also held indirect factors such as the high incidence of strikes accountable for the escalating cost of labor:

> The average increase in strikes of more than 33 per cent, in relation to the labour force during the period 1983–1987, had a negative impact on the labour-intensity of the South African economy, to the same extent as an overall increase of 7.9 per cent in the direct cost of labour (i.e. wages) relative to that of capital.[88]

In other words, from the perspective of the NEM, excessive striking drove up labor costs. According to the NEM, a second indirect influence on the high cost of labor was the level of job security. The NEM acknowledged that job security did have positive effects, such as increased labor productivity due to better training, but the general tone of the document was that employees' rights had been favored over employers' rights. This negatively influenced the ability of employers to compete internationally. The NEM also directly attacked South Africa's unions by explicitly calling for immigration to supplement local shortages in "high-level manpower."[89]

The NEM drew fundamentally different conclusions than the MERG Report on the institutional framework of labor-capital relations. It argued that although industrial councils promoted peace, their centralized wage-determination process handcuffed industry. It felt that the councils did not take into account the "production performance and profitability of individual enterprises" and that their policies would "create labour rigidity by inhibiting labour mobility." The NEM also felt that the councils might lead to high wages in certain industries and, subsequently, to demands for greater protection from cheaper foreign goods.[90] The NEM called for a more decentralized wage structure.

The NEM directly linked high labor costs to South Africa's difficulty in meeting its capital requirements. As real wages increased more rapidly, it felt, the net investment requirements necessary to meet the NEM model's targeted growth rate of 3.6 percent per annum also would increase.[91]

Financing Economic Development in Post-Apartheid South Africa

The RDP's largest challenge was how to finance its ambitious programs. The RDP's and MERG Report's approach to financing was fundamentally different from that of the NP. Not only did the ANC favor demand-led growth, it also blamed South Africa's fifteen years of economic decline on levels of government spending that were too low.[92]

The MERG Report envisioned two phases in South Africa's economic recovery. The first phase, from 1993–1999, would be what it called "the initial public investment–led phase."[93] The report projected that the first phase would lead to real growth in government expenditures of 3.8 percent, but initially only 2 percent growth in GDP.[94] The second phase would be oriented more toward private investment.

According to the MERG Report, even if domestic investment were to increase, the government would have to channel it into the public sector. The report argued that one way that domestic savings could be channeled into the public sector would be to establish "prescribed asset requirements" from capital institutions to fund public-sector investment; in other words, telling banks they had to invest in certain public works. The RDP went as far as to argue that the future government should require financial institutions to lend an increasing share of their assets to Black-owned enterprises. Finally, both the RDP and the MERG Report argued for tighter government control over the Reserve Bank.[95]

However, these policies for guiding the flow of investment from one sector to another would move money around, not create new investment. The MERG Report's conclusion, therefore, was that its macroeconomic policies would work "provided that the foreign-exchange constraint could be avoided."[96] It also argued that South Africa's low-debt ratios would allow for higher levels of foreign borrowing.[97] Dependence on foreign funds was a soft spot in the ANC's demand-driven model. The MERG Report pointed out that access to foreign funds, particularly from the

World Bank, was critical for its plan to convert capital outflows of between 2 and 3 percent to capital inflows of 1 to 2 percent.[98]

There was general agreement across the competing poles of South Africa's political economy that the domestic savings rate would have to promote sustained economic growth. Real gross domestic fixed investment, as a percentage of GDP, had been steadily declining in South Africa. There were fundamental differences, however, on how to increase the level of domestic investment. The NEM focused on constraining domestic consumption, both private and governmental. The NEM, as the reification of NP ideology, was not concerned with job creation. Inflation, on the other hand, was a central concern, as was any demand stimulus (private or public) that could trigger it. It stated: "Any actions causing further increases in these ratios and establishing these expenditure items at permanently higher levels will have catastrophic results for economic growth and employment because of the implications it will have for domestic savings in the longer term."[99] Instead, the NEM called for an increase in gross fixed investment as a percentage of GDP fueled by private business enterprise in the industrial sector.[100] This meant a decrease in taxes, particularly corporate taxes.

Consistent with its monetarist approach, the NEM also focused on reducing the level of inflation. It directly linked the rate of inflation to domestic savings. It argued that the inflation rate, in conjunction with South Africa's nominal exchange rate, influenced the competitive position of South Africa's exports and that this had a direct effect on South Africa's balance of payments, because an increase in demand in relation to supply would have a negative impact on the balance of payments.[101]

The NEM plan was implicitly less dependent on international sources of capital than the RDP and MERG Report approach would be. It was also less sanguine about the possibility of IFIs' funding:

> During the 1970s commercial banks provided developing countries with a substantial part (approximately 75 per cent) of foreign capital. Since the emergence of the international debt problem after 1982, there has been a drastic reduction in the availability of funds for developing countries with serious balance of payments problems.[102]

South Africa's debt crisis of 1985 strongly influenced the NEM's policy. During the 1980s, short-term foreign debt increased sharply in South Africa—from 49.1 percent in 1980 to more than 72 percent in 1986.[103] When the major international banks, led by Citibank, refused to roll over South Africa's short-term debt in 1985, a debt standstill was announced. The NEM argued that the underlying cause of the 1985 crisis was lower rates of direct-investment capital, a response to "the deteriorating political and socio-economic situation in South Africa."[104]

The ANC argued for a relatively loose monetary policy with strong state intervention. Although it rejected the IFIs' policy framework, its approach would lead to greater reliance on IFIs' assistance. To some extent, the ANC may have been blinded by its international image as the giant-killer. The NP, whose policy so closely mimicked that of the IFIs, did not anticipate going to the IFIs and had doubts about the availability of aid from that source. Its historical experience bred caution, while the parvenu ANC's recent history bred optimism.

The projections of the IMF and the NEM concerning the future of South Africa's economy were cut from the same cloth. The IMF model projected 3.5 percent growth in GDP, based on an investment-to-GDP ratio of 27 percent from the 1992 level of 19 percent. The NEM model projected 3.6 percent growth based on an average investment rate of 22.4 percent. In contrast, the MERG program actually fit the IMF's "Scenario 2: Higher Fiscal Deficit," which predicts lower economic growth and employment growth.[105]

The MERG Report projected 1.1 percent growth in 1994 and 3.8 percent growth between 1994 and 2000. It acknowledged that higher domestic savings might be needed, but only if "the foreign borrowing position of the economy remained unchanged."[106] In fact, because the MERG Report model projected that the public debt would initially rise, it projected that the trade deficit would continue. The MERG Report, in fact, argued that the NEM overreacted to the balance-of-payments constraints. This idea was given new impetus by foreign debt restrictions and capital flight since the mid-1980s. Two aspects of this constraint are inadequately investigated in the NEM. Even while proposing a looser fiscal policy, the MERG Report remained optimistic about the future debt level. First, it argued that there is every likelihood of negotiating a favorable foreign debt repayment arrangement, and the advent of a democratic government could reduce the reluctance of banks to lend to South Africa and to roll over existing credits. Second, it posited a strong possibility of new foreign capital inflows.[107]

The tug-of-war for the ideological heart of South Africa had interesting implications. Ideology, of course, does not predict policy, especially when it is relatively plastic. The ideological debates captured in the

MERG Report (1993), the RDP (1994), and the NEM (1993) both inform and foreshadow the policy debates of transitional South Africa over manufacturing, trade, and macroeconomics. The debate surrounding the NEM and MERG Report/RDP plans revealed real fissures in transitional South Africa's political economy. The IFIs were central to the discussion as well.[108]

Leading up to the April 1994 elections, the ANC became increasingly business friendly, but it never wavered in support for its bedrock constituency. In February 1994, Mandela argued that job creation was the ANC's highest priority. He also argued: "We are convinced, left to its own devices, the South African business community will not rise to the challenges that face us."[109] In the same month he told workers at a National Union of Mineworkers conference that the ANC-led government would wrest mineral rights from mining houses and place them in the hands of the state.[110]

The position of labor was more clear-cut. COSATU General Secretary Sam Shilewa stated that "[South Africa's] militant and organized workers will not accept a formula for economic growth based on their exploitation." He stressed that the "much-vaunted Asian tiger scenario would lead to widespread social and industrial conflict."[111] COSATU reacted "swiftly and angrily" to bankers' criticism of the RDP.[112]

The business community's reaction to the RDP/MERG Report was mixed. The most stringent criticism came from the banking community. Standard Bank group economist Nico Czypionka stated that the RDP's section on banking was "enough to make one's hair stand on end"; Council of Southern African Bankers (COSAB) Chief Executive Piet Liebenberg stated that much of the RDP was "made from sheer ignorance."[113] A more measured criticism came from Rand Merchant Bank economist Rudolph Gouws, who pointed out that the RDP lacked clarity on its macroeconomic implications and had an overly optimistic view of government expenditure savings. He also noted that the RDP said little about how to reconcile increased wages and the creation of jobs.[114]

General criticisms of RDP/MERG Report programs were directed toward its promotion of an activist state. President de Klerk said that this approach had resulted in the "mess" in which the economy found itself.[115] A book edited by Ben Vosloo, managing director of the Small Business Development Corporation, painted the ANC policy as "a grim picture of the growth of the public sector in [South Africa] to the detriment of the private sector." It also pointed to the Asian newly industrialized countries as a model for future South African policy.[116]

The most controversial element of the ANC's proposed policy was its apparent intention to nationalize the South African mining industry. The MERG Report called for the formation of a mining house cartel to be chaired by the government.[117] The pressure for this policy came most strongly from the National Union of Mineworkers. In February 1994, following its eighth national conference, the union called for the mining industry to be run on socialist principles.[118] It is important to note, however, that the notion of nationalizing the mines was floated as a policy option and was not necessarily fully backed by the ANC.[119]

Just as important was the international reaction to the ANC's socialist mining policy and the ANC's response to that reaction. There were reports that some managers of foreign funds threatened to take their funds out of South Africa.[120] The ANC, while keeping open the "option" of nationalization, backed off the strong nationalization stance. In a response to *Business Day*'s question on each party's respective nationalization policies, the ANC responded, "The ANC has never considered nationalisation to be a panacea for our country's serious economic problems."[121]

The ANC was playing to two constituencies, one domestic and one international. In the same speech where he emphasized the importance of creating jobs and the prominent role of the state for that end, Mandela also stated: "We would like to create a climate conducive to foreign investment through stable, consistent, and predictable policies."[122] The ANC was possibly more self-conscious of its international image than was the NP. The paradox within the ANC's position was that while they were wary of IFIs' influence, their economic blueprint made it more likely that they would need IFIs' help. As it turned out, they managed after April 1994 to largely keep the IFIs at bay.

The interesting paradox in the juxtaposition of the NEM and RDP/MERG Report is that the ANC was at once more wary of IFIs' influence while more likely to have to turn to the IFIs for financial assistance. The policies of the IFIs, nonetheless, were more closely associated with the NEM's recommended policies than with the ANC's.

The RDP and MERG Report explicitly criticized the policies of the IFIs. The MERG Report ran various scenarios through its model to determine the best fiscal policy and concluded that the worst-case scenario would be "succumbing to IMF ideology."[123] MERG coordinator Vella Pillay argued that if IMF conditions attached to the Contingency and Compensatory Financing Facility were to be implemented in South Africa, unemployment would rise to "catastrophic" levels.[124] The RDP reflects a subtler, but nonetheless evident, aversion to IFIs' prescriptions.

Relationships with international financial institutions such as the World
Bank and International Monetary Fund must be conducted in such a way
as to protect the integrity of domestic policy formation and promote the
interests of the South African population and economy. Above all we
must pursue policies that enhance national self-sufficiency and enable us
to reduce dependence on international financial institutions.[125]

But because the RDP would likely be more dependent on IFIs' financing,
the implications of its policies were not necessarily consistent with its
stated intent, which was to keep the IFIs at arm's length.

The MERG Report did acknowledge the importance of the support of
the IFIs: "IMF loans which are a necessary condition for increased private
bank lending may also become available in the near future."[126] It was also
more optimistic about the possibility for new foreign capital and private
bank lending. Nonetheless, prior to the April 1994 elections, there were
already indicators that the reinvestment in South Africa would be tenta-
tive. Even though South Africa liberalized its rules governing potential
investors, new investment had only a short boom in 1997, and it was
concentrated in a few capital-intensive industries.[127] Without such financing, the ambitious demand-driven economic strategy might have to turn
to the IFIs for financing. In fact, after resisting going to the IFIs during
its first year in power, the ANC government turned to the IMF to fund
development programs.[128] The need to go to the IFIs was defended by the
need to fund the RDP.

The NEM model explicitly agreed with the policy prescriptions of the
IFIs. Alan Hirsch, key economic advisor to the ANC, averred that discussions with the World Bank strongly influenced the NEM.[129] Through its
identification with structural adjustment plans, the NEM was consistent
with the policies of the IFIs. The NEM states:

This model is compatible, not only with a post-apartheid dispensation,
but also with virtually all macro-economic stabilization and structural
adjustment programmes in developing countries during the 1980s.[130]

Throughout the document, the program it propounds for South Africa is
referred to as a restructuring program.

The NEM acknowledged the importance of the IFIs by calling for nor-
malization with international organizations such as the IMF and World
Bank. It recognized that IMF bridging facilities (short-term loans) might
be necessary to cover deficits in the current account of the balance of payments and to avoid pressure on the exchange rate. Because the NEM

model incorporated an averaging financing gap of 0.7 percent that would have to be filled by foreign capital, and because many traditional avenues of external finance would not be available, the NEM openly called for closer ties to the IFIs. It expected deficits as South Africa liberalized its trade in an effort to become more competitive. It also expected the world to help South Africa offset an increase in imports that would accompany economic growth and an increase in exports.[131] But because the NEM openly embraced a more disciplined monetary strategy, it would be less likely to lean heavily on the IFIs. It emphasized constraints on balance of payments and savings instead.

The ideological debate in transitional South Africa reflected the political nature of South Africa's economic policymaking. Politics, of course, is driven by material interests. Voters support the party that will make their life better. But how to promote specific interests, say business versus labor, and the policies used for that end have an underlying ideological dimension. Even before the specifics of economic policy are debated, differences in core beliefs about economics are often obvious. This was the case in transitional South Africa. The two most important political parties during transition, the ANC/labor (through COSATU) and the NP, had different underlying philosophies and, just as important, different constituencies. The policy debate in South Africa during the transition was also influenced by the philosophy of the IFIs, although not always as might have been expected. The NP government was less inhibited about going to the IFIs while also more pessimistic about the possibility of new public and private sources of finance. The ANC was highly critical of the IFIs at the same time that it was more optimistic about the possibility of new public and private sources of finance. Members of the ANC who had lived in exile, for instance in Zambia, witnessed firsthand the negative impact of IFIs' ideology.

5

South Africa's Political
Economy in Transition:
Industry and Trade

This chapter offers a commercial variant of liberal theory to explain the preferences of societal actors outlined in Chapter 4. Consistent with the "bottom-up" approach of liberalism, I begin with examining South Africa's manufacturing profile by focusing on specific sectors of its economy, respectively, the capital-intensive and labor-intensive sectors. Chapter 6 complements this chapter by looking at the financial interests within transitional South Africa. The pair completes a commercial explanation and, as well, are linked in South Africa because the financial and manufacturing sectors are intertwined.[1]

There was a general consensus in transitional South Africa that manufacturing would be central to post-apartheid South Africa's economic development.[2] For instance, the South African Chamber of Business's extensive study of South Africa's industrial policy stated that "industrial policy is the policy directed towards the development and growth of the manufacturing sector."[3] If manufacturing was central to post-apartheid South Africa's economic prospects, trade was essential to growth in manufacturing. In South African economist Colin McCarthy's words, "Manufacturing goods are widely traded internationally, and therefore trade policy could be regarded as perhaps a more important policy instrument for industrialization."[4] A growth in the manufactured goods export sector was seen as crucial to overall growth; if the macroeconomic balances were to be maintained, the export economy needed to diversify rapidly.[5] Finally, an economic development policy built on the manufacturing sector and trade would have a strong regional component. In the early 1990s, approximately 25 percent of South Africa's manufactured goods went to the region. The Nedbank Economic Unit study concluded that "once South Africa is accepted politically the region holds tremendous potential for South Africa's exporters."[6] Regional cooperation, therefore, was tied to transitional South Africa's manufacturing and trade policy.

South Africa's Industrial Structure and Trade Regime: The Evolutionary Logic of Apartheid Economics

By the time of its transition, South Africa's industrial and trade policy had gone from inward-looking—import-substitution industrialization (ISI)—to a qualified export-oriented orientation (EOI). However, even within this shift, the bifurcation of its economy crafted by forty years of apartheid continued to shape its underlying political dynamics. Traditionally, South Africa had a highly protected manufacturing sector. Although export promotion was well advanced prior to the transition period, it was also embedded in the political logic of apartheid and promoted highly capital-intensive industries that were typically dominated by large corporations and parastatals.[7] The move from ISI to EOI that predated the transition period only reinforced the dominance of capital-intensive industry in South Africa. South Africa's manufacturing and trade policy was dominated by its mineral sector, the parastatals they nurtured, and political considerations.

The "Pact Government's" Customs Tariff Act of 1925, which changed the tariff structure and reorganized the Bureau of Trade and Tariffs to protect local industries and create jobs for Afrikaners, launched South Africa's ISI policy and its promotion of capital-intensive industry.[8] Three years later, South Africa created the giant parastatal, the Iron and Steel Corporation (ISCOR), which foreshadowed the dominant role parastatals would play in South Africa's industrialization,[9] a reflection of the politically motivated denigration of South Africa's labor-intensive industries.

The traditional lodestar of the South African economy was its mining industry. Gold in particular dominated the economy, in terms of exports as well as share of GDP.[10] It spurred both a manufacturing sector and a demand for skilled labor. But these two demands were in awkward juxta-position throughout the apartheid era. The weak manufacturing sector survived during the apartheid period through state support drawn from the profits of the mining industry.[11] However, South Africa's adoption of an ISI strategy led to a shift from mining to manufacturing.[12] Its large parastatals were created, in effect, to move South Africa away from its reliance on mining. For instance, South Africa created the Industrial Development Corporation (IDC) in 1939 to attract foreign investment to fund the creation of public corporations in partnership with private businesses. However, it did so without stimulating an increase in demand for skilled Black labor.

Therefore, although the aggregate figures on the development of the South African economy support the contention that it moved away from dependence on extraction industries, particularly mining, the manufacturing base was nonetheless closely tied to the mining industry. The African Development Bank study on regional integration in Southern Africa pointed out:

> In spite of the relative size and complexity of its manufacturing sector, South Africa remains very much a mineral-based and mineral-dependent economy. The development, growth and diversification of the manufacturing sector had its origins in the growth of consumer-based and intermediate industries . . . [and] in the expansion of engineering capacity to supply the mining industry. The profits from mining not only facilitated the growth of the manufacturing sector, but the leading houses were able to diversify into manufacturing.[13]

It is impossible to exaggerate the importance of gold to South Africa's economy during the apartheid period. One economist has argued that if smelted metals had been excluded from South Africa's manufactured exports in the late 1980s, the South African manufacturing sector would have been a lower export earner than other upper-middle-income countries such as Brazil, Hong Kong, Singapore, and South Korea.[14] Another economist feels that gold even cushioned periods of economic decline in South Africa during the 1970s,[15] periods typically characterized by anemic manufacturing.

South Africa's giant parastatals were, therefore, the Gordian knot tying manufacturing to mining,[16] and they ultimately dominated South Africa's trade policy. Beginning in the 1920s, the South African state encouraged the development of the manufacturing sector by establishing and providing finance through the IDC for large parastatals such as ISCOR (iron and steel), Eskom (electricity), SASOL (fuel), Foskor (phosphate), and Mossgas (gas). These parastatals were imbued with the political logic of apartheid and concomitantly shaped the character of South Africa's capital-labor relations. In South African political economist Nicoli Nattrass's words: "South Africa's [apartheid] macro-economic and labour policies tended to be highly contradictory attempts to marry the requirements of capitalist growth with the demands of capitalists, white workers, and an ideology of racial segregation."[17] And American political scientist Nancy Clark states that "advanced technology has allowed [apartheid] South African state enterprises to avoid the use of labor that was reputed to be cheap but would in fact have entailed substantial [political] costs."[18] The important point here is that the political and social imperatives of apartheid meant that capital intensity, replacing people with machines, continued to be promoted even as South Africa moved from ISI to a purported focus on EOI. Government policies such as the Physical Planning Act and state-supported investments in capital-intensive industry were central to both the ISI strategy and to the move toward EOI[19] that essentially amounted to a survival strategy for South Africa's conglomerate and parastatal sector. The goal of the export drive of the late 1970s to 1980s was to support capital-intensive industry.

Harry Oppenheimer, then chairman of Anglo-American Corporation, argued in 1950 that although the South African manufacturing industry had taken off after World War II, "manufacturing industry will only be able to serve as a substitute for the wasting asset of our mining industry if it is able to increase exports."[20] By 1972, the limits of further import replacement had been pointed out by the Reynders Commission, which argued for a shift toward greater emphasis on the expansion of manufactured exports. The Van Huysteen Committee's proposals followed, leading to the adoption in 1978 of incentives for exporters that were based on the principle of uniform assistance to exporters and designed to rectify the bias against exports resulting from tariffs on imported inputs.[21] Harry Oppenheimer was worried that mining alone would not drive South Africa's economy and that manufacturing, and in particular manufactured exports, would need to grow. The Reynders Commission, which was appointed by the South African government in 1971 to inquire into the problem of exports and in particular manufactured goods, followed by the Van Huysteen Committee, which was appointed by the government as a follow-up in 1978, argued for a trade-based manufacturing plan. The latter recommended that the South African government adopt export incentives.

One economist argues that there were actually two trade liberalization periods in South Africa, 1972–1976 and after 1983.[22] Beginning in the 1970s South Africa, indeed, pursued a more ambitious export policy, while continuing its ISI policy through protection of domestic industry. South Africa's episodes of liberalization were laced with traditional protectionist pressures, and in both periods, export incentives accompanied trade liberalization. In essence, South Africa wanted to have its cake and eat it too. It wanted to promote trade but also wanted to protect its politically sensitive industries from external competition.

The first liberalization period followed the 1972 Reynders Commission's report, which argued that import replacement could not be counted on to maintain economic growth. Nonetheless, it continued protection in specific sectors. In fact, the report argued for the continuation of infant industry protection and the export of goods in which South Africa had a comparative advantage. The Reynders Commission was followed in succession by the Van Huysteen Committee and the Klue Report, a 1983 government report on the importance of an outward-oriented strategy.[23] Neither strayed far from the traditional policy of protecting South Africa's capital-intensive industry, that is, mining.

As it moved toward an export orientation, South Africa's trade policy could, therefore, be characterized as "embedded ISI"; the key actors in the perpetuation of ISI were the parastatals and large corporations. The GATT trade policy review of South Africa in 1993 stated:

> Since the 1970s[,] direct import controls have, in most instances, been replaced by tariffs. Complementary to the inward-orientation of trade policy has been concessional finance for major projects; through the Industrial Development Corporation, public funds were channeled to capital-intensive projects designed to exploit, *inter alia,* coal iron ore and develop downstream heavy industries such as synthetic fuels and steel.[24]

This was a way to promote an outward-looking manufacturing policy while protecting key domestic industries.

The second period of liberalization began after South Africa's balance-of-payments crisis of 1985, during which there was a large net transfer of resources abroad.[25] South Africa was forced to address its balance of trade in order to pay for essential intermediate and capital goods inputs, goods necessary to keep the capital-intensive industries operating. The export of manufactured goods was key. By the 1980s, the primacy of manufactured exports as a policy objective was firmly established.[26] But it can only be understood as an outgrowth of internal dynamics that promoted capital-intensive industry.

As part of its trade policy reform, apartheid South Africa reduced quantitative restrictions (QRs), such as quotas that limit imports. In 1982, the Department of Trade and Industry appointed an Interdepartmental Import Control Committee to examine the possibility of lowering QRs. Subsequently, the proportion of the value of total imports subject to QRs went from 77 percent in 1982 to 55 percent in 1983, 55 percent in 1984, and 23 percent in 1985. By 1991 it was no more than 11 percent. But manufacturers were allowed to apply for tariff increases in advance of the removal of QRs; this was a way to offset the competition from greater quantities of imports.[27] Finally, in 1985 South Africa moved from a positive list of goods that could be traded to a negative list that indicated goods that could not be imported without approval, further liberalizing the trade regime. This in effect turned the notion of protection on its head; the assumption was that you could now trade unless otherwise noted rather than that you could not trade unless otherwise noted.

Although South Africa was liberalizing its trade regime, it did so within the confines of the apartheid system. In fact, South Africa's trade regime was arguably less liberal than the above summary might indicate. Alan Hirsch, economist for the ANC, has argued that raised duties, particularly formula duties, and the imposition of balance-of-payments-motivated surcharges on imports in 1987 compensated for the removal of QRs.[28] He concluded that the effective rate of protection increased from the early 1980s to the early 1990s.

Further evidence of the protection afforded South African manufacturing was the establishment of the General Export Incentive Scheme (GEIS) in 1990. The GEIS replaced the export incentives of 1980 that were meant to increase exports.[29] It amounted to as much as 20 percent of the export value of manufactured goods.[30]

The promotion of manufactured exports was firmly established in South Africa for at least a decade before the transition. However, EOI was embedded in a highly protected industrial structure. The beneficiaries of this industrial and trade system were the highly capital-intensive parastatals and the large corporations that controlled the mineral/industrial complex. During the 1980s, manufacturing exports grew from 27 percent to 35 percent of South Africa's total exports, and four highly capital-intensive sectors accounted for almost half of those exports—iron and steel, chemicals, nonferrous metals, and pulp and paper.[31]

The residue of apartheid shaped transitional South Africa's industrialization and trade debate. As a 1993 SACOB discussion document stated, "The role of an Industrial Policy and its importance to the growth performance of the South African economy has gained increasing prominence during the political transition stage."[32] This prominence was the result of two factors. First, with the end of economic sanctions against apartheid South Africa, trade became a more important instrument for economic development. Second, and more significant, democratization opened its domestic political arena to more intense competition over economic policy.

Transitional South Africa's Trade Policy Debate

The Industrial Development Corporation's 1990 study *Modification of the Application of Protection Policy* (which was commissioned by the minister of the Department of Trade and Industry) set the stage for transitional South Africa's trade debate. The report advocated a neutral trade regime: formula duties would be eliminated, tariff levels would be reduced, and the scope of the GEIS would be reduced.[33] The plan, however, did favor certain export-promoting schemes, such as the Phase VI of the local content program for motor vehicles to promote the production of cars.[34] One South African analyst described the IDC's proposal thus: "a broad macro-restructuring, primarily centred on a lowering of the company tax rate and the stabilization of some of the main economic variables, while at the same time advocating the introduction of development programmes at the industry level."[35] The IDC study was important for two reasons: it defined the parameters of the industrialization and trade debate, and it foreshadowed the underlying sectoral competitions that drove that debate.

Two central players shaped transitional South Africa's industrial and trade policy debate, the Industrial Strategy Project (ISP) and the Department of Trade and Industry (DTI). The ISP was initiated by COSATU and the Economics Trends Research Group.[36] Since 1992, it had been investigating how competitive South Africa's industries were. Both the ISP and the DTI offered moderate policy prescriptions; both advocated cautious liberalization. However, the ISP was primarily concerned with labor and small enterprises, while the DTI was preoccupied with the status-quo industries—South Africa's established capital-intensive industries.

In its summary report, the ISP stated, "In general, our concern to harness the power of market forces does not imply that policy designed to expose South African firms to unmediated market relations will, in and of itself, revitalize the manufacturing sector."[37] It emphasized, in fact, the production of those tradable goods aimed at small manufacturers,[38] that is, labor-creating enterprises.

The DTI's general argument was less protectionist than the ISP's, although it was more protectionist than the Industrial Development Corporation's original recommendations. The DTI's director, Dr. Stef Naude, outlined the department's policy in a 1992 speech, "Blueprint for Prosperity." Naude recommended:

> The pace and magnitude of tariff reform should be dictated by the progress that is going to be made with the improvement of the competitiveness of manufacturing industry. [This] depends on the ability to afford incentives on the supply for modernisation of productive facilities, training and re-training of labour, development of technology, and the advances that need to be made in improving the investment climate.[39]

In a subsequent paper, Naude reemphasized that "[i]n the case of certain sensitive industries that have to be restructured, the new [GATT] offer provides for a reduction of present rates over a longer period of up to eight years." Although he was aware of the merit of obtaining "developing country" status in GATT and other international forums, Naude further argued that the benefits from such a status were shrinking: "It would not necessarily be in our best interest if recognition as a developing country encouraged us to go on shielding the manufacturing sector from the facts of life."[40] Thus, both the ANC-aligned Industrial Strategy Project and the apartheid government's Department of Trade and Industry advocated export promotion embedded in cautious liberalization. The former, however, remained primarily concerned with the health of labor-intensive industry and the latter with protecting the status-quo capital-intensive industries.

The differences between the ISP and DTI are revealed in the details of their respective positions on three issues defining transitional South Africa's policy debate: the relationship between manufacturing growth and trade; the capital intensity of South Africa's manufacturing industry; and ways to become more competitive.

Manufacturing and Trade in South Africa

Manufacturing is usually credited for the 1960s economic boom in South Africa.[41] However, the debate over the relationship between manufacturing growth and trade was less settled. This is more than a chicken-and-egg debate, because whether one argues that manufacturing stimulates trade or vice versa will influence how one structures trade policy.

The DTI and SACOB argued that an open trade regime preceded gains in production. A World Bank study of South Africa's trade policies that compared two periods, 1972–1983 and 1983–1990, found that the first period corresponded to a period of relative protection and the second period to relative openness and a lower exchange rate in real terms. The study concluded that a significant association between "total factor productivity growth" and export expansion had existed during both periods. Its authors felt that import substitution had not contributed to total factor productivity growth and in fact had had a negative impact in the first period.[42] SACOB also argued that South Africa's disappointing share of world trade led to poor economic growth.[43] The DTI accepted the conclusions of the World Bank and the Industrial Development Corporation.[44] Trade was expected to stimulate productivity.

The Industrial Strategy Project implicitly accepted the assumption that increasing exports would make South African manufacturing more competitive: "[ISP's] own research findings generally support those of the [World Bank] and we agree with most of [the IDC's] proposals for trade policy reform."[45] However, it did so with the caveat that its own research into the link between export expansion and industrial growth "in a number of sectors" did not necessarily support the claim that growth is tied to trade.[46]

Although export promotion was generally encouraged by the ISP, it was not seen as a panacea across all sectors of South Africa's economy, and examining South Africa at the aggregate level ignores important nuances at the sectoral level. If the link between export growth and industrial growth varied across sectors, then an EOI policy would not only potentially threaten ISI-dependent industries but would also gather support from sectors that reflected a positive correlation between trade and growth. Therefore, within the larger debate on industrialization and trade policy, there was the politically contentious issue of what sectors to promote. South Africa's labor-intensive manufacturing sector, in particular, was wary of free trade.

Capital Intensity and Employment in South Africa

South Africa's low industrial growth rate was linked to excessive capital intensity. The ratio of capital to labor in South Africa was approximately two times that of developing countries at comparable levels of development,[47] and the manufacturing sector, which was expected to propel economic growth and provide employment, was the main offender.

However, the level of capital intensity was not uniform across all industries. The growth in the capital intensity of South Africa in the aggregate during certain periods could be explained by trends in particular manufacturing industries: in the 1970s, investment in the iron and steel industry (ISCOR); in the late 1970s and early 1980s, in the chemical and chemical products industry (SASOL); and in the mid-1980s, the paper and paper products industry (Sappi and Mondi).[48] Thus, it was possible to identify less capital-intensive areas that could be targeted for future investment and future employment. As with the debate on the relationship between exporting and industrial growth, disaggregating the capital intensity of South Africa's different industries reveals sectoral differences with important political inferences. That is, different sectors of South Africa's economy had different levels of capital intensity and this would have political ramifications.

The second issue defining the debate concerning South Africa's capital-intensive industry was the question of how it related to employment. One side of the debate claimed that high labor costs had dictated greater capital inputs. And, in fact, labor costs had increased by a factor of three between 1975 and 1980.[49] The profit rates in South Africa were squeezed by Black and White wages rising faster than the profits available for distribution.[50] Nancy Clark supports this claim; she argues that labor costs were always the main challenge to the production costs of the state corporations.[51] But this is only half the story.

While labor was costly, capital was artificially cheap. The state manipulated macroeconomic policies to create artificially low capital costs. For instance, from 1975 to 1980, real interest rates were negative, thus stimulating capital-intensive production.[52] South Africa's high degree of capital intensity came from promoting economic growth through the parastatals. This was done to proscribe Black participation in the industrial sector. Parastatals and large corporations, therefore, would be unlikely avenues for employment growth.[53]

Becoming More Competitive

The underlying purpose of South Africa's economic liberalization was to increase the competitiveness of its industries. But how competitiveness in transitional South Africa was defined also determined what industries were considered competitive.

Revealed comparative advantage, which is based on what a country actually trades, was the dominant approach for determining the competitiveness of South African industries during the early transition. However, this approach had its limitations; it could only measure the results of trade and did not compensate for policy biases that were built into the trade regime. One economist claimed that it was thus impossible for revealed comparative advantage to "yield some 'true' comparative advantage indicator. . . . Perhaps the most serious problem is that comparative advantage analysis can only measure the results of trade. Therefore they cannot compensate for policy biases built into the trade regime and yield some 'true' comparative advantage indicator."[54] This problem had important political implications. Policy biases are grounded in political logic, and in transitional South Africa this led to an emphasis on its traditional export strength in resource-based and large-scale projects.[55] The supporting argument by those in favor of capital-intensive industry was that these sorts of projects, such as the Columbus Stainless Steel Project and the Alusaf Aluminum Project, would provide a trickle-down effect for the rest of the economy. The logic of this argument was that these large projects, which traditionally were the products of Industrial Development Corporation funding, would earn foreign exchange, increase savings, and avoid the problem of high labor costs. Using this logic, only the metal, chemical, and wood and pulp paper sectors looked promising as international competitors.[56] The revealed comparative advantage approach, regardless of its academic merit, had powerful underlying political inferences in transitional South Africa. It framed the debate so that capital-intensive industry would naturally not only take center stage in South Africa but would also shove labor-intensive industry off that stage.

The Industrial Strategy Project, on the other hand, argued that where most of South Africa's investment had gone during the apartheid era, namely chemicals and steel, job creation had been minimal. It argued that job creation would be better in footwear and clothing.[57] These products would be included in "narrow manufactures [light manufactured goods, such as furniture and textiles]," which excluded semi-manufactured exports such as chemicals, iron and steel, and wood pulp. Between 1988 and 1991, exports of narrow manufactures doubled, although admittedly they were still at a very low level. The greatest improvement came in the categories of other transport equipment, autos and parts, and clothing. Hirsch attributed the sudden surge in exports of narrow manufactures to the export incentives put in place in 1989, particularly through the auspices of the GEIS.[58] Because the GEIS provided incentives according to a product's value added, raw materials received no incentives.

Each of the above three debates revealed sectoral competition for influence over trade and manufacturing policy in transitional South Africa's economy. Although there was a general consensus that South Africa needed to improve its export performance, no consensus existed on what to export.

The Political Economy of Industrialization and Trade in South Africa

The central issues of the industrial-trade debate discussed above, trade as promoting manufacturing growth, the capital intensity of the manufacturing sector, and the competitive structure of South Africa's economy, are obviously linked. But, more importantly, an exegesis of the policy debate reveals that examining South Africa in the aggregate "poisons the analytical well." For each issue examined, there is an inherent, if not necessarily apparent, political dimension engendering group competition for influence and advantage. As John Zysman states: "If not all industries are equal, and if governments can create advantage, then trade competition can be seen as a struggle between different paths of economic development or a fight for post position in the economic race."[59]

Most of the relevant South African actors accepted the state as an appropriate venue for promoting competitiveness. This is just as true for the traditional centers of influence in the South African economy as it was for what were to become new centers of power—organized labor and the ANC. SACOB, for instance, supported both a broad-based industrialization strategy and a selected sectoral policy, proposing that South Africa create an Industrial Policy Forum (IPF) similar to the Industrial Structure Council of the Ministry of International Trade and Industry in Japan. The IPF would then work through newly created sectoral strategy committees to direct industrial strategy to specific industries and markets.[60] Kevin Lings, writing for the Nedbank Economic Unit, noted: "[South Africa] should give up the search for the universal Holy Grail of effective export promotion. Its efforts would be better directed at more focused and specific attention and backing for industries with demonstrable export promise and showing competitive advantage."[61] It was never formed.

Support for an industrial policy did not mean a second round of ISI. It did mean enhanced political competition, since such a policy expects that the state will pick, or through economic policy, promote potential trade winners. Hirsch called South Africa's new tilt toward industrial policy with protection the "neostructuralist" position and argued that the Normative Economic Model of 1993 demonstrated that position's growing influence in government.[62] The support for state involvement varied, and this itself had political undertones, but there was little disagreement that the state should play a proactive role in economic development. As one analyst stated, the very success of the IDC (the group closest to supporting a laissez-faire approach in the trade debate) demonstrated the success of this approach.[63]

South Africa, and in particular its conglomerates, had a long history of hiding behind state protection. A 1992 study on the competitiveness of South Africa's manufactures stated that "the acceptance of South Africa into the international community represents a major threat to many manufacturing organizations."[64] As Bell stated, "At the commencement of the government's program for removing QRs there was an outcry from business, which saw this as the abandonment of South Africa's traditional policy of protection."[65] In fact, after the publication of the Klue Report, which did call for continued protection, the government had to publish a white paper stating that it "has never espoused any so-called free trade."[66] Economist Colin McCarthy argued that "[f]rom a policy point of view, even the most convincing arguments for an export-oriented industrial development strategy cannot overcome the practical problems of carrying out such a strategy. Industrialization through protection creates strong vested interests, amongst labour and employers, in the maintenance of protection."[67] The business community felt threatened by the removal of QRs. Years of protection had created a vested interest in that protection and a vested interest in a proactive role for the state.

The practical problems of carrying out trade policy reform in South Africa during transition were further complicated by the complexity of the tariff structure. There was general agreement within South Africa that its tariff structure should be rationalized. The number of tariff lines (tariffs on specific categories of goods) and the degree of variance between those lines would have to be reduced. In fact, the complex tariff structure was "fertile ground for rent seeking and lobbying" and was what the ISP called "an administrative nightmare."[68] South Africa's tariff structure and the large differences in tariff levels among and within sectors created the space for political pressure groups to compete for their sector-specific preferences.

What is interesting, therefore, is which industries were being supported by what means and what this matrix revealed about the links between politics and policy in South Africa.[69] What was South Africa protecting and what was it promoting for export? The link between import protection and export promotion in South Africa was direct because protection created high input cost and a lack of competitiveness for its manufactured goods, which led to export promotion schemes.[70]

Consumer goods had the highest tariff protection, 17.6 percent, followed by capital goods at 7.9 percent and intermediaries at 5.0 percent.[71] Thus, among the most protected industries in South Africa were the mature, labor-intensive textiles, apparel, and footwear industries.[72] But as tariffs and import controls were reduced and eliminated, in many cases formula duties were then used to protect selected industries against competitive low-cost imports as South Africa liberalized its exchange regime. At the same time, formula duties were used in more than 50 percent of imported products in the fertilizer, synthetic resins, tire and other rubber products, clothing, and railway-equipment industries to keep them competitive.[73] All but the final two were typically produced by South Africa's capital-intensive large industries. In fact, the ISP also argued that structural adjustment programs had hurt the lower ends of manufacturing without improving performance at the higher ends of manufacturing.[74]

The debate over how to promote manufacturing and trade contained within it a debate on what had been and was receiving the most protection. This secondary debate, however, was really about which sector of the economy to promote and, of course, the politics of supporting one sector over another. The isolation from the rest of the world that was created by the sanctions campaign against South Africa had triggered protection as a necessary strategic policy. Industries such as engineering, transport, equipment, electronics, and chemical fields were, thus, favored by the state because they were seen as politically and economically essential to apartheid.[75] Lall argues that South Africa's protective regime, in fact, had no underlying strategy related to industrial competitiveness; he feels that it had "many of the non-selective and non-economic aspects of protection."[76] That is to say, it served the political purposes of the state.

High protective tariffs led to compensatory programs to promote trade. In the early stages of the transitional period, South Africa began to directly promote exports through various schemes such as the GEIS, the Export Marketing Scheme (EMS), structural adjustment programs, and tax incentive schemes. The GEIS was introduced in 1990 to help firms offset the price disadvantages South African exporters faced in the international market. These disadvantages were largely due to the high level of protection of intermediaries, goods used to make other goods. SACOB argued, for instance, that South African manufacturing costs were 15 percent higher than they were in OECD countries.[77] The GEIS provided a tax-free financial subsidy to exporters based on the value of exports, the level of processing, and the local content of the product to be exported.

The EMS was also introduced in 1990. It gave partial compensation for transportation costs and subsistence allowances for travel to find export markets. It also promoted trade fairs and the dissemination of information on export markets. South Africa also assisted in the export of large-capital projects, such as power plants. In instances where the export of large-capital projects were repaid over many years, the Department of Trade and Industry subsidized the interest rate and, under the export development financial scheme, the Industrial Development Corporation could finance an increase in export manufacturing capacity at reduced rates.[78]

South Africa's self-imposed SAPs, first introduced in 1988, were industry-specific programs directed at textiles, clothing, and motor vehicles. But the SAPs for clothing and textiles were abandoned at the end of 1993 because they were not considered to be cost effective. Exporters qualified for a duty-free import permit if they exported at least 2.5 percent of their output. The automobile program gave tax relief and export incentives for a final product with a local content of 75 percent and rebates of excise duties based on the percentage of local content.[79]

Finally, in September 1991, a new tax allowance relating to export performance, Section 37E of the Income Tax Act, was introduced specifically for mineral beneficiation, aimed at two large projects—the Columbus Stainless Steel Project and the Alusaf Aluminum Project.[80] ISCOR gave financial assistance to exporters of fabricated products and special price rebates for steel used in the manufacture of export products.

The overall incentive structure for export promotion largely, if not exclusively, favored large capital-intensive industries. Most of South Africa's export incentives did not help smaller firms: the GEIS did little to help smaller firms, duty rebate schemes were not accessible to smaller firms, and Section 37E of the Income Tax Act and the IDC's subsidized loans had a bias toward large capital-intensive schemes. Furthermore, the South African Foreign Trade Organisation (SAFTO), although privatized, was subsidized by the government and represented primarily large firms. Smaller companies could not afford SAFTO, and it was "very white in its make-up and orientation."[81]

The structure of investment, as well, favored South Africa's capital-intensive industries. While the share of total investment in chemical and basic metals grew from 40.4 percent in 1972 to 59.8 percent in 1990, the share in the three most labor-intensive sectors, clothing, leather and footwear, and wood and furniture, declined during the same period from 4 percent to 1.9 percent.[82] Much of the investment in South African manufacturing was state-supported research and development. Government laboratories and public corporations performed the bulk of research and development in South Africa, which concentrated in iron and steel, industrial chemicals, and electrical and nonelectrical machinery.[83]

All of this would be moot if capital-intensive industry provided for job growth. But Hirsch, writing for the ISP, protested: "It would seem that the best way to encourage employment-intensive export industries (in addition to the measures already mentioned) would be . . . to attend more carefully to the needs of small and medium enterprises that seek to enter export markets."[84] Most importantly, these enterprises were labor-intensive. Underwriting the cautious approach to tariff reform promoted by the ISP, among others, was the concern for the effect it would have on employment. The ISP stated, "In particular, the reduction that we propose must be timed so that the impact of employment loss in fundamentally uncompetitive sub-sectors is cushioned."[85] Furthermore, where there is "competitive potential" that can lead to "new employment opportunities," the ISP called for tariff protection.[86] Business, while agreeing on a policy of gradual reform, called for a qualitatively different form of trade protection. SACOB, while tipping its hat to job creation, argued that industrial policy should not cater to "unsustainable employment."[87]

Because transitional South Africa witnessed a bifurcation in trade policy preferences, between support for more-labor-intensive industry and the traditional capital-intensive sectors, it engendered a reexamination of trade promotion policies. The beneficiaries of the status quo, big business, favored the old policies, or possibly a level playing field, because they would capitalize on their post-position. As Kevin Lings could therefore state:

> These enterprises [large capital intensive] have appropriate marketing organization with the necessary expertise in exporting, and there is little reliance on official marketing support. Furthermore, the export performance is related to the conditions of the foreign market and not to the presence of any export incentive scheme.[88]

Labor and small business would logically favor changes in South Africa's trade promotion policy. The divide between big business and labor (and small enterprises) was superimposed on the regional grid. In fact, given the importance of the regional market during decades of formal isolation, regional trade relations were the most politically charged.

The Political Economy of South Africa's Regional Policy

During the apartheid era, South Africa did trade with the outside world. However, the international sanctions campaign made it difficult to develop new markets, and Southern Africa was all the more important. During the transition period, South Africa's manufacturing exports significantly increased, most notably exports to other African countries.[89] GATT's 1993 *Trade Policy Review* pointed out: "Manufactures tend to have a higher importance in regional, intra-African trade than in total trade. Africa accounts for close to one-third of South Africa's manufactured exports, although Africa is a market for just 7 per cent of South Africa's exports."[90] African imports from South Africa increased by 40 percent in 1988–1989 and 22 percent in 1989–1990, faster than South Africa's trade increased outside Africa;[91] Southern Africa was the most important African market for South African manufactured goods. According to one estimate of South Africa's total trade with Africa in 1992, 66.6 percent was with SACU countries, 25 percent was with non-SACU SADC countries, 91.5 percent was with SADC countries, and only 8.5 percent was with non-SADC African countries.[92] Thus, when we speak of South Africa's exports to Africa, it is a reasonable approximation for its exports to Southern Africa.

It was also argued that room remained for South Africa to increase trade with the region. Colin McCarthy posited that South Africa could increase its exports significantly by gaining a greater share of the African market. He felt that if South Africa's share of imports in its "natural" markets was hypothetically set at a 15 percent share or its existing share, whichever was highest, it would more than double its exports to Africa.[93] He blamed the lower percentage (below 15 percent) on political resistance to apartheid. However, even though most of the neighboring countries at the time were members of the anti-apartheid SADCC, they were already above the 15 percent level.[94] The twin assumptions of a fairly high elasticity of demand for South African goods in Africa (particularly Southern Africa) and South Africa's hypothetical ability to meet that demand (elasticity of supply) are more important flaws in McCarthy's model.[95] The demand for South African goods should not be assumed.

South Africa's regional trade relations were congruent with its over-

all industrialization and trade policy. The domestic political pressures embedded in the sectoral competitions outlined above translated into support
for competing regional trade regimes. It is one thing to hypothesize that
South Africa could capture 15 percent of its "natural" market, and another
thing to identify what that market was and whether it could be penetrated by South Africa. South Africa had certain obvious advantages due
to proximity, such as delivery time and familiarity with the regional
markets, that were reinforced by a well-established capability to finance
trade.[96] However, South Africa's manufacturing sector was not competitive on a world scale, as reflected by the many export incentive schemes
created to deal with that fact. One political scientist has argued that
during apartheid, Southern Africa provided a significant market for a
range of manufactured goods that would have been unlikely to find export
markets elsewhere and that South African goods sold in the region may
have cost as much as 15 to 25 percent more than FOB prices of comparable
goods from elsewhere.[97] Exports of capital-intensive goods, iron, steel, and
chemicals totaled $3.13 billion, and narrow manufactures totaled $2.84
billion in exports in 1991. The configuration of South Africa's overall
trade is reflected in the composition of its exports to Africa in general and
to Southern Africa in particular (see Table 1, Appendix). Nevertheless, Africa imported more than 40 percent of South Africa's exports in plastics,
fashion, and machinery and about 33 percent of chemicals, vehicles and
parts, and "other manufactures." South Africa had already gained a significant foothold in the export of capital-intensive goods prior to the transition. On the other hand, labor-intensive goods had done poorly. Africa
took only about 10 percent of South Africa's textiles and paper products.[98]

South Africa's regional trade profile reflects the dominance of its
capital-intensive sector. Table 2 (Appendix) slightly skews South Africa's
trade statistics because it is based on SACU's trade with the region. (South
Africa's trade with its SACU partners is greater than its total trade with
the rest of Africa.) However, SACU is acknowledged to have retarded the
industrial development of the BLS states, and the export statistics for
SACU can be considered a proxy for South Africa's export statistics. This
table shows that South Africa's exports to the region were concentrated in
capital-intensive industries: machinery and appliances, plastics and rubber
products, and chemical products. This advantage was built on decades of
support from the apartheid governments.

This snapshot of South Africa's trade profile, however, is taken with
apartheid as the backdrop. It is no surprise that the capital-intensive industries generally performed best. Future trade relations would depend on

how post-apartheid South Africa's trade regime would be structured. The ability of South Africa to maintain and even increase its share of regional trade would depend, in part, on the competitiveness of different sectors of its economy. Indeed, the performance of the capital-intensive sector seemed to reflect how competitive it was. For instance, it tended to have a lower level of protection.

The textile, apparel, and leather subsector had the highest level of protection, almost three times the average for the manufacturing sector. According to economists Belli et al., the value added by this sector was nearly twice what it would have been in a free trade situation.[99] This sector was not likely to penetrate the regional market for several reasons: South Africa's neighbors produced similar products, and the country had not been competitive by world standards. A free trade approach to regional economic integration would decimate this sector, as cheaper labor-intensive goods from the region flooded South Africa's domestic market. Therefore, if South Africa wanted to pursue a more labor-intensive export policy, as demanded by one side of the trade policy debate, it would have to promote these industries along with the relatively labor-intensive food and beverage industry. The political power of labor-intensive industries embedded in South Africa's powerful unions guaranteed it a voice. But could they make an argument for a larger regional role?

Support for the more-labor-intensive sectors was not without economic merit. In fact, the more-labor-intensive industries in South Africa were becoming the most productive.[100] South Africa's National Productivity Institute created four categories of productivity growth (1971–1988): strong, moderate, below average, and poor. Many labor-intensive industries, such as textiles and cloths and wood products were in the strong category, while many capital-intensive industries were in the poor category, such as chemicals and metal products. It is a paradox that in the seventeen years prior to the transition, productivity growth had been poor in areas it had been able to export. In the areas where it had not penetrated the regional market, and where regional competition was most likely to be strong, it had made gains in productivity. Nonetheless, on a sunken-costs basis, money already invested in an industry, South Africa's advantage was still in capital-intensive upstream products.[101]

The final piece of South Africa's regional trading profile is the politics of policymaking. An important aspect of apartheid-era South Africa's industrial policy that can serve as an analogue for post-apartheid South Africa is its Regional Industrial Development Programme, part of South Africa's program to decentralize industry. It was meant to increase employment in the homelands by creating incentives for industry to relocate there.[102] Between 1976 and 1985, 10.17 percent of South Africa's manufacturing growth came from the homelands. In 1982, manufacturing employment in the homelands accounted for less than 1 percent of total manufacturing employment; in 1988 it accounted for 10 percent. Most important, these jobs were mostly in labor-intensive industries; over 60 percent were in food products, textiles, wearing apparel, wood products, furniture, nonmetallic minerals, and metal products.[103] Thus, although the Regional Industrial Development Programme was politically motivated, and possibly prohibitively expensive, programs meant to accomplish similar objectives and increase employment in disadvantaged areas (or disadvantaged groups) certainly could be imagined. A similarly politically motivated policy of promoting labor-intensive industry would be possible. But it could be accomplished within a regional context only if South Africa abandoned a free market approach. A laissez-faire approach in an environment where the capital-intensive sector has post-position (i.e., starts with a better competitive position) would not trigger new categories of exports because it would benefit only exports from capital-intensive industries. Post-apartheid South Africa's regional trade relations mirrored the challenges its general trade policy would soon face. The one important difference is that its Southern African neighbors would not easily accept a focus on more labor-intensive manufacturing exports. As with the larger debate, South Africa's regional trade policy revolved around promoting either the more established capital-intensive industries or the more-labor-intensive industries.

Apartheid South Africa's regional economic relations were tied to its industrial and trade policies. The political economy of apartheid South Africa's industrial and trade debates spilled over into the debate over regional relations.

Transitional South Africa witnessed parallel debates over its future industrial and trade policy and the institutionalization of regional cooperation. Although not necessarily directly linked, these debates had logical connections that proved to be politically consistent. That is, there was a natural congruence between political support for different forms of institutionalized regional cooperation and political support for capital-intensive over labor-intensive industry.

South Africa's capital-intensive industries had post-position and, even without institutional support, would continue to dominate the region.

Furthermore, other than new infrastructural projects, they had already saturated the regional market. This partially explains why SACOB de-emphasized the region. It also meant that dependence rather than inter-dependence described its regional relations. The prospects for South Africa's labor-intensive industries were much different. It would have been difficult to promote regional exports in this sector, and very difficult to protect politically powerful domestic industries, such as textiles, in a laissez-faire environment.

South Africa's labor-intensive and capital-intensive industries had very different regional footprints and therefore very different ways to promote their regional interests. For labor-intensive industries, there was no natural (or unnatural) competitive advantage in the region. These products would have to compete for markets with similar products made in South Africa's neighboring countries. South Africa's capital-intensive industries had no such competition. A free market approach to regional economic integration/cooperation would not help labor-intensive goods from South Africa penetrate regional markets. As supported by the developmental economic integration/cooperation model, the state would have to play an active role in making sure industries would be spread throughout the region. In this case, South Africa's labor-intensive industry would need political support. Left on its own, it would not survive competition from low labor costs in neighboring countries. Its regional dominance estab-lished, South Africa's capital-intensive sector would benefit from a pas-sive state role. Because it did not like any institutional constraints on its regional plans, the loosest possible form of regional economic integration/cooperation—ad hoc cooperation—was ideal.

The ANC, which allied itself with labor and was supported by small business, propagated developmental cooperation that was necessary to pro-mote and protect labor-intensive industry and small-business interests in the region. There would have been no reason for South Africa's neigh-bors to be sensitive to these sectors without some quid pro quo. For labor-intensive industry in transitional South Africa to increase its regional foot-print, it would be necessary for South Africa to bargain with its neighbors. This sector did not have a regional competitive advantage. This implies a sectoral approach where South Africa makes concessions in one area, for instance energy or transportation, for a concession from its neighbors in another sector, such as trade in labor-intensive goods. The developmen-tal approach reflected in the original SADCC and in the ANC's official position reflected the fact that different sectors of South Africa's economy had different regional footprints and different abilities to export to the region. Regional economic integration/cooperation based on the free market model reflected the other side. South Africa's capital-intensive conglomerates were driven by a very different regional logic.

6

Banking, Finance, Monetary Policy, and Globalization in South Africa

This chapter injects an explicit diachronic dynamic into the overall argument. As Garrett states: "Globalization has been fastest and most recent with respect to financial capital mobility; the growth of trade has been slowest but started earliest; foreign direct investment occupies an intermediate position."[1] The previous chapter focused on the period pre-dating the April 1994 election in South Africa and the evolution of South Africa's trade regime. This chapter transcends that period by looking at how the new ANC government navigated the open seas of globalization, how the need for foreign investment influenced its opening up to international capital, and, finally, the effects of capital mobility on South Africa's political economy.

This chapter primarily focuses on the private banking sector. What kind of economic policy did the banking sector promote and how did it indirectly and directly seek to influence regional economic integration/cooperation in Southern Africa? As Garrett makes clear, on no other sector of a country's political economy has the impact of globalization been greater. This chapter, therefore, will also look at how the new ANC government began to meet the challenges of globalization. This demands, then, an examination of South Africa's exchange-rate policy and of state institutions such as the South African Reserve Bank.

Banking and Finance in Transitional South Africa

The investment and banking industry in transitional South Africa did not support a restructuring of South Africa's economy. This was made clear in its vituperative response to the Reconstruction and Development Programme, as was related at the end of Chapter 4. However, although the banking sector was closely tied to South Africa's conglomerate sector, it had a slightly different regional perspective. First, it had a regional and international competitive advantage in Southern Africa; although transitional South Africa's big-business sector downplayed the importance of the region, South African banks leveraged their regional dominance. South African banks implicitly broke with SACOB's position by emphasizing a strong regional role. Nonetheless, the nature of those ties and the way that South African banks would institutionalize regional relations reinforced the ad hoc form of cooperation favored by the conglomerate sector.

The regional dominance of South African banks was well established before the transition. Rodney Galpin, chairman and chief executive of Standard Chartered Bank, stated that South Africa's "financial and capital markets have much greater depth and sophistication than the rest of Africa. They are in fact more advanced than those in a number of European countries and in most countries in the Far East."[2] Banking was one area where South Africa probably had a true competitive advantage against both local and international competition.[3] In 1992, the World Economic Forum and the International Management Institute studied the economic competitiveness of twenty-two industrialized and fourteen newly industrialized countries. South Africa ranked fourth in finance among the newly industrialized countries.[4] The African Development Bank study concluded that during the transition, South African banks were already displacing extraregional banks in the region.[5] The most aggressive of South Africa's major banks in the region was Standard Bank, which took over ANZ Grindlay's entire African operation with branches in Botswana, Zambia, and Zimbabwe.[6] Although Grindlay had branches outside Southern Africa, Standard Bank stayed focused on the region. For instance, the managing director of Standard's Botswana subsidiary stated that Standard would not be a major international bank—"our view is that we are a major regional bank."[7] South Africa's largest bank, Amalgamated Banks of South Africa, usually considered the most cautious of the major banks, was also regionally inclined. An Amalgamated Banks of South Africa official stated that they, too, expected to expand into the region. He explained that letters of credit for exports were the type of risks the conservative Amalgamated Banks of South Africa liked to take, while for countries outside Southern Africa they would only accept cash or a second bank's guarantee.[8]

Thus, during the transition South African banks were already moving into the region, but their regional role was strictly limited. They were primarily interested in opening up regional retail banking branches, in financing trade, and in penetrating regional markets rather than stimulating development in neighboring countries. One South African banker lamented the unwillingness of South African banks to back production facilities in Africa; they were not willing to take "sovereign risk" in Africa —that is, sink investments in countries that could be nationalized—but were willing to finance trade, which was really not a risk.[9] There was little talk of developmental cooperation and even less talk about a regional organization. The early posturing of South Africa's banks, therefore, was consistent with an ad hoc approach to regional cooperation. The focus on trade finance did not include small enterprises, and pre-export financing for small firms remained a problem.

The march north of South African banks was part of a general pattern. Two and a half years after the April 1994 elections, most investment north of the border was in services. Prominent examples were grocery stores (such as Pic 'n Pay), breweries, hotels, electric power, mining, telecommunications, and railways and ports.[10]

By 1998, South African firms had overtaken Britain to become the leading foreign business licensees in Southern Africa.[11] There was almost no investment in industry (although mining investment, which was typical even throughout the apartheid years, was strong). Hein Marais summarized the situation:

> [South African investments] generally have not been aimed at industrial development. Most corporations have announced expansion plans in other African countries. South African Breweries (SAB) now runs brewing companies in Botswana, Lesotho, Swaziland, Tanzania and Zambia. "Our strategy in Africa," according to SAB's chair, "is to dominate market share." Retail giants like Shoprite-Checkers and Pick 'n Pay have opened operations in Zambia, Mozambique, Namibia, Botswana, Kenya and Zimbabwe. Financial institutions like Standard Bank now operate in 13 other African countries, prompting the African Development Bank to comment that South African institutions have become "increasingly important" in the commercial banking and insurance sectors of the region.[12]

Despite their strong regional presence, South African banks indirectly (through their reluctance to invest in productive enterprises) and directly (through their links with South Africa's large corporations) supported ad hoc cooperation. The powerful conglomerate/banking establishment had already obtained post-position in South Africa. The first ANC administration's eager engagement with international capital markets gave this sector yet more leverage in economic policymaking. The financial/banking sector's regional influence was predicated on apartheid South Africa's policies. If its manufacturing and trade policy shaped its regional relations, its monetary and exchange-rate policy had an equally important influence on its evolving regional economic foreign policy.

To understand how post-apartheid South Africa's monetary policy shapes its political economy, we need to appreciate a little of its history. The new ANC government's room to maneuver was limited, and the trade-offs it made favored the banks and their conglomerate partners.

South Africa's Monetary Policy

Apartheid South Africa's monetary policy did as much to promote the capital-intensive sector and retard development of the labor-intensive sector as did its industrial and trade policy covered in the previous chapter. This was exacerbated (from the perspective of labor-intensive industry) by structural flaws inherited by the post-apartheid economy. Most significant, South Africa's policies guaranteed cheap capital (real interest rates were negative and a low exchange rate maintained), which made it cheaper to promote capital-intensive industry. These policies are largely attributed to South Africa's balance-of-payments problem that resulted from the 1985 decision of international banks not to renew South African loans.

The failure to increase real interest rates in South Africa in the decades before the transition meant that throughout the 1970s and the 1980s, the tax-adjusted cost of borrowing was negative. Inflation was essentially greater than interest rates. The combination of low exchange rates and low interest rates promoted apartheid South Africa's capital-intensive industries.[13] Its monetary policy reinforced the biases of its trade and industrialization policy, and the post-apartheid state inherited an incentive structure that had all but crippled labor-intensive industry's ability to export to the region.

As South Africa adopted a more export-oriented trade regime, exchange-rate policy rose in importance. To promote exports, it adopted a constant exchange-rate regime; a regime that focuses on keeping the value of the rand relatively even relative to other currencies (particularly those of major trading partners). This makes it easier for exporters to calculate the cost of doing business overseas. The economy responded positively but not equally across all of its sectors; the capital-intensive sector outperformed the labor-intensive sector. Why did the capital-intensive sector benefit from an ostensible outward-looking policy? Harvey and Jenkins, well-known Southern African economists, argue that the uneven response to a general real-exchange-rate depreciation is due to the fact that a general trade-weighted exchange-rate policy is misleading because bilateral aspects vary: "[A]s with any average, a trade-weighted real exchange-rate index is only useful if the components of the average move in roughly similar direction and by comparable amounts."[14] In the case of South Africa, this was unlikely, since the inflation rate of its neighbors, at least those outside the Common Monetary Area, is normally much higher than its own. High inflation devalues a country's currency, acting as a de facto devaluation. Table 3 (Appendix) shows South Africa's real exchange rate compared to some neighboring countries.

To simplify, there are two ways to look at the impact of South Africa's exchange-rate regime. First, if South Africa were to lower its exchange rate, then its exports should get cheaper and more easily penetrate regional markets. But that requires a country-by-country comparison to see what the actual effect of a lower exchange rate would be. If the countries whose markets South Africa hoped to penetrate—its neighboring countries—have high inflation, the effect of lower interest rates is nullified. South Africa's traditional exchange-rate policy actually had the effect of limiting its ability to export narrow manufactured (labor-intensive) goods.[15] The result was a crippling of labor-intensive exports.

There is a second explanation for the poor performance of South Africa's labor-intensive goods. The uneven response to the constant exchange rate that South Africa had adopted to promote exports may have been because the structure of trade varied among industries. Textiles, a labor-intensive industry, had the lowest relative depreciation and thus would have the most difficulty penetrating external markets. Apartheid South Africa's monetary and exchange-rate policies combined to limit the ability of narrow manufactured goods to penetrate the regional market; thus, only the capital-intensive sector really benefited.

The third legacy of apartheid South Africa's monetary policy was low domestic savings. The ANC inherited a domestic savings shortfall and hoped to turn on the faucet of international finance. The 1985 South African debt standstill exacerbated this condition. The trigger for that series of events was P. W. Botha's "Rubicon Speech" of August 15, 1985. Chase Manhattan called in South Africa's loans and then refused new loans to

South Africa. Other banks followed its lead. The subsequent political unrest led to plummeting investor confidence and capital flight. Balance of
payments came under severe stress.

In the wake of the 1985 South African debt standstill, the rand
quickly depreciated against a basket of foreign currencies (dollar, yen,
deutsche mark, pound, lira). The positive effect of this depreciation was a
trade surplus (during the sanctions era) that peaked at 17 billion rand in
1990 and was still 15.5 billion rand in 1992. The negative effect was the
choking off of the necessary flow of imports for economic growth. South
Africa's commitment to repay its debt in terms of the Interim Debt Agreement with foreign banks meant that it had to run a current-account surplus on the balance of payments. This was done by suppressing domestic
demand, promoting exports, and maintaining fiscal discipline.[16] South Africa was successful, but at a cost. The subsequent increase in exports and
the decrease in the ratio of imports to GDP were accomplished by reducing domestic investment, which was import intensive.[17] Investment as a
percentage of GDP declined from 26.4 in 1982–1984 to 20.2 in 1985–
1991.[18]

Transitional South Africa had strong banks but a weak savings position. Its capital stock was increasing by about 2 percent per annum; South
Africa's competitor countries had increased theirs by about 8 percent per
annum. Immediately after the "debt crisis," South Africa's annual net investment in the manufacturing sector turned negative.[19]

Therefore, at the cusp of the post-apartheid era, South Africa was
acutely aware of the need for foreign capital. It is ironic that the ambitious
RDP was more sensitive to flows of foreign investment than was the more
conservative NEM. The new government's solution was to open up the old
laager economy—globalization. This opening up has had political costs.

The Globalization of South Africa's Political Economy

Globalization was anticipated as following naturally from the dismantling
of international sanctions against South Africa. In fact, as the ANC placed
its supporters in high government positions, a new élan evolved. Whereas
the old Afrikaner bureaucracy had a stubborn laager mentality tinged with
xenophobia, the new ANC elite were eager to embrace the world. In South
African political scientist Anthoni van Nieuwkerk's words:

> Free from its apartheid isolationist moorings, a broad approach of "uni-
> versality" represented its intention to pursue a diplomacy of active inter-

nationalism which was nevertheless bound by certain ideological incli-
nations, historic alliances and political preferences.[20]

After all, most of that world had supported the dismantling and demise
of apartheid. As Rashad Cassim states, "The new government, under the
auspices of a new breed of bureaucrats, was now bent on renewing its
status in the international and regional arena."[21]

The importance for South Africa of participating in the world economy
was evident early in the transition. The first task of the National Economic
Forum (NEF), a corporatist institution created to plan economic policy
options during the transition, was to put together a GATT offer. South
Africa is one of the original signatories to GATT and has participated in
all the GATT rounds of multilateral trade negotiations. In each round,
participating countries negotiate their individual trade policies within the
GATT process. While South Africa took part in this process, many foreign
governments and corporations limited their trade and investment with
apartheid South Africa from about 1985 to early 1990. With the imminent demise of apartheid, South Africa negotiated its trade policies under
the final GATT round—the Uruguay Round. South Africa went under
GATT's Trade Policy Review Mechanism (TPRM), one of the mid-term
initiatives of the Uruguay Round. The GATT Council, which conducts
the review, ended its formal written concluding remarks by saying:

> In conclusion, the Council recognized that the South African economy
> was subject to many constraints. With sanctions largely dismantled,
> South Africa, as a country undergoing significant transformation, should
> make every effort to align its economy fully with the multilateral trad-
> ing system.[22]

This is essentially what transitional South Africa did.

But as important as international trade was to the emerging post-
apartheid state, international capital markets would prove to be a more important and immediate concern. Capital mobility, the freedom of money
in its many forms to cross national borders, became an important factor in
South Africa's macroeconomic policy,[23] and South Africa underwent a major transition in its external relations concerning international capital.[24]

South Africa's statement to the GATT review process, just prior to the
April 1994 election, argued that to ensure economic growth in transitional South Africa, fixed-capital investment (spending on machinery,
buildings, and technology so the economy can produce more consumer
goods in the future) would have to increase to 24 percent of GDP.[25] This

figure was generally accepted as necessary for 3.5 percent GDP growth in post-apartheid South Africa.[26] It would be difficult to meet. South Africa's gross domestic investment as a percentage of GDP was between 19 and 21 percent during the period 1985–1990. In that time span, its gross domestic savings went from 30 percent of GDP to 25 percent.[27] By 1998, the net national savings rate had fallen to below 14 percent of GDP.[28] All of this meant that it would be difficult to find more money to invest in the economy. The World Bank had argued that only by reviving private investment would post-apartheid South Africa be able to meet the demands of the ANC's economic blueprint, the Reconstruction and Development Programme (RDP).[29]

Furthermore, an "apartheid dividend" to rescue the balance of payments was unlikely. Jeffrey Herbst reported that the best guess was that short-run savings would be 2 to 4 percent of GDP.[30] Some of these savings were expected to come from eliminating the administrative duplication that was endemic to apartheid. But the transitional bargain between the old National Party government and the African National Congress (the so-called "sunset clause"), included pension guarantees and protection for civil servants from being let go. Duplication would likely continue, albeit in a different guise, as the ANC created government positions for its supporters.[31]

In the opening session of the World Economic Forum in Cape Town on June 9, 1994, Mandela stressed that his government would adhere to Western economic policies rather than the socialist policies the ANC had advocated as a banned liberation movement.[32] Shortly after the April 1994 election, the United States held an investment conference for South Africa in Atlanta. Archbishop Desmond Tutu, who joined the delegation, stated, "I was sometimes called Mr. Sanctions, the man most white South Africans loved to hate. Now, I want to be—please allow me to become—Mr. Investment."[33]

To placate both international and domestic capital, the post-apartheid South African government moved away from the Keynesian demand-driven model as originally articulated in the RDP.[34] Political scientists and economists credit the global trend across countries away from Keynesian demand-driven economic policies to those more dependent on monetary policy to the increase in international capital mobility.[35] However, in theory, South Africa could have accelerated or slowed down its integration into the world economy.[36] For instance, it could have maintained or strengthened trade barriers or continued capital controls, such as the dual-exchange-rate system, rather than dismantling them.[37] Given its relatively low level of external debt, the South African state had room to adopt a heterodox development strategy.[38] But resisting the winds of globalization was increasingly difficult in the post–Cold War era, and globalization would have particular sector-specific political ramifications in South Africa.

The new South African government took steps to increase capital mobility between it and the outside world. Two important changes in South Africa during 1995 were South Africa's abolishment of both the "financial rand" system, which was a form of capital control that kept South Africans from investing abroad while accepting investments from abroad, and its import surcharges. The former had been used to protect South Africa's balance of payments and was expected to do so for another decade, according to a senior official at the South African Reserve Bank in 1993.[39] Instead, post-apartheid South Africa signaled its commitment to reducing exchange controls. In 1996, the governor of the Reserve Bank, Chris Stals, listed five steps that had led to South Africa's "gradual" phasing out of exchange controls:

1. South Africa's debt standstill arrangement was terminated at the end of 1993.
2. South African companies are now allowed to make foreign direct investment in cases where it benefits balance of payments.
3. In March 1995 the two-tier foreign-exchange system (finrand) was abolished.
4. In June 1995, permission was given to South African institutional investors to exchange through approved asset swaps, trading part of their South African portfolio for foreign securities.
5. South Africa developed an (ongoing) forward exchange market outside the Reserve Bank.[40]

The five reforms listed above were a response to the challenges created by the ability of capital to move around the world with the touch of a computer keyboard. South Africa's large corporations were (as are large multinational corporations everywhere) increasingly skilled at moving their money around. If they felt uneasy with post-apartheid South Africa's monetary policy, they could move money out of the country, further exacerbating the shortfall of domestic savings and investment. Increasing capital mobility was also expected to bring in foreign capital, and in the immediate years after the 1994 election, this strategy was relatively successful.

South Africa's eager, even anxious, reintegration into international capital markets had a deep domestic impact; it severely strained the ANC-COSATU alliance. The impact of capital mobility on South Africa's monetary policy and the way it affected the domestic political balance of power can be illustrated by using the Mundell-Fleming model. It demonstrates two characteristics of the new South African government's policies: the need for foreign investment placed structural limits on the RDP, and those limits helped shape a foreign-exchange regime that favored the entrenched banking/conglomerate sector.

The Political Economy, Capital Mobility, and Exchange Rate in the New South Africa

In a world where money is relatively free to cross national borders—capital mobility—a state's exchange rate becomes an important, even central, instrument for managing the country's economy. In most cases, this is done through adopting a floating exchange rate (allowing the market to determine the value of a state's currency). As transitional South Africa opened up, globalized exchange rates became a pivotal policy instrument. As Brian Kahn pointed out: "It can be seen, therefore, in both the recommendations and possibly the recent practice of exchange rate policy that the exchange rate is now [early 1990s] being seen as an important part of the overall industrial or trade strategy."[41] It is possible to resist capital mobility by restricting the flow of money in and out of a country, as Malaysia did to some extent in the wake of the East Asian financial crisis of 1997–1998. But in the early years of post-apartheid South Africa, new infusions of capital were considered essential to economic growth.

What this means in practice, and in the specific case of post-apartheid South Africa, is that monetary policy (controlling the money supply) becomes a more effective instrument of macroeconomic management than fiscal policy (taxation) as a tool for macroeconomic policy—monetarism pushes ahead of Keynesianism as an instrument of macroeconomic policy. As Garrett states, "[F]iscal policy is ineffective under capital mobility where the exchange rate floats."[42] It therefore handicaps Keynesian approaches to macroeconomic management and limits the possibility of establishing a Keynesian welfare state. The decision to embrace capital mobility has important political ramifications. There are two dimensions to the politics of South Africa's exchange-rate policy.

First, as political economist Jeffry Frieden states, "In an open economy, the politics of monetary policy tend to be organized around the concentrated effects of exchange rate movements, and thus are likely to resemble interest group politics involving such things as tariffs (for which, after all, a real depreciation can be a substitute)."[43] In the case of post-apartheid South Africa, its export industries are becoming increasingly capital intensive.[44]

In general, South Africa's exchange-rate policy supported its big-business sector. As South African economists Janine Aron and Ibrahim Elbadawi state in their important study of post-apartheid South Africa's macroeconomic policy:

> From the perspective of the relatively sophisticated formal manufacturing and financial sectors, it appears that priority should be accorded to macroeconomic stability (especially exchange rates), to orderly foreign exchange and financial markets and to macroeconomic efficiency.[45]

That is exactly what South Africa did.

The second dimension concerns the relative influence of different departments in the South African government over macroeconomic policy. An increase in capital mobility strengthens the relative role of finance ministries and central banks. For instance, Sylvia Maxfield argues that economic policy is likely to reflect bankers' preferences under three conditions: if there is an independent central bank, if the finance ministry is allied with the central bank and exercises hegemony over other ministries, and if state industrialization or planning authorities have little ability to control the flow of investment funds.[46] Stephen Haggard and Chung Lee argue that a concentration of banking/industrial economic power reinforces the power of groups in favor of economic liberalism.[47] And in fact the South African Reserve Bank and Department of Finance played an increasingly central role in post-apartheid South Africa's macroeconomic policy.

The spending imperatives of the Keynesian Reconstruction Development Plan conflicted with the Reserve Bank's strong emphasis on containing inflation. Using the exchange rate to affect the balance of payments, as in the case of post-1985 South Africa, can actually inhibit economic growth. In effect, in such a situation, domestic savings are being exported rather than being used to promote local industry, and the result is the redistribution of income away from labor.[49] Nonetheless, South Africa embarked on just such a path in the first ANC administration.

South Africa's exchange-rate policy has to be considered in the context of the government's macroeconomic policy. The South African Reserve Bank's first post-apartheid governor, Chris Stals, a holdover from the de

Klerk regime, made it clear prior to the April 1994 election and after it that the Bank's central purpose was to protect the exchange rate of the rand.[50] Stals explained that the Bank's policy was not to use the exchange rate as an anchor for inflation; instead, by fighting inflation, the Reserve Bank could protect the external value of the rand. The goal was a "relatively stable exchange rate."[51] He stated: "Monetary policy should therefore preferably not be applied in an anticyclical manner, or at times to stimulate the economy and at other times to depress it (the so-called 'stop-go' approach)."[52]

Facts on the ground, a lack of foreign investment, and an ideational shift by the ANC led to what was for all intents and purposes a neoliberal macroeconomic framework. The death of a demand-driven model was, in fact, signaled by the apparent demise of the RDP on March 28, 1996. Its replacement with a new economic blueprint, Growth, Employment and Redistribution (GEAR), in June of that year was directly tied to South Africa's exchange-rate regime and, in fact, was based on a South African Reserve Bank model.[53]

> South Africa's first currency crisis—starting in February 1996—quickly overtook [the] debate [over a neoliberal macroeconomic policy], as the value of the Rand dropped by more than 25%. In this context, the government moved quickly to calm domestic capital and foreign currency markets, including senior civil servants, representatives of the Development Bank of Southern Africa, and the World Bank. In June, after considerable internal disagreement within the Tripartite Alliance, Finance Minister Trevor Manuel finally released the new strategy, "Growth, Employment and Redistribution."[54]

GEAR was the ANC's first comprehensive economic plan since its election in 1994. Nico Czypionka, chief economist at Standard Bank, stated that the "debate appeared to have shifted in favor of a free market approach, despite accusations from labor and some in the ANC of such an approach as 'Thatcherite'."[55] GEAR had three main tenets, each signaling a move away from what South African business leader Edward Osborn called the "slick neo-Keynesian notion" of demand-led growth.[56] It called for the South African budget deficit to be reduced from 5.1 percent to 3.0 percent by the year 2000; it called for tight monetary policy with inflation to be kept to an average of 8.2 percent until 2000; and it called for accelerated privatization of the parastatal sector.[57] It was consistent with what many considered the onslaught of neoliberal economics in post-apartheid South Africa, and, in fact, two World Bank economists were employed to help draw up GEAR.[58]

GEAR had been preceded by an internal policy debate pitting labor against business. The business perspective was promoted in the document drafted by the so-called Brenthurst Group (a group of South Africa's captains of industry that was named for mining magnate Harry Oppenheimer's home) in March 1996, "Growth for All"; COSATU, the Federation of South African Labor Unions (FEDSAL), and the National Council of Trade Unions (NACTU), the three main labor unions, responded with their own manifesto, "Social Equity and Job Creation."[59] As Nicoli Nattrass and Jeremy Seekings stated:

> The Strategy [GEAR] rests on the assumption that restrictive fiscal policies will send such positive signals to investors that growth will leap foreword on a wave of confidence-driven investment. Likewise, it is debatable whether the strategy will bring about sufficient job creation to narrow inequality substantially.[60]

Labor was strongly opposed to GEAR. COSATU's mission statement argued that unemployment was still too high because of bad or nonexistent policies from the ministers of trade and industry and of finance. In June 1996, COSATU repeatedly lobbied against a tight monetary policy and called for lower interest rates. In a 1996 draft discussion paper, COSATU lamented that "[n]o one from the ranks of the [labor] movement, except some in government, were involved in [GEAR's] formulation, only orthodox economists from the old order, IMF and World Bank."[61] COSATU and the South African Communist Party condemned GEAR as 'Thatcherite" or "neoliberal" and said that it undermined the RDP's goal of improving the conditions of the impoverished Black masses.[62] At the Communist Party's seventy-fifth anniversary celebration in Cape Town, Sam Shilowa, secretary-general of COSATU, stated that GEAR would never have emerged from the ANC prior to the 1994 general elections and was not in line with the RDP.[63] COSATU called for "flexible independence" from the ANC at its sixth national congress in 1997 because the ANC was the author of GEAR.

The point is that although an increase in capital mobility can have a constraining effect on the range of policy options open to a country, it does not signal the end of partisan policymaking.[64] Rather, it heightens the political significance of exchange-rate policy. As Jeffrey Herbst had predicted, once the ANC was in power it had to make the difficult decision to disappoint part of its constituency.[65]

Early in the transition, the political tension of the post-apartheid era was already anticipated. South African economist Terence Moll, commenting on South Africa's macroeconomic challenge of maintaining a balance between economic growth and an equitable economy in South Africa, observed, "Such goals will entail exceptionally cunning political management if the dangers of excessive macroeconomic expansion are to be avoided."[66] There was a strong possibility, as implied in the RDP, that heavy pressure would be brought to bear on the post-apartheid state to make reparations for the suffering caused by apartheid by redistributing income—particularly by increasing public-sector employment, social spending, and real wages. Without sharp rises in taxes or extensive foreign assistance, an expansionary and ultimately unsustainable macroeconomic environment could emerge—as happened to an extent during the 1980s.[67] The pressure on the ANC to make good on its electoral promises led to predictions that "[a]s far as the future is concerned, high and increasing levels of government spending in South Africa seem unavoidable."[68]

These arguments proved to be only half right. As witnessed by the economic ideology of the RDP, the political pressures for what could be considered an entrenched Keynesian welfare state were indeed powerful, but the dynamics of post-apartheid South African coalitions were much more fluid than the 1993/1994 election period had predicted. And an economy open to international forces engenders new coalitional dynamics. Post-apartheid South Africa was not a highly indebted country, but it was deficient in domestic savings and needed to attract foreign capital and keep domestic capital from fleeing. Subsequently, the foreign-exchange regime developed under Chris Stals supported the status-quo industries.

The structure of transitional South Africa's financial sector and the politics of macroeconomic and monetary policy in an increasingly open economy influenced the political matrix for regional cooperation in transitional South Africa. The more open economy, which the new government pursued from the time of the transition, at once reflects the preferences of South Africa's international-oriented actors and reinforces their influence over state policy. South Africa's banking and investment sectors were the beneficiaries of increased capital mobility, and South African banks were closely tied to the conglomerate sector, which strongly supported ad hoc cooperation. GEAR's exchange-rate policy, which supported the status-quo industries, became increasingly central to trade promotion. Post-apartheid South Africa's exchange-rate regime favored the status-quo industries. Banking and finance, both public and private, indirectly pushed post-apartheid South Africa away from developmental cooperation in Southern Africa.

7

International Influences and
Political Choice in Transitional South Africa

This chapter uses three proxies for the international system to explore international influences on transitional South Africa's regional economic relations: GATT,[1] the IFIs, and the EU.[2]

The International System Matters, But How?

How the international system matters is usually framed by the question, Do international influences inhibit or promote regional economic integration among developing countries? This question casts the debate in a similar way to the larger debate over why states do or do not cooperate. The more interesting question is how the international system shapes the process of cooperation/integration among states.

There are strong arguments that international influences, particularly those from the North, retard economic integration in the South. Many scholars, particularly those from the dependency tradition, offer systemic explanations for the failure of Third World regional integration. Trade between developed and developing countries, they argue, promotes relations of unequal exchange; that is, manufactured goods for primary products. This unequal exchange relationship guarantees that the Third World will not produce manufactured products that can compete with similar products from the industrialized countries. This situation indirectly hurts the prospects for regional integration among developing countries because industrial development is necessary for intraregional trade.[3] Others push the argument farther by claiming that the industrialized countries directly, and purposefully, inhibit Third World regional integration.[4] Proof offered for this assertion includes the fact that official donor assistance (predominantly from the North) is usually bilateral.[5] Thus, divide-and-rule tactics are used to preclude competition from unified groups of southern countries. The IFIs have, some argue, inhibited regional economic integration among developing countries. For instance, structural adjustment programs (SAPs) may inhibit regional economic integration and cooperation in the developing world because they are conceived as national programs and thus lack a regional dimension[6] and because they typically are short-term programs and regional integration is a long-term endeavor.[7] Also, in practice, SAPs have not been used to improve intraregional trade preferences and, in fact, have encouraged trade outside the region more than inside the region. It has also been argued that the marginalization of Africa in the international economy makes South-South economic linkages more difficult.[8]

On the other hand, some argue that certain international pressures promote regional economic integration in the Third World. The relationship of unequal exchange between North and South is the primary motivation for most Third World regional economic integration schemes. Also, as is particularly evident in the case of South Africa, one of the most common arguments in support of some level of regional cooperation is the perception that the international political economy is breaking into competing trading blocs: the EU, NAFTA, and Mercosur (Argentina, Brazil, Paraguay, Uruguay). Björn Hettne has called this neomercantilism.[9]

F. W. de Klerk, for instance, stated, "We live in a shrinking and competitive world where countries on all continents are forming economic blocs and associations to improve their chance of economic survival and prosperity."[10] Africa, and particularly Southern Africa, has no strong ties to any of these blocs.[11] In December 1993, before the formal end of apartheid, Len Van Zyl, chief executive of the South African Foreign Trade Organisation, emphasized that trading blocs are important for negotiating with other trading blocs.[12] The first ANC government made similar assumptions:

> The strength of SADC as a future economic bloc must not be underestimated and must clearly feature prominently in the response of South

Africa and Southern Africa to bloc formation elsewhere. The objective, however, should not be to force confrontation with other blocs but rather to develop mutually beneficial relationships.[13]

Elias Links, former South African ambassador for the ANC to the European Union, offered:

> The EU will be one of the major players in a new world order in a century to be characterized and dominated by globalisation and inter-regional relations. The EU Member States' pooling of sovereignty in their own national interest also offers many interesting pointers for SADC's own regional integration efforts.[14]

In some instances, extraregional actors have actually directly encouraged the creation of regional economic integration schemes. For instance, external influences figured prominently in the formation of the Southern African Development Coordination Conference.[15] In the late 1970s, the Preferential Trade Area (PTA) and the nascent SADCC competed for extraregional support. The UN's Economic Commission for Africa (ECA) was instrumental in the formation of the PTA and attempted to garner European Economic Community support for the PTA while blocking support for the SADCC.[16] However, the SADCC developed the closer relationship with the European Economic Community. The EEC subsidized it early on and maintained the SADCC's historic and current links to the EU.[17]

Today the EU promotes Third World regional integration, at least in its rhetoric.[18] One South African Department of Trade and Industry official felt that the EU would in fact rather deal with an area than with individual countries.[19] The former director general of the Department of Trade and Industry related that even in discussions on bilateral matters, the European countries tended to emphasize regional matters.[20] The SADC itself concluded that "[i]n an increasing number of cases, external partners are making a linkage between an equitable relationship in Southern Africa and South Africa's inclusion on favorable terms in arrangements with external parties. This is particularly notable in the case of the European Community."[21] Like the EU, the IFIs now voice support for regional integration. In general, as Southern Africa expert Gilbert Khadiagala states, "the lifting of the East-West political-military rivalry has, nonetheless, been accompanied by enhanced Western economic intervention via the dominant Bretton Woods institutions, the World Bank, and the International Monetary Fund."[22]

The most immediate impact of the IFIs on the process of regional integration in Africa is through their SAPs, which might actually help promote regional cooperation and integration. The World Bank's 1991 study on intraregional trade in Sub-Saharan Africa begins by stating that the lack of progress with regional trade liberalization stems mainly from inappropriate macroeconomic policies—overvalued exchange rates, excessive fiscal deficits, distorted credit allocation, and heavy domestic-market protection.[23] The focus of the SAPs on the macroeconomic policies of individual countries may in practice engender a convergence of the macroeconomic performance that is necessary for enhanced regional integration; in other words, the different national economies have similar economic indicators such as inflation, national debt, and so forth.[24] Severe macroeconomic problems within national economies make it very difficult for those countries to cooperate with other countries in the region. SAPs may help ameliorate this problem. Regional cooperation could, in fact, build on the SAPs already in place in Southern Africa.[25] Theoretically, the rationalization of the national economies could create conditions that favor regional cooperation.

SAPs are also supposed to improve the mobility of factors of production across borders that would complement the process of regional economic integration.[26] The African Development Bank study on integration in Southern Africa argues that on the macroeconomic level, financial stabilization and structural adjustment programs currently being implemented in Southern Africa need to be sustained and coordinated to promote regional integration. The report adds that SAPs will open up manufacturing sectors and expose them to competition, which will lead to greater convergence of the regional economies.[27] Probably the most important macroeconomic effect of SAPs on the prospects for regional cooperation and integration is their impact on exchange-rate policies; the nonconvertibility of currencies has been one of the most serious blocks to intraregional trade.

The World Bank and the IMF have also indirectly promoted regional economic integration in Southern Africa. For instance, the SACOB study on regional cooperation stated that they expect the World Bank to assist more readily in an economically unified Southern Africa than in the various countries separately.[28] Fantu Cheru states that the World Bank, in fact, pressured South Africa to take the lead in transforming the existing integration efforts in Eastern and Southern Africa.[29] As will be discussed below, the World Bank wanted regional economic integration/cooperation to be based on the market model. At the 1993 Brussels conference on the future relations between the EC and Southern Africa, the World Bank representative stressed the need for a regional approach in Southern Africa and the central role South Africa was expected to play.[30]

On the negative side, regional convergence may mask disruptions in the domestic economies caused by the macroeconomic policies of IFIs. More important, these disruptions affect the industrial and trade structure of the individual countries, thus also affecting the politics of regional cooperation and integration. For instance, South African economics professor Trevor Bell argues that further import liberalization in South Africa through comprehensive tariff reductions, as promoted by the IFIs, aggravates problems confronting macroeconomic stabilization in various ways by increasing imports, reducing fiscal balances by shrinking customs tariffs, and adversely affecting import-competing industries, most importantly labor-intensive ones.[31] Brian Levy's World Bank study addresses these problems by focusing on how to increase the export potential of South Africa's labor-intensive industries, particularly the clothing industry.[32]

International pressures, therefore, are a mixed bag. The international community now more readily accepts regional economic integration among developing countries and in some instances promotes integration of a certain type. This change in attitude is symbolized by the World Bank's evolving view. In 1981, the World Bank published its blueprint for economic development in Sub-Saharan Africa, *Accelerated Development* (also known as the Berg Report).[33] This report sparked a heated debate both inside and outside Africa about what was the right economic development strategy for the continent. It argued for a laissez-faire free trade strategy; Africa was to open up its economy to the rest of the world and through the magic of comparative advantage and competition replicate the Asian miracle that had launched the economies of South Korea, Hong Kong, Singapore, and Taiwan. Africa, specifically the ECA, rejected this model and proposed regional economic integration, the Lagos Plan of Action, as an alternative to the World Bank's export-oriented strategy. The Lagos Plan was adopted at the 1980 OAU Assembly of Heads of State and Government held in Freetown, Sierra Leone. It argued for self-reliant development through delinking Africa from the world economy. Almost a decade later, the World Bank published the successor to *Accelerated Development,* titled *Sub-Saharan Africa: From Crisis to Sustainable Growth.* This study included a short chapter on regional integration drawn from a collection of background papers, *Proceedings of a Workshop on Regional Integration and Cooperation,* with twenty-four contributors, many of them African. As John Ravenhill noted, this report endorsed at length the OAU/ECA's demand for regional economic integration.[34] In fact, as one of South Africa's leading experts on the ties between South Africa's regional and international relations indicated, there was a strong belief in South Africa that it could strengthen its position with the World Bank and the IMF in the post-apartheid era to the extent that it was seen as doing the right thing in the region.[35]

Thus, there is disagreement over how the international system influences integration among developing countries but general agreement that integration should not be discouraged. There has been no such concordance concerning the type of regional economic integration. In particular, there is general disagreement between those promoting a free-market approach and those supporting developmental integration. For instance, the U.S. government promotes a regional FTA in Southern Africa. In 1995, the SADC Secretariat signed a Memorandum of Understanding with the U.S. government, which committed the U.S. to help the SADC with a program of regional trade liberalization. And the U.S.'s African Growth and Opportunity Act lists as one of its eligibility requirements that countries have policies supporting the growth of regional markets within a free trade area framework.

Thinking about Regional Integration

The Ideology of the IFIs and Regional Cooperation in South Africa

By early 1991, the ANC had already met with IFIs' missions to South Africa.[36] The World Bank, in particular, actively participated in the debate over how to institutionalize regional cooperation in post-apartheid Southern Africa. As the SADC's macro-framework study report stated, "the World Bank had established a firm presence among 'opinion leaders' in South Africa on regional issues."[37] Closer economic cooperation and integration in Southern Africa was also one of the main topics of discussion between South African financiers and their African counterparts at the IMF's 1991 annual meeting.[38]

There was some ambiguity in the position of the IFIs concerning the best form of regional economic integration in Southern Africa. In 1992, the IFIs had expressed a preference for the PTA and trade liberalization as the way to foster regional integration.[39] This was largely because the PTA's pursuit of a common market seemed to most closely fit the free trade approach the IFIs favored. But the World Bank sent mixed signals; it praised the SADCC, for example:

SADCC is the economic grouping that tends to be most highly praised in [Sub-Saharan Africa]; largely because it has a small secretariat, works through national governments and has a concrete and limited agenda. The other economic groupings (and any new efforts at regional integration) should be based on the same principles. It may be fruitful to discuss and implement one protocol at a time instead of trying to work ineffectively on a dozen fronts.[40]

In fact, the SADCC's traditional project-based approach to regional integration, with its focus on the coordination of specific sectors, complements both the sector-based SAPs and the project-based lending of the World Bank.

The apparent support of the IFIs, particularly the World Bank for a strong state role, however, is better understood as support for South Africa taking a leading regional role. Ohlson and Stedman, experts on South and Southern Africa, argued that the IFIs (as well as major Western countries and donors) favored a regional system where South Africa would be the hegemon.[41] South Africa was certainly well positioned to dominate infrastructure development in post-apartheid Southern Africa. The SADC had, in fact, expressed concern over South Africa's ability to dominate externally funded projects in their member states: "South African firms have become involved in externally funded projects in several SADC member countries. . . . A number of South African building contracting firms (such as LTA and Murray and Roberts), equipment suppliers and parastatals (like Eskom) have as a consequence significantly increased their involvement in projects in Angola, Mozambique and Zambia, among others."[42] The SADC also stated that the South African Department of Finance and SAFTO promoted South Africa's involvement in regional projects.[43] The African Development Bank study, as well, cautioned that the South African business community perceived reentry to regional markets as an advantage only insofar as it would enable them to compete for aid-funded contracts and expand aid-funded exports.[44]

World Bank programs have supported a project-oriented approach to cooperation; its investment lending, which accounts for approximately three-fourths of all funds it disburses, is usually given to a government or parastatal for a specific project.[45] The World Bank has also indirectly supported the large-corporation and parastatal sector because of the importance of project assistance to Africa. World Bank project lending in Africa increased from under $8 billion in the 1970s to $17 billion in the 1980s, about $1.7 billion annually.[46]

The importance of World Bank contracts to South Africa and South Africa's regional dominance in procuring contracts took off during the transition. From July 1, 1992, to June 30, 1993, South Africa was awarded thirty-three contracts in Southern Africa (Lesotho 9, Malawi 5, Mozambique 8, Zambia 5, and Zimbabwe 6). No other country in the region was awarded a contract for a country outside its own borders. The South African total in dollars for the region was $52,938,748; the sum total for the countries other than South Africa in the region was $55,322,235.[47] The results for the following year are skewed by one contract for Zimbabwe worth $130,804,080. In that year, South Africa had 22 contracts in neighboring countries, while none of the other countries had external contracts.[48]

The approach of the IFIs, using South Africa as the engine of growth in Southern Africa, closely reinforces the ad hoc approach to regional cooperation. But the second and more important element underlying IFIs' support for regional economic integration is their support for market liberalization. As Fantu Cheru noted, "The World Bank's renewed interest in regional integration comes after a period of long opposition to the idea, and it signaled out the PTA and SADCC for financial and technical support."[49] However, as Cheru further noted, the World Bank's vision is fundamentally different from that informing most African integration schemes. The World Bank generally supported outward-looking regional integration in Southern Africa. It feels that instead of pulling away from the international economy, regional integration is a way to reintegrate Africa into the global economy.[50] The Bank argues that supporting regional cooperation is part of the larger process of liberalizing trade and removing controls on the flow of capital across borders.[51]

> As regionalism emerges as an integral part of the world trading environment, it should not be allowed to divert attention from the fact that the first-best policy remains most-favored-nation liberalization and the ultimate goal multilateral free trade. Regional agreements should be implemented in a manner that harnesses them securely to the long-run goal of multilateral liberalization.[52]

There are two sides to the regional integration policy of the IFIs. First, they support a basically laissez-faire approach to regionalism that is consistent with their general propagation of economic liberalism. This approach is expected to be girded by free-market enterprise buttressed by the domestic winners in the trade game. Second, the IFIs frame regional eco-

nomic integration as a problem of national initiative and promote significant state involvement in the process by supporting large regional projects
that are often dominated by the parastatal sector (or large corporations).
In both cases, functional cooperation through project financing and free
market integration, the IFIs found ready allies in South Africa's large-
corporation sector.

GATT's Free Trade Agreement Ideology

GATT is the institutional backbone of the international free trade regime.
It is also typically associated with market integration rather than developmental integration. Article I of GATT contains the most-favored-nation
(MFN) clause, in which members agree to extend unconditionally to all
other GATT members "any advantage, favor, privilege or immunity" that
they give to other countries. There are exceptions, the most well known
being Article 24, which allows for customs unions and free trade areas.
However, GATT also includes the much-ignored "enabling clause," which
opens the door to a more developmental approach to regional integration.
Rosalind Thomas explains that the enabling clause "was specifically designed to appreciate the economic development of LDCs and LLDCs. For
that reason it is more flexible in its application than Article XXIV."[53]

GATT's most important role, nonetheless, is as promoter of the free
trade norm. And regionalism has often been depicted as an alternative, or
parallel, path to free trade.[54] GATT has become so complex, with so many
participants, that one way forward (to free trade) would be to liberalize
commerce on a regional basis and embed these regional schemes in further
rounds of GATT. C. Fred Bergsten, director of the Washington, D.C.–
based Institute of International Economics, for instance, has argued that
regional agreements can speed overall change to more free trade.[55] Article
24 of GATT, in fact, permits a customs-union territory to negotiate in a
GATT round as a contracting party even though the treaty was built on
the MFN principle. For example, Botswana can import and export goods
from its partners in SACU duty free without having to extend similar
treatment to countries outside SACU. In principle, GATT does not pro-
hibit regional economic integration in Southern Africa. But this is not
necessarily the case.

In 1979, at the Tokyo Round of negotiations, GATT adopted an agreement that called for the "differential and more-favorable treatment, reci-
procity and fuller participation of developing countries," creating a permanent legal basis for preferences among least developed countries (LDCs)

and between LDCs and the more industrialized nations. Paragraph two of the agreement outlines its intent:

(a) Preferential tariff treatment accorded developing countries by developed countries in accordance with the GSP.
(b) Differential and more favorable treatment for developing countries in other GATT rules dealing with nontariff barriers
(c) Regional or global arrangements entered into amongst [developing countries] for the mutual reproduction or elimination of tariffs, . . . on products imported from one another;
(d) Special treatment of the least-developed countries in the context of any general or specific measures in favor of developing countries.[56]

This means that within GATT, and now the World Trade Organization, there is room for a less restrictive attitude toward developmental cooperation than that permitted under Article 24.

Nonetheless, GATT remains ideologically committed to the MFN norm and freer trade. It does allow under the "Enabling Clause" for an alternative approach to a customs union and a free trade area for regional economic integration. In practice, however, exceptions are rare and are limited to developing countries.

The European Union, the Lomé Convention, and Regional Integration in Southern Africa

During South Africa's transition, there was little doubt within South Africa's foreign-policy establishment, in either political camp, that the EU favored regional cooperation in Southern Africa, with South Africa playing the leading role. However, the structuring of South Africa's relations with the EU was a contentious issue in transitional South Africa. There were two basic approaches—negotiate a bilateral relationship with the EU or negotiate membership in the Lomé Convention, a trade and aid agreement between the EU and seventy-two African, Caribbean, and Pacific (ACP) countries. It is a preferential trading arrangement between the EU and the ACP countries that exempts the latter from certain tariff and nontariff barriers. The preferences are nonreciprocal and apply to industrial, processed, and agricultural products.

The bilateral approach was supported by business and had been favored by the NP government, particularly by its finance minister, Derek Keys.[57] This approach was supported by studies that demonstrated that the Lomé Convention would not significantly help South Africa's export-

ers; the share of ACP countries of total EC imports from developing countries actually declined from 20.5 percent five years before Lomé (1970) to
16.6 percent ten years after the convention was signed (1985).[58] Big business had a vested interest in ignoring the important gains that could be
made by membership in Lomé because they favored a bilateral approach
and Lomé would primarily help labor-intensive industry. In general, South
Africa's exports to the EC did not face significant tariffs. Only half of its
ten most important exports faced MFN tariffs, and some of these were
relatively light. Overall, less than one-fifth of South Africa's exports that
were already going to EU countries would have benefited from tariff
relief.[59]

But labor, and originally the ANC, had good reason to pursue membership in the Lomé Convention. A 1989 study by McQueen and Stevens
showed that the aggregate figures (like those above) obscured important
gains by the ACP countries. In fact, in certain export categories Africa was
steadily increasing exports to Europe: "Most of the products showing sustained growth are based . . . on the processing of natural resources, for example wood and wood products, leather products, cotton yarn, fabrics and
clothing, canned tuna."[60] Canned fruit was also listed as a growth area.
Although in general South Africa's exports to the EU did not face high
tariffs, specific sectors would benefit from South African membership in
the Convention. Preferences would be important for products that fell outside the top ten, such as fresh and processed fruit and light manufactures
such as textiles and leather goods. The study looked at the potential
growth of South Africa's twenty most important exports into the EU market and concluded that full membership in the Lomé would help South
Africa the most. Most important for South Africa would be the Convention's generous preferences for textile exports from the ACP countries.

In 1994, the post-apartheid South African government commissioned
Christopher Stevens, an academic expert on Africa-EU relations, to study
the possible options open to it for a trade agreement with the EU. His
findings also indicated that Lomé was the best option. The ANC came to
power in 1994 committed to the Lomé option. And as late as 1997, the
South African government cautioned against an FTA approach with the
EU, mentioning specifically the weakness of the clothing, textiles, and
footwear sectors.[61] However, building on the GATT precedent, the EU
considered South Africa a developed country and therefore ineligible for
the asymmetrical preferences granted under Lomé status. This essentially
precluded South Africa from full membership in the Lomé Accord but left
the door open for some sort of partial membership.

Rather than Lomé status, the EU offered South Africa GSP status for industrial products in September 1994 and for agricultural products the following fall. South Africa requested Lomé minus status (without access to the "special protocols" and the European Development Fund). In the spring of 1995, the EU Commission requested a mandate from the Council of Ministers to negotiate with South Africa for the establishment of a free trade area.[62] After rejecting Lomé status for South Africa, on March 24, 1997, the EU agreed to a "Lomé Protocol" that would allow South Africa to become a qualified member of the Lomé Convention. This fell well short of the type of agreement South Africa had pursued. Rather than full Lomé participation, South Africa and the EU agreed to the Protocol and a parallel negotiation over an FTA.[63]

As related above, the EU had a tiered system of trade-preference agreements. Membership in Lomé, simply put, was the best deal they could give a developing country concerning the depth and breadth of goods that would get tariff breaks and the amount and kind of development assistance the EU could offer. South Africa had hoped to get the full range of benefits. Instead, the EU played hardball. Certainly the EU was more powerful and had some leverage as the largest market for South Africa's goods. Part of the ANC's constituency, such as labor, did not like the deal. The ANC, nonetheless, seemed to think that it had to close the deal, one that big business largely favored.

During the transition, the EU voiced support for regional integration in Southern Africa and it signaled a preference for the SADC. Although how the EU would relate to the SADC and the principles on which it would condition its support of regional economic integration/cooperation in Southern Africa would be largely defined by a renegotiated Lomé Accord, the end of apartheid re-energized its interests. In early September 1994, the EU and the SADC agreed on wide-ranging political and economic cooperation. The agreement was reached at a meeting of foreign ministers. It was the first such agreement the EU had reached with Africa. In German Foreign Minister Klaus Kinkel's words, "The time is ripe for co-operation between both our regions to move on to a new stage."[64]

However, the EU also sought to nudge the SADC in the direction of a market approach to regional cooperation. The EU's subsequent negotiations with South Africa over its petition for Lomé Convention membership is proof. The EU's goals for a free trade area with South Africa included "to encourage the smooth and gradual integration of South Africa into the world economy."[65] It saw advocating integration of (semi-)developing countries into the world economy and locking them into a tariff liberalization/

free trade area agreement as one way to do this.[66] Joao de Deus Pinheiro, the EU commissioner in charge of the negotiations with South Africa, defended the EU's position opposing South Africa's membership in the Lomé Convention by arguing that it would work against that country in the long run because it would keep it out of step with the world trend toward the liberalization of commerce.[67]

Transitional South Africa and then post-apartheid South Africa tried to leverage its membership in the SADC for better terms in its talks with the EU. And as it became increasingly evident that the EU would not grant South Africa developing-country status, the new South African government more strongly linked its trade relations with the EU to its regional ties. When talks with the EU stalled because South Africa was not getting what it wanted, Pretoria tied to stress that it was looking out for the entire SADC region. But the EU position remained firm.

It is ironic that the main economic benefit for South Africa would be its ability to apply for European Development Bank projects in all ACP countries.[68] This had not been one of South Africa's negotiating priorities. South Africa would not be eligible for nonreciprocal trade benefits nor would it receive development aid outside the Lomé arrangement. The EU special protocols on bananas, rum, beef and veal, sugar, and coal and steel products would not apply to South Africa. Finally, the EU allowed for only ad hoc South African participation in the Lomé Accord's "cumulation of origin" clause, which allows products exported from one country under the Lomé Accord to incorporate components from another Lomé country. Instead of full Lomé participation, South Africa was offered the opportunity to negotiate a free trade agreement with the EU.

The EU's rejection of South Africa's petition for Lomé status coupled with the proposed free trade agreement was inconsistent with its purported support for regional economic integration in Southern Africa. Of the four institutional alternatives mentioned above for formalizing the EU's relations with South Africa (Lomé, Super GSP, bilateral association agreements, and the Generalized System of Preferences), the Lomé Accord had the best mechanisms for promoting regional integration. This is largely because Lomé, unlike the other arrangements between the EU and developing countries, has a "regional cumulation clause, allowing two or more ACP/EU states to undertake different parts of the production of a good so long as in the aggregate it meets Lomé's rules of origin terms."[69]

The ACP members that were expected to have grave doubts about South Africa's participation agreed to its membership in Lomé. South Africa's participation in Lomé did not necessarily reduce SADC members' exports to the EU, and if South Africa were to negotiate membership in the Lomé Convention, all the ACP states would be de jure parties to the negotiations. From the perspective of the welfare of Southern Africa in general, there was no good reason to exclude South Africa from the Lomé Accord. So the EU opposition to South African membership seemed to contradict its support for regional economic integration/cooperation.

The EU's precursor, the EEC, had played midwife to the Southern African Development Coordination Conference, so it had a vested interest in its success. However, while there were divisions within the EU over what type of regional economic scheme to promote in Southern Africa, it moved away from a developmental approach while ostensibly still supporting the SADC. The EU's approach to its trade negotiations with South Africa, possibly unwittingly, appealed to South African big business. The South African parastatal and conglomerate sector had always favored a bilateral approach for South Africa's regional trade and a free trade agreement with Europe, its most important trading partner, unencumbered by regional arrangements. Stef Naude, former director of the Department of Trade and Industry, had implicitly cautioned against linking South Africa's participation in a formal agreement in Southern Africa with its prospects for an agreement with the EU: "The ideal solution would be a bilateral arrangement between South Africa and the EC based on the realities and needs of the particular situation. An insistence by the Community that its arrangement has to be with a Southern Africa region will seriously delay any bilateral agreement."[70]

The position of big business in South Africa concerning the talks with the EU was a neat complement to its position on regional economic integration/cooperation. First, they did not want to do anything that tied them more closely to the region. Second, they preferred a bilateral to any multilateral approach, particularly a multilateral approach that included the other countries of Southern Africa. Finally, the ANC recognized that they could not ignore the interests of big business.

The Trade, Development and Cooperation Agreement signed between the EU and South Africa in Pretoria on October 11, 1999, is closely linked to the Cotonou Agreement, which replaced the Lomé Convention. The Cotonou Agreement was signed on June 23, 2000, after eighteen months of negotiations, and went into force on April 1, 2003. It was essentially a continuation of Lomé IV but even more strongly propagated neoliberal economics and had a twenty-year framework. It explicitly sought to integrate the ACP countries into the liberal world economy. Article 34(4) of the agreement states that trade relations between the EU and the ACP will be in full conformity with the provisions of the World Trade Organization. Unlike its precursors, the successive Lomé agreements, the Cotonou Agreement split the category of developing nations into two categories, non-LDCs and LDCs. The former will have the possibility to maintain a relationship with the EU based on nonreciprocity (they do not have to reduce their tariffs on EU goods in step with the EU's tariff reductions); the latter will have to negotiate nonreciprocal economic partnership agreements. The Cotonou Agreement also had a strong regional dimension.

From the perspective of the ideological impact of the EU on regional integration in Southern Africa, two aspects of the Cotonou Agreement are important; each was foreshadowed in the negotiations between the EU and South Africa. First, the new agreement between the EU and the ACP countries explicitly stated that the Cotonou Agreement would conform with the rules laid down by the World Trade Organization. Specifically, Article 34(4) states that trade relations between the EU and ACP will be in full conformity with the provisions of the World Trade Organization, and Article 34(1) calls for the "smooth and gradual integration of the ACP States into the world economy."[71] The nonreciprocal Lomé preferences, which allowed the ACP states to have higher tariffs on EU products than vice versa, would be phased out over an eight-year period. The preferences granted in the Lomé Accord would be replaced with new free trade partnerships. Under Article 29, the EU's preference is to negotiate regional economic partnership agreements with groups of the ACP countries that have established free trade areas.[72] This, of course, is a direct attempt to influence the nature of regional economic integration/cooperation among developing states. The EU supported the market approach. Article 30 encourages functional regional cooperation in areas such as infrastructure. An SADC free trade area would be the basis of regional economic partnership agreements between the EU and Southern Africa.[73]

External actors actively participated in transitional South Africa's internal debate over how it would cooperate with its neighbors in the post-apartheid era. The three agencies discussed above, the IFIs, GATT, and the EU, had their own divisions and ambiguities, but each pushed for a market approach over a developmental model. This is a reflection of the ascendance of neoliberal orthodoxy, the belief that market forces would produce the best economic results and that the role of the state should be drastically reduced, in the post–Cold War world. In the EU's case, it also reflected internal political dynamics. Transitional South Africa and the new ANC elite were particularly susceptible to these ideological pressures because they were keen to formally reintegrate into the international economy. Although the IFIs, GATT (World Trade Organization), and the EU are independent, their collective ideological preference for a market approach created a powerful undercurrent in South Africa.

Commercial Influences on the Politics of Regional Integration in South and Southern Africa

The commercial impact of external actors on South Africa's political economy and its ramifications for regional economic integration can be depicted as a three-act play.[74] First, the IFIs helped define the trade debate in transitional South Africa. They provided the backdrop. In a very real sense, the international actors controlled much of the staging for South Africa's emerging role in the region, and so did constrict South Africa's options. Nonetheless, it would be wrong to assume that South Africa had no independence from these international actors. As the concluding chapter will discuss, they made choices, albeit laced with compromises that did indeed promote a form of regional economic integration/cooperation consistent with the developmental approach. The IFIs also influenced the trade pattern in Southern Africa at large through the impact of their structural adjustment programs and, to a lesser extent, the Cross-Border Initiative, as a complement to SAPs. Second, even before the new government was formally ensconced in office, it had committed through its GATT agreement to vast trade liberalization. Third, South Africa negotiated a preferential trade arrangement with the EU that originally sought to mitigate the political fallout of its liberalization program.

The Commercial Impact of the IFIs

The fact that South Africa did not have an SAP meant that the IFIs did not have the same level of influence there as in neighboring countries. It also meant that South Africa continued to export to the region from behind relatively high tariff walls. The IFIs were and are influential in transitional and post-apartheid South Africa. The debate in South Africa during transition was not about whether to get in bed with the IFIs but rather about how comfortable to get.[75]

Nonetheless, South Africa could avoid IMF conditionality by not applying to the third and further tranches of its quota or to the Extended Fund Facility.[76] In either of these two separate cases, South Africa would be in danger of falling into the IFI debt trap. The influence of the IMF is strongest in countries that turn to it for financial assistance and where the

IMF stipulates preconditions and prior actions or where there are quantified performance criteria.[77] Although the IMF influences countries that borrow from it, the level of influence can vary depending on the type of agreement and level of debt assumed by the borrower. As related in Chapter 4, the RDP would actually rely more on external assistance, at least in the short term, than would the NEM plan. One of the first international negotiations the Transitional Executive Council tackled was for a $4.8 billion loan under the IMF's Contingency Financing Facility to repay South Africa's debt to international creditor banks.[78] South Africa also applied for an IMF loan to compensate for the loss of export earnings and higher cost of imports during the first half of 1993.[79] These loans, however, provided the IFIs with little leverage before or after April 1994.[80]

The World Bank quietly influenced the development of South Africa's trade policy. For instance, Alan Hirsch credited the 1993 World Bank discussion paper on South Africa by Belli and colleagues with convincing South Africa's IDC that productivity improvements since the early 1970s were due to its switch from traditional ISI policy to an export-oriented policy.[81] During the transition, both the South African government and the private sector argued in favor of making the reduction of import protection according to the standard World Bank/IMF formula the centerpiece of future trade and industrial policy. This standard embedded in the World Bank's *World Development Report* for 1987 was adopted wholesale by the IDC's study on trade.[82] Also, the 1990 IDC study, which was the baseline for subsequent debate on South Africa's trade policy, borrowed heavily from the World Bank. In the report, the IDC referred to pressure from the World Bank on potential borrowers to adopt outward-oriented strategies[83] and argued that tariffs should be homogenized and lowered so that they would match "World Bank standards for strongly outward-oriented policy."[84]

The Cross-Border Initiative (CBI) is the attempt of the IFIs to integrate the processes of regional integration and structural adjustment. In an update on the CBI, the World Bank explained that the CBI was promoting "integration by emergence" rather than "integration by design."[85] The latter has been typical of most of the developing world and is characterized by formal treaties and organizations. The CBI envisions a process where countries reduce barriers to each others' trade and finance "while in parallel also lowering the barriers to trade with third parties."[86] The CBI is also based on the principle of "variable geometry," where individual countries reduce barriers as they can. The idea is that the countries liberalizing fastest will pressure the laagers to liberalize. The CBI is a variant of market regional economic integration/cooperation. It would fit into the model presented in the Maasdorp Report discussed in Chapter 3.

The IFIs actively propagated economic liberalism and free market integration in Southern Africa. They also directly influenced trade relations of individual SADC countries with South Africa through individual SAPs in Lesotho, Malawi, Mozambique, Tanzania, Zambia, and Zimbabwe.[87] But SAPs by South Africa's neighbors would eviscerate the potential of a regional free trade agreement. Precisely because the IFIs have more influence in highly indebted countries that have repeatedly come to them (such as SADC countries attempting to implement SAPs) than in countries that are not debt distressed, such as South Africa, tariff barriers are lowered among regional countries at different rates. Many SADC countries have lowered their tariffs far below their World Trade Organization commitments.[88] One South African trade expert has gone as far as to suggest that these countries need to raise tariffs again within the SADC context to, among other reasons, "ensure that they do not undermine regional strategies and are able to give something in return for concessions received."[89] From South Africa's perspective, this would mean that its partners in the SADC would have to raise their external tariffs vis-à-vis countries outside of the SADC higher than the tariff they would apply to South Africa as a quid pro quo for South Africa's asymmetrical tariff cuts. Finally, the SAPs reduce the potential gains from a regional FTA. As two South African experts argued, "Creating a FTA for SADC, as envisaged in the (SADC) Trade Protocol, appears to be superfluous if special disposition is to be made in favor of states in the region."[90]

The approach of the IFIs to regional cooperation/integration could have an indirect impact on the political dynamics within South Africa over the future of its regional relations. The World Bank's approach relies on the private constituencies that would benefit from economic integration to lobby for regional integration and thus enhance the prospects of success;[91] it emphasizes unilateral action and national decisions.[92] The importance of the domestic sources of regional cooperation and integration is reflected in the "Desk Study on Regional Integration in Eastern and Southern Africa: Constraints to Intra-Regional Payments, Trade and Investment," partially attributable to the World Bank. The "Concept Paper" that accompanied this study stated: "The underlying hope is that the private sector will no longer feel constrained to the national market, rather it will consider widening opportunities of a subregional rather than a national market, and develop an investor culture to exploit such opportunities." Most significant, the study's focus was on "national selection" and "self selection."[93]

That is, although the study promoted regional cooperation and integration, specifically cross-border trade and investment, it argued that the process that would accomplish this would begin at the national level. This is consistent with the neoclassical political logic of reform of the IFIs:[94] trade liberalization creates domestic winners who will then support the liberalization process. This is a form of ad hoc regional integration rather than economic regional integration. Individual countries, South Africa in this case, would be able to avoid mutual dependence (interdependence) with its neighbors.

The implication of this public-choice logic, the idea that the economic winners of a program will both lobby hard for that program while gaining strength from that program and thus be a more effective pressure group, is that if the private sector is the winner, the public sector is the loser. The World Bank was correct to anticipate counterpressures to liberalization from the losses because it would accelerate the necessary but "politically difficult" restructuring of a large number of nonviable enterprises, most of which were in the public sector.[95] In transitional South Africa's context, the dominance of its capital-intensive industries would be strengthened and could be expected to promote their interests and preferences regarding how to further regional cooperation. The CBI would have the Darwinian effect of rewarding the strong—South Africa's capital-intensive industry— while allowing the weak—labor-intensive industry—to die. This obviously also strengthens the capital-intensive industry's domestic position politically.

The Economic Impact of South Africa's GATT Accord

South Africa's GATT offer was put together by the National Economic Forum just before the April 1994 democratic election. Given the very fluid nature of South African politics and institutions at the time, it basically became the government's position, and the talks were dominated by NP bureaucrats.[96] As South African economist Rashad Cassim noted, the government had not had the opportunity to deal with a significant anti-liberalization lobby, partly because liberalization had not progressed far enough for the losers to identify their interest.[97] In fact, South Africa's financial ambassador to Europe just before the ANC took office had anticipated that South African labor would make GATT negotiations difficult.[98] Any reduction in tariffs, as would follow a new agreement with GATT, would open up South Africa's labor-intensive industries to greater competition from abroad.

South Africa's years of quasi-isolation made it aware of the benefits of participating in the international economy. This partially explains the quick commitment to GATT, which was made even as South Africa was negotiating the end of apartheid rule. It committed post-apartheid South Africa to sweeping tariff reductions and to phasing out layers of support schemes, such as the General Export Incentive Scheme (GEIS), once used to promote otherwise uncompetitive exports.

South Africa was under pressure from the Uruguay Round of GATT to make deep cuts in its tariff levels and to rationalize its complex tariff structure.[99] It sought developing-country status under GATT, which divides contracting parties into developed countries, developing countries, and least-developed countries. The latter two are entitled to "special and differential treatment."[100] For South Africa, this would have given some sensitive industries breathing room by extending the life of the GEIS another eight years (under GATT's trade-related investment rule, the GEIS would have to be phased out in two years).[101] South Africa's push for developing-country status under GATT was symptomatic of the politics of trade liberalization.

During GATT's Trade Policy Review of South Africa in 1993, it cautioned South Africa against remaining in "transition" indefinitely. Developing-country status was brought up in South Africa's opening statement at GATT's Trade Policy Review procedure, but the United States responded that South Africa, as a founding member of GATT and one of the top thirty trading nations with a strong manufacturing base, did not fit the developing-nation criteria.[102] South Africa's response was that "the Government was not the sole actor in the transition process."[103] It pointed to domestic pressures on the government, noting that the push for developing-country status was rooted in specific sectoral interests such as labor-intensive industry.

The business community supported a laissez-faire trade regime and lobbied against developing-country status. For instance, Paul Hatty, chairperson of the Industrial Planning Committee of SACOB argued that "[t]he business perspective is that South Africa must remain a committed member of GATT to ensure that we are able to retain world markets and that these markets are available on a most favored nation basis."[104] Commenting on South Africa's request for developing-country status, the ex-director of the Department of Trade and Industry, Steph Naude, noted that "none of the delegations from the other major contracting parties—the EC and Japan—was more positive [about the benefits of development status for South Africa]—not even in private."[105] There was, in fact, a close relationship between the Normative Economic Model, which argued for a free market economy, and the plan South Africa proposed to GATT to reform and reduce its tariffs. The text of South Africa's GATT offer emphasized that the NEM was a trade-based economic strategy for post-apartheid South Africa[106] but that adhering too quickly to GATT standards could cause the post-apartheid economy to be stillborn. Nonetheless, GATT was central to transitional South Africa's economic strategy, and the fact that the newly formed National Economic Forum's first priority was South Africa's GATT offer is proof of the importance of the free trade principle in transitional South Africa.

South Africa was ultimately refused developing-country status. If it had been granted that status, certain sensitive industries in South Africa would have benefited. This was particularly true for its textile industry. Article 6 of the 1994 GATT accords granted developing countries "differential and more favorable treatment" for their textiles industries during a transition period. Developing countries are also granted special provisions on subsidies and on "safeguard action" to protect domestic industry.[107] In November 1993, Trevor Manuel, head of the ANC's economic department, stated that GATT rules were unfair and that the clothing industry would be at the forefront of South Africa's future industrial policy, because it was characterized by the small- and medium-sized enterprises to which the ANC was committed. His argument was that the GEIS was instrumental in the ability of the textile and clothing industries to survive and that GATT demands would have a negative impact on the ANC's ability to carry out its industrial strategy and its ability to placate an important constituency.[108] South Africa's Textile Federation and the National Clothing Federation, who were traditionally at odds, actually formed a common front to lobby for continued GEIS support.[109]

After the GATT review process, South Africa was able to conclude a new agreement determining its tariff schedules just before the final round of GATT and the creation of the World Trade Organization. South Africa's tariff agreement, which was signed in Morocco in the spring of 1994 and would come into effect on July 4, 1995, brought wide-ranging reform in its tariff structure, but not evenly across all sectors. South Africa's access to all its main markets improved and it exhibited a substantial capacity to export to new countries around the world.[110] South Africa agreed to lower its tariffs by an average of 40 percent over five years and to simplify its tariff structure.[111] Ninety-eight percent of South Africa's tariffs lines will be bound (cannot be increased without going to the GATT), versus only

15 percent before the agreement.[112] In other areas, though, tariff reform was minimal. Steel tariffs, although they were already relatively low, were virtually unchanged; they could be between 10 percent and 15 percent compared to the old ceiling of 5 percent. Thus, ISCOR could actually apply to the Board on Tariffs and Trade for a tariff increase. Other industries that got generous concessions from GATT included the motor industry, some chemical and electronics companies, and certain paper products companies. Starting in 1994, clothing and textiles had twelve years to adjust (tariffs on imported clothing will decrease from 100 percent to 45 percent over 12 years), with no reduction in tariffs in the first four years. Although South Africa's GATT accord garnered some praise there, it was also challenged by some as favoring large producers.[113] The IDC predicted that South Africa's GATT agreement would, in fact, cause sectors such as textiles and car-making to suffer a 4 to 5 percent decline in employment, despite the fact that heavily unionized and labor-intensive industries were granted between eight and twelve years to phase in tariff reductions.[114]

GATT influenced South Africa's balance of payments as well as its trade and industrial strategy. As a result of the 1985 debt crisis, exports continued to be a necessary remedy for the current-account problems that South Africa faced during the transition. This made many manufacturers nervous about the potential loss of the GEIS. (As mentioned earlier, schemes that countries use to support exports are typically outlawed by GATT rules. In South Africa, GEIS is one such scheme.) For instance, the NEM stated: "South Africa cannot afford to abolish the GEIS in the short term, until an alternative export-promotion system is put in its place to relieve the pressure on the current account of the balance of payments and exchange rate."[115] Most important, whatever replaces the GEIS will need to be cleared through GATT.[116] With the completion of its GATT agreement, South Africa was also prohibited from using surcharges to ease balance-of-payments pressures.

South Africa's GATT accord handcuffed the new government in subsequent trade talks. The GATT negotiations were not merely between South Africa and GATT. In fact, it is better appreciated as an implicit two-dimensional bargaining process: international, between South Africa and GATT, and domestic, between the South African state and domestic interests. At the international level, "every protection weakening exercise is a potential bargaining chip in relation to multilateral trade institutions and bilateral agreements, so the government must be wary of cashing in

chips for no advantage."[117] At the domestic level, each relationship between South Africa and an external player would have a cascading effect
on domestic politics.

The international system helped shape South Africa's domestic political matrix and how it would, in turn, shape regional economic relations.
First, GATT, the IFIs, and the EU all promoted regional cooperation in
Southern Africa. And while they have been treated separately in this chapter, they could also be seen as a tightly woven cloth that sometimes seemed
to smother South Africa's economic foreign policy. South Africa's negotiations with the EU were embedded in the process of globalization strengthened by the institutional sinews of the IFIs, GATT, and the EU. For example, the Lomé Accord tied access to macroeconomic finance to ACP
countries' implementation of SAPs.[118] The EU used GATT as leverage in
their talks with South Africa by asserting that it would not give developing status to a country to which GATT had already refused such status.
The establishment of the World Trade Organization in 1994 was said by
the director-general of GATT to go hand in hand with increased cooperation with the IMF and World Bank.[119] The Cotonou Agreement defended
changes to the Lomé Accord by arguing that the EU needed to conform to
the rules of the World Trade Organization.[120] This whole cloth, then, represents a powerful ideological pull away from developmental cooperation
and toward market cooperation or ad hoc cooperation.

The commercial impact is less conclusive. The natural ally of the IFIs
is South Africa's conglomerate sector, and through their SAPs and the
CBI they supported a free trade approach. Through the project approach,
the IFIs seemed to support ad hoc cooperation. But they also supported
an underlying philosophy based on neoclassical political logic; trade liberalization creates domestic winners, who will then support the liberalization process. South Africa's status-quo industries maintained, or even enhanced, their economic position after apartheid.

However, South Africa's negotiations with the EU hint at a different
political logic. The SAPs in the region and South Africa's GATT agreement painted South African labor into a corner. The political mandate in
its negotiations with the EU was to look out for the labor-intensive sector. In fact, South Africa had not pushed for participation in the European Development Fund projects for ACP countries. What turned out to
be a very contentious negotiation process had two important political
ramifications that would influence post-apartheid South Africa's regional
economic relations. First, as the EU backed South Africa into a corner, the

new South African government played the regional hand; it tried to argue that it was looking out for the region and thus needed more concessions from the EU. Second, labor and its strong representation in Parliament began a counteroffensive. The following chapter will examine this process in more detail.

8

The Post-Apartheid State and Policy Process

The architecture of the South African state influences its regional relations. Interests alone cannot explain policy formation. State institutions privilege certain interests over others. Also, state actors, such as bureaucrats, have some autonomy and their own interests and pursue their own agendas and, by definition, a South Africa in transition threatened preordained institutional advantages held by the old political elite. In the first instance, for example, agricultural interests in the U.S., although typically located in sparsely populated states, have as many senators (two) as the most densely populated states—thus the stubborn persistence of farm subsidies. In the second case, bureaucrats often have a vested interest in existing policies.

A republican explanation of policy formation in transitional South Africa is of particular interest because the state itself was an arena under, if not quite reconstruction, certainly renovation. In Moravcsik's words:

> While ideational and commercial liberal theory, respectively, stress demands resulting from particular patterns of underlying societal identities and economic interests, republic liberal theory emphasizes the ways in which domestic institutions and practices aggregate those demands, transforming them into state policy.[1]

This could also be framed from a public policy perspective. As Anthoni van Nieuwkerk offers, policy decisions involve a series of points in time and space when and where a decision is made by some official or body to adopt, modify, or reject a preferred policy.[2] The previous chapters dealt with the apposite point in time when preferences were formulated. The republican dimension of the policy process is the focus of the present chapter.

South Africa's negotiated transition to democracy signaled the beginning of the formal struggle over the shape and purpose of the post-apartheid state; the shape of the state itself was open for negotiation.[3] The negotiations were carried out under the auspices of the Convention for a Democratic South Africa (CODESA) I and II. CODESA I first met in December 1991 and included 238 delegates from nineteen parties; the guiding principle was "sufficient consensus of major protagonists."[4] What this meant, in effect, was that the ANC and the NP worked together to shape the negotiated settlement that ended apartheid.

Although this study is not about South Africa's transition to full democracy, the nature of that transition is important. Samuel Huntington has outlined four types of transitions: transformation, replacement, interventions, transplacements.[5] South Africa is typically categorized as a transplacement, where reformers in the ruling regime meet moderates in the opposition regime. The typical product of this type of transition is an economically and socially conservative dispensation.[6] The South African transition is often characterized as "elite pacting."[7] In fact, a Gramscian "war of position" marked apartheid's denouement. The moderate wing of the ANC, along with business and strong international backing, came out on top. But as Robert Horwitz argues, South Africa's transition "was fundamentally the product of a general mass movement, a phenomenon downplayed or even neglected by most transition theory, and a historical fact disregarded by many South African commentators."[8] The Government of National Unity which took power in 1994 under ANC leadership in fact played to two audiences. South Africa has been engaged in a Janus-like political balancing act[9] between its commitments to neoliberal economic reform and the demands of its base constituency. In Padraig Carmody's words," the South African government is attempting a compromise between globalization and social democracy."[10]

South Africa's balancing act has been somewhat successful thus far for two reasons. First, although the failures of Southern Africa's neoliberal economic plan (GEAR) are legend,[11] there has been fundamental change. One of the central promises of the RDP, returning the mineral wealth underneath the ground to the people, began to gather steam in 2002. Second, the ANC made a successful transition from a revolutionary party to a ruling party.

The policy debate in transitional South Africa, therefore, went from the ideological to the technical realm; there was less debate on the under-lying principles of economic management (Keynesian versus monetarist) and more on crafting specific economic policy.[12] In fact, the GEAR strategy was consistently tied to the philosophy of the RDP, and the COSATU/SACP members of the ANC government voted unanimously in favor of it.[13] South African economists Nicoli Nattrass and Jeremy Seekings have shown that although public opinion on the ANC's performance was largely negative midway through its first term (October 1996), support for the ANC itself was still very strong.[14] They cite a poll that states that two-thirds of ANC supporters saw trade and investment as necessary for economic growth, despite the fact that "for the first time in South Africa, the governing party does not represent any of the existing capitalist classes."[15]

An important part of the technical struggle for dominance was over the nature of the post-apartheid state. Both sides were quite aware that the new state would influence their ability to carry out their respective agendas. As Anthony Payne states in his review of regionalism, "First, each position now accepts that political competition does not take place on an even terrain and that there is such a thing as structured privilege, which can be enjoyed by a particular group or individual."[16] In the case of transitional South Africa, the state was not only the playing field, but the design of that field was part of the political process.

A republican explanation of policy thus has two related tasks. First, how does the "state" privilege certain interests? This entails looking at the institutional infrastructure within South Africa. Second, what are the preferences of state actors who are positioned to influence policy? That is, within those institutions how might personal preferences come into play? While the transition period, and in particular the 1994 electoral campaign, determined the new hierarchy, the way that the state would take account of societal interests and demands was evolving. The nature of the game changed once the ANC gained power. Its members were not incumbents. The "purposefully vague anti-capitalist rhetoric" of the ANC leadership gave it "considerable ideological leeway successfully to stitch together a loosely defined coalition of interest groups that included workers and aspirant entrepreneurs, Christians and Communists, and the unemployed and middle class, around a shared objective of dismantling *apartheid*."[17]

But the prominence of the ideological component of the ANC's message faded during the transition period, and it went from engaging primarily in a "discourse of radical need" to a "discourse of means," that is, from a focus on how to overthrow the state to one of how to govern the state.[18] This also meant that the economic discourse moved from the ideological plane to the technical plane of crafting economic policy.[19] Ideology had to be translated into policy, but that also meant that the practical took precedence over the ideal.

The level of economic expertise within the ANC was limited, making it susceptible to external (and internal) advice or ideas.[20] The ANC's interlocutors were no longer just radicals and revolutionaries from the Eastern Bloc but representatives of international capital. Also, "The party leadership, after three decades in exile and therefore living in physical and ideological proximity to Eastern Europe, cannot have failed to see the looming disillusionment from below that has fueled the social revolutions there."[21] The new ANC government came to power after the collapse of the Soviet Union. The failure of the socialist experiment and the disillusionment of the people who live under communist rule registered with the new government. On top of the Cold War victory for the West, globalization and its neoliberal principle seemingly swept all competitors into the dustbin of history. Post-apartheid's embrace of globalization (as discussed in the previous chapter) translated into support for big business beyond what one might have anticipated. Although not quite left behind, grassroots members of the anti-apartheid struggle, particularly labor, were disappointed.

Thus, while the struggle for influence over policy in the new South Africa continued after the 1994 election, a new dimension to that struggle emerged. As the new South Africa navigated its formal reintegration into the world economic system, powerful international pressures influenced, if not determined, the shape of the post-apartheid state. The new South African state emerged from a dialectical struggle between pressures from powerful international entities to globalize and the domestic political imperatives for a (re)distributive state. The former inhibited the ability of the ANC to make good on the institutional changes it had promised during the transition. The latter pitted populist demands against South Africa's emerging neoliberal economic orthodoxy. Post-apartheid South Africa had to placate foreign investors while trying not to ignore the demands of its own constituency.[22]

The Globalization of the State:
Neoliberal Orthodoxy in Post-Apartheid South Africa

After the April 1994 election, the new ANC government pursued a policy that embraced globalization.[23] Globalization can skew state development. Leo Panitch captures the relationship between state development and globalization when he argues that globalization not only affects interests within states but has impact on the architecture of the state. Power is likely to become more centralized.[24] As Sylvia Maxfield argues, economic policy is most likely to reflect bankers' preferences under three conditions: 1. an independent central bank; 2. if the finance ministry is allied with the central bank; and 3. if the state has little ability to control the flow of investment funds.[25] In post-apartheid South Africa, indeed, globalization led to a concentration of power in the Department of Finance and the South African Reserve Bank.

But given the entrenched institutional power of the interests that had benefited from forty years of apartheid, particularly South Africa's large conglomerates, the ANC was expected to pursue institutional change. In situations where tension exists between economic imperatives for growth and distributive demands, such as in transitional South Africa, "governments may have incentives to change the institutional structure of their polities so as to mitigate the tension between distributional politics and economic performance."[26] Early in the transition, in fact, the ANC did call for wide-ranging institutional renovations, particularly in the areas of finance and investment. But it did not carry them through. This is partially because a rise in the relative scarcity of foreign exchange can change the relative balance of power within governments:[27] the availability of foreign credit strengthens "spending ministries," and reduced access to foreign credit strengthens orthodox forces, supporters of neoliberal economics.[28]

The new government apparently did make a turn to the political right. The fact that the only two holdovers from the old regime were the governor of the South African Reserve Bank, Chris Stals, and the finance minister, Derek Keys, indicates that South Africa was sending signals to the international financial community that there would be no radical change in its economic policy. Specifically, the demand-driven model of Keynesianism would not be adopted.[29] When Derek Keys resigned early in the ANC's first administration, ex-banker Chris Liebenberg replaced him. Liebenberg was considered to be close to Reserve Bank governor Chris Stals, leading one Johannesburg banker to say, "The two of them would be singing out of the same hymn book."[30] In fact, the ANC's monetary and macroeconomic policy after the April 1994 elections was seen as both moderate and business friendly. Characterizations of the ANC leadership during its first year in power emphasized a neoliberal turn and apparently offered proof of the state-bending pressures of globalization.

Jay Naidoo, the ex-head of the Congress of South African Trade Unions (COSATU) and the new Government's minister in charge of implementing the RDP, was once described as looking like Satan, sounding like

Marx, and acting like Mephistopheles. As Minister he was described as
a figure of flawless economic orthodoxy. Alec Erwin, the new Government's deputy minister of finance, an ex-unionist, was labeled a convert
to economic orthodoxy.[31]

Economic orthodoxy in the context of the post–Cold War world meant the
market-driven model of the West. The pressures of globalization, which
were as much ideational as material, seemingly created a group of converts
at the apex of South Africa's government, particularly in positions that
dealt with economic policy. The culmination of the government's conver-
sion to neoliberal economic orthodoxy was signaled by the apparent demise of the Reconstruction and Development Programme on March 28,
1996, and its replacement with the new GEAR economic blueprint in
June 1996. The RDP was not dismantled, but the RDP portfolio was
closed, and the RDP fund was reallocated to the Department of Finance
and the office of Deputy President Thabo Mbeki.[32] Mandela's spring 1996
Cabinet shuffle, which scrapped Jay Naidoo's Reconstruction and Development portfolio and raised Mbeki to the position of South Africa's "growth
czar," symbolized the ANC's shift in policy emphasis from development
to growth. Mbeki was reported to have been deeply skeptical about the
RDP at the outset; "he knew the government's delivery promises would
lead it up a dead-end."[33] Further evidence of the ANC's shift came when
it replaced Minister of Posts, Telecommunications and Broadcasting Pallo
Jordan with Jay Naidoo. Jordan was possibly the most powerful proponent
of the ANC's Keynesian wing and reportedly clashed often with Mbeki.

But while South Africa committed to a neo-orthodox economic program, this did not mean that its leadership changed their ideological
stripes. It meant that it accepted the causal argument of the Washington
Consensus and thought it must do so in order to attract foreign investment. Recall that the ANC's economic model was always predicated on a
greater flow of foreign funds than the Normative Economic Model would
have likely required. In fact, the troika of ANC economic leadership,
Trevor Manuel, Alec Erwin, and Jay Naidoo, were labor leaders. Trevor
Manuel was the ANC's "economic policy czar" during the transition and
rose to become the finance minister in the first ANC government. The
title of a *Newsweek* interview with him in 1994 was "No Adam Smith Fans
Here."[34] Jay Naidoo, the former head of COSATU, stated in 1992 that "we
need to block government policies that are going to entrench things and
make it impossible for a democratic government to meet the needs of the
people and address the inequalities of apartheid."[35] Alec Erwin, who represented COSATU on the National Economic Forum (NEF) and became

deputy finance minister in the new government and its leading trade official, stated during the transition, "We do not accept a simple macroeconomic formula, such as the IMF's labour elasticity model, in assessing job growth in SA."[36] The pressures of globalization seemingly created
a group of converts at the apex of South Africa's government, particularly in positions that dealt with economic policy. Finally, Tito Mboweni
(the former labor minister) and a critic of GEAR, replaced Chris Stals
as governor of the Reserve Bank at the end of the ANC's first election
term.

Nonetheless, globalization, manifested in both its ideational and material power, strongly influenced the new South Africa. It may have height-
ened the importance of the South African Reserve Bank and the Department of Finance. But the ideology of these state institutions should not be
assumed to be neoliberal economic orthodoxy, nor should we assume that
they supported market cooperation/integration. The South African Reserve Bank adopted an unofficial rule of treating investment in Africa more
leniently in terms of exchange control and other restrictions.[37] And the
Reserve Bank created an investment window for South African capital des-
tined for the region.[38] The South African leadership may have embraced
neoliberal economic policy prescriptions, but this does not necessarily
mean that they either changed their "consensual beliefs" or abandoned
their core constituency.

Whether the ANC's shift to the right was purely political or based on
economic pragmatism is difficult to say. What matters is that the political
posturing that began early in the transition period continued into the
post-apartheid era. And South Africa's regional economic policy can be
understood as a reflection of competing interests with the conglomerates
maintaining their position after apartheid and small business and labor
fighting for a voice. The institutionalization of the post-apartheid state
was part of the struggle.

Politics and Institutions in the Post-Apartheid State

The battle over the shape and purpose of the post-apartheid state engaged
three arms of the post-apartheid government's policy-making apparatus—
the National Economic Development and Labour Council (NEDLAC),
Parliament, and the relevant government bureaucracies, in particular the
Department of Trade and Industry, the Department of Foreign Affairs,
and the Department of Finance. Two processes shaped the "new" South
African state. First, the basic character of the "new" South African state

evolved out of a struggle between its corporatist and pluralist impulses, represented, respectively, by NEDLAC and Parliament. The outcome would affect the ability of different groups to influence ANC foreign economic policy. Second, the old-guard government bureaucracy was slowly replaced with ANC stalwarts and supporters. This group had a very different approach to regional economic cooperation/integration than the cadre that had cohered around the Maasdorp Report in 1994. Figure 8.1 depicts foreign economic policymaking in post-apartheid South Africa in the first ANC administration.[39]

The Corporatist State versus the Pluralist State

Following Anna Seleny's lead, what is important here is "analyzing political relations *within* corporatist institutions, on the one hand, and *between* them and parliament and parties, on the other."[40] The pluralist post-apartheid South African state was more open to domestic influences than had been the apartheid government. Greg Mills states that the Department of Foreign Affairs was increasingly willing to interact with civil society.[41] Anthoni van Nieuwkerk states that "the transition saw procedural shifts towards policymaking that was more open and inclusive."[42] The South African Chamber of Industries (representing 690 corporate members) hired its first political analyst during the transition. This analyst, an Afrikaner, averred that contrary to the past, "lobbying" would be more important in the future South Africa because the past regime was relatively closed.[43] Gavin Maasdorp commented in 1993 that there would be "increased pressure under a new government in order to protect domestic employment."[44]

A pluralistic polity implies the presence of groups that will want to influence government decisions affecting their interests. But a corporatist structure can be used to centralize state power. It is also assumed to be a natural concomitant of globalization. As Timothy Shaw cautions, globalization may lead toward corporatism where only a few established groups' interests will be incorporated.[45]

With the COSATU-led initiative to create a National Economic Forum, transitional South Africa witnessed the development of corporatist structures.[46] One report described the creation of NEF thus: "South Africans may be trying to re-invent the wheel with their search for a corporatist solution to economic policymaking."[47] Corporatism is expected to strengthen the hand of the state; an archetypical example is South Korea under Syngman Rhee.[48] The NEF, which was formally launched on Octo-

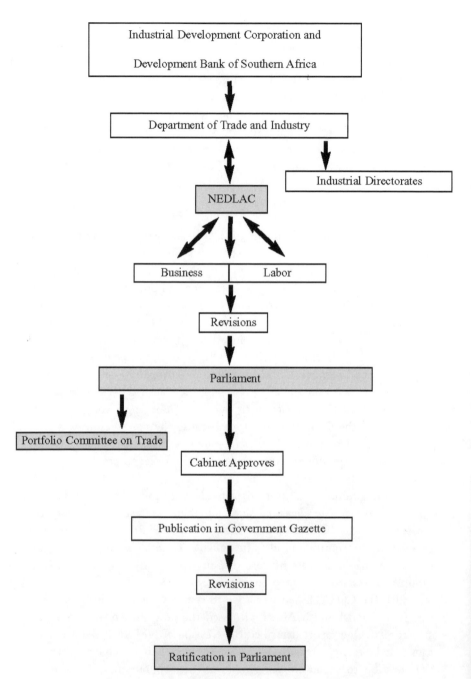

Figure 8.1.

ber 29, 1992, was a tripartite body that evolved out of an arrangement that allowed the government to interact with trade unions in the clothing, textile, and mining industries.[49] It was a forum consisting of representatives from government, business, and organized labor. The NEF's statement of intent called for a "consensus-geared co-operative body to deal with economic and related socio-economic issues and the economic challenges facing the country." However, although it was corporatist in form, the NEF signaled the growing inclusiveness of the South African state:

> Government broke with a long tradition of secrecy in the formulation of the national Budget, when, in December 1992, it briefed the NEF on the fiscal constraints and options identified by treasury officials. This was done some months before the Budget was finalized and made public. Labour and business used the opportunity to set out their respective views on the criteria to be applied when evaluating the Budget.[50]

Corporatism in South Africa, in fact, was the paradoxical product of pluralism. The NEF operated parallel to the multiparty negotiations on constitutional reform and debated all aspects of economic policy. Its first priority was South Africa's trade policy, specifically regarding its new negotiations with GATT, as well as debate on the Normative Economic Model (NEM). The most significant accomplishment of the NEF was its successful offer to the Uruguay Round of GATT, an agreement that did not sit well with labor.

On February 18, 1995, the NEF was changed to the National Economic Development and Labour Council (NEDLAC).[51] Mandela stated:

> This crucial body [NEDLAC] will bring together representatives of government, labour, capital, and civil society. . . . We trust that the representatives that sit on NEDLAC will, in turn, reach out to their own constituencies to inform and involve them in the decisions, which bear, among other things, on the disbursement of public funds.[52]

NEDLAC had the statutory power to devise a national policy to promote exports and new labor-market laws, while its raison d'être was to short-circuit lobbying of the government by vested interests.[53] But NEDLAC did not evolve into a corporatist body that would make globalization easier; instead its forums worked to construct a "democratic and socially transformative version of corporatism."[54]

While it was created at the initiative of COSATU,[55] the NEF and its prodigy, NEDLAC, did not always promote labor interests. COSATU participated in the NEF/NEDLAC, but it increasingly resented and resisted the privileged place of business in those bodies. As South African journalist Marais points out, South African labor had actually become more "reticent towards tripartism [corporatism],"[56] largely because it was used to depoliticize the globalization process. Labor nonetheless used its participation in NEDLAC to gain some institutional weight to counter the power of globalization. NEDLAC's first brief was to create a new labor law, and in 1996 South Africa passed the Labour Relations Act.

> In February 1991, the LRA was finally amended. The new act was hailed as the first piece of post-apartheid legislation and consolidated a democratic industrial relations system accepted by labor, employers, and the state. The timing of these reforms was crucial for the entire transition process: the labor movement entered the transition phase not as a wounded giant hobbled by an authoritarian regime but as a movement with unprecedented freedom.[57]

It was described as "the first major test of the relations of the 'social partners'—labour and business—to the ANC in government, and therefore too a test of tripartism and NEDLAC in a democratic South Africa."[58] COSATU commented: "Two years after [the] implementation [of the Labour Relations Act], COSATU remains convinced that [it] remains a legislative milestone in our new democracy."[59]

Possibly because it was a labor initiative, NEDLAC could hardly be seen as an instrument to increase the speed of the globalization process.[60] It is particularly sensitive to labor interests,[61] even though the business lobby through the early years of post-apartheid rule was far better organized. One NEDLAC representative who dealt directly with the EU and SADC talks related that the government did not want to listen to "tainted lobbies" such as the Chamber of Mines.[62]

NEDLAC continued to play an important role in post-apartheid South Africa. South African business, particularly as represented by SACOB, had early successes within the NEF, as represented by the GATT agreement. However, labor learned its lesson and NEDLAC became better attuned to the interests of labor, as evidenced in the Labour Relations Act.

While the new South African Parliament got off to a slow start, by 1998 it was no longer a rubber stamp for the government.[63] South African political scientist Tom Lodge depicts the parliament as possibly the most important South African institution for creating and maintaining an open political culture.[64]

The new South African Parliament began to flex its muscles during

South Africa's trade talks with the EU, with a specific concern for how an EU agreement would affect the region, and the Reconstruction and Development Programme. The South African Parliament called for any agreement with the EU to "contribute positively to placing the South African economy on a new-development growth path."[65] Or, more bluntly, as MP Rob Davies stated:

> Among the principles underlying the trade and development agreement are that any trade arrangement should be supportive of the RDP [Reconstruction and Development Programme] process, should be mutually beneficial and balanced, should remove discrimination against South African goods in the EU market, should encourage investment in Southern Africa, should build regional integration and should be asymmetrical in both content and timing.[66]

A trade agreement with the EU would have to be both vetted and ratified by the South African Parliament, which was a central part of trade policymaking in South Africa. Parliament used its power. Davies's Portfolio Committee on Trade held hearings on South Africa's EU negotiations and held up the talks because of its concern over the proposed "rules of origin" section.[67] The EU proposed an ad hoc rule of origin, which the Committee argued would inhibit closer regional ties. In the summer of 1996, three committees that covered portfolios that were most directly impacted by the EU talks (agriculture, trade and industry, and foreign affairs) prepared a joint submission on the South African government's negotiation mandate. Davies explained, "Our involvement stemmed from a sense that the responsibility given to us, as public representatives, required rather more of us than passively waiting for an agreement to be presented for ratification."[68] Max Sisulu, chief whip of the majority party in Parliament, organized a Southern Africa regional conference of parliamentarians in 1998 to discuss the two sets of talks: South Africa's trade talks with the EU and upcoming talks within the SADC over trade. He invited Trevor Manuel and Alec Erwin, the government's two top trade officials, to the conference.[69] The South African Parliament obviously had begun to play a central institutional role in trade policy. How did this affect the politics of special interests?

The South African Parliament is more closely aligned with labor than with business. First, approximately fifty COSATU officials became members of Parliament after the first election.[70] Second, the chair of the Trade and Industrial Policy Group, Professor Ben Turok, as well as Rob Davies, both central players in Parliament on trade matters, have long been associated with the left of the ANC and are considered to be close to labor. A statement by an allied MP, Mr. C. Dlamini, a former COSATU member, catches the labor position:

> I hope the DP [Democratic Party] and NP will begin to realise that organised labour, particularly COSATU, has always fought to defend and liberate our country from being politically emasculated and economically paralysed by forces which are not very sympathetic to our cause. . . . It is because of this understanding that we should say as South Africans that the offer of the free-trade agreement as spelled out by the European Union cannot go unchallenged, as it is unacceptable.[71]

The South African Parliament was most representative of the more populist demands in South Africa, and the leadership, particularly in trade issues, tended to support labor interests over business.

So how does the post-apartheid state privilege certain interests? The corporatist impulse, possibly a product of globalization, could be expected to mitigate pressures on the state from particular interests. In South Africa's case, however, it was more an arena for competition between labor and business. Parliament's growing role in policymaking promotes the interests of the ANC's core constituency—labor. In any case, bureaucrats in key positions brought their own preferences to office. New players within the state played a key role in shaping the architecture of post-apartheid South Africa's regional relations.

The Changing of the Guard

The changing of the guard had two dimensions; first, the "sunset clause" which was meant to protect the jobs of the old civil service, actually resulted in early retirement. And labor's interest was well represented, as the *SA Labour Bulletin* reported in 1996: "[T]he presence of labour organizers in key posts, stoking what was regarded as the engine of the new government, was cause for considerable gratification."[72] For example, the successful negotiations around the Labour Relations Act were partially attributed to the number of Labor Minister Tito Mboweni's advisors that came from labor's ranks.[73] The institutional dynamics in post-apartheid South Africa were different than in apartheid South Africa. The Development Bank of Southern Africa (DBSA) played a more central role in advising the government on regional economic integration than did the IDC, and the DTI played a more central role than did the Department of Foreign Affairs.[74]

In both cases, the new powers favored a more developmental approach over market regional economic integration/cooperation.

Although part of South Africa's transitional bargain between the Afrikaner ruling party and the African National Congress was the so-called "sunset clause," which guaranteed the positions of the old Afrikaner bureaucracy, those bureaucrats held little sway over policy in the years after the April 1994 election. As Peter Hall notes, a bureaucracy's influence increases during normal periods;[75] the transition was no such time. More important, in South Africa the old bureaucracy, while formally employed, was replaced with ANC stalwarts.[76] While the "sunset clause" meant that many of the old guard (NP bureaucrats) still haunted the halls of government, ANC loyalists were making the important decisions. In the Department of Foreign Affairs, for instance, prior to April 30, 1996, 259 retirement packages were approved, and from July 1996 to January 1997, an additional 112 applications for severance packages were received.[77]

The central institutional player in the formulation of post-apartheid South Africa's regional trade policy was the Department of Trade and Industry,[78] which was the focal point of support for market cooperation/integration in 1993/1994. It now simply had new faces and new ideas. I conducted interviews with South African officials in 1994 and 1998; in 1998, none of the officials I had interviewed in 1993/1994 still played a central role in South Africa's regional economic foreign policy. For instance, the head of the Africa Division of DTI in 1998 was Mfundo C. Nkuhlu. In 1993 he had presented a paper at a workshop that rejected the market cooperation promoted by his predecessor in favor of a developmental approach.[79] He was also one of the co-authors of a key MERG study. By 1998, Alan Hirsch, a lead architect of the Industrial Strategy Project's trade policy, was chief director of the Industrial and Technology Strategy, and Faizel Ismail of the ANC was chief director of foreign trade relations in the Department of Trade and Industry.[80]

The DBSA played an increasingly central role in post-apartheid South Africa's regional economic relations. This was foreshadowed in the transition period, as Mfundo C. Nkuhlu noted in 1993.[81] In fact, the DBSA had two members on the Transitional Executive Council, which dealt with South Africa's future regional relations. In 1993, the DBSA organized a meeting in Gaborone to discuss the future of SACU. Max Sisulu remembers the meeting as a forum for "listening to the region."[82] The connection between the DBSA and the government is not always indirect. Nkuhlu's top official at DTI, Marina Mayer, who plays a central role in formulating

South Africa's foreign economic policy with the EU and SADC region, had formerly worked at the DBSA.

The post-apartheid state had new institutional dynamics and new personnel. Both NEDLAC and Parliament influenced trade policy, and both were open to domestic pressure. The IDC and DBSA played key advisory roles, the latter carving out a key role in the debate over regional foreign policy. Within the government, the Department of Trade and Industry eclipsed the Department of Foreign Affairs, and it took a relatively pro-development approach.

During the push to end apartheid, there was some coincidence of interest between business and labor because each suffered in its own way from apartheid. But once this political objective was obtained, conflicting economic interests would end this awkward arrangement.[83] For instance, late in the transition, the head of NAFCOC, the Black business association, related that the alliance between Black business and Black labor would likely end after the election.[84] Labor and big businesses had clear preferences on the direction of South Africa's economy and regional relations grounded in both their respective ideologies and in their material interests. The institutions of the post-apartheid state and the ANC bureaucrats that staffed the apposite institutions dealing with South Africa's regional relations facilitated the pursuit of a new regional order in Southern Africa. Unlike the robust big-business roots of South Africa's political economy, the state itself was easier to rid of the apartheid hold. Because the politics of how to redesign regional relations in South Africa were filtered through a new state, this is where the ANC had the most autonomy. The following chapter looks at what these dynamics created.

9

Conclusion:
Post-Apartheid South Africa's
Regional Relations

Peter Evans has said that "presenting complicated pictures of institutional configurations that are very much rooted in particular historical settings should be applicable to other cases."[1] In order to validate even an exercise in mid-range theorizing, as proffered here, explanations must be valid across cases. The argument here, thus far, is that integration and cooperation theory have been closed models. The decision to cooperate or not is explained by exogenous factors, while preferences for how to cooperate, rather than deciding to cooperate or not, are ignored. The question of why or, more important, how to cooperate demands that the model be opened up. First, it means understanding the domestic configuration of forces across three dimensions: ideological, material, and republican. As Söderbaum asks, "What [are] the driving forces of the regionalization process?"[2] Or, more simply, it means understanding the dictates of a country's political economy. It also means understanding how external forces interact with these domestic interests. I have offered a liberalist theoretical approach as a way to open up the model while acknowledging the powerful pull of external influences, particularly on developing or emerging economies.

The history of South Africa's regional relations validates this approach.

South Africa's regional relations between the founding of the apartheid state and F. W. de Klerk's presidency can only be understood within the context of its domestic dynamics and a desire for international legitimacy. Certain themes, as well, connect the old South Africa to the new. For instance, even as the apartheid regime tried to protect itself from the "winds of change" and emphasized its European identity, it was often preoccupied with regional relations. This was most evident in its patterned demand for absorbing the High Commission Territories or the dream of incorporating Rhodesia (Zimbabwe).

In the waning years of apartheid, leading up to the April 1994 election, South Africa openly debated the future of regional cooperation in Southern Africa. Three types of cooperation were considered in this debate: developmental integration/cooperation, market integration/cooperation, and ad hoc cooperation. By 1990, each type of cooperation had established an institutional presence anchored in, respectively, the SADC, SACU, and existing bilateral trade agreements and cross-border projects. The Transitional Executive Committee's subcommittee on regional relations reflected the diversity of opinion in South Africa. Two of its members were also members of the Development Bank of Southern Africa, two were members of the ANC, one was a high-level government official, and one was a prominent academic economist.

The different approaches to regional economic cooperation in transitional South Africa were grounded in differentiated interdependence. South Africa's labor-intensive industry has strong competition from South Africa's neighbors; capital-intensive industry does not. Simply put, the region means different things to different people. If interdependence is acknowledged as the catalyst for cooperation and if there is more than one way to cooperate, then identifying the differentiated character of interdependence and its political inferences will help explain preferences for models of regional cooperation. Economic interdependence with other states is grounded in domestic political and economic imperatives, which are in turn shaped by a combination of ideological and material factors. This book builds a framework for understanding how South Africa shaped its regional economic foreign policy, specifically the form that regional economic integration/cooperation would take, by looking at how domestic political competitions among groups that would like to influence policy are shaped by ideology, commercial interests, and the institutions of the post-apartheid South African state.

Developmental cooperation—cooperation that would facilitate economic development of all of South Africa's economy—was the stated preference of the ANC during the transition. It was supported by labor, the ANC's most important electoral ally, and by small Afrikaner businesses, as represented by Die Afrikaans Handelsinstituut. A market or ad hoc approach to regional economic cooperation would not have served their regional interests; it would have reinforced the dominance of South Africa's status-quo industries. Although the ANC would later change its position, during the transition it preferred a Keynesian, if not quite a socialist, economic philosophy. This ideological stance also informed its position in the relevant policy debates. Within the ANC alliance, the philosophy of economic growth that favored the strong state was spearheaded by labor and, in particular, COSATU. The arguments of the Reconstruction and Development Programme introduced the ANC's policy preferences and their constituent support into the policy debate in South Africa. In juxtaposition with the old NP regime and its own constituent support, the RDP revealed an economic blueprint for regional economic integration/cooperation. The developmental approach, with its implied state-managed process, was consistent with the ANC's ideological bent during the transition, supporting a strong state role for promoting economic development.

Market cooperation, often also labeled the laissez-faire approach, would have benefited the bureaucrats that dominated the Southern African Customs Union. To the extent that South African businesses had profited from South Africa's dominance of SACU, they also benefited from a free market approach, although it was their second-best choice. Market cooperation had powerful ideological support from external actors. The EU, while voicing ideological support for developmental cooperation, had material interests—gains to be made from trade with South Africa—in a growing free market, and the Cotonou Agreement pushed this even farther than had the Lomé Accord. The IFIs and GATT strongly promoted regional integration through the expansion of free trade. They found ready partners, to some extent, with big business and the old regime, because they shared support for neoliberal orthodoxy.

Ad hoc cooperation was the residue of the hoary notion of the hub-and-spoke approach to regional cooperation and had strong ideological and material support from the old regime and from big business and the parastatals. Post-apartheid South African firms were benefiting from the dependence of neighboring countries on South Africa's regional telecommunications, electricity grid, and railroads.[3] These big-business interests rejected, to various degrees, both the prominence of Southern Africa in the ANC's foreign policy and the premise of regional interdependence. Their dominance of the economy and their political power in South Africa have been well documented in this book. It started with the growth of a powerful parastatal sector and large capital-intensive industries with the banking/financial sector backing them. The apartheid government supported them through both its manufacturing and trade policy and though it macroeconomic and finance policy. They had, simply put, post-position as South Africa entered its transition. Their tangible dominance was augmented by a creeping ideological coup that brought neoliberal economics to the ANC.[4] Any institutional framework, particularly one smelling of developmental cooperation, would only tie their hands. As Andrew Hurrell states, "[I]f the hegemon is in an extremely dominant position the very extent of that power may make institutions and, in this case, institutionalized regionalism unnecessary or at least marginal."[5] This explains the business position in South Africa. The IFIs, particularly the World Bank, promoted bilateral projects and, at least indirectly through their advocacy of South Africa's leading regional role, the hub-and-spoke approach.

The Janus-faced nature of South Africa's politics has led to a natural tension within its foreign policy that seemed to embrace neoliberalism and free trade while arguing for greater equity in international relations.[6] Philip Nel has coined the phrase "ambiguous globalism" to describe post-apartheid South Africa's uncertain position, and its foreign policy is a direct extension of this position.[7] The government must balance competing interests within South Africa while walking a tightrope between international and domestic politics. As democratic post-apartheid South Africa enters its consolidation stage, its foreign policy, particularly regional relations, is best understood as a compromise between key political constituencies. This explains, in part, the debate within South Africa between those who see South Africa as the benevolent hegemon versus those who see it as an ambitious middle power.[8] It is pursuing a strategy for regional economic integration/cooperation that has elements of both ad hoc cooperation and developmental integration/cooperation as a way to placate two important constituencies—labor and big business.

Shaping the Future: South Africa's Regional Relations in the Post-Apartheid Era

The starting point for understanding regional cooperation/integration is with the constituent parts of the system—states. And South Africa is the regional leader in Southern Africa. Its manufactured valued-added is five times the size of the rest of the SADC countries combined; its massive trade surplus in the region (the ratio of exports to imports) was over seven to one in 1995; and between 1994 and 1995 (immediately after the 1994 election), South Africa's exports to the region increased by 59 percent, from 7.5 percent to 10.6 percent of total international trade. Finally, 70 percent of South African exports to the region were manufactured goods.[9] South Africa also continues to dominate the infrastructure of Southern African trade: Zambia, Zimbabwe, Botswana, Democratic Republic of Congo, Malawi, and Mozambique routed 80 percent of their trade through South African ports and railroads.[10] None of this should be surprising. Free from the taint of apartheid and the constraints of economic sanctions, South Africa was bound to expand its two-tailed comparative advantage: primary products outside of Africa and manufactured goods to Africa. In fact, this was the unspoken assumption of the ad hoc approach and, to a lesser extent, the market approach.

There was, however, still no clear consensus in post-apartheid South Africa over how to institutionalize regional economic relations. As Colin Legum states, "Pretoria has clearly been having difficulty in deciding its own role as the engine of the region."[11] South Africa took two directions, which, depending on the political drivers of regionalism in South Africa, could either be divergent or convergent paths. On one hand, it has used the SADC as the institutional anchor for regional relations. And some argue that the ANC clearly adopted a developmental approach as the basic architectural principle.[12] In David Simon's words, "[I]n southern Africa, SADC is the foremost development-oriented regional institution."[13] On the other hand, it has promoted functional or project cooperation in the region, sometimes very much outside the ambit of the SADC's institutional influence. And some would argue that this is CONSAS redux. There is disagreement, therefore, about exactly what path South Africa is taking (as well as about what path it should take). Part of the problem is understanding how the three strains—developmental cooperation, market cooperation, and functional cooperation—fit together. They fit, I would argue, as pieces of a political puzzle rather than as parts of a coherent and cohesive regional strategy. Developmental and functional cooperation are the most prominent, largely because the ideological and material interest behind them is strongest in post-apartheid South Africa.

As would be expected, cooperation has not been institutionalized neatly along the lines of any one of the three models offered in this book, developmental, market, or ad hoc. Nonetheless, and most certainly, the process of cooperation was a clear change from apartheid South Africa's regional relations. The new emphasis was on cooperation, not destabilization. Some promoted interdependence rather than one-sided dependence, and regional ties and regional development assumed a central place in South Africa's foreign economic policy.

SACU and market cooperation, while not irrelevant, has had little institutional impact. However, as an integral part of South Africa's regional relations, it cannot be ignored. In the fall of 2002, a new SACU agreement was reached that simplified tariffs, opened decision making, and revealed a new revenue-sharing formula.[14] But the long, drawn-out negotiations on reforming SACU reflect its diminishing prospects as the institutional anchor for regional relations. Discussions concerning the SADC, for instance, seemed more important. A Customs Union Task Team, which included participants from each SACU country, renegotiated SACU.

The most contentious issue was the revenue-sharing formula, which during the apartheid era had more of a political that an economic rationale. Under the new arrangement a pool of revenue will not be administered by one country, as it was in the past. The new customs revenue formula will determine each country's share based on its contribution to intra-SACU imports. Excise revenue will be calculated based on each country's gross domestic product. It is weighted to help the less-developed members of SACU. For instance, although South Africa contributes close to 80 percent of the customs pool, it will get only 50 percent back. The new revenue arrangement also calls for the establishment of a development fund that depends on the level of development of each SACU member state. During apartheid, South Africa, in particular the Department of Foreign Affairs, was willing to use the revenue-sharing formula (which was a transfer of funds from South Africa to its SACU partners) as political capital. This issue has been exacerbated by South Africa's trade agreement with the EU because that agreement reduces the total revenue pool since the reduction in tariffs subsequent to the agreement reduces the pool of money that can be shared. Finally, the debate over SACU and a "variable geometry" approach to freer regional trade has been overtaken by the SADC's free trade agreement protocol, while SACU's effect on greater industrialization in the BLSN countries remains contentious. The variable geometry approach was a prominent part of the plan outlined by Gavin Maasdorp. It would have brought different countries into an association with SACU and South Africa at different levels, for example free trade agreement, custom union, common market, economic union. The renegotiated SACU agreement has not deepened or widened SACU and the compensation for polarization that SACU's transfer payments are meant for does nothing to specifically counter polarization.[15] It is too little too late.

The SADC

The Southern African Development Community is the institutional anchor of South Africa's regional relations, but it has been redefined. South Africa joined the SADC in 1994 and was put in charge of the newly created financial sector. But the SADC, in anticipation of South African membership, had gone through some interesting contortions.

The difficulties in the marriage of the SADC and South Africa are largely due to what is called the "hegemon's dilemma." South Africa's neighbors both acknowledge the positive potential of South Africa's membership and fear its dominance. The early response of South Africa's neighboring countries, in fact, was to try to lock it into a favorable bilateral deal before the 1994 election. Among other reasons, the neighboring states understood that the old regime was, in a great irony, more politically pliable than an ANC-led government might be. While the departing NP government was the pariah, the incoming ANC government was the parvenu. But the transitional South African government, already by April 1994 a de facto partnership between the NP and ANC, refused to renegotiate bilateral treaties.

The SADC's collective response to the hegemon's dilemma was curious in some respects. Originally a prototype of developmental cooperation, the SADC embraced a free market approach, as embodied in the IMF's Cross-Border Initiative.[16] The new SADC moved away from the project cooperation of its precursor and toward closer political cooperation among its member states in order to "establish the conditions for equitable trade integration."[17] In August 1996, SADC members signed a free trade protocol calling for a free trade area within ten years in Southern Africa. The new protocol was based on neoclassical economics rather than development economics.[18] It favored further liberalization of trade in goods and services and provided for the reduction and eventual elimination of protective tariffs on goods that originated in member states.[19] But the trade protocol did not include measures to ensure that industries would be distributed equitably throughout the region and thus did not have provisions to prevent polarization.[20] The SADC's executive secretary, Kaire Mbuende, tried to assuage the fear of the region's smaller economies about South Africa's dominance by stating that the smaller economies would benefit from a wider market.[21] It is, of course, difficult to square a market approach with a developmental logic, leading one long-time observer to comment that the SADC was only "formally" a developmental organization.[22] It was (and is) too early to evaluate the SADC's new mission.

But it is ironic that South Africa, as the country most likely to benefit from a free trade agreement, challenged the free trade approach embraced by the SADC. After South Africa joined the SADC, a Department of Trade and Industry delegation visited the SADC's Industry and Trade Coordination Division in Dar es Salaam and registered concern about the neoclassical approach.[23] Two studies assessed the impact a free trade area would have on the SADC region, as proposed by the SADC Trade Protocol.[24] One study, commissioned by the SADC, argued that a free trade area would benefit the whole region. Another study, conducted by the Industrial Development Corporation, came up with a fundamentally different conclusion:

> South Africa stood to gain from a free trade agreement in terms of increased GDP, total exports and manufactured exports. In contrast, four of the remaining non-SACU SADC countries were likely to experience a negative impact on their economies, primarily in the form of de-industrialization, as a result of increased competition to domestic industry from South Africa.[25]

The IDC's position was supported and reinforced by the Development Bank of Southern Africa. As many had expected, the DBSA played an increasingly central role in the framing of post-apartheid South Africa's regional relations.

The SADC and developmental cooperation had strong support within the South African state. The Department of Trade and Industry dominated foreign economic policy with a limited amount of support from the Department of Foreign Affairs. As Rashad Cassim, an important outside advisor, stated, "The main drivers are a new generation of bureaucrats in the Department of Trade and Industry,"[26] and the DTI was a strong proponent of the developmental approach. For instance, it tied its trade talks with the EU to the development of the region. Faizel Ismail, chief director of foreign trade relations at the DTI, felt that the South African delegation to the EU should be "diplomats in service of development."[27]

The South African Department of Foreign Affairs has played second fiddle to the Department of Trade and Industry in the formation of South Africa's trade policy. Nonetheless, in 1996, even Foreign Affairs Minister Alfred Nzo wrote that

> The promotion of economic development of the Southern African region is of paramount importance as the economies of the countries of the region are intertwined to such an extent that, for South Africa to believe that it could enter a prosperous future in isolation without taking neighboring countries with her, would be unrealistic and hazardous.[28]

The Department of Trade and Industry and the Department of Foreign Affairs largely agreed that economic development of the region was essential to South Africa's future.

It is not surprising that the South African Parliament was the strongest advocate of developmental cooperation. The ANC leadership of the Parliament, particularly in trade issues, had a long record of support for the SADC and developmental cooperation. And the Parliament was more closely aligned with labor than with business. The ties between Parliament and labor are the clearest proof of how domestic interests impact policymaking in the South African democracy. First, as discussed in Chapter 8, the chairs of the Trade and Industrial Policy Group, Professor Ben Turok and Rob Davies, both central players in Parliament on trade matters, have long been associated with the left of the ANC and considered to be close to labor. Second, the South African Parliament is most representative of the more populist demands in South Africa. And the most sensitive economic sector was labor-intensive industries.

Gavin Maasdorp and Alan Whiteside's 1993 study had anticipated the problems a free trade area in Southern Africa would cause in South Africa. They were correct. They had noted in particular the politically sensitive agricultural subsidies enjoyed by South African farmers and the quotas on clothing imports, specifically from Zimbabwe.[29] Colin McCarthy made a similar argument six years later when he stated that market integration would lead to polarized development and that South Africa's clothing, textile, and footwear firms would have a difficult adjustment.[30] When the South African–EU trade talks stalled in 1997, the South African government regrouped and called for a "consultation period" to examine the EU offer's impact on South Africa's political economy. The consultation period in South Africa triggered by its dissatisfaction with the EU's position led to detailed directives to its negotiation team, which were finalized on June 20, 1997, that would deal with the "sensitive products and sub-sectors" in South Africa. Included were textiles, cars, television assembly and parts, oil production from coal, footwear, small arms and ammunition, dairy products, beef and veal, and sugar.[31] These were primarily labor-sensitive areas.

Table 4 (Appendix 1) shows that South Africa imports mainly labor-intensive goods from the SADC countries; those countries continue to have a comparative advantage in specific labor-intensive sectors.[32] It would be difficult for South Africa to compete with the other SADC countries in labor-intensive exports. This only strengthens the domestic position of South Africa's capital-intensive industries. But clothing and textile industries, where non-SACU SADC countries have a potential to grow, remain a source of discontent to South Africa and its neighbors.[33] A free trade agreement would decimate many labor-intensive industries in South Africa. Table 5 (Appendix 1) shows that during the transition, South Africa continued to export primarily capital-intensive products to the region. Although there was some growth in labor-intensive exports (albeit from a low base), mineral products (the heart of South Africa's capital-intensive complex) grew by 35.3 percent, about three times more than the next-highest category.

Predictably, South Africa's proposed trade and tariff offer to the SADC in 1998 drew concern from the labor-intensive clothing and textile sector, even though special arrangements for "sensitive" products, which included dairy products, wheat, sugar, cotton knitted or crocheted fabrics, clothing products, leather footwear, and vehicles, were included.[34] The clothing and textile sectors—which jointly employed about 215,000 workers—felt particularly vulnerable to "illegal" imports that might be routed through SADC states to South Africa.[35] Thus, as Steve Atkins and Alan Terry argued, production in the region would not necessarily be located in the lowest-cost areas; the position becomes more complicated when the political imperative of creating jobs is added,[36] an issue that is particular sensitive in South Africa.

The post-apartheid South African administration did not accept a laissez-faire approach to regional cooperation. In fact, South Africa offered to open up its trade (reduce tariffs) more quickly than it would demand that its neighbors further reduce their own trade barriers to South African goods. South African political scientists Nana Poku and Maxi Schoeman explain: "Trade liberalism would therefore need an asymmetrical arrangement (with greater access to South African markets than vice versa), a contradiction in terms, but one pointing again to the need for political involvement in the economic strategies of the region."[37] This is not necessarily generosity. Free trade is a threat to South Africa's sensitive labor-intensive sector, which translates to a political threat for the ANC. From South Africa's perspective, because a free trade area would be negotiated sector by sector, it would not be necessarily the same as a laissez-faire approach to regional cooperation.

The Development Bank of Southern Africa, the Department of Trade and Industry, Parliament, even the Industrial Development Corporation all propagated a developmental approach. This included strong criticism of the SADC's trade protocol. The most important piece of the political puzzle here is labor. A free trade area would kill off South Africa's labor-intensive sector. The other piece of the political puzzle is, of course, big business, which was doing fine. It could maintain its position after apartheid without formal institutional support.

Functional Cooperation

The second process driving post-apartheid South Africa's regional relations was functional cooperation, or project cooperation. Functional cooperation connotes a return to the hub-and-spoke approach and carries the baggage of the ideology that led to CONSAS. This is particularly true of South Africa's "spatial developmental initiatives" (SDIs), which were launched in 1995 and are jointly sponsored by the Department of Trade and Industry and the Department of Transportation. SDIs are efforts to match potential investors (by the government, parastatals, and private investors) with viable projects that enhance regional cooperation. SDI projects seek to generate sustainable economic growth and employment and to "maximize the extent to which private sector investment and lending can be mobilized into the SDI area."[38] Three areas made up the bulk of the region's functional cooperation: transportation, hydroelectric power, and shared water resources. In early 1999, the portfolio of all SDIs had identified 661 investment opportunities at a cost of U.S.$22 billion. As of 2000, eleven SDIs had been established in South Africa, and more are being planned.[39] The Maputo Development Corridor (MDC), a road and rail link running from Witbank (about 100 kilometers from Johannesburg) to the port of Maputo in Mozambique, is the flagship of the SDIs.[40] It was begun in 1997 and includes industrial projects such as the Mozal aluminum smelter in Maputo; agricultural projects, such as the Bushbuckridge coffee plantation; tourism, such as the Maputo Polana Hotel; mining projects, such as the Tzaneen ilmenite plant; and gas and slurry pipelines. It involves private and public partnerships, including strong parastatal support from the DBSA and the IDC in South Africa.[41]

The SDIs have been characterized as an extension of neoliberal economic orthodoxy. First, they are intended to attract private investment.[42] For example, the Mozal smelter in Maputo is owned by an international consortium led by London-based Billiton (47 percent), South Africa's IDC

(24 percent), Japan (25 percent), and the government of Mozambique (4 percent).[43] Second, South Africa's parastatals have been major partners. As Söderbaum explains:

> DBSA . . . has seconded staff and offices to project managers, housing budgets. . . . The IDC has been engaged in identifying "bankable" investment projects, while the CSIR has re-oriented some of its activities to support the programme.[44]

The DBSA's Private Sector Investment Unit offers this profile:

> The Private Sector Investment Unit of the Development Bank of Southern Africa (DBSA) plays a unique role in facilitating private sector provision of infrastructure in support of sustainable economic development in the SADC region.
>
> The unit was established in 1996 in response to a worldwide trend towards increased private sector involvement in infrastructure, and in recognition of the need for an appropriate source of financial support for Public Private Partnerships (PPPs) in Southern Africa.[45]

Third, similar to the logic underwriting the ad hoc approach to regional cooperation, "[T]he institutional structure of the MDC is non-bureaucratic, with a more or less minimalist approach to institutions."[46] Finally, the SDIs are considered a natural concomitant to GEAR.[47] Legum explains:

> The list of South Africa's involvement in what has been described as "a constellation of Southern African economies led by private capital," enjoys the active encouragement of the South African Government through its Macro-economic Growth, Employment, and Redistribution (GEAR) policy.[48]

Söderbaum calls the MDC the practical implementation of GEAR.[49]

The SDIs can be seen as a neoliberal approach to regionalism. But they are not the same as CONSAS, nor, strictly speaking, ad hoc cooperation. The SDI program is coordinated by the intersectoral Overall SDI Coordinating Committee (OSDICC), which reports to the Cabinet Investment Cluster (CIC). The CIC is made up of national ministers whose portfolios include infrastructure and economic development. Paul Jourdan,[50] Deputy Director of DTI, is South Africa's point man for the SDIs. Jourdan has described SDIs as a way to link up developing areas with economic potential and to create jobs.[51]

The South African state has continued to emphasize the developmental purpose of the SDIs. It has done more than merely facilitating investment, as the neoliberal model would expect.[52] In launching the Mozal smelter, the South African government stated: "The Mozal smelter is a practical illustration of this foreign policy and its public private partnership will become a catalyst to economic development in the region."[53] As Thabo Mbeki stated when he was vice president:

> Focusing on areas of untapped economic potential, [SDIs] facilitate re-
> gional integration by promoting investment, employment and wealth
> creation, as well as infrastructure development. SDIs demonstrate the
> paradigm shift from the protected and isolated approach to economic
> development of the past towards regional co-operation and integration.[54]

Functional cooperation has been the leading edge of post-apartheid South Africa's regional initiatives. The SDIs have a superficial resemblance to ad hoc cooperation; they reflect the interests of big business and are promoted by their parastatal patrons. But is functional cooperation, as distinct from ad hoc cooperation, necessarily incongruent with developmental cooperation? The answer is no.

Functionalism within a Developmental Context?

Functional cooperation within the context of South Africa's basic architectural design for regional relations is not necessarily inconsistent with the developmental approach. Gavin Maasdorp, reflecting on the new realities, stated in 1996:

> If this paper had been written a few years ago, it might have discussed
> the pros and cons of trade integration as compared with sectoral coop-
> eration (or functional cooperation). Today it can do both.[55]

Colin McCarthy made a similar argument:

> However, if the trade focus is broadened to include not only primary
> products and manufactures, but also tourism and non-tradeables such as
> water and electricity, the scope for a profitable two-way trade is extended
> considerably.[56]

And that is what South Africa did. Mfundo Nkuhlu, director of the DTI's Africa Bilateral Trade Relations, has been consistent in relating the positive synergies of the two:

This restructuring of [regional] relations is intended to promote: i. Co-ordinated regional development through the cluster approach as well as spatial development initiatives; ii. Project-oriented approach to infra-structure rehabilitation and reconstruction; iii. Measures to give the less developed regional states access to the South African Market in an iso-metric fashion, as well as coordination of macro-policies.[57]

He also stated:

This integration [SADC] is seen as occurring in the terms of the devel-opmental paradigm, which places emphasis on infrastructural develop-ment alongside trade promotion.[58]

In fact, post-apartheid South Africa's use of public enterprises such as Transnet and Eskom in a public-works program, which was to help rebuild and revitalize the economy, was good old-fashioned Keynesianism.[59] Their use in regional projects is akin to state-led development.

Infrastructural development, therefore, is not necessarily the same as ad hoc cooperation. Ad hoc cooperation was a blunt instrument in the "hub-and-spoke" approach that typically encouraged bilateral arrange-ments, or what Eliot Berg advocated as "ad hoc regionalism"—where the institutional form of cooperation depends on the immediate task at hand, such as the West African Examinations Council and the East African Wildlife Society.[60] But the project cooperation promoted in post-apartheid South Africa, while certainly benefiting the conglomerate sector, was in-consistent with the logic of the ad hoc approach.

The key difference is that the ad hoc approach saw regional interdepen-dence as anathema and was against the creation of regional institutions that would formalize cooperation/integration. The project approach advo-cated by post-apartheid South Africa strengthens regional interdependency, and in some cases it actually highlights asymmetrical advantages that fa-vor South Africa's neighbors. The new functionalism is embedded in a multilateral approach. Functional cooperation in post-apartheid Southern Africa reflects and strengthens interdependence in the region. While it plays to the strengths of South Africa's dominant corporations, it also points to South Africa's vulnerabilities.

South Africa is vulnerable in three areas necessary to develop its indus-trial infrastructure: energy, water, and transportation. In each of these three areas, South Africa depends on its regional neighbors to gain ac-cess to the resources it needs. Hydroelectric energy sources are the biggest exception to South Africa's regional dominance.[61] Up until the transition period, energy cooperation was built on bilateral agreements, the most important instance being the use of the Cahora Bassa Dam in Mozambique. South Africa had traditionally been a net exporter of power. In 1991, Eskom supplied power worth 155.5 million rand to six SADC member countries and imported power worth 11.3 million.[62] However, Eskom's long-range plans include a regional power grid that would tie together a number of the projects Eskom was already supporting in various neighboring countries. The DBSA recognized this and argued that a regional approach to power system development could end up saving $3 billion between 1995 and 2010 and $400 million annually in operating costs.[63] This would call for a multilateral power authority and tariff-setting agency. In June 1996, power executives from South Africa, Zimbabwe, Botswana, Zambia, and Zaire met in Kinshasa to discuss plans for expanding the regional electricity grid.[64] Interestingly, this has been a private-led initiative. The Southern Africa Power Pool (SAPP) was established in 1995 with the signing of the Inter-Governmental Memorandum of Understanding, with the help of the SADC Energy Sector's Technical and Administrative Unit. Eskom is but one of twelve participating utilities. Eskom's plans for the region cannot be fulfilled through a bilateral approach (the old CONSAS plan). Because of the nature of the challenges it faces, is has embraced a multilateral approach to functional cooperation and is thus not necessarily inconsistent with a developmental approach to regional economic integration/cooperation.

The industrial heartland of South Africa, the Witwatersrand, will become increasingly dependent on imported water.[65] Political scientist Larry Swatuk notes that water and power provide contexts for functional cooperation between the new South Africa and the SADCC: "at the very least, the SADCC states have water which South Africa needs."[66] As the former director of the Hydrological Research Unit at the University of Witwatersrand pointed out, "[T]he relatively developed dry southern subcontinent of Africa contrasts markedly with the less-developed but well-watered north."[67] The model for cooperation in water resources was the Lesotho Highlands Water Project (LHWP), phase one of which is complete. This huge project has been undertaken on a purely bilateral basis. South Africa typically used "joint technical commissions" for such projects, with such neighboring countries as Namibia, Botswana, Mozambique, Swaziland, and Lesotho. South Africa's future water needs, however, will likely require a multilateral approach. Within fifty years, South Africa will have used all its surface water and will have to go to the Zambezi. This project has to be multilateral, and it needs to start soon (the LHWP was first discussed in 1954, a lead time of forty years). Discussion on the Zambezi project, which will certainly be more complex than the LHWP, would need at least as much lead time, and Botswana, Zambia, and Zimbabwe would have to participate.[68]

The bilateral approach may be most efficient for the transportation sector. In 1993, the position of the Department of Transportation was to continue transportation cooperation under the relevant SACU committee and to pursue bilateral agreements with states outside SACU. Existing bilateral relations were particularly strong in shipping.[69] But transportation also requires multilateral cooperation in Southern Africa. Railway cooperation in Southern Africa is well advanced; this was true even during apartheid. In fact, there were parallel South African groups working on regional transportation cooperation, one cooperating informally with the SADC, and the other formally cooperating with regional actors. In 1992, SADCC approached Spoornet, the South African railroad parastatal, to merge the two groups. Transportation is one of the areas where the SADC had most successfully institutionalized cooperation, and Spoornet favored the SADC as the umbrella organization for regional cooperation in transportation.[70]

The Maputo Corridor Project with Mozambique includes building a toll road between Witbank in South Africa and Maputo in Mozambique, rebuilding the adjacent railway line, and modernizing Maputo Harbour. The last symbolizes South Africa's new approach to the region; Maputo Harbour at one time carried 40 percent of the old Transvaal Province's (now Gautang Province) foreign trade. Apartheid South Africa's "transport diplomacy" and destabilization campaign reduced the percentage to five. The modernization is a multisectoral approach whose goal is to stimulate tourism, agriculture and forestry, mining, construction, energy, finance, and services. The Corridor connects South Africa and Mozambique, but the regional governments of Mozambique, South Africa, Zimbabwe, Swaziland, and Botswana have set up the Maputo Corridor Company. The Maputo Corridor Project is a good example of a hybrid approach to regional economic integration/cooperation. It is a functionalist approach to development.

In the three major functional areas where ad hoc cooperation was deemed appropriate, in fact, a more formalized multilateral approach is developing. Functionalism is increasingly identified with developmental integration in Africa. In long-time observer Timothy Shaw's words,

the continent's new post-1980s agenda opens up prospects for new *functionalist* arrangements, such as over tropical forests, ivory and diamond trades, drought management, refugee repatriation, water distribution, oil and natural gas pipelines, container transportation, cellular telephones, computer networks, satellite television, regional capital and stock markets, etc.[71]

As Larry Swatuk points out, South Africa focused on functional cooperation and SADC is using protocols to manage them.[72]

However, function does not always predict form.[73] It is important to note that while interdependence in water and electricity may make multilateral cooperation logical, a country may be willing to incur "irrational costs" to avoid interdependence. Thus, as South African scholar D. C. Midgley noted in 1988, "For progress to be made it is essential that the notion of dependence be replaced by that of interdependence."[74]

Interdependence and Regional Cooperation in Southern Africa

Functional cooperation and how it relates to the SADC's mission is central to the developmental approach. There are two ways developmental cooperation can gain traction in Southern Africa. First, a "harmony of interest" between South Africa and its neighbors is possible. If this were to happen, its regional identity would become more powerful than its country identity. But more likely, South Africa will pursue its national self-interest. Although South Africa is the regional hegemon, the rationale for interdependence must be strong enough to mitigate the region's dependence on South Africa. And these interdependencies must be linked under the umbrella of a regional regime. U.S. political scientist Robert Keohane explains:

> Clustering of issues under a regime facilitates side payments among those issues: more potential quids are available for the quo. Without international regimes linking clusters of issues to one another, side payments and linkages would be difficult to arrange in world politics.[75]

Without the institutional sinews to connect interdependent states, the strongest state could leverage its advantage in any dyadic approach to regional bargaining. South Africa would dominate in any regional pairing. If South Africa pursues its own national interests, there must be a political benefit from regional interdependence that is greater than the advantages of bilateralism.

The nature of interdependence in South Africa is two-dimensional. The first dimension is reflected in functional cooperation, and its central domestic constituency in South Africa is the status-quo industries—the large conglomerates and the parastatals. The second dimension is regional trade, and its central constituency is labor-intensive industries.

It is ironic that functional cooperation in Southern Africa creates more quids for the quo precisely because it brings in issues where South Africa's neighbors have an advantage. Before the 1994 election, one DBSA researcher listed the key issues as:

> [d]eveloping Southern Africa as an integrated economic region and in particular the need to promote sensible and genuine economic interdependence at the structural level, as opposed to the previous one-sided dependence. Building upon South Africa's increasing reliance on SADCC countries for hydro-electrical power generation, water resources supply, and the provision of transport services would be sound (if inadequate) examples to support such a broad development strategy.[76]

A 1997 DBSA paper emphasized that nontraditional tradables, such as water and electricity, could balance South Africa's overwhelming trade advantage.

> The potential for the importation of water and energy by South Africa from the rest of the region should be explored. Given the abundant endowments of these resources in the region and South Africa's diminishing domestic resources, accompanied by rising demand, energy and water emerge as areas where intra-regional trade may be enhanced and the current trade imbalance redressed.[77]

After the 1994 election, the DBSA advocated a developmental approach built on the twin pillars of multilateral linkages and functional cooperation.[78] The principles of "equity, balance and mutual benefit" were important components of the DBSA's approach.[79] The development bank was very critical of the free trade approach. The South African government mandated the DBSA to include the region in SDIs and infrastructural projects in order to counter the polarization effects of South Africa's dominance of the region. The other component of South Africa's regional interdependence is the economic weakness of its politically powerful labor-intensive sector.

South African political scientists Glen Adler and Eddie Webster noted that creating jobs for South African Blacks along with the water problem created powerful regional interdependencies.[80] Jobs and water create greater interdependency between South Africa and the regions because South Africa is dependent on the region for water and must control immigration to protect jobs at home. These interdependencies mean that the

SADC free trade protocol has political implications. The prospects for South Africa's labor-intensive industries and job growth in South Africa are tied to its ability to reach an agreement with its neighbors that is politically acceptable to labor. The ANC-COSATU alliance depends on this. Poku and Schoeman capture how free trade applies to South Africa:

> In unilaterally freeing its market, or freeing it in those sectors where neighboring countries have a comparative advantage that might therefore benefit them, South Africa might place its own industries at risk. This is particularly true of its textile, footwear and furniture industries. . . . Therefore, moves to benefit neighboring manufacturing capacity by opening up South Africa's markets may not only have economic repercussions (e.g. increased unemployment), but are also politically risky in terms of political support, potential labour unrest and further alienation of the trade union movement in South Africa.[81]

This is particularly evident in the strained relationship between South Africa and Zimbabwe. Trade unions and employers in South Africa's textile industry are strongly opposed to opening up South Africa's markets to Zimbabwean textiles, even though this might make sense in terms of regional economic interdependence. South Africa already has a 30 percent unemployment rate and its textile industry employs 250,000 people; proposals that might harm that industry have enormous political significance.[82] This is why COSATU has argued for a regional industrial development strategy to precede any reduction in trade barriers under a regional free trade area.[83] After South Africa's offer to SADC was gazetted on September 11, 1998, textile and clothing union officials challenged the impact it would have on their industries.[84] The free trade agreement talks have yet to be completed.

The politics of interdependence in South Africa pull South Africa in two different directions. Geoffrey Garrett has succinctly captured this pattern:

> The most important distributional cleavage in the industrial democracies has long been between those who support the market allocation of wealth and risk—the natural constituency of right-wing parties—and those who favor government efforts to alter market outcomes—the left's core base of support.[85]

The fact that post-apartheid South Africa is a semi-industrialized economy, with a foot in two worlds, only exacerbates that cleavage. Labor and nontraditional exports need help. The status-quo industries do not. Southern

Africa could become South Africa's captured market; a South African min-ing executive referred to South Africa's relationship with its "near abroad" as akin to Russia's claims of special privilege in the former Soviet repub-lics.[86] But post-apartheid South Africa's regional relations will reflect the institutional configurations and interests shaping its foreign economic policy.

This book treats regionalism as a state-led process.[87] It assumes the that political considerations are the most important factors in policy-making.[88] I examined the South African state with an emphasis on trade flows, competitiveness, and macroeconomic policy to explain the prefer-ences of societal actors[89] and the ways they work their way through the institutional gateways, such as the IMF, the World Bank, the World Trade Organization, and the EU, in post-apartheid South Africa. As in the do-mestic political economy, in regional relations South Africa's left benefits from intervening (an active state role) and the right benefits from not in-tervening (a passive state role).[90] The argument of the book also includes external influences on the political dynamics of preference formation in South Africa.

The ANC came to power in 1994 in the wake of an overwhelming election victory. In 1999, the ANC fell one seat short of a two-thirds ma-jority in Parliament (266 out of 400 seats), which would have allowed it to unilaterally change the country's constitution. Nonetheless, like any elected government, the ANC responds to domestic pressures. That is the point of this book. As former speaker of the U.S. House of Representatives Tip O'Neil once said, "All politics is local."

Thus, to understand how post-apartheid South Africa would build a new relationship with its neighbors and in particular how it would ap-proach regional economic integration/cooperation, I posited that we must first understand how the constituent parts of its political economy view regional relations. In transitional South Africa this meant a political fault line that separated big-business interests from labor interests. I borrowed Moravcsik's liberal theory that links social preferences to state behavior. Moravcsik argues that a bottom-up approach to understanding policy should include ideological, commercial, and republican components.

From the ideological perspective, the ANC would be expected to pur-sue a Keynesian, if not necessarily socialist, economic program. Labor, in particular COSATU, which formally aligned with the ANC, continues to argue for such a program. In the form of regional economic cooperation/integration, this would support a more developmental approach over either a market or ad hoc approach. The ANC, however, seemingly took a right turn, and this was in part due to the powerful pull of ideas from the IFIs and other international organizations such as the EU and World Trade Organization.

Post-apartheid South Africa's commercial relations seem to reflect its big-business interests. Undoubtedly, the power of big business could not and was not ignored in post-apartheid South Africa. The GEAR plan seemed to cement its hold on South Africa, and the IFIs seemed to act, from labor's perspective, as partners in crime to big business. Big business and labor had very different commercial interests in the region. But in post-apartheid South Africa, although big business remained powerful, labor could not be ignored. Between Nelson Mandela's inauguration on May 10, 1994 and mid-August of that same year, more working days were lost through strikes than in any other year since 1987.[91] In one incident, the South African government used soldiers to clear 700 truckers who were blocking a highway in demand of higher wages. Nelson Mandela's response to labor unrest so early in his first term is telling. In September 1994, he told labor unions that strikes would scare off the foreign investors necessary for rejuvenating the economy.[92] Thus, post-apartheid South Africa was quite sensitive to business interests. The weakest political player in post-apartheid South Africa that propagated a particular form of regional economic integration/cooperation (in this case market cooperation) was the old bureaucracy. In fact, many of the new class of ANC bureaucrats in the relevant departments helped draft the MERG report and the RDP.

Mediating the power struggle between business and labor with their respective ideological and commercial interests is the South African state. The republican part of a bottom-up understanding of apartheid South Africa's regional relations is probably where the ANC/labor ideology and commercial interests have the greatest traction. The ANC government is full of men and women who contributed to the original RDP and to groups such as MERG and ISP. Thus, even with the combined power of big business and the IFIs in post-apartheid South Africa, regional relations have not taken a sharp right turn.

Post-apartheid South Africa under the ANC rejected both the market and ad hoc approaches to regional economic integration/cooperation. The SADC has been the institutional anchor for its regional economic relations, and developmental cooperation has been the guiding philosophy. However, South Africa has grafted onto its core belief in developmental regional economic integration/cooperation elements of both the market approach and ad hoc cooperation. SACU was renegotiated but did not become the center of South Africa's regional plan as envisioned in the Maas-dorp Report. Ad hoc cooperation, such as bilateralism, is also present in South Africa, but it has been incorporated into the developmental model.

In contrast to the argument made in this book, much of the literature on post-apartheid South Africa's regional relations sees its regional role as a projection of captured interests, for instance, big business. I argue that post-apartheid South Africa's regional relations more closely represent a political compromise that reflects the different visions of South Africa's regional role and their respective political bases. Its regional economic relations represent a de facto political compromise between developmental cooperation and project, or functional, cooperation. Each has a strong constituency in South Africa to whom the ANC listens. Developmental cooperation is supported by labor and still has large ideological appeal within the ANC. But, as has been well chronicled and documented, the ANC has also been responsive to the demands of big business.[93] Business profits from and supports a less institutionalized form of regional cooperation, in this case project cooperation. The IFIs have been powerful proponents of a free trade agreement and functional cooperation. Their influence in South Africa is palpable.

South Africa's regional foreign policy represents an attempt to square the political circle. It has managed to placate big business and the IFIs (largely through the GEAR plan) without accepting their architectural plan for the region. Only the next decade will tell if, in fact, South Africa's neighbors can advance economically as the regional power continues to try to face its own domestic challenges.

This book does not claim to give a complete picture for regionalism in Southern Africa. Many actors, including neighboring states, and many influences within South Africa have not been addressed. As well, the focus has been on the narrow domain of regional economic cooperation. In reality, it cannot be divorced from the larger picture which would include: regional security issues, informal economies, nascent regional civil society, the crime problem in post-apartheid South Africa, the issue of immigration, and the devastating spread of AIDs. Nonetheless, the prospects for regional cooperation and integration in Southern Africa begin with decisions made in Pretoria. Understanding what is happening within South Africa, and why, is a good starting place and an essential piece of the Southern African puzzle.

Appendix 1: Tables

Table 1. South African Exports by Product Category, 1988–91
(in current US$billion)

	1988	1989	1990	1991
A Food	1.14	1.66	1.63	1.68
B Raw Materials	0.94	0.97	0.88	0.79
C Ores and Minerals	1.82	1.98	1.82	1.56
D Fuels	1.23	1.23	1.45	1.46
E Non-Ferrous Metals	0.79	0.83	0.72	0.74
F Total Primary	5.91	6.67	6.50	6.23
G Iron and Steel	1.80	2.02	2.15	2.16
H Chemicals	0.76	0.84	0.84	0.97
I Other Semi-Manufactured	1.82	2.46	2.88	2.82
J Total Machine & Trans.	1.18	1.33	1.94	2.28
J1 Mach. & Trans. Equip	0.59	0.66	0.97	1.14
J2 Power & Gen. Equip.	0.01	0.01	0.02	0.02
J3 Other Non-Elec. Equip	0.25	0.23	0.29	0.35
J4 Office Machinery	0.05	0.06	0.07	0.09
J5 Electrical Machinery	0.06	0.07	0.11	0.09
J6 Auto Parts & Assem.	0.14	0.17	0.25	0.32
J7 Other Transport Equip	0.08	0.12	0.23	0.27
K Textiles	0.10	0.11	0.17	0.16
L Clothing	0.5	0.05	0.8	0.13
M Other Consumer Products	0.16	0.18	0.24	0.26
N Manufactures (G–M)	5.87	6.99	8.29	8.78
Other*	10.62	9.43	9.81	9.64
O Total	22.41	23.09	24.60	24.65
P Broad Manufactures (E–M)	6.66	7.82	9.01	9.64
Q Narrow Manufactures (J–M)	1.49	1.67	2.43	2.84
R Intermediaries (E,G,H,I)	5.17	6.15	6.58	6.68

*Not classified by source; largely gold exports
Source: IDC Data Base (Hirsch, Trading Up, p. 73).

Table 2. Exports of the Common Customs Area of Botswana, Lesotho, Namibia, South Africa, and Swaziland to the Rest of Southern Africa, January–December 1992

Section	Value R 000	% Total Exports to Africa	% Total Exports in Section (all areas)
1. Animals & Products	56,906	1.3	7.3
2. Vegetable Products	302,856	6.9	13.2
3. Animal &Vegetable Fats	76,997	1.7	50.8
4. Foodstuffs & Beverages	356,205	8.1	19.2
5. Mineral Products	236,195	5.3	3.3
6. Chemical Products	642,511	14.6	19.9
7. Plastic & Rubber Products	241,950	5.5	32.5
8. Hides, Skins, & Leather	5,023	0.1	1.2
9. Wood & Articles	22,379	0.5	5.9
10. Pulp, Paper, & Products	143,112	3.2	7.5
11. Textiles	182,866	4.1	10.1
12. Footwear & Related	12,035	0.3	22.2
13. Stone & Related Products	70,438	1.6	19.1
14. Jewelry	1,421	>0.1	>0.1
15. Articles of Base Metals	639,455	14.5	6.7
16. Machinery & Appliances	804,755	18.4	37.4
17. Vehicles & Related	484,680	11.0	20.8
18. Optical Equipment	42,567	1.0	24.5
19. Misc. Manufactures	73,955	1.7	24.3
20. Art	244	>0.1	1.3
21. Unclassified	8,440	0.2	>0.1
TOTAL	4,407,012	73.7	6.5

Source: Monthly Abstract of Trade Statistics: Foreign Trade Statistics of the common customs area of Botswana, Lesotho, South Africa, and Swaziland released by the Commissioner for Customs and Excise of the Republic of South Africa, January–December 1992, Pretoria, 1993. Cited in Robert Davies et al., *Reconstructing Economic Relations with the Southern African Region: Issues and Options for a Democratic South Africa* (Cape Town: MERG, 1993), p. 73.

Table 3. South African Real Exchange Indices against Selected Southern African Countries

Botswana	+ 9.1
Malawi	−13.5
Zambia	+12.0
Zimbabwe	+13.7

Source: Harvey and Jenkins, "The Unorthodox Response of the South African Economy to Changes in Macroeconomic Policy." Draft, unpublished paper, March 12, 1992.

Table 4. SACU Shares of Imports by Commodity from SADC (%)[1]

CH22	Description	1991	1992	1993	1994	1995	1996	1997	1998
01	Live animals, animal products	3.1	2.8	3.4	3.3	4.1	2.4	2.4	2.0
02	Vegetable products	11.1	9.3	16.3	11.1	9.2	7.1	9.8	9.3
03	Animal, vegetable fats & oils	0.7	1.7	1.1	1.4	0.3	0.7	1.0	0.8
04	Prepared foodstuffs, beverages, tobacco	29.6	21.7	19.0	14.5	17.6	17.5	13.7	17.5
05	Mineral products	8.8	8.3	6.9	4.5	4.1	21.6	15.1	6.9
06	Products of chemical or allied industries	1.1	1.6	1.8	1.8	1.9	1.3	1.3	1.5
07	Plastics and rubber	1.7	2.4	2.2	1.9	2.0	1.7	1.9	2.0
08	Raw hides and skins, leather	1.7	1.9	1.9	2.4	2.3	1.3	0.8	0.8
09	Wood, cork, straw	3.5	6.4	5.0	5.9	7.5	7.1	6.1	5.3
10	Pulp, paper & paperboard, books	0.9	1.0	1.2	1.1	1.5	1.6	1.9	1.1
11	Textiles, fabrics, clothing	18.4	19.9	16.9	25.5	20.6	18.5	25.7	30.0
12	Footwear, headgear, umbrellas	1.6	2.7	3.4	2.4	3.0	1.3	0.7	0.6
13	Articles of stone, asbestos, ceramics	0.5	0.6	0.6	0.7	0.8	0.7	0.9	0.8
14	Precious metals	0.4	0.3	0.6	1.7	1.8	0.3	0.2	0.4
15	Base metals	8.1	10.6	9.2	11.1	11.5	7.4	7.3	9.4
16	Machinery, mechanical, electrical	3.8	4.8	6.2	5.5	5.4	4.5	5.3	6.6
17	Vehicles, aircraft, ships	1.8	2.2	1.4	2.3	2.0	1.7	1.8	1.5
18	Optical photo, measuring, musical instruments	0.3	0.2	0.4	0.3	0.4	0.6	2.0	1.5
20	Misc. manufactured articles	1.3	1.6	2.4	2.7	3.0	2.4	2.1	1.9
21	Works of art collectors pieces & antiques	0	0	0	0.2	0.1	0.2	0.1	0.1
22	Other unclassified goods	1.7	0	0	0	0.9	0	0	0
	Total	100	100	100	100	100	100	100	100

Source: TIPS Database[2]   *Notes:* 1. As in Chapter 5, SACU can be used as a proxy for South Africa.   2. Kalenga, "Regional Trade," p. 12.

Table 5. SACU Exports by Commodity to SADC (million rand, 1995 constant prices)

CH22	Description	1991	1992	1993	1994	1995	1996	1997	1998	1999	2000	Growth
01	Live animals, animal products	127	115	160	175	218	215	295	301	309	248	11.3%
02	Vegetable products	274	481	339	339	562	884	431	942	787	441	8.9%
03	Animal, vegetable fats & oils	100	121	147	108	154	172	146	144	138	129	2.5%
04	Prepared foodstuffs, beverages, tobacco	492	499	555	653	791	961	1,023	972	1,035	1,167	11.0%
05	Mineral products	142	346	295	178	1,375	1,815	1,931	1,243	1,374	2,439	35.3%
06	Products of chemical or allied industries	981	1,026	1,158	1,494	1,326	1,696	1,799	1,838	1,808	2,064	8.7%
07	Plastics and rubber	367	390	436	476	569	630	721	676	768	791	9.6%
08	Raw hides and skins, leather	10	8	9	8	15	19	15	12	12	11	4.8%
09	Wood, cork, straw	30	45	82	88	99	56	69	78	77	91	7.7%
10	Pulp, paper, paperboard, books	264	250	302	571	392	672	442	456	475	523	7.9%
11	Textiles, fabrics, clothing	349	317	305	419	368	401	526	315	337	371	1.2%
12	Footwear, headgear, umbrellas	14	20	33	37	35	80	43	34	42	50	11.3%
13	Articles of stone, asbestos, ceramics	118	121	137	125	126	194	191	156	186	162	5.2%
14	Precious metals	5	4	4	64	6	5	9	6	7	11	4.4%
15	Base metals	1,019	1,012	996	1,002	1,751	1,401	1,484	1,331	1,636	1,687	6.4%
16	Machinery, mechanical, electrical	978	1,305	1,400	1,461	2,020	2,570	2,423	2,360	2,316	2,178	9.9%

CH22	Description	1991	1992	1993	1994	1995	1996	1997	1998	1999	2000	Growth
17	Vehicles, aircraft, ships	707	745	843	954	968	1,354	1,368	1,157	1,276	1,169	7.1%
18	Optical photo, measuring, musical instruments	63	73	94	121	128	137	166	180	158	144	10.9%
20	Misc. manufactured articles	85	115	146	151	149	229	220	202	220	219	10.4%
21	Works of art collectors pieces & antiques	0	0	0	5	1	1	1	6	1	1	13.6%
22	Other unclassified goods	39	0	0	0	125	0	0	0	0	0	0.0%
	Total	6,163	6,990	7,442	8,430	11,179	13,492	13,308	12,426	12,972	13,898	10%

Source: http://www.tips.org.za/research/Focus/aug2002.pdf

Appendix 2: Chronology

1910 The Union of South Africa is established, comprising Transvaal, the Orange Free State, Natal, and the Cape

1912 The South African Native National Council (SANNC) is launched (changes its name to the African National Congress in 1923)

1941 The African Mineworkers Union is formed

1948 The National Party under Daniel Malan is voted into power, beginning forty years of apartheid rule

1952 The ANC Defiance Campaign starts

1955 The ANC publishes its "Freedom Charter"

1958 Hendrik Verwoerd, grand architect of apartheid, becomes president

1959 The Pan Africanist Congress (PAC) is formed under Robert Sobukwe

1960 Police shoot at pass-law protestors at Sharpeville

1960 Prime Minister Harold MacMillan of Great Britain gives his "Winds of Change" speech in front of the South African Parliament
The ANC and the PAC are banned
The ANC adopts a policy of armed struggle under Umkhonto weSizwe (Spear of the Nation)

1962 Nelson Mandela is arrested for plotting against the government

1969 The South African Students' Organization is formed under Steve Biko
The Southern African Customs Union is renegotiated

1974 Portugal announces its withdrawal from Angola and Mozambique

1975 The South African army invades Angola

1976 Protest against the use of Afrikaans in Black schools initiates riots

1977 Black consciousness activist Steve Biko dies in detention

1978 Vorster resigns and Minister of Defense P. W. Botha replaces him

1980 Zimbabwe becomes independent
The Southern African Development Coordination Conference is formed (changed to the Southern Africa Development Community in 1992)

1983 The United Democratic Front—a coalition of trade unions, women's groups, and youth organizations—is established
New constitution allows for a "Coloured" Parliament, but not for the 24 million Blacks

1984 Archbishop Desmond Tutu is awarded the Nobel Peace Prize
Nkomati Accords—South Africa and Mozambique agree not to support insurgencies in their respective countries

1984– Township revolt, state of emergency
1989

1985 Start of economic sanctions against South Africa by countries around the world

1986 The Congress of South African Trade Unions (COSATU) is formed

1987 P. W. Botha's televised "Rubicon" speech on South Africa's commitment to change is broadcast to Western industrial democracies
1988 "Trek to Lusaka" begins
1989 Pass laws and the Mixed Marriages Act are abolished
F. W. de Klerk replaces P. W. Botha as president, meets Mandela. Public facilities desegregated. Many ANC activists freed.
1990 On February 2, de Klerk unbans the ANC, the PAC and the SACP
On February 11, Nelson Mandela is released
1991 The National Peace Accord is signed by all major political players other than the right wing
1992 The Convention for a Democratic South Africa (CODESA) is launched on December 20 at the World Trade Center in Kempton Park
1993 The UN lifts sanctions against South Africa (with the exceptions of arms and oil) in October
De Klerk and Mandela are jointly awarded the Nobel Peace Prize
Agreement on interim constitution
1994 First post-apartheid elections held in April; Nelson Mandela elected president
South Africa signs a new GATT accord and joins the WTO
1996 The ANC government under President Nelson Mandela adopts its new economic policy: Growth, Employment and Redistribution (GEAR)
1999 Second post-apartheid election; Thabo Mbeki elected president

Appendix 3: Key Committees, Commissions, and Economic Plans

Committees and Commissions

Reynders Commission (1971)

Appointed by the South African government to inquire into the problem of exports, particularly manufactured goods. The 1972 Reynders Report argued for a shift toward greater emphasis on the expansion of manufactured exports.

Wiehahn Commission (1977)

Appointed by Prime Minister John Vorster essentially as a complement to the Riekert Commission; the Wiehahn Commission looked at job reservation affecting Blacks and the apartheid system of industrial relations and trade union rights. The commission recommended that Section 77 of the Industrial Conciliation Act of 1956, which established the job reservation system, be abolished. P. W. Botha accepted this recommendation in 1979.

Van Huysteen Committee (1978)

Recommended (after Reynders) that the South African government adopt export incentives.

Erasmus Commission (1978)

Appointed by the South African government to look into the Infogate scandal, which concerned illegal activities by staff at the Information Department, particularly by Dr. Eschel Rodie, Secretary of Information and Minister of Information. It concluded its first report in December 1978 and led to Prime Minister Vorster's resignation on June 4, 1979.

Riekert Commission (1978)

Established by the South African government to look at the state-controlled movement of Africans from rural "homelands" to industrial cities. In its 1978 report (published in 1979) it recommended that restrictions of Black Africans in the townships be eased. This effectively marked the end of the National Party's notion of the urban Black worker as transient and recognized the permanence of the urban Black.

Economic Plans

Normative Economic Model (NEM, 1993)

The economic plan of the NP; it was drafted by the Central Economic Advisory Service, in consultation with the South African Reserve Bank, government departments, and the special economic advisor to the minister of finance. Its document, "The Restructuring of the South African Economy: A Normative Model Approach," promoted a free market economy and leaned toward supply-side economics.

MERG Report (1993)

The Macroeconomic Research Group was set up by the ANC in 1991. Its main report, *Making Democracy Work*, was published in late 1993. The MERG report agreed with most of the recommendations of the ANC's Reconstruction Development Programme, such as unbundling and deracializing ownership of corporations; public-sector provision of basic needs (such as housing, electricity, and water); a living wage; training for workers; land reform; and fiscal restraint. However, the Macroeconomic Research Group leaned farther to the left than the ANC with recommendations such as the nationalization of the South African Reserve Bank.

Reconstruction and Development Programme (RDP, 1994)

The economic blueprint of the ANC, the RDP was the product of broad-based cooperation by the ANC, COSATU, the SACP, the South African Council of Churches, and the South African National Civic Organization. In many instances, it promulgated a Keynesian approach to the post-apartheid South African economy.

Maasdorp Report (1994)

"A Vision for Economic Integration and Cooperation in Southern Africa," prepared for the South African Department of Trade and Industry, March 1994. Headed by Professor Gavin Maasdorp, Economic Research Unit, University of Natal, Durban. The report argued for a linear process of regional economic cooperation, which emphasized trade liberalization and possibly monetary cooperation. It promulgated using the SACU as the institutional anchor and adding other countries at variable levels of cooperation (i.e. free trade, customs union, common market, economic union) over time.

Notes

1. Introduction

1. Colleen Lowe Morna, "Frontline States Prepare for Competition with South Africa," *African Business* (October 1990): 17.

2. Erich Leistner, "Issues of Economic Integration in Southern Africa," Konrad-Adenauer-Stiftung Occasional Papers 7, Johannesburg, September 1992, 10.

3. Gilbert M. Khadiagala, "Regional Dimensions of Sanctions," in *How Sanctions Work: Lessons from South Africa,* ed. Neta C. Crawford and Audie Klotz (New York: St. Martin's Press, 1999), 255. Some of these deaths should be attributed to the internal dynamics of the Angola and Mozambique civil wars.

   Rearguard action is the attempt of the South African government to weaken the neighboring states hosting anti-apartheid forces (such as the MK). South Africa invaded Angola in 1980, conducted an air strike against ANC bases in Mozambique in 1983, and conducted commando raids into Zimbabwe in 1982 and 1986 and Botswana in 1985 and 1986.

4. Peter Batchelor and Susan Willett, *Disarmament and Defense Industrial Adjustment in South Africa* (New York: Oxford University Press, 1998), 191.

5. The neighboring countries that hosted anti-apartheid forces and, in general, supported the anti-apartheid movement had taken a costly gamble in confronting the regional power.

6. Leistner, "Issues of Economic Integration," 10.

7. President Clinton, "Remarks Announcing Assistance to South Africa," May 5, 1994, *1994 Public Papers of the President,* vol. 1 (Washington, D.C.: GPO, 1995).

8. *The Star* (Johannesburg), February 28, 1994.

9. Peter Gourevitch, *Politics in Hard Times: Comparative Responses to International Economic Crisis* (Ithaca, N.Y.: Cornell University Press, 1986), 34; G. John Ikenberry, "Creating Yesterday's New World Order: Keynesian 'New Thinking' and the Anglo-American Postwar Settlement," in *Ideas and Foreign Policy: Beliefs, Institutions, and Political Change,* ed. Judith Goldstein and Robert O. Keohane (Ithaca, N.Y.: Cornell University Press, 1993), 59.

10. A. A. H. Aly, *Economic Cooperation in Africa: In Search of Direction* (Boulder, Colo.: Lynne Rienner, 1994), 35–41.

11. Scholars have expressed doubts about whether conventional approaches to analyzing integration are relevant in the context of regional economic integration in the Third World. See Peter Robson, "Regional Economic Cooperation among Developing Countries: Some Further Considerations," *World Development* 6 (1978): 776; Constantine Vaitsos, "Crisis in Regional Economic Cooperation (Integration) among Developing Countries: A Survey," *World Development* 6 (1978): 719–769.

12. Steven Weber, "The European Bank for Reconstruction and Development," *International Organization* 48 (1994): 3.

13. This is generic to most social theory on institutions. Paul DiMaggio and

Walter Powell, "The Iron Cage Revisited: Institutional Isomorphism and Collective Rationality in Organizational Fields," *American Sociological Review* 48 (1983).

14. Andrew Hurrell, "Explaining the Resurgence of Regionalism in World Politics," *Review of International Studies* 21 (1995): 338.

15. Richard Sandbrook, *The Politics of Africa's Economic Recovery* (New York: Cambridge University Press, 1993), 39.

16. Jeffrey Herbst, "War and the State in Africa," *International Security* 14 (1990): 126–127. Herbst also argues that African countries' fiscal structures were a legacy of colonial rule. See also Jeffrey Herbst, *State and Power in Africa* (Princeton, N.J.: Princeton University Press, 2000), 117.

17. Rolf J. Langhammer, "The Developing Countries and Regionalism," *Journal of Common Market Studies* 31 (1993): 218.

18. Rod Falvey and Cha Dong Kim, "Timing and Sequencing Issues for Trade Liberalization," in *Trade and Fiscal Adjustment in Africa,* ed. David Bevan, Paul Collier, Norman Gemmell, David Greenaway (New York: St. Martin's Press, 2000), 28.

19. World Bank, Economics and Finance Division, Technical Division, Africa Region, "Intra-Regional Trade in Sub-Saharan Africa," unpublished report, World Bank, Washington, D.C., 1991, 1.

20. Bela Balassa, *The Theory of Economic Integration* (Homewood, Ill.: R. D. Erwin, 1961); Albert Hirschman, *The State of Economic Development* (New Haven, Conn.: Yale University Press, 1958); Gunnar Myrdal, *Economic Theory and Underdeveloped Regions* (London: Duckworth Press, 1957).

21. Balefi Tsie, "States and Markets in the Southern African Development Community (SADC): Beyond the Neo-Liberal Paradigm," *Journal of Southern African Studies* 22 (1996): 93.

22. James Mittelman, *The Globalization Syndrome: Transformation and Resistance* (Princeton, N.J.: Princeton University Press, 2000), 117.

23. The OAU was formed in 1963 as the first intergovernmental organization composed of all independent African states to promote African political cooperation. The Lagos Plan of Action was adopted at the 1980 OAU Assembly of Heads of State and Government in Freetown, Sierra Leone. The Plan pursued self-reliance by delinking the African continent from the international economic system.

24. John Ravenhill, "Africa's Continuing Crisis: The Elusiveness of Development," in *Africa in Economic Crisis,* ed. John Ravenhill (New York: Columbia University Press, 1986), 2.

25. John Ravenhill, "Redrawing the Map of Africa?" in *The Precarious Balance: State and Society in Africa,* ed. Donald Rothchild and Naomi Chazan (Boulder: Westview Press, 1988), 282.

26. Moravcsik has moved away from this, as is evident in his "Taking Preferences Seriously: A Liberal Theory of International Politics," *International Organization* 51 (1997): 513–554. Nonetheless, even in this article there is some tendency to accept a dichotomous choice—between cooperating and not cooperating—while implying that the nature of interdependence influences the "form, substance, and depth of cooperation" (520; see also 543).

27. Two caveats are necessary at this point. First, I am talking about institutions, not regimes, because the regimes imply the limitation of independent decisionmaking. The ad hoc form of cooperation is built on protecting independent decision making. This is a real option that has strong support in South Africa. Second, institutions can be either cooperative or conflictual (Wendt, "Anarchy Is What States Make of It," *International Organization* 46 [1992]: 399), but the focus here is on cooperative institutions. However, although the ad hoc approach to regional relations in postapartheid Southern Africa was usually depicted as a specific cooperative approach, its

antecedent in Southern African history, the Constellation of Southern African States (CONSAS) that was promoted by South Africa during apartheid, was certainly conflictual.

28. Tony Hawkins, "Economic Integration in Southern Africa," paper presented at the African Regional Workshop on Economic Integration, Capetown, South Africa, March 2–4, 1994.

29. These are often offered as the possible forms for regional cooperation in Africa. For instance, John Ravenhill outlined the three possible forms as "largely unregulated unions/common markets," "common markets with industrial planning with, possibly, explicit counter-dependency objectives," and "functional cooperation." John Ravenhill, "Collective Self-Reliance or Collective Self-Delusion: Is the Lagos Plan a Viable Alternative?" in *Africa in Economic Crisis,* ed. John Ravenhill (New York: Columbia University Press, 1986), 97.

30. For instance, Gavin Maasdorp, who was a strong proponent of the market approach during the transition, later said, "If this paper had been written a few years ago, it might have discussed the pros and cons of trade integration as compared with sectoral cooperation or functional cooperation. Today you can do both." Gavin Maasdorp, "Can Regional Integration Help Southern Africa?" in *Can South Africa and Southern Africa Become Globally Competitive Economies?* ed. Gavin Maasdorp (New York: St. Martin's Press, 1996), 45.

31. Gavin Maasdorp and Alan Whiteside, *Rethinking Economic Cooperation in Southern Africa: Trade and Investment* (Johannesburg: Konrad-Adenauer Stiftung, 1993), 35; C. G. Gore, "International Order, Economic Regionalism and Structural Adjustment: The Case of Sub-Saharan Africa," in *Progress in Planning,* ed. D. Diamond, B. McLoughlin, and B. Massam (New York: Pergamon Press, 1992), 192.

32. Mfundo Nkuhlu, "Southern Africa After Apartheid: Perspectives on Institutional Arrangements for Multi-Lateral Relations," paper prepared for Workshop on the Correlation of Political Systems and Economic Development in Southern Africa, University of Fort Hare, November 1–2, 1993, 11; Greg Mills, "Introduction," in *War and Peace in Southern Africa,* ed. Robert I. Rotberg and Greg Mills (Washington, D.C.: Brookings Institution Press, 1998), 21.

33. A third organization, the Preferential Trade Area (PTA), which was changed to the Common Market for Eastern and Southern Africa (COMESA), is not considered here because it included states outside of the region and was largely dismissed in South Africa as a vehicle for regional cooperation/integration. Christopher Clapham called it "amorphous and virtually meaningless"; *Africa and the International System: The Politics of State Survival* (New York: Cambridge University Press, 1996), 118. The African Development Bank's extensive study on regional integration in Southern Africa also focused on the SADC rather than the PTA. There was a considerable amount of debate, nonetheless, over splitting COMESA into a northern and southern region; the latter would be absorbed into the SADC.

34. Although Namibia did not join until independence, when South Africa took over the territory in 1915, it treated the territory as part of the Customs Union.

35. Gore, "International Order," 207.

36. Mfundo Nkuhlu even states that "SACU was never established as an institution intended to foster economic integration." Nkuhlu, "Southern Africa After Apartheid," 6.

37. The original 1969 agreement did have a provision for infant industry protection (Article 6), but any action had to be agreed upon by South Africa. Also, a secret memorandum was attached requiring that protection under Article 6 be used only if such an infant industry could supply at least 60 percent of the Customs Union's demands. James Sidaway and Richard Gibbs label SACU a revenue-sharing agreement

between South Africa and its SACU partners in "SADC, COMESA, SACU: Contradictory Formats for Regional Integration in Southern Africa: Reconfiguring the Region," in *South Africa in Southern Africa: Reconfiguring the Region,* ed. David Simon (Athens: Ohio University Press, 1998), 171.

38. Carol Thompson, "African Initiatives for Development: The Practice of Regional Economic Cooperation in Southern Africa," *Journal of International Affairs* 46 (1992): 132. See also Richard Gibb, "Regional Integration in Post-Apartheid Southern Africa: The Case for Renegotiating the Southern African Customs Union," *Journal of Southern African Studies* 23 (1997): 67–86.

39. Reginald Green, "The Economic Implications of Post-Apartheid Southern Africa: How to Add Ten and One," paper presented at a Conference of the Africa Leadership Forum, Windhoek, September 8–10, 1991.

40. "Botswana Country Paper," prepared for the Workshop on Reconstituting and Democratising the Southern African Customs Union, Gaborone, Botswana, March 7, 1994, 8.

41. Gibb, "Regional Integration in Post-Apartheid Southern Africa," 78. See also Sidaway and Gibb, "SADC, COMESA, SACU: Contradictory Formats for Regional Integration in Southern Africa," 171–173.

42. Michael Matsebula and Vakashile Simelane, "Small Countries within Regional Integration," in *Can South and Southern Africa Become Globally Competitive Economies?* ed. Gavin Maasdorp (New York: St. Martin's Press, 1996), 57.

43. Fredrik Söderbaum, "The New Regionalism and the Quest for Development Cooperation and Integration in Southern Africa," Minor Field Study Series 73, Department of Economics at Lund University, 1996; Paul Kalenga, "Regional Trade Integration in Southern Africa: Critical Policy Issues," Working Paper no. 00/42, Development Policy Research Unit, University of Cape Town, September 2000, 8. There is some evidence, however, that there has been some convergence in terms of GNP growth between the BLSN states and South Africa relative to other countries in the region; ibid.

44. Botswana broke with the Rand Monetary Area, the Common Monetary Area precursor, in 1976 when it created its own currency, the pula, which is not fixed to the rand.

45. When their economies became monetized in the second half of the nineteenth century, the BLS states adopted the South African currency. Namibia did the same after World War I. After the establishment of the South African Reserve Bank in 1921, the South African pound became the sole legal tender in what is today the Common Monetary Area when Bechuanaland (Botswana) joined. The arrangement was formalized in 1974 when Lesotho, Swaziland, and South Africa formed the Rand Monetary Area, although Botswana dropped out. Each country used its own currency for internal transactions and the South African rand for foreign-exchange transactions. All foreign-exchange reserves were held by the South African Reserve Bank in rand. In 1986, a trilateral monetary agreement created the Common Monetary Area, replacing the Rand Monetary Area. It essentially gave the members more autonomy from South Africa. In 1992, Namibia became a member of the Common Monetary Area. The members share a common pool of exchange reserves and maintain current accounts in the South African Reserve Bank, while each can use its own currency (the dollar in Namibia, the lilangeni in Swaziland, and the loti in Lesotho), held at par value with the rand.

46. Colin McCarthy, "SACU and the Rand Zone," in *Regionalisation in Africa: Integration and Disintegration,* ed. Daniel C. Bach (Bloomington: Indiana University Press, 1999), 162.

47. It later added Mauritius, the Democratic Republic of Congo, and the Seychelles.

48. The original members of the Front-Line States were Angola, Botswana, Mozambique, Tanzania, Zambia, and Zimbabwe, and Namibia joined when it became independent. It was formed in 1976. Botha reiterated South Africa's CONSAS idea in 1979.

49. Thompson, "African Initiatives for Development," 132.

50. SADC Secretariat, "Management of Regional Cooperation," unpublished paper, SADC, Gaborone, 1994, 9.

51. James Mittelman, *The Globalization Syndrome: Transformation and Resistance* (Princeton, N.J.: Princeton University Press, 2000), 116.

52. Balefi Tsie, "States and Markets in the Southern African Development Community (SADC): Beyond the Neo-Liberal Paradigm," *Journal of Southern African Studies* 22 (1996): 75.

53. Fredrik Söderbaum, "The New Regionalism in Southern Africa," *Politeia* 17 (1998): 85.

54. See, for instance, the Development Bank of Southern Africa (DBSA) study, Lolette Kritzinger-van Niekerk, ed., *Towards Strengthening Multisectoral Linkages in SADC* (Midrand: DBSA, March 1997).

55. Hurrell, "Explaining the Resurgence of Regionalism," 336.

56. Arne Tostensen, "What Role for SADC(C) in the Post-Apartheid Era?" in *Southern Africa After Apartheid: Regional Integration and External Resources,* ed. Bertil Odén (Uppsala: Scandinavian Institute of African Studies, 1993), 151.

57. Simba Makoni, "Getting Down to Brass Tacks," *Southern African Economist* 4, no. 2 (April/May 1991): 13. See also South African Consulate General, "Interdependence and Co-operation in Southern Africa," South African Briefing Paper no. 3/90, February 1990, for an analysis of South Africa's regional role that has an implicit bias toward bilateralism.

58. Carol Thompson, *Harvests under Fire: Regional Cooperation for Food Security in Southern Africa* (Atlantic Highlands, N.J.: Zed Books, 1991), 5.

59. South African Consulate General, "Interdependence and Co-operation in Southern Africa," 3.

60. Tostensen, "What Role for SADC(C)?" 150. Mfundo Nkuhlu called it the default option. Nkuhlu, "Southern Africa After Apartheid," 13.

61. Söderbaum, "The New Regionalism," *Politeia* 17 (1998): 86.

62. Michael Schulz, Fredrik Söderbaum, and Joakim Ojendal, "Introduction: A Framework for Understanding Regionalism," in *Regionalization in a Globalizing World,* ed. Michael Schulz, Fredrik Söderbaum, and Joakim Ojendal (London: Zed Books, 2001), 28.

63. Although I do not build on the "New Regionalism" approach, my framework can complement such an approach. Björn Hettne, for instance, stated that it was appropriate to explore the options of single states and the underlying power structures determining their external orientation. "The New Regionalism: A Prologue," in *The New Regionalism and the Future of Security and Development,* ed. Björn Hettne, András Inotai, and Osvaldo Sunkel (New York: St. Martin's Press, 2000), xix.

64. Andrew Moravcsik, "Taking Preferences Seriously: A Liberal Theory of International Politics," *International Organization* 51 (1997): 517.

65. Ibid., 515.

66. Ibid., 533.

67. Oran Young, "Political Discontinuities in the International System," *World Politics* 20 (1968): 369–392. Haas also acknowledged this shortcoming; *The Uniting of*

Europe: Political, Social and Economic Forces, 1950–1957 (Stanford, Calif.: Stanford University Press), xiv–xv.

68. Andrew Axline, "Underdevelopment, Dependence and Integration: The Politics of Regionalism in the Third World," *International Organization* 37 (1977): 101.

69. Richard Higgott, "Africa and the New International Division of Labour," in *Africa in Economic Crisis,* ed. John Ravenhill (New York: Columbia University Press, 1986), 297.

70. William Martin, "Region Formation under Crisis Conditions: South vs. Southern Africa in the Interwar Period," *Journal of Southern African Studies* 16 (1990): 112–138. In 1929, the Southern Rhodesian government requested a revision of the customs agreement with South Africa of 1925. But South Africa used the occasion to press for greater trade advantages. In particular, it sought to limit Southern Rhodesia's exports of tobacco and cattle, further enhancing South Africa's trade surplus with Southern Rhodesia.

71. Björn Hettne explains that in the case of Latin America, the failures of regional cooperation were due to the market-oriented mode of integration, which reproduced *dependencia* within the region. Björn Hettne, "Neomercantilism and the Pursuit of Regionalism," *Cooperation and Conflict* 28 (1993): 226.

72. C. S. Eliot Kang, "Regulating Inward Foreign Direct Investment," *International Organization* 51 (1997): 307. For a discussion on how an open-economy approach and the institutionalist approach are natural complements, see Robert Keohane, "Problematic Lucidity: Stephen Krasner's 'State Power and the Structure of International Trade'," *World Politics* 50 (1997): 169.

73. Björn Hettne, "Globalization and the New Regionalism: The Second Great Transformation," in *Globalism and the New Regionalism,* ed. Björn Hettne, András Anotai, and Osvaldo Sunkel (New York: St. Martin's Press, 1999), xv.

74. The linkage between finance and industrial capital is important for two reasons: industrialists can finance expansion without state funds and will share bankers' policy preferences; Sylvia Maxfield, *Governing Capital: International Finance and Mexican Politics* (Ithaca, N.Y.: Cornell University Press, 1990), 49.

75. Michael Bratton and Nicolas van de Walle, *Democratic Experiments in Africa: Regime Transitions in Comparative Perspective* (New York: Cambridge University Press, 1997), 10.

76. Ibid.

2. Setting the Stage

1. Peter B. Evans, Dietrich Rueschemeyer, and Theda Skocpol, "On the Road toward a More Adequate Understanding of the State," in *Bringing the State Back In,* ed. Peter B. Evans, Dietrich Rueschemeyer, and Theda Skocpol (New York: Cambridge University Press, 1985), 348.

2. Ian Taylor, *Stuck in Middle GEAR: South Africa's Post-Apartheid Foreign Relations* (Westport, Conn.: Praeger, 2001), 38.

3. The apartheid state's foundation was well established before Afrikaner rule; its basic form was the colonial state. See Clifton Crais, *The Politics of Evil: Magic, State Power, and the Political Imagination in South Africa* (New York: Cambridge University Press, 2002), 31. Apartheid's immediate roots can be traced to the 1920s, as symbolized by the 1927 Native Administrative Act. Ibid., 146.

4. Some South Africa politicians, as well, imagined southern Mozambique being incorporated into a larger union.

5. Peter C. J. Vale, *Security and Politics in South Africa: The Regional Dimension* (Boulder, Colo.: Lynne Rienner, 2003), 50.

6. Merle Lipton, *Capitalism and Apartheid: South Africa, 1910–1986* (London: Wildwood House, 1989), 22.

7. James Barber and John Barratt, *South Africa's Foreign Policy: The Search for Status and Security 1945–1988* (New York: Cambridge University Press, 1990), 29.

8. The three processes are my categorization of Alf Stadler's explanation of the rise of White power in South Africa in *The Political Economy of Modern South Africa* (London: Croom Helm, 1987), 76–77.

9. Hermann Giliomee, *Surrender without Defeat: Afrikaners and the South African Miracle* (Johannesburg: South African Institute of Race Relations, 1997), 11.

10. Stephen John Stedman, "South Africa: Transition and Transformation," in *South Africa: The Political Economy of Transformation,* ed. Stephen John Stedman (Boulder, Colo.: Lynne Rienner, 1994), 11.

11. Peter Vale notes that as early as the late 1960s, the O'Dowd thesis, which stated that apartheid would be brought down by capitalism, was debated within South Africa. Vale, *Security and Politics,* 75.

12. At this time, though it was dominated by Afrikaners, the United Party was the National Party's opposition in Parliament.

13. Barber and Barratt, *South Africa's Foreign Policy,* 31.

14. Lipton, *Capitalism and Apartheid,* 40.

15. Andre du Pisani, "Ventures into the Interior: Continuity and Change in South Africa's Regional Policy (1948–1991)," in *Southern Africa at the Crossroads: Prospects for the Political Economy of the Region,* ed. Anthoni van Nieuwkerk and Gary van Staden (Johannesburg: South African Institute of International Affairs, 1991), 191.

16. The CCTA consisted of two representatives each from the governments of Belgium, France, Portugal, the Federation of Rhodesia and Nyasaland, the Union of South Africa, and the United Kingdom.

17. The members of the CSA were appointed by the CCTA and were not government representatives.

18. In 1922, despite Smuts's intense lobbying, Southern Rhodesia rejected incorporation into the Union of South Africa by a vote of 8,774 to 5,989. Antony Verrier, *The Road to Zimbabwe* (London: Jonathan Cape, 1986), 30.

19. At the Lobatse Conference in October 1962, it became the official military wing of the ANC.

20. D. Hobart Houghton, *The South African Economy* (London: Oxford University Press, 1980), 212–232.

21. A "laager" is the traditional Afrikaner circling of the wagons, connoting a stubborn resistance to outward pressures. Barber and Barratt, *South Africa's Foreign Policy,* 91.

22. Ibrahim A. Gambari, "The United Nations," in *From Cape to Congo: Southern Africa's Evolving Security Challenges,* ed. Mwesiga Baregu and Christopher Landsberg (Boulder, Colo.: Lynne Rienner, 2003), 266.

23. The 1956 Tomlinson Commission's study on South Africa's homeland policy in fact included the HCT states.

24. Deon Geldenhuys, *The Diplomacy of Isolation: South African Foreign Policy Making* (New York: St. Martin's Press, 1984), 25.

25. Kenneth Grundy, *Confrontation and Accommodation in Southern Africa* (Berkeley: University of California Press, 1973), 38.

26. F. J. Cronje, "Can a Free Trade Association Be Created in Southern Africa?" *Optima* 15 (1965): 113–118.

27. Hein Marais, *South Africa: Limits to Change: The Political Economy of Transition* (New York: Zed Books, 1998), 38. Marais is regarded as one of South Africa's best political journalists and is the former editor of *Work in Progress.*

28. Nicoli Nattrass and Jeremy Seekings, "Growth, Democracy, and Expectations in South Africa," in *Economic Globalization and Fiscal Policy,* ed. Iraj Abedian and Michael Biggs (Cape Town: Oxford University Press, 1998), 27–35.

29. Houghton, *The South African Economy,* 230. The tension between the ruling NP and South African business was not new. During Verwoerd's premiership, the South African Chamber of Industries had called for consultation between Blacks and Whites for greater peace and stability.

30. Ibid., 216.

31. Stephen Lewis, *The Economics of Apartheid* (New York: Council on Foreign Relations, 1990), 24. It is important to note that the 10 percent share of mining was a historical low just before the freezing of the international gold price in 1971.

32. Houghton, *The South African Economy,* 231.

33. Deon Geldenhuys, *The Diplomacy of Isolation: South African Foreign Policy Making* (New York: St. Martin's Press, 1984), 30.

34. Joseph Hanlon, *Beggar Your Neighbours* (Bloomington: Indiana University Press, 1986), 11.

35. Robert Davies and Dan O'Meara, "The State of Analysis of the Southern African Region: Issues Raised by South African Strategy," *Review of African Political Economy* No. 29 (1984): 68.

36. Marais, *South Africa: Limits to Change,* 46.

37. Houghton, *The South African Economy,* 242.

38. Anthony W. Marx, *Lessons of Struggle: South African Internal Opposition, 1960–1990* (New York: Oxford University Press, 1992), 149.

39. Albert Robinson, "Statement of the Chairman to the Annual Meeting of the Johannesburg Consolidated Investment Co.," Johannesburg, November 1977, 3, cited in Robert Price, *The Apartheid State in Crisis: Political Transformation in South Africa* (New York: Oxford University Press, 1991), 90.

40. Lipton, *Capitalism and Apartheid,* 179.

41. The title of a 1961 pamphlet, *Looking Outward,* published by the South African Institute of Race Relations (SAIRR), was the first use of the term.

42. Ariston Chambati, "South Africa in African Politics," paper prepared for the South African Institute of International Affairs Symposium, June 6–7, 1975, Johannesburg, South Africa, 1.

43. Ibid., 9.

44. *Southern Africa Record,* no. 3 (Johannesburg: South African Institute of International Affairs), 31–32, cited in Ronald Ballinger and Gerrit Olivier, "Détente in Southern Africa: Two Views" (Johannesburg: The South African Institute of International Affairs, 1976).

45. *Southern Africa Record,* no. 2 (Johannesburg: The South African Institute of International Affairs), 10, cited in Ballinger and Olivier, "Détente in Southern Africa."

46. One of the underlining causes for the "Lisbon Coup" was the strain of fighting the anticolonial forces in Angola and Mozambique. Both became independent in 1975.

47. Barber and Barratt, *South Africa's Foreign Policy,* 181.

48. "Statement by the South African Prime Minister, The Hon. B. J. Vorster, in the Senate, Cape Town, 23 October, 1974," cited in Denis Worrall, "The Republic of South Africa and Detente," edited version of an address to a meeting of the Institute of International Affairs, Salisbury, June 24, 1974, 5.

49. Grundy, *Confrontation and Accommodation in Southern Africa,* 269.

50. Colin Legum, *Vorster's Gamble for Africa: How the Search for Peace Failed* (London: Rex Collings, 1976), 28–29.

51. Grundy, *Confrontation and Accommodation in Southern Africa,* 252.

52. Barber and Barratt, *South Africa's Foreign Policy,* 134.

53. Grundy, *Confrontation and Accommodation in Southern Africa,* 34.

54. SAIIA and SAIRR are both prominent academic think tanks in South Africa. SAIIA is an independent nongovernmental organization which aims to promote a wider and more informed understanding of international issues among South Africans. SAIRR, which was founded in 1929, supports the struggle for constitutional and economic liberalism.

55. Barber and Barratt, *South Africa's Foreign Policy,* 114.

56. Price, *The Apartheid State,* 158.

57. Stephen Lewis, *The Economics of Apartheid,* 23, 29.

58. Lipton, *Capitalism and Apartheid,* 53.

59. For instance, Vorster had sought to reform sports, but that caused a right-wing backlash in some public facilities; he also sought less strict enforcement of the Mixed Marriages and Immorality Acts. Botha accepted the 1979 Riekert Commission's recommendation that restrictions on Black African businessmen in townships be relaxed and the Wiehahn Commission's recommendation that the exclusion of Blacks from certain jobs be ended. Botha's break with Verwoerd's policy of suppressing the development of a Black middle class was a conscious effort to create a Black segment of the population with a stake in the system.

60. Barber and Barratt, *South Africa's Foreign Policy,* 292.

61. T. R. H. Davenport, *South Africa: A Modern History,* 3rd ed. (South Africa: Macmillan, 1987), 452, cited in Barber and Barratt, *South Africa's Foreign Policy,* 291.

62. Price, *The Apartheid State,* 196.

63. *Leadership* 7, no. 6 (1988): 32, cited in Robert Price, "Majority Rule in South Africa: The Role of Global Pressure," in *Toward Peace and Security in Southern Africa,* ed. Harvey Glickman (Philadelphia: Gordon and Breach Science Publishers, 1990), 95.

64. Marx, *Lessons of Struggle,* 168.

65. Colin Vale, "South Africa on a Derelict Continent," Occasional Paper no. 6, South African Institute of International Affairs, Johannesburg, 1982, 20.

66. Ibid.

67. Deon Geldenhuys, "South Africa: The Politics of International Unpopularity," paper presented at the South African Institute of International Affairs and the South African Institute of Race Relations symposium Where in the World Is South Africa? Johannesburg, November 1977, 6.

68. Robert Davies and Dan O'Meara, "Total Strategy in Southern Africa: An Analysis of South African Regional Policy Since 1978," *Journal of Southern African Studies* 11 (1985): 188.

69. Robert Rotberg, "Decision Making and the Military in South Africa," in *South Africa and Its Neighbors: Regional Security and Self-Interest,* ed. Robert Rotberg, Henry Bienen, Robert Legvold, and Gavin Maasdorp (Lexington, Mass.: Lexington Books, 1985), 21.

70. "South Africa: The Government in Shadows," *Africa Confidential* 28, no. 14 (1987): 1. The most important study of the role of South Africa's security establishment in the formation and direction of the Total National Strategy is Philip Frankel's *Pretoria's Praetorians: Civil-Military Relations in South Africa* (Cambridge: Cambridge University Press, 1984).

71. The first six points dealt essentially with domestic political matters: 1) multinationalism; 2) vertical differentiation and self-determination; 3) a constitutional structure for Blacks; 4) the division of power between Whites and the Indian and Coloured populations; 5) separate communities/group areas; and 6) removing hurtful and unnecessary discriminatory measures. Point 7 addressed the South African economy with specific reference to the interdependence between the different ethnic

groups of South Africa. The eleventh and twelfth points were, at their core, also domestic factors: 11) to facilitate effective decision making by the state; and 12) to promote free enterprise.

72. Deon Geldenhuys, "Some Foreign Policy Implications of South Africa's 'TNS' with Particular Reference to the 12 Point Plan," South African Institute of International Affairs, Johannesburg, March 1991.

73. Peter C. J. Vale, "Some Thoughts on the Political Economy of Control," in *The Constellation of States,* ed. Willie Breytenbach (Johannesburg: South Africa Foundation, 1980), 28.

74. Deon Geldenhuys and Denis Venter, "A Constellation of States: Regional Co-operation in Southern Africa," *International Affairs Bulletin* 8, no. 3 (1979): 40.

75. Geldenhuys, "Some Foreign Policy Implications," 19.

76. Jesmond Blumenfeld, *Economic Interdependence in Southern Africa: From Conflict to Cooperation* (New York: St. Martin's Press, 1991), 152.

77. Theo Malan, "The South African Black States' and Neighboring Black Africa's Response to South Africa's Proposed Constellation of Southern African States," in *The Constellation of States,* ed. Willie Breytenbach (Johannesburg: South Africa Foundation, 1980), 63.

78. Davies and O'Meara, "Total Strategy in Southern Africa," 198.

79. Hanlon, *Beggar Your Neighbours,* 2.

80. For a review of the bureaucratic infighting during this period, see Elling Njal Tjonneland, "Pax Pretoria: The Fall of Apartheid and the Politics of Regional Destabilization," Discussion Paper 2, Scandinavian Institute of African Studies, Uppsala, 1989, 19–29; and Geldenhuys, *The Diplomacy of Isolation.*

81. Hanlon, *Beggar Your Neighbours,* 2.

82. Price, *The Apartheid State,* 95.

83. Barber and Barratt, *South Africa's Foreign Policy,* 321.

84. There is a vast amount of literature on the sanctions campaign against South Africa. An excellent recent compendium is Neta Crawford and Audie Klotz, eds., *How Sanctions Work: Lessons from South Africa* (New York: St. Martin's Press, 1999).

85. Barber and Barratt, *South Africa's Foreign Policy,* 324.

86. Rotberg, "Decision Making and the Military in South Africa," 1.

87. Gilbert M. Khadiagala, "The Front Line States, Regional Interstate Relations and Institution Building in Southern Africa," in *Toward Peace and Security in Southern Africa,* ed. Harvey Glickman (Philadelphia: Gordon and Breach Science Publishers, 1990), 133.

88. Davies and O'Meara, "Total Strategy in South Africa," 205.

89. For a detailed and thorough analysis of CODESA II, see Steven Friedman, ed., *The Long Journey: South Africa's Quest for a Negotiated Settlement* (Johannesburg: Raven Press, 1993); and Timothy Sisk, *Democratization in South Africa: The Elusive Social Contract* (Princeton, N.J.: Princeton University Press, 1995).

90. Friedman, *The Long Journey,* 156.

91. Ibid., 179.

3. Debating the Future

1. "SA, SADC to Meet to Form Regional Trade Bloc," *Southern African Report* 9, no. 8 (February 22, 1991): 12. NAFCOC, which was founded in 1964, is an independent and nonprofit business association that represents the joint interest of South Africa's Black traders and manufacturers. During the apartheid regime, the visibility of NAFCOC was limited by legislation aimed at minimizing the influence of Black business entities. But in the wake of the political reforms in the early 1990s, the organization positioned itself as a vocal force for Black economic empowerment in the

new South Africa. It focused particularly on supporting small- and medium-sized enterprises, which constitute 90 percent of NAFCOC's membership base.

Despite NAFCOC's increased political profile, the organization has continuously found it difficult to make a significant impact on the conditions of the private business sector, mainly because NAFCOC has been financially and operationally constrained by a lack of financial resources and manpower. As a result, in September 2002, a new executive body was elected at the annual NAFCOC Federal Council summit. The new management immediately initiated a restructuring process with the objective of positioning NAFCOC as a more efficient business association that focused on creating a better business environment. The newly structured organization seeks to lead the unity process between Black and White businesses in the country.

2. *The Star* (Johannesburg), June 1, 1993, 2B.

3. ANC, "Ready to Govern: ANC Policy Guidelines for a Democratic South Africa Adopted at the National Conference, 28–31 May 1992" [1992].

4. Author's interview with David Brink, Chief Executive, Sankorp Limited, member of National Economic Council, Business Forum, Sandton, South Africa, February 3, 1994.

5. The TEC was composed of representatives of political parties that had settled upon a draft constitution in December 1993. It became operational in January 1994 and was granted some autonomous power vis-à-vis the de Klerk government. It operated in practice as a parallel or partner body to the government.

6. Robert Davies, "Emerging South African Perspectives on Regional Cooperation and Integration After Apartheid," *Transformation* 20 (1992): 75.

7. Robert Davies, R. Keet, and M. Nkuhlu, "Reconstructing Economic Relations with the Southern African Region: Issue and Options for a Democratic South Africa," Centre for Development Studies, Cape Town, September 1993, 1.

8. What is important is that the extent of institutionalization depends on the preference of policymakers and interest groups. Edward Mansfield and Helen Milner, "The New Wave of Regionalism," *International Organization* 53 (1999): 617.

9. Fredrik Söderbaum, "The New Regionalism and the Quest for Development Cooperation and Integration in Southern Africa," Minor Field Study Series 73, Department of Economics, Lund University, 1996.

10. "ANC's Foreign Policy Must Catch Up with a Reinvented World," *Business Day* (Johannesburg), April 8, 1994, 6.

11. Arne Tostensen, "What Role for SADC(C) in the Post-Apartheid Era?" in *Southern Africa After Apartheid: Regional Integration and External Resources,* ed. Bertil Odén (Uppsala: The Scandinavian Institute of African Studies, 1993), 152. Tostensen is an expert on Southern Africa and the SADCC/SADC who was directly involved in debate concerning the role of the SADC. He is co-author of *Southern Africa: In Search of a Common Future*, which was commissioned and published by the SADC.

12. Chris Alden, "From Liberation Movement to Political Party: ANC Foreign Policy in Transition," *South African Journal of International Affairs* 1 (1993): 77.

13. ANC, "Ready to Govern," 44.

14. Chris Louw, "Manuel Warns of Apartheid Web," *Die Suid-Afrikaan,* October–November 1992, 2–22, cited in Thomas Ohlson and Stephen John Stedman, *The New Is Not Yet Born: Conflict Resolution in Southern Africa* (Washington, D.C.: The Brookings Institution, 1994), 265.

15. Trevor Manuel, "Address to the SADC Annual Consultative Conference," unpublished paper, January 16–31, 1993, Harare, Zimbabwe. Available at SADC headquarters in Gaborone, Botswana.

16. Business, of course, while not the ANC's core constituency, had gone a long way toward improving relations with the ANC. In a curious final act, it was an

Anglo-American Corporation private jet that ferried the negotiating parties back and forth and led to an eleventh-hour agreement between the ANC and Inkatha Freedom Party that allowed the April 1994 election to go forward.

17. Thus, although the ANC remained an elite organization, it also was concerned with subaltern politics. Clifton Crais, *The Politics of Evil: Magic, State Power, and the Political Imagination in South Africa* (New York: Cambridge University Press, 2002), 143.

18. Trevor Manuel, "Address to the SADC Annual Consultative Conference."

19. Robert Davies, R. Keet, and M. Nkuhlu, "Reconstructing Economic Relations with the Southern African Region: Issue and Options for a Democratic South Africa," 1st ed., Centre for Development Studies, Cape Town, September 1993, 62.

20. Thabo Mbeki, Speech to the South African Institute of International Affairs, Jan Smuts House, Johannesburg, November 25, 1993.

21. Nelson Mandela, "South Africa's Future Foreign Policy," *Foreign Affairs* 72 (1993): 88.

22. Chinyamata Chipeta and Robert Davies, "Regional Relations and Cooperation: Post-Apartheid Southern Africa—A Macro Framework Study Report," SADC, Gaborone, 1993, 2.

23. ANC, "Reconstruction and Development Programme" (draft for discussion purposes only, for ANC regions and departments only), February 17, 1994, 6. (Hereafter RDP.)

24. Davies, Keet, and Nkuhlu, "Reconstructing Economic Relations with the Southern African Region," 33.

25. Alfred Nzo, "Address to SADCC," May 5–8, 1990, 4.

26. Dot Keet, "Labour Issues in Southern Africa: Critical Choices for Trade Unions," in *Prospects for Progress: Critical Choices for Southern Africa,* ed. Minnie Venter (Cape Town: Longman, 1994), 127.

27. Gavin Maasdorp and Alan Whiteside, "Project on Rethinking Economic Cooperation in Southern Africa," paper prepared for the Regional Integration Conference, Harare, 1992, 52.

28. Robert Davies and Judith Head, "The Future of Mine Migrancy in the Context of Broader Trends in Migration in South Africa," *Journal of Southern African Studies* 21 (1995): 440; Gavin Maasdorp and Alan Whiteside, *Rethinking Economic Cooperation in Southern Africa: Trade and Investment* (Johannesburg: Konrad-Adenauer Stiftung, 1993), 45.

29. RDP, 6.

30. The SADC's post-apartheid call for a free trade area did have a backlash within South Africa's labor-intensive sector.

31. Keet, "Labour Issues in Southern Africa," 127.

32. SATUCC is a body formed to coordinate the trade union activities of the SADC. All major national trade union centers from the Southern African region are affiliated with SATUCC. It served as a major avenue of influence for COSATU in the process of regional integration/cooperation in Southern Africa.

33. Drew Forrest, "COSATU Drive Fuels Regional Movement," *Weekly Mail,* May 10, 1991, 11.

34. "Draft Social Charter of Fundamental Rights of Workers in Southern Africa" [1991], cited in Robert Davies, "Emerging South African Perspectives on Regional Cooperation and Integration After Apartheid," *Transformation* 20 (1992): 75–87.

35. Keet, "Labour Issues in Southern Africa," 119.

36. See Evance Kalula, "Labour Perspectives in Regional Interdependence," in *Prospects for Progress: Critical Choices for Southern Africa,* ed. Minnie Venter, 108–115 (Cape Town: Longman, 1994), 113.

37. This group is usually considered to be conservative and is more likely to move to the right of the NP, to the Conservative Party, than to the left.

38. Author's interview with Erich Leistner, Former Director, Africa Institute, Pretoria, November 8, 1993; author's interview with A. J. Jacobs, Senior Economist, ABSA Bank, Johannesburg, November 15, 1993.

39. Author's interview with Professor Joseph Poolman, Executive Director, Afrikaans Handelsinstituut, Pretoria, April 20, 1994.

40. Robert Davies, "Emerging South African Perspectives," 80; Davies, Keet, and Nkuhlu, "Reconstructing Economic Relations with the Southern African Region," 34.

41. *Financial Times* (London), November 17, 1992.

42. Gilbert M. Khadiagala, "Southern Africa's Transition: Prospects for Regional Security," in *South Africa: The Political Economy of Transformation,* ed. Stephen John Stedman (Boulder, Colo.: Lynne Rienner, 1994), 176. Ohlson and Stedman call this the "cooperation without transformation" approach; *The New Is Not Yet Born,* 278.

43. Naomi Chazan, Robert Mortimer, John Ravenhill, and Donald Rothchild, *Politics and Society in Contemporary Africa,* 2nd ed. (Boulder, Colo.: Lynne Rienner, 1992), 82.

44. Robert Davies, "Creating an Appropriate Institutional Framework," in *Prospects for Progress: Critical Choices for Southern Africa,* ed. Minnie Venter (Cape Town: Longman, 1994), 5.

45. Jan Isaksen, "Prospects for SACU," in *Southern Africa After Apartheid: Regional Integration and External Resources,* ed. Bertil Odén (Uppsala: The Scandinavian Institute of African Studies, 1993), 189.

46. Bill Keller, "Same Old Bureaucracy Serves New SA," *New York Times,* June 4, 1994.

47. The coordinator of the International Relations Department of the DBSA stressed the importance of the view the new government would inherit from the old system. Author's interview with Brian Bench, Coordinator of International Relations, Development Bank of Southern Africa, Midrand, South Africa, February 14, 1994. The political analyst for the Northern Transvaal Chamber of Commerce averred that the influence of the South African civil service in the short term would grow. Author's interview with Dr. Booysen, Political Analyst, Northern Transvaal Chamber of Industries, Pretoria, South Africa, February 10, 1994.

48. Hermann Giliomee, "The Last Trek? Afrikaners in the Transition to Democracy," *South African International* 22 (January 1992): 118.

49. *Business Day* (Johannesburg), November 11, 1993.

50. Patti Waldmeir, "A New Nation Takes Shape," *Business Day* (Johannesburg), November 22, 1993, 5.

51. Author's interview with C. T. Hattingh, South Africa Department of Trade and Industry, Pretoria, South Africa, February 28, 1994. SACOB's nonparticipation in subsequent meetings may have been due to its strong support for ad hoc cooperation.

52. Gavin Maasdorp, "A Vision for Economic Integration and Cooperation in Southern Africa," Department of Trade and Industry, Government of South Africa, March 1994, 3 (hereafter Maasdorp Report).

53. Author's interview with C. T. Hattingh, South Africa Department of Trade and Industry, Pretoria, South Africa, November 8, 1994.

54. "SADCC's Arrival a Damp Squid," *Weekly Mail,* April 15, 1993.

55. Umesh Kumar, "Uruguay Round and the Southern African Customs Union," paper presented at the Workshop on Reconstituting and Democratising the Southern African Customs Union, Gaborone, Botswana, March 6–8, 1994, 105.

56. Peter C. J. Vale, *Security and Politics in South Africa: The Regional Dimension* (Boulder, Colo.: Lynne Rienner, 2003), 36.

57. Author's interview with David Brink, Sandton, South Africa, February 3, 1994. Brink was the former CEO of Murray and Roberts, one of South Africa's largest construction firms, and head of the National Economic Forum's Business Forum.

58. Maasdorp Report, 23.

59. Author's interview with Theo Malan, Central Economic Advisory Service, Pretoria, South Africa, February 18, 1994.

60. Maasdorp Report, 23.

61. The European Free Trade Association consisted of most European countries who were not members of the EU. These countries have now joined the EU.

62. Maasdorp Report, 26.

63. Ibid., 26.

64. Gilbert Khadiagala, "Southern Africa's Transitions," 176.

65. Fantu Cheru, *The Not So Brave New World! Problems and Prospects of Regional Integration in Post Apartheid Southern Africa* (Johannesburg: South African Institute of International Affairs, 1992), 26.

66. P. Smit, "Regional Challenges Facing South Africa," *Southern African Forum Position Paper* 12, 3rd quarter (1989): 11.

67. Dr. Paul J. Vorster, "Interdependence of States in Southern Africa," *Southern African Forum Position Paper* 12, 4th quarter (1989): 1–2.

68. Davies, "Emerging South African Perspectives," 84. One government official stated that Zambia was working behind the scenes for a preferential trade agreement with South Africa. Author's interview with C. T. Hattingh, Department of Trade and Industry, Pretoria, South Africa, February 28, 1994. Zambia, Malawi, and Mozambique had also approached South Africa about bilateral monetary arrangements. Author's interview with P. E. Immelman, Director, Africa Multilateral Department, Department of Foreign Affairs, Pretoria, South Africa, November 8, 1993.

At the time Rob Davies, an expert on regional economic integration/cooperation, was a well-known academic who was closely aligned with the ANC. He had also done work for the SADC. He later became an important ANC member of the South African Parliament.

69. Chinyamata Chipeta and Robert Davies, "Regional Relations and Cooperation: Post-Apartheid Southern Africa—A Macro Framework Study Report," SADC, Gaborone, 1993, 31.

70. This document was prepared for SACOB by Dr. Erich Leistner of the Africa Institute in Pretoria.

71. *Business Day* (Johannesburg), February 25, 1994.

72. SACOB, "South Africa's Options for Future Relations with Southern Africa and the European Community: Discussion Document," October 19, 1992, i.

73. Ibid.

74. Edward Osborn, "An Organization for Southern African Co-operation," *Nedbank Quarterly Guide to the Economy* (Johannesburg: Nedbank Economic Unit, February 1993), 5.

75. SACOB, "South Africa's Options for Future Relations with Southern Africa," 5.

76. Ibid., 1–2.

77. SACOB, "South Africa's Options for Future Relations with Southern Africa," 2. The SACOB view is closer to a "realist" perspective, which sees interdependence as an anathema. The anarchy assumption that all states must provide for their own security in the neorealist tradition leads to the conclusion that states will actively avoid situations of interdependence. The most forceful exposition of this position remains that of Kenneth Waltz. See his *Theory of International Politics,* particularly chapter 7,

and Kenneth N. Waltz, "Reflections on *Theory of International Politics:* A Response to My Critics," in *Neorealism and Its Critics,* ed. Robert O. Keohane (New York: Columbia University Press, 1986).

78. SACOB, "South Africa's Options for Future Relations with Southern Africa," 2.

79. Letter from Edward Osborn to Trevor Manuel, May 5, 1993. COMESA was established under the auspices of the Lagos Plan for Action. As mentioned briefly in the introduction, many attempts at regional economic integration/cooperation in the developing world in general and Africa in particular adopted a model based on the West European experience—the market approach. COMESA was one such case. It formally came into existence in December 1994 but was originally created as the Preferential Trade Area in 1981. It included countries from two different regions, East Africa (as far north as Djibouti and Sudan) and Southern Africa. It did not have a development component and would suffer from the inequalities endemic to market cooperation among developing states. This is, in fact, partially what doomed the East Africa Community (1967–1976) of Kenya, Uganda, and Tanzania. South Africa did not join COMESA. But Osborn's objection to COMESA was as much ideological as practical. COMESA was the creation of the UN East African Commission. So even its relatively limited institutional framework (compared to the SADC) was still seen as a way of making South Africa more interdependent with the rest of Africa.

80. Letter from Edward Osborn to Trevor Manuel, May 5, 1993, 3.

81. SACOB, "South Africa's Options for Future Relations with Southern Africa," 19. For more detail on the notion of the OECD as the model for regional cooperation in Southern Africa, see Erich Leistner, "Designing the Framework for a Southern African Development Community," *Africa Insight* 22, no. 1 (1992): 8–11.

82. Gavin Reilly, "Southern Africa: The Challenges of the 90s—Summary of Workshop and Keynote Address" (Harare: The Institute of Directors, Zimbabwe Division, 1991), 60.

83. Winnie Graham, "SA to Get Chunk of UN's Spending," *Financial Mail,* January 31, 1992. SAFTO, which originated as a service of DTI, provides consultancy services, international market research, market and trade information, training, and networking assistance for companies trying to become involved in exporting. Most of these activities have recently been assumed directly by the DTI and SAFTO has been closed down. The banks provide export financing, including credit guarantees and other assistance programs, as well as export consulting services.

84. Chinyamata Chipeta and Robert Davies, "Regional Relations and Cooperation: Post-Apartheid Southern Africa—A Macro Framework Study Report," SADC, Gaborone, 1993, 26.

85. *The Star* (Johannesburg), May 10, 1994, 6.

86. Davies, "Emerging South African Perspectives," 79.

87. "Don't Presume Too Much! African Trade Doors Are Opening Wider But the Big Uncertainty Is Payment," *Financial Mail,* January 31, 1992.

88. Author's interview with Michael McDonald, Head of Economics Division, Steel and Engineering Industry, Federation of South Africa, Johannesburg, South Africa, March 15, 1994. The NEF was launched by the South African government in October 1992 one year after it was called for by COSATU. It is formally a corporatist body (labor, business, government) that is used to shape a consensus on economic policy.

4. Ideology and the Political Economy of Transitional South Africa

1. Stephen Krasner, "Approaches to the State: Alternative Conceptions and Historical Dynamics," *Comparative Politics* 16 (1984): 228.

2. Emanuel Adler, *The Power of Ideology: The Quest for Technological Autonomy in Argentina and Brazil* (Berkeley: University of California Press, 1987), 11.

3. Michael Bratton and Nicholas van de Walle, *Democratic Experiments in Africa: Regime Transitions in Comparative Perspective* (New York: Cambridge University Press, 1997), 25.

Ideology, however, should not be confused with ideas. Judith Goldstein and Robert Keohane distinguish among three types of beliefs (ideas): worldviews, principled beliefs, and causal beliefs. Judith Goldstein and Robert Keohane, eds., *Ideas and Foreign Policy* (Ithaca, N.Y.: Cornell University Press, 1993). The first two could be included in what John Jacobson calls "consensual beliefs," which, he argues, shape the legitimate ends of economic activity. Jacobson argues that causal beliefs, which would include what he called economic ideas, are the means to achieve socially approved ends. John Kurt Jacobson, "Much Ado about Ideas: The Cognitive Factor in Economic Policy," *World Politics* 47 (1995): 287. As Thomas Biersteker points out, the change in development discourse evident in the resurgence of neoliberalism is an example of ideas as causal beliefs. Thomas Biersteker, "The 'Triumph' of Liberal Economic Ideas in the Developing World," in *Global Change, Regional Responses,* ed. Barbara Stallings (New York: Cambridge University Press, 1995), 180. In this process, economic ideas, or in more general terms, "stated causal beliefs," are instrumental for pursuing particular ends defined as "consensual beliefs." Ideology comes closer to the notion of "consensual beliefs." Thus, although the substantive issue area of this chapter is economic policy, including economic ideas, it concerns basic ideological beliefs and, therefore, is about socially approved ends, not "causal beliefs." Judith Goldstein, *Ideas, Interests, and American Trade Policy* (Ithaca, N.Y.: Cornell University Press, 1993), 11.

4. James J. Hentz, "The Two Faces of Privatization: Political and Economic Logics in Transitional South Africa," *Journal of Modern African Studies* 38 (2000): 203; Thomas A. Koelble, *The Global Economy and Democracy in South Africa* (New Brunswick, N.J.: Rutgers University Press, 1998).

5. "Trade Minister Prescribes Middle Route between Laissez Faire and Intervention," BBC Summary of World Broadcasts, September 6, 1995.

6. Tom Lodge, *Politics in South Africa: From Mandela to Mbeki* (Bloomington: Indiana University Press, 2002), 21–22.

7. Ketso Gordhan, "Should South Africa Get Involved with the International Monetary Fund and the World Bank?" in *What Has the IMF in Store for South Africa? Proceedings of a Symposium Held on 27th July 1991 at the Soweto College of Education* (Johannesburg: Institute for African Alternatives, 1991), 9–12.

8. GATT, *Trade Policy Review: The Republic of South Africa,* vol. 1 (Geneva: GATT, 1993), 12.

9. ISI is a policy by which a country tries to substitute its imports, particularly light manufactured goods such as furniture, textiles, and shoes, with its own manufactured goods.

10. "Introduction," in *State and Market in Post-Apartheid South Africa,* ed. Merle Lipton and Charles Simkins (Boulder, Colo.: Westview Press, 1993), 9–10.

11. Ibid., 15.

12. Ian Taylor, *Stuck in Middle GEAR: South Africa's Post-Apartheid Foreign Relations* (Westport, Conn.: Praeger, 2001), 58.

13. Kevin Davie, "The New South African Economy," in *What Has the IMF in Store for South Africa? Proceedings of a Symposium Held on 27th July 1991 at the Soweto College of Education* (Johannesburg: Institute for African Alternatives, 1991), 3–6.

14. Patrick Bond, *Elite Transition: From Apartheid to Neoliberalism in South Africa* (London: Pluto Press, 2000), 97–102.

15. Anthony W. Marx, *Lessons of Struggle: South African Internal Opposition, 1960–1990* (New York: Oxford University Press, 1992).

16. Ibid., 120.

17. Ibid., 138.

18. Robert Britt Horwitz, *Communication and Democratic Reform in South Africa* (New York: Cambridge University Press, 2001), 14.

19. Ibid., 257.

20. Author's interview with T. Malan, Economist, Central Economic Advisory Service, Pretoria, March 18, 1994. Malan pointed out that, in fact, the document was accompanied with a disclaimer stating that it was not an NP policy document.

21. Greta Stein, "MERG Poses Serious Challenge to Government's Economic Model," *Business Day* (Johannesburg), December 1, 1993, 10.

22. On the limited impact of MERG on actual policy, see Taylor, *Stuck in Middle GEAR*, 71–74; and Hein Marais, *South Africa: Limits to Change: The Political Economy of Transition* (New York: Zed Books, 1998), 158–160.

23. Bond states that the RDP became policy in 1994 largely because of COSATU, which was directly tied to MERG; *Elite Transitions*, 89. In fact, while MERG quickly faded from the front lines of the debate, the RDP reflects the tension between the ANC leadership and its base. Taylor, *Stuck in Middle GEAR*, 73.

24. Horwitz, *Communication and Democratic Reform*, 16; Peter C. J. Vale, *Security and Politics in South Africa: The Regional Dimension* (Boulder, Colo.: Lynne Rienner, 2003), 79. Keynesianism supports government intervention to maintain adequate levels of employment and to smooth out the bumps in the business cycle.

25. Bond, *Elite Transitions*, 97.

26. Desmond Lachman and Kenneth Bercuson, "Economic Policies for a New South Africa," Occasional Paper 91, International Monetary Fund, Washington, D.C., January 1992, vii.

27. Marais, *South Africa: Limits to Change*, 150.

28. Lodge, *Politics in South Africa*, 21.

29. Lipton and Simkins, eds., *State and Market*, 15.

30. Marina Ottaway, *South Africa: The Struggle for a New Order* (Washington, D.C.: The Brookings Institution, 1993), 48.

31. Jeffrey Herbst, "Economic Crisis and Distributional Imperative," in *South Africa: The Political Economy of Transformation*, ed. Stephen John Stedman (Boulder, Colo.: Lynne Rienner, 1994), 33.

32. Peter Vale labeled the Freedom Charter as Keynesianism; *Security and Politics*, 78.

33. MERG, *Making Democracy Work: A Framework for Macroeconomic Policy in South Africa: A Report to the Democratic Movement of South Africa* (Bellville, South Africa: Centre for Development Studies: 1993), 25. (Hereafter MERG Report.)

34. RDP, 40. On the privatization process in South Africa, see James J. Hentz, "The Two Faces of Privatization."

35. Andre du Pisani, "Post-Settlement South Africa and the Future of Southern Africa," *Issue: A Journal of Opinion* 21 (1993): 64.

36. "Policy Plan Omits Forced Unbundling: MERG Proposes Anti-Trust Caution," *Business Day* (Johannesburg), December 6, 1993, 1. Padraig Carmody, in fact, has shown that unbundling ultimately led to an increase in the Afrikaner share of the Johannesburg Stock Exchange from 24 to 36 percent from 1996–1999. "Between Globalization and (Post) Apartheid: The Political Economy of Restructuring in South Africa," *Journal of Southern African Studies* 28 (2002): 265.

37. MERG Report, 215.

38. The BTI was responsible for setting tariff levels and administering tariff policies in apartheid South Africa. Its policies were largely responsible for building South Africa's mineral-energy complex. After a drawn-out bureaucratic battle during the transition period, the BTI was renamed the Trade and Industry Advisory Board. The BTI's new role was to advise the Department of Trade and Industry. Ben Fine and Zavareh Rustomjee, *The Political Economy of South Africa* (London: Westview Press, 1996), 202.

39. Ibid.

40. Ibid. However, parastatals used the IDC to finance the development of heavy industry through support for state corporations.

41. Marx, *Lessons of Struggle.*

42. RDP, 40.

43. MERG Report, 266.

44. Ibid., 265.

45. RDP, 42, 41, 46.

46. "Foreword" in *The Reconstruction of the South African Economy: A Normative Model Approach,* compiled by the Central Economic Advisory Service, in close consultation with the South African Reserve Bank, government departments, and other bodies and the Special Economic Adviser to the Minister of Finance who acted as coordinator (Pretoria, March 1993). Hereafter NEM.

47. NEM, 53.

48. NEM, 25.

49. NEM, 29. Public-fixed investment is government investment in tangible assets such as roads.

50. Ibid., 209.

51. Ibid., 34, 250, 232, 3.

52. The World Bank and the IMF are not always in agreement. In fact, the World Bank has advised some African countries against further borrowing from the IMF on conventional terms. Dr. Japie Jacobs, special economic advisor to the South African Minister of Finance, says that although there is a general opinion that the roles of the IMF and the World Bank in the developing world are converging, the World Bank does not impose the same standards of conditionality and is more lenient about fiscal discipline. Japie Jacobs, "The IMF and South Africa: Implications for Fiscal Policy," address at the Workshop on Democratisation in South Africa: Economic Structural Adjustment and the Role of the IMF, The Strand, November 18, 1993, 4.

53. The IMF is traditionally more concerned with finance, that is, with balance-of-payments constraints; the World Bank, with project lending. The line distinguishing their missions, however, has become increasingly blurred.

54. MERG Report, 6.

55. World Bank, "An Economic Perspective on South Africa," World Bank, Southern Africa Department, Washington, D.C., May 1993, 5.

56. Ibid., 10.

57. NEM, 29.

58. World Bank, "An Economic Perspective on South Africa," 15.

59. Ibid., 7.

60. Lachman and Bercuson, "Economic Policies," 13; World Bank, "An Economic Perspective on South Africa," 7.

61. It should be noted that the time frame of the study is the medium term. Lachman and Bercuson, "Economic Policies," 14.

62. World Bank, "An Economic Perspective on South Africa," 1.

63. Lachman and Bercuson, "Economic Policies," 14; World Bank, "An Economic Perspective on South Africa," 6; NEM, 6; MERG Report, 71, 6. While the IFIs

were more closely aligned ideologically with the NP and with the NEM, their ideas did influence the ANC. It would be pushing the argument too far to say that the ANC was compelled to accept IFI ideas. Rather, they were convinced. As South African political scientist Tom Lodge reports, critics of ANC economic policy accused top ANC economic staffers such as Trevor Manuel and Tito Mboweni of being intellectually corrupted by encounters with officials of the World Bank. Lodge, *Politics in South Africa,* 22.

64. MERG Report, 3.

65. RDP, 45.

66. However, the manufacturing sector is a poor producer and, because it is so import-dependent, contributes little to the accumulation of foreign exchange. Ibid., 40.

67. MERG Report, 223.

68. RDP, 50.

69. Ibid., 172.

70. Ibid.

71. Ibid.

72. MERG Report, 155.

73. NEM, 169, 176.

74. Ibid., 26.

75. Ibid., 26.

76. Ibid., 34, 180.

77. Sven Lunsche, "Pay Cut Will Boost Jobs, Claims IMF," *Sunday Times/Business Times* (Johannesburg), March 27, 1994, 3.

78. World Bank, "An Economic Perspective on South Africa," 13.

79. Ibid., 12.

80. MERG Report, 152–153.

81. The MERG Report states on the first page of chapter 7: "MERG supports the approach taken by the industrial strategy project (ISP) sponsored by COSATU. . . . This chapter draws freely upon ISP work" (212).

82. MERG Report, 152.

83. Lunsche, "Pay Cut Will Boost Jobs, Claims IMF," 5.

84. MERG Report, 161.

85. NEM, 39.

86. Ibid.

87. Ibid., 53, 47.

88. Ibid., 43.

89. Ibid., 45, 30.

90. Ibid., 49.

91. Ibid., 97.

92. The MERG Report argues that the government in the past has focused much too much on inflation; 71.

93. Ibid. 7.

94. Ibid., 52.

95. Ibid., 256; RDP, 43; MERG Report, 16.

96. MERG Report, 48.

97. Ibid., 12.

98. MERG Report, 61.

99. NEM, 62.

100. Ibid., 95.

101. Ibid., 191, 57.

102. Ibid., 117.

103. Ibid., 115.

104. NEM, 115. The MERG Report blames the 1985 debt crisis on a failure of government policy. It states, "The uncontrolled accumulation of short-term debt in the early 1980s has made a major contribution to the severity of the debt crisis. The Reserve Bank appeared to have had no idea of the extent of foreign debt, or the nature of the maturity structure" (69).

105. Lachman and Bercuson, "Economic Policies," 1; NEM, 104; Lachman and Bercuson, "Economic Policies," 16.

106. MERG Report, 60.

107. Ibid., 27, 48, 6.

108. Greta Steyn, "MERG Poses Serious Challenge to Government's Economic Model," *Business Day* (Johannesburg), December 1, 1993, 10.

109. "State Intervention to Help Business," *Business Day* (Johannesburg), February 15, 1994, 5.

110. Sven Lunsche, "An Underground Struggle," *The Star* (Johannesburg), February 12, 1994, 1.

111. Erica Jankowitz, "Cheap Labour Is No Panacea, Says Shilowa," *Business Day* (Johannesburg), December 2, 1993, 4.

112. Claire Gebhardt, "Bankers under the Whip," *The Star* (Johannesburg), February 4, 1994, 12.

113. Claire Gebhardt, "Bankers Hammer ANC Proposals," *The Star* (Johannesburg), February 3, 1994, 1.

114. Edward West, "Bank Says ANC Plan Lacks Clarity," *Business Day* (Johannesburg), April 22, 1994, 4.

115. Claire Gebhardt, "National Party Messed Up," *The Star* (Johannesburg), February 10, 1994.

116. Kevin Dacie, "Economic Freedom Paves Way to Success," *Sunday Times, Business Times* (Johannesburg), March 6, 1994.

117. Ciaran Ryan, "Anger over ANC's Ideas on Mining," *Sunday Times, Business Times* (Johannesburg), January 30, 1994, 3.

118. "NUM Urges Socialist Running of Mines," *The Star* (Johannesburg), February 17, 1994, 1.

119. The more radical element of the ANC dominated its mining policy.

120. Ciaran Ryan, "Anger over ANC Ideas on Mining," *Sunday Times, Business Times* (Johannesburg), January 30, 1994, 3; Sven Lunsche, "An Underground Struggle," *The Star* (Johannesburg), February 12, 1994, 13.

121. "To Nationalize or Not to Nationalize: That Is the Question," *Business Day* (Johannesburg), February 11, 1994, 12.

122. "State Intervention to Help Business," *Business Day* (Johannesburg), February 15, 1994, 5.

123. MERG Report, 40.

124. "Government Should Spur Demand," *Business Day* (Johannesburg), November 17, 1994, 3. The Compensatory Financing Facility was established in 1963 to help countries cope with temporary exogenous shocks that affected export earnings without resorting to undue and unnecessary adjustment. Once eligibility has been established and access determined (based on the size of the shock and an assessment of the member's past and future cooperation with the Facility), a purchase is made available with no further conditions attached. Coverage was expanded in 1979 to include shortfalls in receipts from tourism and workers' remittances and again in 1981 to include higher costs of cereal import.

125. RDP, 74.

126. MERG Report, 68.

127. Klaus Meyer, Saul Estrin, Suman Bhaumik, Stephen Gelb, Helb Handooussa, Maryse Louis, Subir Gokarn, Laveesh Bhandari, Nguyen Than Ha, and Nguyen Vo Hung, "Foreign Direct Investment in Emerging Markets: A Comparative Study in Egypt, India, South Africa and Vietnam," paper presented at the 6th conference of the European Association of Comparative Economic Studies, Forli, Italy, June 2002, 8.

128. Gumisiai Mutume, "South Africa's Economy Joining the World Loan Queue?" Inter Press Service, October 12, 1995. South Africa successfully reached an agreement with the IMF to facilitate repayment to its international creditor banks. *The Citizen,* September 28, 1994, 1.

129. Alan Hirsch, "Trading Up: Towards a Trade Policy for Industrial Growth in South Africa," Industrial Strategy Project Draft Final Report, Development Policy Research Unit, University of Cape Town, August 1993, 54–55.

130. NEM, 4. In stark contrast, the RDP states, "The pressure of the world economy and the operations of international organizations such as the International Monetary Fund (IMF), World Bank, and GATT affect our neighbors and South Africa in differing ways. In the case of our neighbors, they were pressured into implementing programmes with adverse effects on employment and standards of living" (6).

131. NEM, 22, 57, 61, 172.

5. South Africa's Political Economy in Transition

1. For a history of the relationship between finance capital and industry in South Africa, see Ben Fine and Zavareh Rustomjee, *The Political Economy of South Africa* (Boulder: Westview Press, 1996).

2. Colin McCarthy, "Structural Development of South African Manufacturing Industry—A Policy Perspective," *The South African Journal of Economics* 56 (1988): 3.

3. SACOB, "The Formulation of a New Industrial Policy for South Africa: Discussion Document," Johannesburg, South Africa, September 1993, 4.

4. McCarthy, "Structural Development of South African Manufacturing Industry," 3.

5. Renfrew Christie, "Report to Jim Mullins on South Africa's National Research Strategy," University of the Western Cape, November 23, 1992, 1.

6. Magan Mistry, "The Trade Pattern of Southern Africa," *Nedbank Guide to the Economy,* Nedbank Economic Unit, Johannesburg, February 1992.

7. Charles Harvey and Carolyn Jenkins, "The Unorthodox Response of the South African Economy to Changes in Macroeconomic Policy," draft, March 12, 1992, 19. In author's possession.

8. Merle Lipton, *Capitalism and Apartheid: South Africa, 1910–1986* (London: Wildwood House, 1989), 57; Stephen Lewis, *The Economics of Apartheid* (New York: Council on Foreign Relations, 1990), 11. The Pact Government was an alliance of the NP and Labour that won the election in 1924.

9. South Africa actually has a long tradition of state involvement in the economy. Nancy Clark, for instance, states that "[t]he origins of direct state intervention in the South African economy rest in policies adopted in the nineteenth century by the government of the Zuid Afrikaansch Republic (ZAR) to strengthen itself against African neighbors and British imperialists." *Manufacturing Apartheid* (New Haven, Conn.: Yale University Press, 1994), 13.

10. Lewis, *The Economics of Apartheid,* 58.

11. Stadler, *The Political Economy of Modern South Africa,* 33.

12. Lewis, *The Economics of Apartheid,* 24.

13. African Development Bank, "Economic Integration in Southern Africa: Executive Summary," African Development Bank, Abidjan, Ivory Coast, [1993], 255.

The African Development Bank was established in 1963 by the OAU to promote economic and social development in Africa.

14. Lewis, *The Economics of Apartheid,* 57.

15. Nicoli Nattrass, "Economic Power and Profits in Post-War Manufacturing," in *The Political Economy of South Africa,* ed. N. Nattrass and E. Ardington (Cape Town: Oxford University Press, 1990), 117.

16. In his seminal 1938 study, S. H. Frankel argued that the South African government was siphoning off profits from gold mining and using the money to protect uneconomic manufacturing; *Capital Investment in Africa: Its Courses and Effects* (London: Oxford University Press, 1938), 114–118.

17. Nattrass, "Economic Power and Profits in Post-War Manufacturing," 123.

18. Clark, *Manufacturing Apartheid,* 10.

19. Anthony Black, "The Role of the State in Promoting Industrialization," in Lipton and Simkins, eds., *State and Market,* 230.

20. Harry Oppenheimer, *The Future of Industry in South Africa* (Johannesburg, 1950), cited in Clark, *Manufacturing Apartheid,* 134.

21. Black, "The Role of the State in Promoting Industrialization," 208.

22. Trevor Bell, "Should South Africa Further Liberalise Its Trade?" in Lipton and Simkins, eds., *State and Market,* 83.

23. The former called for uniformity in assistance and thereby for giving more importance to the market. The Kleu Report argued for a greater role for exports in industrial policy to facilitate more cooperation between import replacement and export promotion but with the caveat that there should be moderate protection so that a significant part of the South African market could be preserved for its own manufactures.

24. GATT, *Trade Policy Review,* vol. 1, 3.

25. Ibid.

26. Bell, "Should South Africa Further Liberalise Its Trade?" 95, 209.

27. Ibid., 87–89.

28. Alan Hirsch, "Trading Up: Towards a Trade Policy for Industrial Growth in South Africa," Industrial Strategy Project Draft Final Report, Development Policy Research Unit, University of Cape Town, Cape Town, South Africa, August 1993, 26. Formula duties were South Africa's attempt to protect certain goods without using an ad valorem tariff (which charges a specified percentage of the value of an imported good). Formula duties in South Africa were a nontransparent system of import reference prices (that is, the tax depended on a specified import price).

29. GATT, *Trade Policy Review,* vol. 1, 5.

30. Under the GEIS, with certain exceptions, all exports qualify for assistance, which is tied to the stage of production and local content of the export. The GEIS was considered a success, although it did more for South Africa's traditional capital-intensive industries than for labor-intensive industries.

31. GATT, *Trade Policy Review,* vol. 1, 26. Nonferrous metals contain either no iron or only insignificant amounts used as an alloy. Some of the more common nonferrous metals that steelworkers work with are copper, brass, bronze, copper-nickel alloys, lead, zinc, tin, aluminum, and duralumin.

32. SACOB, "The Formulation of a New Industrial Policy for South Africa," Foreword.

33. Black, "The Role of the State in Promoting Industrialization," 213–214. Formula duties are aimed at low-price imports. They have the effect of protecting certain uncompetitive industries and allowing them to remain uncompetitive. See also Alan Hirsch, "Trading Up," viii.

34. Black, "The Role of the State in Promoting Industrialization," 216. The

local-content program for motor vehicles was part of the so-called structural reforms. Under the structural adjustment program, by exporting, South Africa producers could import duty-free intermediaries or finished goods.

35. Kevin Lings, "Export Incentives in South Africa," *Nedbank Guide to the Economy* (Johannesburg: Nedbank Economic Unit, November 1991).

36. Economic Trends Research Group was a research and policy outfit for the ANC and COSATU from the late 1980s to the early 1990s. It was initially led by South African economist Stephen Gelb.

37. ISP, "Industrial Strategy Project," 1993, 19.

38. Avril Joffe, David Kaplan, Raphale Kaplinsky, and David Lewis, "Meeting the Global Challenge: A Framework for Industrial Revival in South Africa," in *South Africa and the World Economy in the 1990s,* ed. Pauline Baker, Alex Boraine, and Warren Krafchik (Washington, D.C. Brookings Institution, 1993), 92.

39. Hirsch, "Trading Up," 52.

40. Steph Naude, "Evolving International Trade Policy in South Africa," South Africa Department of Trade and Industry, October 28, 1993, 20, 22.

41. See D. Hobart Houghton, *The South African Economy* (London: Oxford University Press, 1980), 216.

42. Pedro Belli, Michael Finger, and Amparo Ballivian, "South Africa: A Review of Trade Policies," Discussion Paper 4, The World Bank, Southern Africa Department, Washington, D.C., 1993, 28–29.

43. SACOB, "The Formulation of a New Industrial Policy for South Africa," 13. M. Holden's study of the relationship between growth in exports and manufacturing in South Africa between 1947 and 1987 was less conclusive. Total exports and manufacturing output had "bi-directional causality" in the sense that exports influenced manufacturing growth and in turn manufacturing growth influenced export growth. M. Holden, "The Choice of Trade Strategy," in Nattrass and Ardington, eds., *The Political Economy,* 263.

44. The African Development Bank study states that the IDC's approach in most respects is identical to the World Bank's position on trade reform. African Development Bank, "Economic Integration in Southern Africa," 274.

45. Joffe, Kaplan, Kaplinsky, and Lewis, "Meeting the Global Challenge," 99.

46. Ibid.

47. GATT, *Trade Policy Review,* vol. 1, 10–11.

48. Edward Osborn and Kevin Lings, "Capital Intensity in the Manufacturing Sector," paper presented at the EBM Research Conference, Vista University, Port Elizabeth, South Africa, November 30–December 1, 1992, 14.

49. GATT, *Trade Policy Review,* vol. 1, 10.

50. Nattrass, "Economic Power and Profits in Post-War Manufacturing," 115–116.

51. Clark, *Manufacturing Apartheid,* 117.

52. GATT, *Trade Policy Review,* vol. 1, 10.

53. However, there is not total agreement on this. Colin McCarthy argued, "On the basis of the 1970–82 growth experience, it appears justifiable to conclude that the conventional wisdom, which holds that consumer-oriented light industries such as food, clothing, textiles, and furniture are the ideal vehicles for the promotion of direct employment opportunities, may be doubted. The 1970–82 experience indicates that there is no reason why these industries should receive priority in an employment-oriented development over industries such as the chemical and metal sectors." McCarthy, "Structural Development of South African Manufacturing Industry," 13.

54. Hirsch, "Trading Up," 85.

55. For the export of large capital projects, for instance, the Department of Trade and Industry subsidized the interest rate to the same level as the consensus interest

rate of the OECD countries. Paul R. Hatty, "The South African Trade Policy Debate: A Business Perspective," in Baker, Boraine, and Krafchik, eds., *South Africa and the World Economy in the 1990s*, 132–133.

56. Chris Alexander Pagel, "Areas of Competitive Advantage in South African Manufacturing" (MA Thesis, Rand Afrikaans University, November 1992), 49.

57. ISP, "Industrial Strategy Project," 5.

58. Hirsch, "Trading Up," 73.

59. John Zysman, *Governments, Markets, and Growth: Financial Systems and the Politics of Industrial Change* (Ithaca, N.Y.: Cornell University Press, 1983), 37.

60. SACOB, "The Formulation of a New Industrial Policy for South Africa," 24–25.

61. Lings, "Export Incentives in South Africa."

62. Hirsch, "Trading Up," 19.

63. Black, "The Role of the State in Promoting Industrialization," 231.

64. Deloitte and Touche, "Building Global Manufacturing Competitiveness: Annual International Manufacturing Survey 1993 South African Results," internal company report for Deloitte and Touche, [1993], 4.

65. Bell, "Should South Africa Further Liberalise Its Trade?" 88.

66. McCarthy, "Structural Development of South African Manufacturing Industry," 19. The Klue Report was commissioned in 1983 by South Africa. It argued for an outward-looking policy.

67. Ibid., 16.

68. ISP, "Industrial Strategy Project," 19. Rent-seeking here refers to the state's behavior of using its position in the economy to extract resources.

69. Here I am not interested in which sectors are more or less competitive but rather in the link between policy and politics.

70. Because most of South Africa's export had components that were imported, paradoxically making imports more expensive also made the final product for export more expensive.

71. Belli, Finger, and Ballivian, "South Africa: A Review of Trade Policies," Table 6.

72. Sanjaya Lall, "What Will Make South Africa Internationally Competitive?" in Baker et al., eds., *South Africa*, 61.

73. Hirsch, "Trading Up," 43.

74. ISP, "Industrial Strategy Project," 18.

75. Colin McCarthy, "South Africa as a Cooperative Partner in Southern African Trade and Investment," paper presented at the Regional Economic Integration Conference, Harare, December 3–4, 1992, 12.

76. Lall, "What Will Make South Africa Internationally Competitive?" 61.

77. SACOB, "A Concept for the Development of a New Industrial Policy for South Africa," SACOB, Johannesburg, May 30, 1991, Table 14, 44.

78. Belli, Finger, and Ballivian, "South Africa: A Review of Trade Policies," 21.

79. The local-content program began in 1961 with Phase I, whose goal was to increase local content of cars by mass or weight from 15 percent to 40 percent. By stages the local content was increase to 66 percent by 1982.

80. Sheila Page and Christopher Stevens, "Trading with South Africa: The Policy Options for the EC," ODI Special Report, Overseas Development Institute, London, 1992, 35.

81. Hirsch, "Trading Up," xi, 132.

82. Joffe, Kaplan, Kaplinsky, and Lewis, "Meeting the Global Challenge," 95.

83. Lall, "What Will Make South Africa Internationally Competitive?" 65.

84. Ibid., 147.

85. ISP, "Industrial Strategy Project," 20.

86. Ibid.

87. SACOB, "The Formulation of a New Industrial Policy for South Africa," 9. There were claims that capital-intensive industry would best promote employment growth. Pagel, for example, argues, "These sectors, iron and steel, chemicals, metal and pulp paper, are not only the large exporters in manufacturing, but they also constitute the large employers." Pagel, "Areas of Competitive Advantage."

88. Lings, "Export Incentives in South Africa."

89. Jonathan Garner and Lynne Thomas, "South Africa's Trade Partners, 1986–1991," Research Paper no. 6, Centre for the Study of the South African Economy and International Finance, London, 1991, 1.

90. GATT, *Trade Policy Review,* vol. 1, 31.

91. Page and Stevens, "Trading with South Africa," 24.

92. Maasdorp Report, 10.

93. Ibid.

94. Of the six non-SACU countries that are members of the SADC, only two, Angola and Tanzania, were under 15 percent.

95. For a thorough discussion of this, see Rashad Cassim, "The Determinants of Intra-Regional Trade in Southern Africa with Specific Reference to South Africa and the Rest of the Region," Development Policy Research Unit, Working Papers no. 01/51, June 2001.

96. An example of South Africa's trade finance capability is the "export credit re-insurance" scheme of the Department of Trade and Industry and the Credit Guarantee Insurance Corporation of Africa, Ltd., which provides insurance and financing facilities to exporters to cover commercial, political, and transfer risks.

97. Robert Davies, "Emerging South African Perspectives on Regional Cooperation and Integration After Apartheid," *Transformation* 20 (1992): 77–78.

98. Page and Stevens, "Trading with South Africa," 27.

99. Belli, Finger, and Ballivian, "South Africa: A Review of Trade Policies," 18.

100. For a similar argument, see Leo Katzen, "The Employment Problem in Post-Apartheid South Africa," in *Sustainable Development for a Democratic South Africa,* ed. Ken Cole (New York: St. Martin's Press, 1994), 52. He argues that chemicals have a comparatively poor production record compared with clothing, footwear, wood products, and furniture.

101. Brian Levy, "How Can South African Manufacturing Efficiently Create Employment? An Analysis of the Impact of Trade and Industrial Policy," Southern Africa Department, World Bank, Washington, D.C., 1992, 45.

102. For an overview of South's Africa's regional industrial policy see A. H. Black, "Decentralization Incentives and Investment in the South African Periphery," in *Industrialization and Investment Incentives in Southern Africa,* ed. Alan Whiteside (Portsmouth, N.H.: Heinemann, 1989).

103. African Development Bank, "Economic Integration, Executive Summary," 257–258.

6. Banking, Finance, Monetary Policy, and Globalization in South Africa

1. Geoffrey Garrett, "Governing in the Global Economy: Economic Policy and Market Integration around the World," paper presented at the American Political Science Association 1998 Annual Meeting, Boston, Mass., 1998, 6.

2. Rodney Galpin, "Southern Africa: A Region of New Potential," *Modern Africa* (April/May 1992): 15.

3. South Africa's history is as much about banking and finance as it is about mining. For an interesting narrative, see Geoffrey Wheatcroft, *The Landlords: The Exploits and Exploitations of South Africa's Mining Magnates* (New York: Atheneum, 1986).

4. Patrick Bond, *Elite Transition: From Apartheid to Neoliberalism in South Africa* (London: Pluto Press, 2000), 47.

5. African Development Bank, "Economic Integration in Southern Africa: Executive Summary," African Development Bank, Abidjan, Ivory Coast [1993], 7.

6. Author's interview with Bryan Bench, Coordinator of International Relations, Development Bank of Southern Africa, Midland, South Africa, February 14, 1994.

7. Author's interview with Dave Brown, Managing Director, Stanbic Bank, Botswana Unlimited, Gaborone, Botswana, March 23, 1994.

8. Author's interview with Herbie E. Schultz, International Relations Department, Amalgamated Banks of South Africa, Johannesburg, South Africa, November 15, 1993.

9. Author's interview with Alister Morphet, Head, Africa Division, First Merchant Bank, Johannesburg, South Africa, March 1, 1994.

10. Howard W. French, "Out of South Africa, Progress (Apartheid's End Is Helping Revitalize a Continent)," *The New York Times,* July 6, 1995, Sec. D, 1.

11. Lynne Duke, "South Africans Looks North, Invests in Neighbors," *Washington Post,* November 6, 1997, A30.

12. Hein Marais, *South Africa: Limits to Change: The Political Economy of Transition* (London: Zed Books, 1998), 136.

13. Charles Harvey and Carolyn Jenkins, "The Unorthodox Response of the South African Economy to Changes in Macroeconomic Policy," draft, unpublished paper, March 12, 1992, 22.

14. Harvey and Jenkins, "The Unorthodox Response," 8.

15. Chris Stals, "South African Exchange Rate Policy: A Reserve Bank Perspective," in *South Africa and the World Economy in the 1990s,* ed. Pauline Baker, Alex Boraine, and Warren Krafchik (Washington, D.C.: Brookings Institution, 1993), 138.

16. GATT, *Trade Policy Review,* vol. 2, 39, 16.

17. Trevor Bell, "Should South Africa Further Liberalise Its Trade?" in *State and Market in Post-Apartheid South Africa,* ed. Merle Lipton and Charles Simkins (Boulder, Colo.: Westview Press, 1993), 95.

18. Brian Kahn, Abdel Senhadji, and Michael Walton, "South Africa: Macroeconomic Issues for Transition," *Informal Discussion Papers on Aspects of the Economy of South Africa* 2 (1992): 4–6, cited in Jeffrey Herbst, "Economic Crisis and Distributional Imperative," in *South Africa: The Political Economy of Transformation,* ed. Stephen John Stedman (Boulder, Colo.: Lynne Rienner, 1994), 31.

19. ISP, "Industrial Strategy Project (ISP)," unpublished paper, 1993.

20. Anthoni van Nieuwkerk, "Foreign Policy-Making in South Africa: Exploring Context, Actors, and Processes," paper presented at the 19th World Congress of the International Political Science Association, Durban, South Africa, July 1, 2003, 11.

21. Rashad Cassim, "The Political Economy of Trade Negotiations in Post-Apartheid South Africa," paper presented at the Conference on the Politics of Economic Reform, University of Western Cape, Cape Town, South Africa, January 16–18, 1998, 18.

22. GATT, *Trade Policy Review: The Republic of South Africa,* vol. 2 (Geneva: GATT, 1993), 6.

23. I use David Andrews's definition for capital mobility: "The capacity of capital to cross borders rather than the actual flows of money." Andrews, "Capital Mobility and State Autonomy," *International Studies Quarterly* 38 (1994): 195.

24. Janine Aron and Ibrahim Elbadawi, "Reflections on the South African Rand Crisis of 1996 and Policy Consequences," Centre for the Study of African Economics, Working Paper Series no. 97, Institute of Economics and Statistics, Oxford University, 5. Available online at http://www.bepress.com/cgi/viewcontent.cgi?article=1098&context=csae.

25. GATT, *Trade Policy Review,* vol. 2, 29.

26. Herbst, "Economic Crisis and Distributional Imperative," 35.

27. African Development Bank, "Finance," in *Regional Integration in Southern Africa,* vol. 2 (Abidjan: African Development Bank, 1994), 3/189–190.

28. Aron and Elbadawi, "Reflections on the South African Rand Crisis of 1996," 15.

29. "World Bank Takes a Delicate Approach to SA," *Business Day* (Johannesburg), December 7, 1993, 4.

30. Herbst, "Economic Crisis and Distributional Imperative," 35.

31. Such duplication could be expected not only for typical patronage reasons but also to keep tabs on suspect Afrikaner civil servants. The "sunset clause," originally the idea of Joe Slovo, a leader of the South Africa Communist Party, guaranteed civil servants their jobs if the ANC won. Of course the ANC did win, and through early buyouts and other mechanisms it was able replace NP loyalists with ANC personnel more quickly.

32. "Mandela: Africa Can Succeed," Associated Press, June 9, 1994.

33. "South Africa Looks to Equality in U.S. Trade Relations," Reuters News Service, June 5, 1994.

34. See Margaret Hanson and James J. Hentz, "Neocolonialism and Neoliberalism in South Africa and Zambia." *Political Science Quarterly* 114 (1999): 479–502.

35. There is a large literature on this, from both theoretical and policy perspectives. For the former, see Robert Keohane and Helen Milner, eds., *Internationalization and Domestic Politics* (New York: Cambridge University Press, 1996), particularly Geoffrey Garrett and Peter Lang's contribution. For a critical analysis of the effects of increased capital mobility, see Will Hutten, "Relaunching Western Economies: The Case for Regulating Financial Markets," *Foreign Affairs* 75 (1996): 8–12.

36. See, for instance, Paul Williams and Ian Taylor, "Neoliberalism and the Political Economy of the 'New' South Africa," *New Political Economy* 5 (2000): 36.

37. Capital controls and trade barriers were common across many developing countries in the 1960s. Richard Cooper, *The Economics of Interdependence* (New York: Council on Foreign Relations, 1968), 143.

38. Padraig Carmody, "Between Globalisation and (Post) Apartheid: The Political Economy of Restructuring in South Africa," *Journal of Southern African Studies* 28 (2002): 257.

39. Author's interview with Pete Gloster, Assistant General Manager, GM Exchange Control, South African Reserve Bank, Pretoria, South Africa, November 23, 1993.

40. Address of Dr. Chris Stals, Governor of the South African Reserve Bank, at the Europe and Africa Business and Finance Forum, Cannes, June 17, 1996.

41. Brian Kahn, "South African Exchange Rate Policy, 1979–1991," Research Paper no. 7, Centre for the Study of the South African Economy and International Finance, London School of Economics, 1992, 10.

42. Geoffrey Garrett, "Capital Mobility, Exchange Rates and Fiscal Policy in the Global Economy," *Review of International Political Economy* 7 (2000): 166.

43. Jeffry Frieden, "Economic Integration and the Politics of Monetary Policy in the United States," in *Internationalization and Domestic Politics,* ed. Robert Keohane and Helen Milner (New York: Columbia University Press, 1996), 111.

44. See Nicoli Nattrass and Jeremy Seekings, "Two Nations? Race and Economic Inequality in South Africa Today," *Daedalus* 130 (2001): 62.

45. Aron and Elbadawi, "Reflections on the South African Rand Crisis of 1996," 14.

46. Sylvia Maxfield, *Governing Capital: International Finance and Mexican Politics* (Ithaca: Cornell University Press, 1990), 26.

47. Stephen Haggard and Chung Lee, "The Political Dimension of Finance in Economic Development," in *The Politics of Finance in Developing Countries,* ed. Stephen Haggard, Chung Lee, and Sylvia Maxfield (Ithaca: Cornell University Press, 1993), 16.

48. "S. Africa's Unions Still Arguing Over Economic Plan," Reuters News Service, August 6, 1996.

49. Brian Kahn, "South African Exchange Rate Policy, 1979–1991," Research Paper no. 7, Centre for the Study of the South African Economy and International Finance, London School of Economics, June 1992, iv.

50. Aron and Elbadawi, "Reflections on the South African Rand Crisis of 1996," 2–3.

51. Chris Stals, "South African Exchange Rate Policy: A Reserve Bank Perspective," in *South Africa and the World Economy in the 1990s,* ed. Pauline Baker, Alex Boraine, and Warren Krafchik (Washington, D.C.: Brookings Institution, 1993), 148.

52. Stals, "South African Exchange Rate Policy," 149.

53. Ian Taylor, *Stuck in Middle GEAR* (Westport, Conn.: Praeger, 2001), 80.

54. Glenn Adler and Eddie Webster, "Bargained Liberalisation: The Labour Movement, Policy-Making and Transition in Zambia and South Africa," paper presented at the 17th World Congress of the International Political Science Association, Seoul, South Korea, August 17–21, 1997.

55. "Markets Tense as S. Africa Weighs Growth Strategy," Reuters News Service, June 11, 1996.

56. Reuters News Service, March 12, 1996.

57. "South Africa Aims for European Investment Boost," Reuters News Service, June 17, 1996.

58. Ian Taylor, *Stuck in Middle GEAR,* 64.

59. NACTU was established in October 1986 through the merger of smaller unions that identified with the Black Consciousness Movement. It was seen as an alternative to the more mainstream COSATU.

60. Nicoli Nattrass and Jeremy Seekings, "Growth, Democracy, and Expectations in South Africa," in *Economic Globalization and Fiscal Policy,* ed. Iraj Abedian and Michael Biggs (Cape Town: Oxford University Press, 1998), 32.

61. "COSATU Discussion Paper: A Draft Programme for the Alliance," November 22, 1996, 2–3; available online at http://www.cosatu.org.za/docs/discuss.html. Two World Bank economists were employed to help draw up GEAR; Taylor, *Stuck in Middle GEAR,* 64.

62. "South Africa Unions Still Arguing Over Economic Plan," Reuters News Service, August 6, 1996.

63. "South Africa: Shilowa Predicts 'Crisis' Within ANC, SACP COSATU Alliance," July 22, 1996, Foreign Broadcast Information Service/Africa.

64. Andrews, "Capital Mobility and State Autonomy," 194.

65. Herbst, "Economic Crisis and Distributional Imperative."

66. Terence Moll, "Macroeconomic Policy in Turbulent Times," in *State and Market in Post-Apartheid South Africa,* ed. Merle Lipton and Charles Simkins (Boulder, Colo.: Westview Press, 1993), 235.

67. Ibid., 259.

68. P. J. Mohr, "Fiscal Policy in South Africa," in *Leading Issues in South African*

Economics, ed. Philip A. Black and Brian Dollery (Johannesburg: Southern Book Publishers, 1989), 287.

7. International Influences and Political Choice in Transitional South Africa

1. "GATT" is used here because most of the interaction I discuss predates the World Trade Organization.

2. There are, of course, other important agencies of the international system that significantly influenced regional economic integration/cooperation in post-apartheid Southern Africa and that actively participated in the debate on the regional dispensation in transitional Southern Africa. For instance, the African Development Bank and the United Nations (particularly through UNCTAD and the ECA) both actively participated in the debate over how to institutionalize the post-apartheid regional dispensation. The African Development Bank's study on regional integration in Southern Africa is the most comprehensive sectoral study on regional integration. However, although the African Development Bank and UN will be mentioned, they are not handled as separate agencies of the international system. In both cases, Southern African countries are important members and in effect could have a strong influence on those agencies' policies.

3. Elaine Friedland, "The Southern African Development Co-ordination Conference and the West: Cooperation or Conflict?" *Journal of Modern African Studies* 23 (1985): 289–290.

4. N. Mwase, "Regional Cooperation and Socialist Transformation in Southern Africa: Problems and Prospects," *Journal of African Studies* 13 (1980): 23; Constantine Vaitsos, "Crisis in Regional Economic Cooperation (Integration) among Developing Countries: A Survey," *World Development* 6 (1978): 727.

5. Richard Weisfelder, "The Southern African Development Coordination Conference (SADCC)," *South Africa International* 13 (1982): 87. Data from the Organisation for Economic Co-operation and Development show that 51 percent of official development assistance from members of its Development Assistance Committee is tied or partially tied to goods and services from the home country; African Development Bank, "Economic Integration in Southern Africa: Executive Summary," African Development Bank, Abidjan, Ivory Coast, 1993, 304.

6. See Jean-Claude Boidin, "Regional Cooperation in the Face of Structural Adjustment" (*The Courier* 112 [1988]: 67) for a thorough description of the national character of SAPs. A similar point is made by the African Development Bank study, "Economic Integration in Southern Africa: A Report for the African Development Bank," African Development Bank, December 1992, Abidjan, Ivory Coast, 1/12; and Thandika Mkandawire, "Dependence and Economic Cooperation: The Case of SADCC," *Zimbabwe Journal of Economics* 2 (1985): 3.

7. Richard Synge, "SADC Tackles Donor Doubts," *Africa Recovery* 7, no. 1 (June 1993), 10.

8. John W. Harbeson and Donald Rothchild, "Africa in Post–Cold War International Politics: Changing Agendas," in *Africa in World Politics,* ed. John W. Harbeson and Donald Rothchild (Boulder, Colo.: Westview Press, 1991), 13.

9. Björn Hettne, "Neomercantilism and the Pursuit of Regionalism," *Cooperation and Conflict* 28 (1993) : 211–232.

10. *Sowetan,* July 11, 1993, 4.

11. It is assumed that the Lomé Accords linking most of Africa to the EU will become weaker rather than stronger over time. The relative importance of Africa in trade with the EU has been declining. In 1976, 11 percent of Europe's imports from outside the European Economic Community originated in Africa; by 1991 it was

8 percent. Christopher Stevens, "Global Trends and Implications for Southern Africa," paper presented at a Workshop on Reconstituting and Democratising the Southern African Customs Union, Gaborone, Botswana, March 6–8, 1994, 4. However, the EU may in fact actually be strengthening its ties to Southern Africa.

12. Author's interview with Len Van Zyl, Chief Executive, South African Foreign Trade Organisation, Sandton, South Africa, December 14, 1993.

13. South African Department of Foreign Affairs, "South African Foreign Policy Discussion Document," Department of Foreign Affairs, Pretoria, [1996].

14. Talitha Bertelsmann-Scott, "The European Union and South Africa: Reaching Agreement?" *SAIIA Reports,* 1998, vi.

15. In fact, until 1984, the SADCC office in Gaborone was staffed by British nationals, who also created its institutional structure.

16. For a detailed chronology of this, see I. Mandaza and A. Tostensen, *Southern Africa in Search of a Common Future: From Conference to a Community* (Gaborone: Southern African Development Community, 1994), 17–23.

17. The European Economic Community originally saw the SADCC as both a way to reduce Southern Africa's dependence on South Africa and a way to provide stability and development. Talitha Bertelsmann-Scott, "The European Union," in *From Cape to Congo: Southern Africa's Evolving Security Challenges,* ed. Mwesiga Baregu and Christopher Landsberg (Boulder, Colo.: Lynne Rienner, 2003), 307, 309.

18. Ravenhill relates that 10 percent of the total development funds to be made available by the European Community under the Lomé Convention has been set aside for the financing of regional development projects; "Regional Integration and Development in Africa," *The Journal of Commonwealth and Comparative Politics* 17 (1978): 245.

19. Author's interview with C. T. Hattingh, South Africa Department of Trade and Industry, Pretoria, South Africa, February 28, 1994.

20. Author's interview with Stef Naude, Former Director-General, Department of Trade and Industry, Pretoria, South Africa, April 26, 1994.

21. Chinyamata Chipeta and Robert Davies, "Regional Relations and Cooperation: Post-Apartheid Southern Africa—A Macro Framework Study Report," SADC, Gaborone, 1993, 42.

22. Gilbert M. Khadiagala, "Southern Africa's Transitions: Prospects for Regional Security," in *South Africa: The Political Economy of Transformation,* ed. Stephen John Stedman (Boulder, Colo.: Lynne Rienner, 1994), 172.

23. World Bank, "Intra-Regional Trade in Sub-Saharan Africa," Economics and Finance Division, Technical Division, Africa Region, World Bank, Washington, D.C., 1991, iii.

24. Tony Hawkins, "Economic Integration in Southern Africa" paper presented at the African Regional Workshop on Economic Integration, Capetown, South Africa, March 2–4, 1994. One 1992 study stated that SAPs had already begun to harmonize exchange rates in Southern Africa; Imani Development Ltd., "Desk Study on Regional Integration in Eastern and Southern Africa: Constraints to Intra-Regional Payments, Trade and Investment," vol. 1: Main Report, January 23 1992, 12.

25. World Bank et al., "Concept Paper: Initiative to Facilitate Cross-Border Private Investment, Trade and Payments in Eastern and Southern Africa and the Indian Ocean," unpublished paper, June 24, 1993, 2.

26. Ibid., 67.

27. African Development Bank, "Economic Integration in Southern Africa, Executive Summary," vi, 16.

28. SACOB, "South Africa's Options for Future Relations with Southern Africa and the European Community: Discussion Document," SACOB, Johannesburg, October 19, 1992, 2.

29. Fantu Cheru, *The Not So Brave New World! Problems and Prospects of Regional Integration in Post-Apartheid Southern Africa* (Johannesburg: South African Institute of International Affairs, 1992), 38.

30. Erich Leistner, "Brussels Conference on Future Relations between the EC and Southern Africa," November 9, 1993 (draft), 2. Leistner was reporting on a meeting convened by the Club de Bruxelles in October 1993.

31. Trevor Bell, "Should South Africa Further Liberalise Its Trade?" in Lipton and Simkins, eds., *State and Market in Post-Apartheid South Africa* (Boulder, Colo.: Westview Press, 1993), 113.

32. Brian Levy, "How Can South African Manufacturing Efficiently Create Employment? An Analysis of the Impact of Trade and Industrial Policy," Southern Africa Department, World Bank, Washington, D.C., 1992.

33. World Bank, *Accelerated Development in Sub-Saharan Africa: An Agenda for Action* (New York: Oxford University Press, 1982).

34. John Ravenhill, "A Second Decade of Adjustment: Greater Complexity, Greater Uncertainty," in *Hemmed In: Response to Africa's Economic Decline,* ed. Thomas Callaghy and John Ravenhill (New York: Columbia University Press, 1993), 25.

35. Author's interview with Erich Leistner, Former Director, Africa Institute, Pretoria, South Africa, November 8, 1993.

36. Ketso Gordhan, "Should South Africa Get Involved with the International Monetary Fund and the World Bank?" in *What Has the IMF in Store for South Africa? Proceedings of a Symposium Held on 27th July 1991 at the Soweto College of Education* (Johannesburg: Institute for African Alternatives, 1991), 9. For a brief review of the involvement of IFIs in South Africa in the early transition period, see Vishnu Padayachee, "Development Implications for South Africa of Using IMF and World Bank Loans and Resources," in *South Africa and the World Economy in the 1990s,* ed. Pauline Baker, Alex Boraine, and Warren Krafchik (Washington, D.C.: Brookings Institution, 1993), 195–199.

37. Chipeta and Davies, "Regional Relations and Cooperation," 33.

38. *The Star* (Business), October 10, 1991.

39. Imani Development, "Desk Study of Regional Integration in Eastern and Southern Africa," 11.

40. Ibid., 64.

41. Thomas Ohlson and Stephen John Stedman, *The New Is Not Yet Born: Conflict Resolution in Southern Africa* (Washington, D.C.: The Brookings Institution, 1994). The Clinton administration's focus on "big emerging markets" included South Africa.

42. Chipeta and Davies, "Regional Relations and Cooperation," 26.

43. Ibid.

44. African Development Bank, "Economic Integration in Southern Africa: A Report for the African Development Bank," December 1992, 1/12.

45. Peter R. Fallon, "The Implications for South Africa of Using World Bank Facilities," in *South Africa and the World Economy in the 1990s,* ed. Pauline Baker, Alex Boraine, and Warren Krafchik (Washington, D.C.: Brookings Institution, 1993), 206.

46. Percy Mistry, "The Present Role of the World Bank in Africa," edited version of a lecture delivered at the Institute for African Alternatives, October 16, 1989, Johannesburg, South Africa, 9.

47. Calculated from *Prior Review Contracts Approved by the World Bank in FY93 by Country of Supplier,* unpublished report, Operations Policy Department, Procurement Policy and Coordination Unit, World Bank, Washington, D.C., January 1994.

48. Calculated from *Prior Review Contracts Approved by the World Bank in FY94 by Country of Supplier,* unpublished report, Operations Policy Department, Procurement Policy and Coordination Unit, World Bank, Washington, D.C., September 1994.

49. Cheru, *The Not So Brave New World!*, 2.

50. Ibid.

51. Robert Davies, "South Africa Joining SADCC or SADCC Joining South Africa? Emerging Perspectives on Regional Cooperation After Apartheid" in Anthoni van Nieuwkerk and Gary van Staden, eds., *Southern Africa at the Crossroads: Prospects for the Political Economy of the Region* (Johannesburg, South African Institute of International Affairs, 1991), 241.

52. World Bank, *Global Economic Prospects and the Developing Countries, 1995* (Washington, D.C.: World Bank, 1995), 21.

53. Rosalind Thomas, "A South African Perspective on SADC Trade and Development Protocol," South Africa, 1997.

54. See Robert Lawrence, *Regionalism, Multilateralism, and Deeper Integration* (Washington, D.C.: The Brookings Institution, 1996), 27–28.

55. David E. Sanger, "Trade Agreement Ends Long Debate, But Not Conflicts," *New York Times,* December 12, 1994, 1.

56. Thomas, "A South African Perspective on SADC Trade and Development Protocol," 15.

57. "Rift Over Ties with EU," *Sunday Times* (Johannesburg), October 17, 1993, 2.

58. Matthew McQueen and Christopher Stevens, "Trade Preferences and Lomé IV: Non-Traditional ACP Exports to the EC," *Development Policy Review* 7 (1989): 239.

59. Christopher Stevens, Jane Kennan, and Richard Ketley, "EC Trade Preferences and Post-Apartheid South Africa," *International Affairs* 69 (1993): 90.

60. McQueen and Stevens, "Trade Preferences," 255.

61. South Africa Department of Trade and Industry, "Basis for Negotiations for a Trade and Development Agreement between the Republic of South Africa and the European Union," cited in *Trading on Development: South Africa's Trade and Development Relations with the European Union,* ed. Rachel Hougton (Johannesburg: Foundation for Global Dialogue, 1997), 164.

62. The mandate from the Council of Ministers was announced in June 1995. It was followed by a second mandate dealing with the particulars of the negotiations between South Africa and the EU.

63. South Africa's SACU partners did not favor a free trade agreement because they would lose the nonreciprocal trade preferences granted under Lomé.

64. Judy Dempsey, "EC and SADC Unveil Plans for Closer Links," *Financial Times,* September 6, 1994.

65. European Union, "Note from the Permanent Representatives Committee to the Council of Ministers on the Subject of South Africa," Brussels, June 14, 1995, in *Trading on Development,* ed. Rachel Houghton, 134.

66. Anne Graumans, "The European Union—South African Negotiations," draft, prepared for the Netherlands Institute for Southern Africa, 1998, 10.

67. *Sunday Times* (Johannesburg), May 21, 1995, 1.

68. The European Development Bank is an EU institution analogous to the World Bank.

69. Stevens, Kennan, and Ketley, "EC Trade Preferences and Post-Apartheid South Africa," 97.

70. Steph Naude, "Evolving International Trade Policy in South Africa," unpublished paper, October 28, 1993, 30.

71. Stephen R. Hurt, "The EU and Africa after the Cold War," in *Africa in International Politics: External Involvement on the Continent,* ed. Ian Taylor and Paul Williams (New York: Routledge, 2004), 164–165.

72. Patricia Lenaghan and Xavier Philippe, "Contents and Influence of the Cotonou Agreement on the Trade and Development Cooperation Agreement," avail-

able online at http://www.uwc.ac.za/ECSA-SA/projects/papers/cotonouagreement.htm; Margaret Lee, "The European Union–South Africa Free Trade Agreement: In Whose Interest?" *Journal of Contemporary African Studies* 20 (2002): 81. The regional economic partnership agreements will enter into force in January 2008 but could have a transition period of twelve years.

73. Clara Mira Salama and Stephen Dearden, "The Cotonou Agreement," Discussion Paper no. 20, European Developmental Policy Study Group, Department of Economics, Manchester Metropolitan University, 2001, 27, 9. Available online at http://www.edpsg.org/Documents/Dp20.doc.

74. The commercial explanation examines South Africa's industrial/trade policy and its macroeconomic/finance policy.

75. Although there were some significant elements in South Africa against any involvement with the IFIs (most representative of this group was the Institute for African Alternatives, a liberal pro-ANC think tank in Johannesburg and its influential director, Ben Turok), the ANC's general stance toward the IFIs became much more moderate.

76. Japie Jacobs, "The IMF and South Africa: Implications for Fiscal Policy," address at the Workshop on Democratisation in South Africa: Economic Structural Adjustment and the Role of the IMF, November 18, 1993, 2. Dr. Jacobs was special economic advisor to the minister of finance in 1993.

77. Graham Bird, "The International Monetary Fund and Developing Countries: A Review of the Evidence and Policy Options," *International Organization* 50 (1996): 477.

78. "The IMF Will Fund SA—Mandela," *The Citizen* (Johannesburg), October, 27, 1993. The ANC's Trevor Manuel was part of the South African negotiating team, which was led by Derek Keys.

79. Jacobs, "The IMF and South Africa," 1.

80. Patrick Bond, *Elite Transition,* 180–181; Hein Marais, *South Africa: Limits to Change,* 157.

81. Alan Hirsch, "Trading Up: Towards a Trade Policy for Industrial Growth in South Africa," Industrial Strategy Project Draft Final Report, Development Policy Research Unit, University of Cape Town, Cape Town, South Africa, August 1993, 16.

82. Alan Hirsch, "The External Environment and the South African Trade Debate," Economic Trends Working Paper no. 13, Development Research Unit, University of Cape Town, Cape Town, 1992, 1, 7.

83. Hirsch, "Trading Up," 51.

84. Industrial Development Corporation, "Modification of the Application of Protection Policy," Industrial Development Corporation, Sandton, South Africa, 1990, 4.

85. World Bank, "Cross-Border Initiative in Eastern and Southern Africa: Regional Integration by Emergence," *Findings* 166 (September 2000); available online at http://www.worldbank.org/afr/findings/english/find166.htm.

86. Ibid.

87. Mauritius was the seventh SADC member to negotiate an SAP with the IMF.

88. Rashad Cassim and Marina Mayer, "Regional Industrial Development," in *Toward Strengthening Multisectoral Linkages in SADC,* ed. Lolette Kritzinger-van Niekerk (Midrand: Development Bank of South Africa, 1997), 57.

89. Rosalind Thomas, "A South African Perspective on the SADC Trade and Development Protocol," paper prepared for the Friedrich Ebert Stiftung Institute, Johannesburg, South Africa, April 1997, 27.

90. Marina J. Mayer and Rosalind Thomas, "Trade Integration in the Southern African Development Community: Prospects and Problems," paper prepared for the Development Bank of Southern Africa, Midrand, 1997, 6.

91. World Bank, "Intra-Regional Trade in Sub-Saharan Africa," World Bank, Economics and Finance Division, Technical Division, Africa Region, Washington, D.C., 1991, iv–v.

92. United Nations Economic and Social Council, "Which Way Economic Integration in Southern Africa? A Review of the Studies Carried Out by the World Bank/IMF/EU and the African Development Bank," paper presented at the African Regional Workshop on Regional Integration, Cape Town, March 24, 1994, 2.

93. Staff of the World Bank, the African Development Bank, the International Monetary Fund, and the Commission of the European Communities, "Concept Paper: Initiative to Facilitate Cross-Border Private Investment, Trade and Payments in Eastern and Southern Africa and the Indian Ocean," June 4, 1993.

94. See Thomas Callaghy, "Africa and the World Economy: Caught between a Rock and a Hard Place," in *African in World Politics,* ed. John Harbeson and Donald Rothchild (Boulder, Colo.: Westview Press, 1991), 60.

95. World Bank, "Intra-Regional Trade Sub-Saharan Africa," 1.

96. Ian Taylor, *Stuck in Middle GEAR,* 107.

97. Rashad Cassim, "The Political Economy of Trade Negotiations in Post-Apartheid South Africa," paper presented at the Conference on the Politics of Economic Reform, Cape Town, South Africa, January 16–18, 1988, 2.

98. *Business Day* (Johannesburg), October 31, 1993, 5.

99. Hirsch, "Trading Up," 4. The Uruguay Round ended in Marrakesh in April 1994. It created the World Trade Organization.

100. Umesh Kumar, "Uruguay Round and the Southern African Customs Union," paper presented at the Workshop on Reconstituting and Democratising the Southern African Customs Union, Gaborone, March 6–8, 1994, 5.

101. Hirsch, "Trading Up," 120. South Africa used another agency of the international system, the World Bank, to support its argument that the GEIS was important, stating that an unpublished World Bank report argued that the GEIS "played a crucial role" in increasing exports. GATT, *Trade Policy Review,* vol. 2, 131.

102. Naude, "Evolving International Trade Policy in South Africa," 22.

103. GATT, *Trade Policy Review,* vol. 2, 144.

104. Paul R. Hatty, "The South African Trade Debate: A Business Perspective," in *South Africa and the World Economy in the 1990s,* ed. Pauline Baker, Alex Boraine, and Warren Krafchik (Washington, D.C.: Brookings Institution, 1993), 134.

105. Naude, "Evolving International Trade Policy in South Africa," 22.

106. GATT, *Trade Policy Review,* vol. 1, 3.

107. Kumar, "Uruguay Round and the Southern African Customs Union," 7, 9–10.

108. "GATT Rules Are Unfair—Manuel," *Business Day* (Johannesburg) November 25, 1993, 3–4.

109. "GATT Rules Are Unfair—Manuel," 3.

110. Christopher Stevens, "Global Trends and Implications for Southern Africa," paper presented at a Workshop on Reconstituting and Democratising the Southern African Customs Union, Gaborone, Botswana, March 6–8, 1994, 8.

111. "South Africa Makes Late Start in Meeting GATT Obligation," January 6, 1995, Xinhua News Agency.

112. John B. Rehm and Leora Blumberg, "South Africa Lowers Lofty Barriers to Trade: Country Ushers in a Liberalized Import Regime," *New York Law Journal* November 21, 1994.

113. Ibid.

114. "South Africa Set to Soften Tariff Blow," February 25, 1994, *Financial Times*; Taylor, *Stuck in Middle GEAR,* 108.

115. NEM, 184.

116. Hirsch, "Trading Up," xii.

117. Hirsch, "Trading Up," 136.

118. Gordon Crawford, "Whither Lomé? The Mid-Term Review and the Decline of Partnership," *Journal of Modern African Studies* 34 (1996): 505.

119. "WTO Role 'Crucial' in Bilateral Disputes," *Financial Times,* February 16, 1994.

120. Stephen R. Hurt, "The EU and Africa After the Cold War," in *Africa in International Politics: External Involvement on the Continent,* ed. Ian Taylor and Paul Williams (New York: Routledge, 2004), 164.

8. The Post-Apartheid State and Policy Process

1. Andrew Moravcsik, "Taking Preferences Seriously: A Liberal Theory of International Politics," *International Organization* 51 (1997): 530.

2. Anthoni van Nieuwkerk, "Foreign Policy-Making in South Africa: Exploring Context, Actors, and Processes," paper presented to the 19th World Congress of the International Political Science Association, Durban, July 1, 2003, 4.

3. Horwitz, *Communication and Democratic Reform in South Africa,* 326.

4. There is a body of literature on this process; for a thorough account, see Timothy Sisk, *Democratization in South Africa: The Elusive Social Contract* (Princeton, N.J.: Princeton University Press, 1995); for a critical account, see Patrick Bond, *Elite Transition: From Apartheid to Neoliberalism in South Africa* (London: Pluto Press, 2000); and Thomas A. Koelble, *The Global Economy and Democracy in South Africa* (New Brunswick, N.J.: Rutgers University Press, 1998).

5. Samuel Huntington, *The Third Wave: Democratization in the Late Twentieth Century* (Norman: University of Oklahoma Press, 1991).

6. Horwitz, *Communication and Democratic Reform in South Africa,* 6.

7. Ian Taylor, *Stuck in Middle GEAR;* Patrick Bond, *Elite Transition;* Hein Marais, *South Africa: Limits to Change;* Thomas A. Koelble, *The Global Economy and Democracy.*

8. Horwitz, *Communication and Democratic Reform in South Africa,* 12.

9. Koelble, *The Global Economy and Democracy,* 182.

10. Padraig Carmody, "Between Globalisation and (Post) Apartheid: The Political Economy of Restructuring in South Africa," *Journal of Southern African Studies* 28 (2002): 261.

11. From 1996 to 2002, when neoliberal reforms were introduced, more than a half a million jobs were lost (the government had expected that 600,000 would be created). Padraig Carmody, "Between Globalisation and (Post) Apartheid," 256. Mamphela Ramphele argues that the level of inequality within South Africa has increased, particularly among Blacks; "Citizenship Challenge for South Africa's Young Democracy," *Daedalus* 130 (2001): 12.

12. Marais, *South Africa: Limits to Change,* 158; Taylor, *Stuck in Middle GEAR,* 69.

13. Koelble, *The Global Economy and Democracy,* 193.

14. Nicoli Nattrass and Jeremy Seekings, "Growth, Democracy, and Expectations in South Africa," in *Economic Globalization and Fiscal Policy,* ed. Iraj Abedian and Michael Biggs (Cape Town: Oxford University Press, 1998).

15. Ibid., 43, 33.

16. Anthony Payne, "The New Political Economy of Regional Studies," *Millennium* 27 (1998): 267.

17. Martin Murray, *Revolution Deferred: The Painful Birth of Post-Apartheid South Africa* (London: Verso, 1994), cited in Paul Williams and Ian Taylor, "Neoliberal-

ism and the Political Economy of the 'New' South Africa," *New Political Economy* 5 (2000): 26.

18. John Muller and Nico Cloete, "Social Scientists and Social Change in South Africa," *International Journal of Contemporary Sociology* 28 (1991): 177; see Michael Macdonald and Wilmot James, "The Hand on the Tiller: The Politics of State and Class in South Africa," *Journal of Modern African Studies* 31 (1993): 387–405.

19. Marais, *South Africa: Limits to Change,* 158.

20. Paul Williams and Ian Taylor, "Neoliberalism and the Political Economy of the 'New' South Africa," *New Political Economy* 5 (2000): 26.

21. Muller and Cloete, "Social Scientists and Social Change," 173.

22. Taylor, *Stuck in Middle GEAR,* 145.

23. Horwitz, *Communication and Democratic Reform in South Africa.*

24. Leo Panitch, *Globalization and the State* (Mexico City: Universidad Nacional Autónoma de México, 1994), 14.

25. See Sylvia Maxfield, *Governing Capital: International Finance and Mexican Politics* (Ithaca, N.Y.: Cornell University Press, 1990), 27.

26. Geoffrey Garrett and Peter Lange, "Capital Mobility, Trade, and Domestic Politics of Economic Policy," in *Internationalization and Domestic Politics,* ed. Robert Keohane and Helen Milner (New York: Columbia University Press, 1996), 54.

27. Douglas North and Barry Weingast, "Constitutions and Commitment: The Evolution of Institutions Governing Public Choice in Seventeenth Century England," *Journal of Economic History* 49 (1989) : 803–832; Robert Cox, "Global Perestroika," in *New World Order? The Socialist Register,* ed. R. Miliband and L. Panitch (London: Merlin, 1992), 30–31.

28. Stephen Haggard and Sylvia Maxfield, "Political Explanations of Financial Policy in Developing Countries," in *The Politics of Finance in Developing Countries,* ed. Stephen Haggard, Chung Lee, and Sylvia Maxfield (Ithaca, N.Y.: Cornell University Press, 1993), 314.

29. Michel Camdessus, the head of the IMF, reportedly put pressure on the ANC to keep Chris Stals and Derek Keys. Bond, *Elite Transition,* 178.

30. "Dismay at Keys Move but Liebenberg Can Fill Gap," Reuters News Service, July 6, 1994.

31. Tony Hawkins, "Love in That May Not Last," *Financial Times* (London), July 18, 1994, 4.

32. Prior to succeeding Nelson Mandela, Thabo Mbeki said, "The ANC is not a socialist party. It has never pretended to be one, it has never said it was, and it is not trying to be. It will not become one by decree or for the purpose of pleasing its 'left critics.'" Thabo Mbeki, "The Fatton Thesis: A Rejoinder," *Canadian Journal of African Studies* 18 (1984): 609.

33. "Issues: A View of South African Political Trends," Communications Services, Johannesburg, June 1996, 5. This policy shift was evident as early as mid-1995, when Mbeki and others had concluded that economic growth was more important than growth and redistribution. Willie Esterhuyse, "What Happened to the Reconstruction and Development Programme?" unpublished paper, June 28, 1996, 2.

34. "No Adam Smith Fans Here," *Newsweek,* February 7, 1994, 48.

35. Marais, *South Africa: Limits to Change,* 234.

36. Sven Lunsche, "Pay Cut Will Boost Jobs, Claims IMF," *Sunday Times/Business Times,* March 27, 1994, 3.

37. Rashad Cassim and Marina Mayer, "Regional Industrial Development," in *Toward Strengthening Multisectoral Linkages in SADC,* ed. Lolette Kritzinger-van Niekerk (Midrand: Development Bank of South Africa, 1997), 54.

38. Mfundo Nkuhlu, "South Africa's Trade Policy with SADC and Africa," in *Trading on Development: South Africa's Trade and Development Relations with the European Union,* ed. Rachel Houghton (Braamfontein: Friedrich Ebert Stiftung, 1997), 84.

39. Of course, there is room to explore within these boxes. For example, although I am dealing with the first ANC administration, under the second ANC administration and President Mbeki, there was a movement toward a more centralized foreign policy making process. See Anthoni van Nieuwkerk, "Foreign Policy Making in South Africa" for an excellent explanation of the inner workers of the executive branch under Mbeki.

40. Anna Seleny, "Old Political Rationalities and New Democracies: Compromise and Confrontation in Hungary and Poland," *World Politics* 51 (July 1999): 512.

41. Greg Mills, "South Africa's Foreign Policy: From Isolation to Respectability?" in *South Africa in Southern Africa: Reconfiguring the Region,* ed. David Simon (Athens: Ohio University Press, 1998), 73.

42. Anthoni van Nieuwkerk, "Foreign Policy-Making in South Africa," 9.

43. Author's interview with Dr. Booysen, political analyst, Northern Transvaal Chamber of Industries, Pretoria, February 10, 1994.

44. Gavin Maasdorp and Alan Whiteside, *Rethinking Economic Cooperation in Southern Africa: Trade and Investment* (Johannesburg: Konrad-Adenauer Stiftung, 1993), 10.

45. Timothy M. Shaw, "Africa in the Global Political Economy: Globalization, Regionalization, or Marginalization?" in *The New Regionalism and the Future of Security and Development,* ed. Björn Hettne, András Inotai, and Osvaldo Sunkel (New York: St. Martin's Press, 2000), 110.

46. For an excellent explanation of the role of labor in creating "national forums," see Horwitz, *Communication and Democratic Reform in South Africa,* 14–15.

47. "South Africa Economy: Recovery Sought Via 'Corporatism,'" *Economist Intelligence Unit: Business Europe,* March 7, 1995.

48. Stephen Haggard and Chung-in Moon, "The South Korean State in the International Economy: Liberal, Dependent or Mercantile?" in *The Antinomies of Interdependence: National Welfare and the International Division of Labor,* ed. John Ruggie (New York: Columbia University Press, 1983).

49. *The Financial Mail* reported that the NEF was formed because there was debate over economic policy at CODESA (Convention for a Democratic South Africa), which was preoccupied with the new political dispensation in South Africa (April 3, 1992, 33–35).

50. Ebrahim Patel, "New Institutions of Decision-Making," in *Engine of Development?,* ed. Ebrahim Patel (Kenwyn, South Africa: Juta, 1993), 6–7.

51. NEDLAC established four "negotiating chambers"—public finance and monetary policy, trade and industry, labor market, and socioeconomic development. The first three include representatives from the labor, government, and business sectors. In public finance and monetary policy, the South African Reserve Bank was present as well. In socioeconomic development, community groups were also present.

52. Nelson Mandela's Address to the Opening of the 2nd Parliament, February 17, 1995; PR Newswires Associates, February 21, 1995.

53. "South Africa Economy: Recovery Sought via 'Corporatism,'" *Economist Intelligence Unit: Business Europe,* March 7, 1995.

54. Horwitz, *Communication and Democratic Reform in South Africa,* 17.

55. For a discussion with Sam Shilowa, then assistant general-secretary of COSATU, on the formation of the NEF, see "National Economic Forum," *SA Labor Bulletin* 16 (1992): 13–18.

56. Marais, *South Africa: Limits to Growth,* 232.

57. Glenn Adler and Eddie Webster, "Bargained Liberalisation: The Labour Movement, Policy-Making and Transition in Zambia and South Africa," paper prepared for 17th World Congress of the International Political Science Association, August 17–21, 1997, Seoul, South Korea, available online at http://www.antenna.nl/~waterman/adler.html.

58. Karl von Holdt, "The LRA Agreement: 'Worker Victory' or 'Miserable Compromise'?" *SA Labour Bulletin* 19 (1995): 16.

59. "COSATU Press Statement Marking the 2nd Anniversary of the LRA," November 12, 1998; available online at http://www.cosatu.org.za/press/1998/pr1112.txt.

60. Garrett demonstrates that the notion that the market has come to dominate the less well off and their power at the ballot box and using only one model of political economy are theoretically and empirically wrong. Geoffrey Garrett, *Partisan Politics in the Global Economy* (New York: Cambridge University Press, 1998).

61. Author's interview with Michael McDonald, NEDLAC representative and Head, Economic Division, Steel and Engineering Industries Federation of South Africa, Johannesburg, August 7, 1998.

62. Author's interview with Sam Ramburuth, National Economic Development and Labour Council, Trade and Industry Chamber, Johannesburg, August 5, 1998.

63. Mills, "South Africa's Foreign Policy," 79.

64. Lodge, *Politics in South Africa: From Mandela to Mbeki* (Bloomington: Indiana University Press, 2002), 165.

65. Paul Goodison, "The EU's Trade and Development Policy: South Africa and the SADC," in *Trading on Development: South Africa's Trade and Development Relations with the European Union,* ed. Rachel Houghton (Braamfontein, South Africa: Friedrich Ebert Stiftung, 1997), 47.

66. Republic of South Africa, Debates of the National Assembly, *Hansard No. 17, Third Session–1st Parliament, 5–7 November 1990,* 5181.

67. Rules of origin define what is considered a country's (or region's product); for instance, the percentage of the components that go into an automobile that must be local and the percentage that can be imported.

68. Republic of South Africa, Debates of the National Assembly, *Hansard No. 17, Third Session–1st Parliament, 5–7 November 1990,* 5180.

69. Author's interview with Max Sisulu, Chief Whip Majority Party (ANC), Cape Town, August 13, 1998.

70. However, labor did not form a caucus in Parliament. They were elected as ANC members, and a clause in the new Constitution stipulated that if a member switched parties, he/she lost his or her seat. In this way, the ANC leadership could more easily direct economic policy without worrying about a revolt in the ranks.

71. Republic of South Africa, Debates of the National Assembly, *Hansard, No. 17: Third Session–1st Parliament, 5–7 November 1990,* 5192.

72. "COSATU Regaining Lost Ground," *SA Labour Bulletin* 20 (1996): 12.

73. Karl von Holdt, "The LRA Agreement: 'Worker Victory' or 'Miserable Compromise'?" *SA Labour Bulletin* 19 (1995): 23.

74. Anthoni van Nieuwkerk, "Economic Policy-Making in South Africa: Exploring Context, Actors, and Processes," paper presented at the 19th World Congress of the International Political Science Association, Durban, South Africa, July 1, 2003, 13.

75. Peter A. Hall, "Conclusion," in *The Political Power of Economic Ideas,* ed. Peter A. Hall (Princeton, N.J.: Princeton University Press, 1989), 375.

76. Author's interview with Neil van Heerden, Executive Director, South Africa Foundation, Johannesburg, South Africa, August 20, 1998. Rashad Cassim also makes this point in "The Political Economy of Trade Negotiations in Post-Apartheid South

Africa," paper presented at the Conference on the Politics of Economic Reform at the ISP workshop, January 16–18, 1998, 6. The first wave of ANC civil servants into the DTI, for instance, began in 1999; author's interview with Marina Mayer, South Africa Department of Trade and Industry, Pretoria, August, 6, 1998.

77. Mills, "South Africa's Foreign Policy, 78.

78. The Department of Foreign Affairs played a diminishing role in South Africa's regional economic policymaking. This is possibly because the focus of South Africa's regional ties during the apartheid era was on maintaining some kind of foreign relations in the face of growing isolation. Thus, the Department of Foreign Affairs backed SACU while the Department of Finance did not. In the post-apartheid era, from a foreign relations perspective, political capital was less of an incentive than economic gains.

79. Mfundo Nkuhlu, "Southern Africa After Apartheid: Perspectives on Institutional Arrangements for Multi-Lateral Relations," paper presented at the Workshop on the Correlation on Political Systems and Economic Development in Southern Africa, Harare, Zimbabwe, November 1–2, 1993.

80. Faizel Ismail was a top ANC economic advisor during the transition. He joined the first ANC government in 1994 and led the South African government's negotiation team on the trade agreement with the EU. In 1995 he was chief director of foreign trade relations at the Department of Trade and Industry.

81. "[The DBSA] has in recent times gained considerable clout and may be well-placed to play a significant role in the future of the region"; Nkuhlu, "Southern Africa After Apartheid," 6.

82. Author's interview with Max Sisulu, Chief Whip Majority Party (ANC), Cape Town, South Africa, August 13, 1998.

83. Bratton and van de Walle, *Democratic Experiments,* 107. For an excellent elaboration of the argument that apartheid was challenged by assaults from both business and labor (particularly urban dwellers), see Nicoli Nattrass and Jeremy Seekings, "Growth, Democracy, and Expectations in South Africa," in *Economic Globalization and Fiscal Policy,* ed. Iraj Abedian and Michael Biggs (Cape Town: Oxford University Press, 1998).

84. Author's interview with Max Tlakula, First Vice President and Acting Director, National African Chamber of Commerce, Johannesburg, South Africa, March 2, 1994.

9. Conclusion

1. Peter Evans, "The Role of Theory in Comparative Politics: A Symposium," *World Politics* 48 (1995): 5.

2. Fredrik Söderbaum, "The New Regionalism in Southern Africa," *Politeia* 17 (1998): 86.

3. William Reno, *Warlord Politics and African States* (Boulder, Colo.: Lynne Rienner, 1998), 59.

4. It has been argued that big business has driven post-apartheid South Africa's regional foreign policy. Hein Marais, *South Africa: Limits to Change: The Political Economy of Transition* (London: Zed Books, 1998), 132.

5. Andrew Hurrell, "Explaining the Resurgence of Regionalism in World Politics," *Review of International Studies* 21 (1995): 343.

6. Ian Taylor, *Stuck in Middle GEAR:South Africa's Post-Apartheid Foreign Relations* (Westport, Conn.: Praeger, 2001), 87.

7. Philip Nel, "The Power of Ideas: 'Ambiguous Globalism' and South Africa's Foreign Policy," paper presented at the International Political Science Association, Durban, South Africa, July 2003.

8. Anthoni van Nieuwkerk, "Foreign Policy-Making in South Africa: Exploring Context, Actors, and Processes," paper presented at the International Political Science Association, Durban, July 1, 2003, 22.

9. Fred Ahwireng-Obeng and Patrick J. McGowan, "Partner or Hegemon? South Africa in Africa," *Journal of Contemporary African Studies* 16 (1993): 3, 20, 12.

10. Adebayo Adedeji, *South Africa and Africa: Within or Apart* (Atlantic Highlands, N.J.: Zed, 1996), cited in Reno, *Warlord Politics and African States,* 59.

11. Colin Legum, "Balance of Power in Southern Africa," in *The Uncertain Promise of Southern Africa,* ed. York Bradshaw and Stephen N. Ndegwa (Bloomington: Indiana University Press, 2000), 14. Percy Mistry argues that in general there is no wide consensus on either what kinds of regional arrangements should emerge among developing countries or how they should be institutionalized. "Regional Integration and Economic Development," in *The New Regionalism and the Future of Security and Development,* ed. Björn Hettne, András Inotai, and Osvaldo Sunkel (New York: St. Martin's Press, 2000), 27.

12. Talitha Bertelsmann, "Regional Integration in Southern Africa," unpublished paper, South African Institute of International Affairs, Johannesburg, South Africa, 1998, 10.

13. David Simon, "Regional Development—Environment Discourses, Policies and Practices in Post-Apartheid Southern Africa," revised version of the paper presented at the International Geographical Union Congress, Durban, South Africa, August 4–7, 2002, 6.

14. Ranjeni Munusamy, "Customs Pact Ushers in Free Trade," *Sunday Times* (Johannesburg), October 20, 2002.

15. Colin McCarthy, "SACU and the Rand Zone," in *Regionalisation in Africa: Integration and Disintegration,* ed. Daniel C. Bach (Bloomington: Indiana University Press, 1999), 168.

16. Balefi Tsie, "States and Markets in the Southern African Development Community (SADC): Beyond the Neo-Liberal Paradigm," *Journal of Southern African Studies* 22 (1996); see also Richard Gibb, "Regional Integration in Post-Apartheid Southern Africa: The Case of Renegotiating the Southern Africa Customs Union," *Journal of Southern Africa Studies* 23 (1997): 84.

17. Gavin Maasdorp and Alan Whiteside, *Rethinking Economic Cooperation in Southern Africa: Trade and Investment* (Johannesburg: Konrad-Adenauer Stiftung, 1993), 35.

18. Rosalind Thomas, "A South African Perspective on the SADC Trade and Development Protocol," paper prepared for the Friedrich Ebert Stiftung Institute, Johannesburg, South Africa, April 1997.

19. "Protocols Signed at the Maseru Summit," *SADC Today,* n.d., SADC, Gaborone.

20. Rashad Cassim and Marina Mayer, "Regional Industrial Development," in *Toward Strengthening Multisectoral Linkages in SADC,* ed. Lolette Kritzinger-van Niekerk (Midrand: Development Bank of Southern Africa, 1997), 59.

21. "Southern Africa: SADC Official Says Regional Free Trade Zone Will Also Benefit Smaller Economies," Reuters Textline: BBC Monitoring Service, August 27, 1996.

22. Sheila Page, "Some Questions for Industrial Research in SADC," unpublished paper, June 1998, 59.

23. Rosalind Thomas, "A South African Perspective on the SADC Trade and Development Protocol," unpublished paper, DBSA, Midrand, 1997, 2.

24. For an excellent review of this debate and the relative studies, see Paul Kalenga, "Regional Trade Integration in Southern Africa: Critical Policy Issues," De-

velopment Policy Research Unit, Working Paper no. 00/42, University of Cape Town, September 2000.

25. Thomas, "A South African Perspective on the SADC Trade and Development Protocol," 20.

26. Rashad Cassim, "The Political Economy of Trade Negotiations in Post-Apartheid South Africa," paper prepared for the Conference on the Politics of Economic Reform at the ISP Workshop, Cape Town, January 16–18, 1988.

27. Talitha Bertelsmann, "The European Union and South Africa: Reaching Agreement?" *SAIIA Reports,* South African Institute of International Affairs, Johannesburg, 1998, 29.

28. Quoted in "South African Foreign Policy Discussion Document," South African Government, Department of Foreign Affairs, Pretoria, 1996, 19.

29. Gavin Maasdorp and Alan Whiteside, *Rethinking Economic Cooperation in Southern Africa: Trade and Investment* (Johannesburg: Konrad-Adenauer Stiftung, 1993), 19.

30. McCarthy, "SACU and the Rand Zone," 166–167.

31. Anne Graumans, "The European Union—South African Negotiations," prepared for the Netherlands Institute for Southern Africa, July 1998, 4.

32. The SADC is a competitive exporter of some products to the rest of the world that South Africa imports from. Kalenga, "Regional Trade Integration in Southern Africa," 11.

33. Ibid., 6.

34. *Financial Mail,* October 16, 1998.

35. Ibid.

36. Steve Atkins and Alan Terry, "The Changing Role of Sugar as an Economic Vehicle for Economic Development within South Africa," in *South Africa in Southern Africa: Reconfiguring the Region,* ed. David Simon (Athens: Ohio University Press, 1998), 142.

37. Nana Poku and Maxi Schoeman, "Regional Integration in Southern Africa: A Cautionary Note," paper presented at the 39th Convention of the International Studies Association, Washington, D.C., September 2–5, 1999, 8.

38. Industry Canada's Web site has an excellent summary of South Africa's SDIs at http://strategis.ic.gc.ca/SSG/dd74196e.html.

39. Fredrik Söderbaum, "Institutional Aspects of the Maputo Development Corridor," research report presented at the Regional Workshop, Development Policy Research Unit's Southern Africa Project, Windhoek, South Africa, September 28–29, 2000, 7–9.

40. For more about the Maputo Development Corridor, see http://www.africansdi.com/members/iii/sdi.nsf/0/c753c11985c9099242256dd7004320fb?OpenDocument. For a thorough analysis of the SDIs, see Fredrik Söderbaum and Ian Taylor, eds., *Kick-Starting Development? Reconstructing the Maputo Corridor in the Context of Globalisation* (London: Ashgate, 2003).

41. Söderbaum, "Institutional Aspects of the Maputo Development Corridor," 13.

42. Ibid., 23.

43. For more on Mozal, see James J. Hentz, "The Mozal Aluminum Smelter—Partnership for Exploitation or Development?" in *Kick-Starting Development? Reconstructing the Maputo Corridor in the Context of Globalisation,* ed. Fredrik Söderbaum and Ian Taylor (London: Ashgate, 2003), 83–94.

44. Söderbaum, "Institutional Aspects of the Maputo Development Corridor," 13.

45. International Marketing Council of South Africa, "Public-Private Sector Partnerships," available online at http://www.southafrica.info/doing_business/investment/opportunities/public-private.htm.

46. Söderbaum, "Institutional Aspects of the Maputo Development Corridor," 21.

47. Ian Taylor, "Globalization and Regionalization in Africa: Reactions to Attempts at Neo-Liberal Regionalism," *Review of International Political Economy* 10 (2003): 318.

48. Legum, "Balance of Power in Southern Africa," 16.

49. Söderbaum, "Institutional Aspects of the Maputo Development Corridor," 7.

50. As a member of the ANC's Department of Economic Planning during the transition, Jourdan argued that business had no representation in the ANC. He also noted, however, that the ANC had a short window of opportunity while its ideology was strong. Author's interview with Paul Jourdan, Department of Economic Planning, ANC, Johannesburg, South Africa, November 3, 1993. After the 1994 election, Jourdan became the deputy director of the Department of Trade and Industry.

51. Legum, "Balance of Power in Southern Africa," 18.

52. David Simon, "Regional Development—Environment Discourses, Policies and Practices in Post-Apartheid Southern Africa," revised version of the paper presented at the International Geographical Union Congress, Durban, South Africa, August 4–7, 2002, 16.

53. "President Thabo Mbeki's Visit to Mozambique," press release issued by the Office of the President, September 19, 2000.

54. "Infrastructure and Development in Southern Africa: Speech by the Executive Deputy Present," Development Bank of Southern Africa, Midrand, South Africa, July 31, 1998.

55. Gavin Maasdorp, "Can Regional Integration Help Southern Africa?" in *Can South and Southern Africa Become Globally Competitive Economies?* ed. Gavin Maasdorp (New York: St. Martin's Press: 1996), 45.

56. McCarthy, "SACU and the Rand Zone," 166.

57. Mfundo Nkuhlu, "South Africa's Trade Policy with SADC and Africa," in *Trading on Development: South Africa's Trade and Development Relations with the European Union,* ed. Rachel Houghton (Braamfontein: Friedrich Ebert Stiftung, 1997), 83.

58. Mfundo Nkuhlu, "Southern Africa After Apartheid: Perspectives on Institutional Arrangements for Multi-Lateral Relations," prepared for Workshop on the Correlation of Political Systems and Economic Development in Southern Africa, November 1–2, 1993, 11.

59. "Public Enterprise to Play a Key in Economic Development," BBC Summary of World Broadcasts, June 28, 1994.

60. Eliot Berg, *Regionalism and Economic Development in Sub-Saharan Africa,* 2 vols. (Alexandria, Va.: Applied Development Economics, 1988), cited in C. G. Gore, "International Order, Economic Regionalism and Structural Adjustment: The Case of Sub-Saharan Africa," in *Progress in Planning,* ed. D. Diamond, B. McLoughlin, and B. Massam (New York: Pergamon Press, 1992), 184–249.

61. Tore Horvei, "Powering the Region: South Africa and the Southern African Power Pool," in *South Africa in Southern Africa: Reconfiguring the Region,* ed. David Simon (Athens: Ohio University Press, 1998), 147.

62. Robert Davies, R. Keet, and M. Nkuhlu, "Reconstructing Economic Relations with the Southern African Region: Issue and Options for a Democratic South Africa," Centre for Development Studies, Cape Town, September 1993, 8.

63. Mills, "South Africa's Foreign Policy," 83–84.

64. In fact, Eskom apparently lobbied for the Democratic Republic of Congo's membership in the SADC, which had repeatedly been denied in the past.

65. Davies, Keet, and Nkuhlu, "Reconstructing Economic Relations with the Southern African Region," 7.

66. Larry Swatuk, "Power and Water: The Coming Order in Southern Africa," in

The New Regionalism and the Future of Security and Development, ed. Björn Hettne, András Inotai, and Osvaldo Sunkel (New York: St. Martin's Press, 2000), 211.

67. D. C. Midgley, "Co-operative Development of Water and Hydroelectric Potential," in *South Africa in Southern Africa: Economic Interaction,* ed. Erich Leistner and Pieter Esterhuysen, 158–176 (Pretoria: Africa Institute of South Africa, 1988), 163.

68. Author's interview with N. M. Krige, Deputy Director-General for Water Resource Development, Department of Water Affairs and Forestry, Pretoria, South Africa, February 28, 1994.

69. Author's interview with J. Geringer, South African Department of Transportation, Pretoria, South Africa, March 8, 1994.

70. Author's interview with Andre Heydenryah, Business Manager (Africa), Spoornet, Johannesburg, South Africa, November 22, 1993.

71. Shaw, "Africa in the Global Political Economy," 110.

72. Swatuk, "Power and Water," 239.

73. In fact, some scholars argue that functionalism benefits the strongest state. Michael Schulz, Fredrik Söderbaum, and Joakim Ojendal, eds., *Regionalization in a Globalizing World: A Comparative Perspective on Forms, Actors, and Processes* (London: Zed Books, 2001). For this argument applied to South and Southern Africa, see James J. Hentz, "The Southern African Security Order: Regional Integration and Security among Developing States," paper presented at the International Political Science Association Meeting, Durban, South Africa, June 29–July 4, 2003.

74. D. C. Midgley, "Co-operative Development of Water and Hydroelectric Potential," in *South Africa in Southern Africa: Economic Interaction,* ed. Erich Leistner and Pieter Esterhuysen (Pretoria: Africa Institute of South Africa, 1988), 163.

75. Robert Keohane, *After Hegemony: Cooperation and Discord in the World Political Economy* (Princeton, N.J.: Princeton University Press, 1984), 91.

76. Johan van Zyl, "Southern Africa: Towards Closer Economic Co-operation in the 1990s—A Discussion Paper," Development Bank of Southern Africa, Midrand, South Africa, November 1990.

77. Marina J. Mayer and Rosalind Thomas, "Trade Integration in the Southern African Development Community: Prospects and Problems," paper prepared for the Development Bank of Southern Africa, Midrand, 1997, 20.

78. The DBSA consist of many independent analysts, so characterizing it as having a uniform approach must be accompanied with the caveat that it may not be a unanimous approach.

79. Marina J. Mayer, "Introduction and Overview," in *Towards Strengthening Multisectoral Linkages in SADC,* ed. Lolette Kritzinger Niekerk (Midrand: Development Bank of Southern Africa, 1997).

80. Glen Adler and Eddie Webster, "Bargained Liberalisation: The Labour Movement, Policy-Making and Transition in Zambia and South Africa," paper prepared for 17th World Congress of the International Political Science Association, August 17–21, 1997, Seoul, South Korea, 143.

81. Poku and Schoeman, "Regional Integration," 10.

82. Sue Kell and Troy Dyer, "Economic Integration in Southern Africa," in *The Uncertain Promise of Southern Africa,* ed. York Bradshaw and Stephen Ndegwa (Bloomington: Indiana University Press, 2000), 385.

83. Bob Deacon, "The Social Dimension of Regionalism: A Constructive Alternative to Neo-liberal Globalization?" Globalization and Social Policy Programme (GASPP) Occasional Paper no. 8/2001, June 2001, available online at http://www.gaspp.org/publications/occasional%20papers/gaspp8–2001.pdf.

84. *Financial Mail,* October 16, 1998. They included the argument that South Africa's administrative capacity to police a free trade agreement was limited.

85. Geoffrey Garrett, *Partisan Politics in the Global Economy* (New York: Cambridge University Press, 1998), 7.

86. Reno, *Warlord Politics and African States,* 56.

87. Anthony Payne and Andrew Gamble, "Introduction: The Political Economy of Regionalism and World Order," in *Regionalism and World Order,* ed. Anthony Payne and Andrew Gamble (New York: St. Martin's Press, 1996), 2.

88. Anthony Payne, "The New Political Economy of Regional Studies," *Millennium* 27 (1998): 269.

89. This is consistent with Andrew Moravcsik's approach as outlined in the introduction. For a recent defense of this approach, see Moravcsik, "The Future of European Integration Studies: Social Science or Social Theory," *Millennium* 28 (1999): 371–392.

90. This is borrowed from Garrett's work on globalization. Garrett, *Partisan Politics in the Global Economy,* 7.

91. "Black Workers Feel Cold Shouldered in New South Africa," Reuters News Service, August 15, 1994.

92. "South Africa Truckers' Strike Ends," Associated Press, September 21, 1994.

93. Patrick Bond, *Elite Transition: From Apartheid to Neoliberalism in South Africa* (London: Pluto Press, 2000); Marais, *South Africa: Limits to Change;* Ian Taylor, "Globalization and Regionalization in Africa: Reactions to Attempts at Neo-Liberal Regionalism," *Review of International Political Economy* 10 (2003), 310–330; Taylor, *Stuck in Middle GEAR;* Paul Williams and Ian Taylor, "Neoliberalism and the Political Economy of the 'New' South Africa," *New Political Economy* 5 (2000), 21–40; Thomas A. Koelble, *The Global Economy and Democracy in South Africa* (New Brunswick, N.J.: Rutgers University Press, 1998).

Bibliography

Abegunrin, Olayiwola. *Economic Dependence and Regional Cooperation in Southern Africa.* Lewiston, N.Y.: Mellon Press, 1990.

Adler, Emanuel. "Imagined (Security) Communities: Cognitive Regions in International Relations." *Millennium* 26 (1997): 249–278.

———. *The Power of Ideology: The Quest for Technological Autonomy in Argentina and Brazil.* Berkeley: University of California Press, 1987.

Adler, Glenn, and Eddie Webster. "Bargained Liberalisation: The Labour Movement, Policy-Making and Transition in Zambia and South Africa." Paper prepared for 17th World Congress of the International Political Science Association, August 17–21, 1997, Seoul, South Korea.

African Development Bank. "Economic Integration in Southern Africa: Executive Summary." African Development Bank, Abidjan, Ivory Coast, 1993.

———. "Economic Integration in Southern Africa: A Report for the African Development Bank." African Development Bank, Abidjan, Ivory Coast, December 1992.

———. "Finance." In *Regional Integration in Southern Africa.* Vol. 2. Abidjan: African Development Bank, 1994.

———. *Regional Integration in Southern Africa.* Vol. 2. Abidjan: African Development Bank, 1994.

African National Congress (ANC). *Discussion Document on Regional Co-operation and Integration in Southern Africa After Apartheid.* ANC Department of Economic Planning, 1993.

———. "Ready to Govern: ANC Policy Guidelines for a Democratic South Africa Adopted at the National Conference, 28–31 May 1992" [1992].

———. "Reconstruction and Development Programme." Draft for discussion purposes only, for ANC regions and departments only. February 17, 1994.

Ahmad, Aly. *Economic Cooperation in Africa.* Boulder, Colo.: Lynne Rienner, 1994.

Ahwireng-Obeng, Fred, and Patrick J. McGowan. "Partner or Hegemon? South Africa in Africa." *Journal of Contemporary African Studies* 16 (1993): 5–38.

Alden, Chris. "From Liberation Movement to Political Party: ANC Foreign Policy in Transition." *South African Journal of International Affairs* 1 (1993): 63–81.

Altmann, J. "South-South Cooperation and Economic Order." *Intereconomics* (May/June 1982): 143–147.

Aly, A. A. H. *Economic Cooperation in Africa: In Search of Direction.* Boulder, Colo.: Lynne Rienner, 1994.

Amin, Samir, Derrick Chitali, and Ibbo Mandaza. *SADCC: Prospects for Disengagement and Development in Southern Africa.* London: Zed Books, 1987.

Andrews, David. "Capital Mobility and State Autonomy." *International Studies Quarterly* 38 (1994): 193–218.

Anglin, Douglas. "Economic Liberation and Regional Cooperation in Southern Africa: SADCC and PTA." *International Organization* 37 (1983): 681–713.

———. "SADCC After Nkomati." *African Affairs* 84 (1985): 163–181.

Appel, Hilary. "The Ideological Determinants of Liberal Economic Reform: The Case of Privatization." *World Politics* 52 (2000): 520–529.

Aron, Janine, and Ibrahim Elbadawi. "Reflections on the South African Rand Crisis of 1996 and Policy Consequences." Centre for the Study of African Economies, Working Paper Series no. 97. Institute of Economics and Statistics, Oxford University, 1999. Available online at http://www.bepress.com/cgi/viewcontent.cgi?article=1098&context=csae.

Atkins, Steve, and Alan Terry. "The Changing Role of Sugar as an Economic Vehicle for Economic Development within South Africa." In *South Africa in Southern Africa: Reconfiguring the Region,* ed. David Simon, 129–145. Athens: Ohio University Press, 1998.

Austen, Ralph. *Africa in Economic History.* Portsmouth, N.H.: Heinemann, 1987.

Axelrod, Robert. *The Evolution of Cooperation.* New York: Basic Books, 1984.

———, and Robert Keohane. "Achieving Cooperation under Anarchy: Strategies and Institutions." In *Neorealism and Neoliberalism: The Contemporary Debate,* ed. James Baldwin, 85–115. New York: Columbia University Press, 1993.

Axline, Andrew. "Underdevelopment, Dependence and Integration: The Politics of Regionalism in the Third World." *International Organization* 37 (1977): 82–104.

Baker, Pauline, Alex Boraine, and Warren Krafchik, eds. *South Africa and the World Economy in the 1990s.* Washington, D.C.: Brookings Institution, 1993.

Balassa, Bela. *The Theory of Economic Integration.* Homewood, Ill.: R. D. Erwin, 1961.

———, and Ardy Stoutjesdijk. "Economic Integration among Developing Countries." In *Economic Integration and Third World Development,* ed. Pradip Ghosh, 33–50. Westport, Conn.: Greenwood Press, 1984.

Baldwin, David. "Neoliberalism, Neorealism, and World Politics." In *Neorealism and Neoliberalism: The Contemporary Debate,* ed. David Baldwin, 3–28. New York: Columbia University Press, 1993.

Ballinger, Ronald, and Gerrit Olivier. "Détente in Southern Africa: Two Views." South African Institute of International Affairs, Johannesburg, 1976.

Barber, James, and John Barratt. *South Africa's Foreign Policy: The Search for Status and Security 1945–1988.* New York: Cambridge University Press, 1990.

Barnett, Michael, and Emanuel Adler. "Studying Security Communities in Theory, Comparison, and History." In *Security Communities,* ed. Emanuel Adler and Michael Barnett, 413–441. New York: Cambridge University Press, 1998.

Batchelor, Peter, and Susan Willett. *Disarmament and Defense Industrial Adjustment in South Africa.* New York: Oxford University Press, 1998.

Bates, Robert. *Markets and States in Tropical Africa: The Political Basis of Agricultural Policies.* Berkeley: University of California Press, 1981.

Bayart, Jean-François. *The State in Africa: The Politics of the Belly.* Translated by Mary Harper, Christopher Harrison, and Elizabeth Harrison. London: Longman, 1993.

Beaudet, Pierre, and Nancy Thede, eds. *A Post-Apartheid Southern Africa?* London: Macmillan Press, 1993.

Bell, Trevor. "Should South Africa Further Liberalise Its Trade?" In *State and Market in Post-Apartheid South Africa,* ed. Merle Lipton and Charles Simkins, 81–128. Boulder, Colo.: Westview Press, 1993.

Belli, Pedro, Michael Finger, and Amparo Ballivian. "South Africa: A Review of Trade Policies." Discussion Paper 4. The World Bank, Southern Africa Department, Washington, D.C., 1993.

Bertelsmann, Talitha. "The European Union and South Africa: Reaching Agreement?" *SAIIA Reports,* South Africa Institute for International Affairs, Johannesburg, 1998.

———. "The European Union." In *From Cape to Congo: Southern Africa's Evolving Security*

Challenges, ed. Mwesiga Baregu and Christopher Landsberg, 301–316. Boulder, Colo.: Lynne Rienner, 2003.

———. "Regional Integration in Southern Africa." Unpublished paper, South African Institute of International Affairs, Johannesburg, South Africa, 1998.

Bienen, Henry. "The Political Economy of Trade Policy Reform in Africa." Unpublished paper, 1987.

Biersteker, Thomas. "The 'Triumph' of Liberal Economic Ideas in the Developing World." In *Global Change, Regional Responses,* ed. Barbara Stallings. 174–196. New York: Cambridge University Press, 1995.

Bird, Graham. "The International Monetary Fund and Developing Counties: A Review of the Evidence and Policy Options." *International Organization* 50 (1996): 477–512.

Black, A. H. "Decentralization Incentives and Investment in the South African Periphery." In *Industrialization and Investment Incentives in Southern Africa,* ed. Alan Whiteside, 121–142. Portsmouth: Heinemann, 1989.

Black, Anthony. "The Role of the State in Promoting Industrialization." In *State and Market in Post-Apartheid South Africa,* ed. Merle Lipton and Charles Simkins, 203–234. Boulder, Colo.: Westview Press, 1993.

Black, Philip A., and Brian Dollery, eds. *Leading Issues in South African Economics.* Johannesburg: Southern Book Publishers, 1989.

Blomqvist, Hans C., Christian Lindholm, Mats Lundahl, and Sven Schauman. "Some Experiences from Regional Cooperation between Third World Countries." In *Southern Africa After Apartheid: Regional Integration and External Resources,* ed. Bertil Odén, 48–70. Uppsala: The Scandinavian Institute of African Studies, 1993.

Blumenfeld, Jesmond. *Economic Interdependence in Southern Africa: From Conflict to Cooperation.* New York: St. Martin's Press, 1991.

Boidin, Jean-Claude. "Regional Cooperation in the Face of Structural Adjustment." *The Courier: Africa—Caribbean—Pacific—European Community* 112 (November–December 1988): 67–69.

Bond, Patrick. *Elite Transition: From Apartheid to Neoliberalism in South Africa.* London: Pluto Press, 2000.

"Botswana Country Paper." Prepared for the Workshop on Reconstituting and Democratising the Southern Africa Customs Union, Gaborone, Botswana, March 7, 1994.

Bowman, Larry, W. "The Subordinate State System of Southern Africa." *International Studies Quarterly* 12 (1968): 231–262.

Bratton, Michael, and Nicholas van de Walle. *Democratic Experiments in Africa: Regime Transitions in Comparative Perspective.* New York: Cambridge University Press, 1997.

———. "Neopatrimonial Regimes and Political Transitions in Africa." *World Politics* 46 (1994): 453–490.

Brown, A. J. "Economic Separatism vs. a Common Market in Developing Countries." *Yorkshire Bulletin* 19 (1961): 33–40.

Burley, Ann Marie, and Walter Mattli. "Europe before the Court: A Political Theory of Legal Integration." *International Organization* 47 (1993): 41–77.

Callaghy, Thomas. "Africa and the World Economy: Caught between a Rock and a Hard Place." In *Africa in World Politics,* ed. John Harbeson and Donald Rothchild, 39–68. Boulder, Colo.: Westview Press, 1991.

———. "Political Passions and Economic Interest." In *Hemmed In: Responses to Africa's Economic Decline,* ed. Thomas Callaghy and John Ravenhill, 463–519. New York: Columbia University Press, 1993.

———. "The State and the Development of Capitalism in Africa: Theoretical, Historical and Comparative Reflections." In *The Precarious Balance: State and Society in Africa,* ed. Donald Rothchild and Naomi Chazan, 67–99. Boulder, Colo.: Westview Press, 1988.

———. *The State-Society Struggle: Zaire in Comparative Perspective.* New York: Columbia University Press, 1984.

Callaghy, Thomas, and John Ravenhill, eds. *Hemmed In: Responses to Africa's Economic Decline.* New York: Columbia University Press, 1993.

Caporaso, James. *Functionalism and Regional Integration: A Logical and Empirical Assessment.* Beverly Hills, Calif.: Sage Publications, 1977.

Carl, Beverly May. *Economic Integration among Developing Nations: Law and Policy.* Philadelphia: Praeger, 1986.

Carmody, Padraig. "Between Globalisation and (Post) Apartheid: The Political Economy of Restructuring in South Africa." *Journal of Southern African Studies* 28 (2002): 255–276.

Cassim, Rashad. "The Determinants of Intra-Regional Trade in Southern Africa with Specific Reference to South Africa and the Rest of the Region." Working Papers no. 01/51, Development Policy Research Unit, University of Cape Town, Cape Town, South Africa, June 2001.

———. "The Political Economy of Trade Negotiations in Post-Apartheid South Africa." Paper prepared for the Conference on the Politics of Economic Reform at the ISP Workshop, Cape Town, South Africa, January 16–18, 1988.

———, and Marina J. Mayer. "Regional Industrial Development." In *Towards Strengthening Multisectoral Linkages in SADC,* ed. Lolette Kritzinger-van Niekerk, 43–68. Midrand, South Africa: Development Bank of Southern Africa, 1997.

Chambati, Ariston. "South Africa in African Politics." Unpublished paper prepared for the South African Institute of International Affairs, Johannesburg, June 6–7, 1975.

Chazan, Naomi, Robert Mortimer, John Ravenhill, and Donald Rothchild. *Politics and Society in Contemporary Africa,* 2nd ed. Boulder, Colo.: Lynne Rienner, 1992.

Cheru, Fantu. "Food Development and Institutional Development in SADCC." In *Poverty Policy, and Food Security in Southern Africa,* ed. Coralie Bryant, 250–273. Boulder, Colo.: Lynne Rienner, 1988.

———. *The Not So Brave New World! Problems and Prospects of Regional Integration in Post-Apartheid Southern Africa.* Johannesburg: South African Institute of International Affairs, 1992.

Chipasula, James. "South Africa and SADCC in the Post-Apartheid Era: Conflict or Cooperation." In *South Africa's Dilemmas in the Post-Apartheid Era,* ed. James Chipasula and Alifeyo Chilivumbo, 155–167. London: University Press of America, 1993.

Chipeta, C., and M. L. Mkandawire. "Monetary Harmonization in Southern Africa." Research Paper 30. African Economic Research Consortium, Nairobi, 1994.

Chipeta, Chinyamata, and Robert Davies. "Regional Relations and Cooperation: Post-Apartheid Southern Africa—A Macro Framework Study Report." SADC, Gaborone, Botswana, 1993.

Christie, Renfrew. "Report to Jim Mullins on South Africa's National Research Strategy." Unpublished paper. University of the Western Cape. November 23, 1992.

Clapham, Christopher. *Africa and the International System: The Politics of State Survival.* New York: Cambridge University Press, 1996.

———. "The African State." In *Africa 30 Years On,* ed. Douglas Rimmer, 91–104. London: James Curry, 1991.

Clark, Nancy. *Manufacturing Apartheid.* New Haven, Conn.: Yale University Press, 1994.

Cohen, Benjamin. *The Geography of Money.* Ithaca, N.Y.: Cornell University Press, 1998.

——. "The Political Economy of International Trade." *International Organization* 44 (1990): 261–281.

Cole, Ken, ed. *Sustainable Development for a Democratic South Africa.* New York: St. Martin's Press, 1994.

Congress of South African Trade Unions (COSATU). "COSATU Discussion Paper: A Draft Programme for the Alliance." November 22, 1996. Available online at http://www.cosatu.org.za/docs/discuss.html.

Cooper, Richard. "Economic Interdependence and Foreign Policies in the 1970s." *World Politics* 24 (1972): 159–181.

——. *The Economics of Interdependence.* New York: Council on Foreign Relations, 1968.

——. "Monetary Theory and Policy in an Open Economy." In *Economic Policy in an Interdependent World,* ed. Richard Cooper, 179–198. Cambridge, Mass.: MIT Press, 1986.

"COSATU Regaining Lost Ground." *SA Labour Bulletin* 20 (1996): 7–9.

Cox, Robert. "Global Perestroika." In *New World Order? The Socialist Register,* ed. R. Miliband and L. Panitch, 26–43. London: Merlin, 1992.

Crais, Clifton C. *The Politics of Evil: Magic, State Power, and the Political Imagination in South Africa.* New York: Cambridge University Press, 2002.

Crawford, Gordon. "Whither Lomé? The Mid-Term Review and the Decline of Partnership." *The Journal of Modern African Studies* 34 (1996): 503–518.

Crawford, Neta, and Audie Klotz, eds. *How Sanctions Work: Lessons from South Africa.* New York: St. Martin's Press: 1999.

Cronje, F. J. "Can a Free Trade Association Be Created in Southern Africa?" *Optima* 15 (1965): 113–118.

Davie, Kevin. "The New South African Economy." In *What Has the IMF in Store for South Africa? Proceedings of a Symposium Held on 27th July 1991 at the Soweto College of Education.* Johannesburg: Institute for African Alternatives, 1991.

Davies, Robert. "Creating an Appropriate Institutional Framework." In *Prospects for Progress: Critical Choices for Southern Africa,* ed. Minnie Venter, 2–13. Cape Town: Longman, 1994.

——. "Economic Growth in a Post-Apartheid South Africa: Its Significance for Relations with other African Countries." *Journal of Contemporary African Studies* 11 (1992): 51–69.

——. "Emerging South African Perspectives on Regional Cooperation and Integration After Apartheid." *Transformation* 20 (1992): 75–87.

——. "Key Issues in Reconstructing South-Southern African Economic Relations After Apartheid." Centre for Southern African Studies, University of Western Cape, November 1990.

——. "South Africa Joining SADCC or SADCC Joining South Africa? Emerging Perspectives on Regional Cooperation After Apartheid." In *Southern Africa at the Crossroads: Prospects for the Political Economy of the Region,* ed. Anthoni van Nieuwkerk and Gary van Staden, 235–246. Johannesburg: South Africa Institute for International Affairs, 1991.

——. "The Southern African Customs Union: Background and Possible Negotiating Issues Facing a Democratic Government." Paper presented at the Workshop on Reconstituting and Democratising the Southern African Customs Union, Gaborone, Botswana, March 6–8, 1994.

——. "The State of Analysis of the Southern African Region: Issues Raised by South African Strategy." *Review of African Political Economy,* no. 29 (1984): 64–77.

——, and Judith Head. "The Future of Mine Migrancy in the Context of Broader

Trends in Migration in South Africa." *Journal of Southern African Studies* 21 (1995): 439–450.

———, R. Keet, and M. Nkuhlu. "Reconstructing Economic Relations with the Southern African Region: Issues and Options for a Democratic South Africa." MERG Occasional Paper Series. The Centre for Development Studies, Cape Town, South Africa, September 1993.

———, and Dan O'Meara. "The State of Analysis of the Southern African Region: Issues Raised by South African Strategy." *Review of African Political Economy* No. 29 (1984): 64–76.

———, and Dan O'Meara. "Total Strategy in Southern Africa: An Analysis of South African Regional Policy Since 1978." *Journal of Southern African Studies* 11 (1985): 183–210.

de Kock, G. C. P. "Economic Growth and Foreign Debt: The South African Case." In *Leading Issues in South African Economic,* ed. Philip A. Black and Brian Dollery, 268–278. Johannesburg: Southern Book Publishers, 1989.

———. "The Gold Price and the South African Economy." In *Leading Issues in South African Economics,* ed. Philip A. Black and Brian Dollery, 222–228. Johannesburg: Southern Book Publishers, 1989.

Deloitte and Touche. "Building Global Manufacturing Competitiveness: Annual International Manufacturing Survey 1993 South African Results." Internal company report for Deloitte and Touche, [1993].

Deng, Francis, and I. William Zartman. *A Strategic Vision for Africa.* Washington, D.C.: Brookings Institution, 2002.

Development Bank of Southern Africa. "Infrastructure and Development in Southern Africa: Speech by the Executive Deputy Present." Midrand, South Africa: Development Bank of Southern Africa, July 31, 1998.

DiMaggio, Paul, and Walter W. Powell. "The Iron Cage Revisited: Institutional Isomorphism and Collective Rationality in Organizational Fields." *American Sociological Review* 48 (1983): 147–160.

du Pisani, Andre. "Post-Settlement South Africa and the Future of Southern Africa." *Issue: Journal of Opinion* 21 (1993): 60–70.

———. "Ventures into the Interior: Continuity and Change in South Africa's Regional Policy (1948–1991)." In *Southern Africa at the Crossroads: Prospects for the Political Economy of the Region,* ed. Antoni van Nieuwkerk and Gary van Staden, 188–234. Johannesburg: South African Institute of International Affairs, 1991.

Esterhuyse, Willie. "What Happened to the Reconstruction and Development Programme?" Unpublished paper. June 28, 1996.

Etzioni, Amitai. *Political Unification.* Huntington, N.Y.: Krieger, 1974.

Evans, Graham. "Myths and Realities in South Africa's Foreign Policy." *International Affairs* 67 (1991): 709–721.

Evans, Peter B. "The Role of Theory in Comparative Politics: A Symposium." *World Politics* 48 (1995): 1–49.

———, Dietrich Rueschemeyer, and Theda Skocpol. "On the Road toward a More Adequate Understanding of the State." In *Bringing the State Back In,* ed. Peter B. Evans, Dietrich Rueschemeyer, and Theda Skocpol, 347–366. New York: Cambridge University Press, 1985.

Fallon, Peter R. "The Implications for South Africa of Using World Bank Facilities." In *South Africa and the World Economy in the 1990s,* ed. Pauline Baker, Alex Boraine, and Warren Krafchik, 204–211. Washington, D.C.: Brookings Institution, 1993.

Falvey, Rod, and Cha Dong Kim. "Timing and Sequencing Issues for Trade Liberalization." In *Trade and Fiscal Adjustment in Africa,* ed. David Bevan, Paul Collier, Norman Gemmell, and David Greenaway, 13–35. New York: St. Martin's Press, 2000.

Fine, Ben, and Zavareh Rustomjee. *The Political Economy of South Africa.* London: Westview Press, 1996.

Frank, Andre Gunder. "Latin American Economic Integration." In *Latin America: Underdevelopment or Revolution?* ed. Andre Gunder Frank. New York: Monthly Review Press, 1969.

Frankel, Philip. *Pretoria's Praetorians: Civil-Military Relations in South Africa.* Cambridge: Cambridge University Press, 1984.

Frankel, S. H. *Capital Investment in Africa: Its Courses and Effects.* London: Oxford University Press, 1938.

Frieden, Jeffry. "The Dynamics of International Monetary Systems: International and Domestic Factors in the Rise and Demise of the Classical Gold Standard." In *Coping with Complexity in the International System,* ed. Robert Jervis and Jack Snyder, 137–162. Boulder, Colo.: Westview Press, 1993.

———. "Economic Integration and the Politics of Monetary Policy in the United States." In *Internationalization and Domestic Politics,* ed. Robert Keohane and Helen Milner, 108–136. New York: Columbia University Press, 1996.

———. "National Economic Policies in a World of Global Finance." *International Organization* 45 (1991): 425–452.

Friedland, Elaine. "The Southern African Development Co-ordination Conference and the West: Cooperation or Conflict?" *Journal of Modern African Studies* 23 (1985): 287–314.

Friedman, Steven, ed. *The Long Journey: South Africa's Quest for a Negotiated Settlement.* Johannesburg: Raven Press, 1993.

Galpin, Rodney. "Southern Africa: A Region of New Potential." *Modern Africa* (April/ May 1992): 15–16.

Gambari, Ibrahim A. "The United Nations." In *From Cape to Congo: Southern Africa's Evolving Security Challenges,* ed. Mwesiga Baregu and Christopher Landsberg, 255–274. Boulder, Colo.: Lynne Rienner, 2003.

Garner, Jonathan, and Lynne Thomas. "South Africa's Trade Partners, 1986–1991." Research Paper no. 6. Centre for the Study of the South African Economy and International Finance, London, 1991.

Garrett, Geoffrey. "Capital Mobility, Exchange Rates and Fiscal Policy in the Global Economy." *Review of International Political Economy* 7 (2000): 153–170.

———. "The European Community's Internal Market." *International Organization* 46 (1992): 533–560.

———. "Governing in the Global Economy: Economic Policy and Market Integration around the World." Paper presented at the American Political Science Association Annual Meeting, Boston, Mass., September 2–6, 1998.

———. *Partisan Politics in the Global Economy.* New York: Cambridge University Press, 1998.

———, and Peter Lange. "Internationalization, Institutions, and Political Change." In *Internationalization and Domestic Politics,* ed. Robert Keohane and Helen Milner, 48–75. New York: Cambridge University Press, 1996.

———, and Barry Weingast. "Ideas, Interest, and Institutions: Constructing the European Community's Internal Market." In *Ideas and Foreign Policy,* ed. Judith Goldstein and Robert Keohane, 173–206. Ithaca, N.Y.: Cornell University Press, 1993.

GATT. *Trade Policy Review: The Republic of South Africa 1993.* 2 vols. Geneva: GATT, September 1993.

Gelb, Stephen, ed. *South Africa's Economic Crisis.* London: Zed Books, 1991.

Geldenhuys, Deon. *The Diplomacy of Isolation: South African Foreign Policy Making.* New York: St. Martin's Press, 1984.

———. "Some Foreign Policy Implications of South Africa's 'TNS' with Particular

Reference to the 12 Point Plan." South African Institute of International Affairs, Johannesburg, March 1991.

———. "South Africa: The Politics of International Unpopularity." Paper prepared for the South African Institute of International Affairs (SAIIA) and the South African Institute of Race Relations (SAIRR) Symposium Where in the World Is South Africa? Pretoria, South Africa, November 1977.

———, and Denis Venter. "A Constellation of States: Regional Co-operation in Southern Africa." *International Affairs Bulletin* 8, no. 3 (1979): 36–73.

Ghai, Dharam P. "Alternative Concepts of Economic Integration." In *Economic Integration and Third World Development,* ed. Pradip Ghosh, 67–73. Westport, Conn.: Greenwood Press, 1984.

Ghosh, Pradip. *Economic Integration and Third World Development.* Westport, Conn.: Greenwood Press, 1984.

Gibb, Richard. "Regional Integration in Post-Apartheid Southern Africa: The Case of Renegotiating the Southern Africa Customs Union." *Journal of Southern Africa Studies* 23 (1997): 67–86.

Giliomee, Hermann. "The Last Trek? Afrikaners in the Transition to Democracy." *South African International* 22 (January 1992): 111–120.

———. *Surrender without Defeat: Afrikaners and the South African Miracle.* Johannesburg: South African Institute of Race Relations, 1997.

Glickman, Harvey, ed. *Toward Peace and Security in Southern Africa.* Philadelphia: Gordon and Breach Science Publishers, 1990.

Goldstein, Judith. *Ideas, Interests, and American Trade Policy.* Ithaca, N.Y.: Cornell University Press, 1993.

———. "The Political Economy of Trade: Institutions of Protection." *The American Political Science Review* 80 (1986): 161–184.

———, and Robert O. Keohane, eds. *Ideas and Foreign Policy: Beliefs, Institutions, and Political Change.* Ithaca, N.Y.: Cornell University Press, 1993.

Goodison, Paul. "The EU's Trade and Development Policy: South Africa and the SADC." In *Trading on Development: South Africa's Trade and Development Relations with the European Union,* ed. Rachel Houghton, 38–57. Proceedings of a Workshop Organized by the Foundation for Global Dialogue and the Trade and Industrial Policy Secretariat, May 1997. Braamfontein, South Africa: Friedrich Ebert Stiftung, 1997.

Goodman, John, and John Pauly. "The Obsolescence of Capital Controls." *World Politics* 46 (1993): 50–83.

Gordhan, Ketso. "Should South Africa Get Involved with the International Monetary Fund and the World Bank?" Paper prepared for the Symposium What Has the IMF in Store for South Africa?" Johannesburg, Institute for African Alternatives, July 27, 1991.

Gore, C. G. "International Order, Economic Regionalism and Structural Adjustment: The Case of Sub-Saharan Africa." In *Progress in Planning,* ed. D. Diamond, B. McLoughlin, and B. Massam, 184–249. New York: Pergamon Press, 1992.

Gourevitch, Peter. *Politics in Hard Times: Comparative Responses to International Economic Crisis.* Ithaca, N.Y.: Cornell University Press, 1986.

Graumans, Anne. "The European Union—South African Negotiations." Draft, prepared for the Netherlands Institute for Southern Africa, 1998.

Green, Reginald. "Constellation, Association, Liberation: Economic Coordination and the Struggle for South Africa." *African Contemporary Record* 12 (1979–1980): A32–A46.

———. "The Economic Implications of Post-Apartheid Southern Africa: How to Add Ten and One." In *The Challenges of Post-Apartheid South Africa: Conclusions and Pa-*

pers Presented at a Conference of the Africa Leadership Forum, September 8–10, ed. Felix Mosha, 77–122. Windhoek, 1991.

———. "Southern African Development Coordination: Toward a Functioning Dynamic?" *IDS Bulletin* 11 (1980): 53–58.

———, and Carol Thompson. "Political Economies in Conflict: SADCC and South Africa." In *Destructive Engagement: Southern Africa at War,* ed. Phyllis Johnson and David Martin. New York: Four Walls Eight Windows, 1988.

Grieco, Joseph M. *Cooperation among Nations: Europe, America and Non-Tariff Barriers.* Ithaca, N.Y.: Cornell University Press, 1990.

———. "The Relative Gains Problem for International Relations." *American Political Science Review* 87 (1993): 729–735.

Grundy, Kenneth. *Confrontation and Accommodation in Southern Africa.* Berkeley: University of California Press, 1973.

———. "Intermediary Power and Global Dependency: The Case of South Africa." *International Studies Quarterly* 20 (1976): 553–581.

Gupta, Vijay. "SADCC and Racist Machinations of South Africa." In *Regional Organizations,* ed. Rama Melkote, 134–154. New Delhi: Sterling Publishers Private Limited, 1990.

Gutkind, Peter, and Immanuel Wallerstein, eds. *Political Economy of Contemporary Africa.* Beverly Hills, Calif.: Sage, 1985.

Gwaradzimba, Fadzai. "The Southern African Development Coordination Conference (SADCC): Search for Autonomy and Regional Security in Southern Africa, 1980–1990." Ph.D. diss., Johns Hopkins University, 1992.

Haas, Ernst. "The Study of Regional Integration." *International Organization* 24 (1970): 3–42.

———. "Turbulent Fields and the Theory of Regional Integration." *International Organization* 24 (1976): 173–212.

———. *The Uniting of Europe: Political, Social and Economic Forces, 1950–1957.* 2nd ed. Stanford, Calif.: Stanford University Press, 1968.

Haggard, Stephen, and Chung Lee. "The Political Dimension of Finance in Economic Development." In *The Politics of Finance in Developing Countries,* ed. Stephen Haggard, Chung Lee, and Sylvia Maxfield, 3–22. Ithaca, N.Y.: Cornell University Press, 1993.

Haggard, Stephen, and Sylvia Maxfield. "Political Explanations of Financial Policy in Developing Countries." In *The Politics of Finance in Developing Countries,* ed. Stephen Haggard, Chung Lee, and Sylvia Maxfield, 293–326. Ithaca, N.Y.: Cornell University Press, 1993.

———, and Chung-in Moon. "The South Korean State in the International Economy: Liberal, Dependent or Mercantile?" In *The Antinomies of Interdependence: National Welfare and the International Division of Labor,* ed. John Ruggie, 131–190. New York: Columbia University Press, 1983.

———, and Beth Simmons. "Theories of International Regimes." *International Organization* 41 (1987): 491–517.

Hall, Peter A. "Conclusion: The Politics of Keynesian Ideas." In *The Political Power of Economic Ideas: Keynesianism across Nations,* ed. Peter A. Hall, 361–391. Princeton, N.J.: Princeton University Press, 1989.

Hanlon, Joseph. *Beggar Your Neighbours: Apartheid Power in Southern Africa.* Bloomington: Indiana University Press, 1986.

———. "SADCC in the 1990s: Development on the Front Line." Special Report no. 1158. *The Economist Intelligence Unit,* September 1989.

Hanson, Margaret, and James J. Hentz. "Neocolonialism and Neoliberalism in South Africa and Zambia." *Political Science Quarterly* 114 (1999): 479–502.

Harbeson, John W., and Donald Rothchild. "Africa in Post–Cold War International Politics: Changing Agendas." In *Africa in World Politics,* ed. John W. Harbeson and Donald Rothchild, 1–18. Boulder, Colo.: Westview Press, 1991.

Harvey, Charles, and Carolyn Jenkins. "The Unorthodox Response of the South African Economy to Changes in Macroeconomic Policy." Draft, unpublished paper. March 12, 1992.

Hatty, Paul R. "The South African Trade Policy Debate: A Business Perspective." In *South Africa and the World Economy in the 1990s,* ed. Pauline H. Baker, Alex Boraine, and Warren Krafchik, 127–136. Washington, D.C.: Brookings Institution, 1993.

Hawkins, Tony. "Economic Integration in Southern Africa." Paper presented at the African Regional Workshop on Economic Integration, Capetown, South Africa, March 2–4, 1994.

Hazlewood, Arthur. *African Integration and Disintegration: Case Studies in Economic and Political Union.* New York: Oxford University Press, 1967.

Hentz, James J. "The Mozal Aluminum Smelter—Partnership for Exploitation or Development?" In *Kick-Starting Development? Reconstructing the Maputo Corridor in the Context of Globalisation,* ed. Fredrik Söderbaum and Ian Taylor. London: Ashgate, 2003.

———. "Multinational Corporations at the Interstices of Domestic and International Politics: The Case of the H. J. Heinz Company in Zambia and Zimbabwe." *Journal of Commonwealth and Comparative Politics* 32 (1994): 200–230.

———. "The New Regionalism." *Cooperation and Conflict* 37 (2002): 350–356.

———. "The Southern African Security Order: Regional Integration and Security among Developing States." Paper presented at the International Political Science Association Meeting, Durban, South Africa, June 29–July 4, 2003.

———. "The Two Faces of Privatization: Political and Economic Logics in Transitional South Africa." *Journal of Modern African Studies* 38 (2000): 163–202.

Herbst, Jeffrey. "Economic Crisis and Distributional Imperative." In *South Africa: The Political Economy of Transformation,* ed. Stephen John Stedman, 29–46. Boulder, Colo.: Lynne Rienner, 1994.

———. *State and Power in Africa.* Princeton, N.J.: Princeton University Press, 2000.

———. "War and the State in Africa." *International Security* 14 (1990): 117–139.

Hettne, Björn. "Neomercantilism and the Pursuit of Regionalism." *Cooperation and Conflict* 28 (1993): 211–232.

———. "The New Regionalism: A Prologue." In *The New Regionalism and the Future of Security and Development,* ed. Björn Hettne, András Inotai, and Osvaldo Sunkel, xviii–xxxii. New York: St. Martin's Press, 2000.

———. "Globalization and the New Regionalism: The Second Great Transformation." In *Globalism and the New Regionalism,* ed. Björn Hettne, András Anotai, and Osvaldo Sunkel, xv–xxx. New York: St. Martin's Press, 1999.

———, András Inotai, and Osvaldo Sunkel, eds. *The New Regionalism and the Future of Security and Development.* New York: St. Martin's Press, 2000.

Higgott, Richard. "Africa and the New International Division of Labour." In *Africa in Economic Crisis,* ed. John Ravenhill, 286–306. New York: Columbia University Press, 1986.

Hirsch, Alan. "The External Environment and the South African Trade Debate." Economic Trends Working Paper no. 13. Development Research Unit, University of Cape Town, Cape Town, South Africa, 1992.

———. "Trading Up: Towards a Trade Policy for Industrial Growth in South Africa." Industrial Strategy Project Draft Final Report, Development Policy Research Unit, University of Cape Town, Cape Town, South Africa, August 1993.

Hirschman, Albert. "Against Parsimony: Three Easy Ways of Complicating Some Categories of Economic Discourse." *The American Economic Review* 74 (1984): 89–96.

———. *The State of Economic Development.* New Haven, Conn.: Yale University Press, 1958.

Holden, M. "The Choice of Trade Strategy." In *The Political Economy of South Africa,* ed. N. Nattrass and E. Ardington, 260–274. Cape Town: Oxford University Press, 1990.

Horvei, Tore. "Powering the Region: South Africa and the Southern African Power Pool." In *South Africa in Southern Africa: Reconfiguring the Region,* ed. David Simon, 146–163. Athens: Ohio University Press, 1998.

Horwitz, Robert Britt. *Communication and Democratic Reform in South Africa.* New York: Cambridge University Press, 2001.

Houghton, D. Hobart. *The South African Economy.* London: Oxford University Press, 1980.

Houghton, Rachel, ed. *Trading on Development: South Africa's Trade and Development Relations with the European Union.* Proceedings of a Workshop Organized by the Foundation for Global Dialogue and the Trade and Industrial Policy Secretariat, May 1997. Braamfontein, South Africa: Friedrich Ebert Stiftung, 1997.

Huntington, Samuel. *The Third Wave: Democratization in the Late Twentieth Century.* Norman: University of Oklahoma Press, 1991.

Hurrell, Andrew. "Explaining the Resurgence of Regionalism in World Politics." *Review of International Studies* 21 (1995): 331–358.

Hurt, Stephen R. "The EU and Africa after the Cold War." In *Africa in International Politics: External Involvement on the Continent,* ed. Ian Taylor and Paul Williams, 155–173. New York: Routledge, 2004.

Hutten, Will. "Relaunching Western Economies: The Case for Regulating Financial Markets." *Foreign Affairs* 75 (1996): 8–12.

Ikenberry, G. John. "Creating Yesterday's New World Order: Keynesian 'New Thinking' and the Anglo-American Postwar Settlement." In *Ideas and Foreign Policy: Beliefs, Institutions, and Political Change,* ed. Judith Goldstein and Robert O. Keohane, 57–86. Ithaca, N.Y.: Cornell University Press, 1993.

———, David Lake, and Michael Mastanduno. "Introduction: Approaches to Explaining American Foreign Economic Policy." *International Organization* 42 (1988): 1–14.

Imani Development Ltd. "Desk Study on Regional Integration in Eastern and Southern Africa: Constraints to Intra-Regional Payments, Trade and Investment." Vol. 1, Main Report. Prepared by Richard Hess for the Commission of European Communities, the World Bank, and the Preferential Trade Area for Eastern and Southern African States. January 23, 1992.

Industrial Development Corporation (IDC). *Competitive Advantage and the Promotion of Export Growth.* Sandton, South Africa: IDC, 1993.

———. "Modification of the Application of Protection Policy." Industrial Development Corporation, Sandton, South Africa, 1990.

Industrial Strategy Project (ISP). "Industrial Strategy Project 1993." Unpublished paper.

Isaksen, Jan. "Prospects for SACU." In *Southern Africa After Apartheid: Regional Integration and External Resources,* ed. Bertil Odén, 182–200. Uppsala: The Scandinavian Institute of African Studies, 1993.

Ismail, Faizel. "South Africa's Trade and Investment Policy and Its Negotiations with the EU." In *Trading on Development: South Africa's Trade and Development Relations with the European Union,* ed. Rachel Houghton, 86–92. Braamfontein, South Africa: Friedrich Ebert Stiftung, 1997.

Jacobs, Japie. "The IMF and South Africa: Implications for Fiscal Policy." Address by Dr. Japie Jacobs, Special Economic Adviser to the Minister of Finance, at the Workshop on Democratisation in South Africa: Economic Structural Adjustment and the Role of the IMF, The Strand, November 18, 1993.

Jacobson, John Kurt. "Much Ado about Ideas: The Cognitive Factor in Economic Policy." *World Politics* 47 (1995): 283–310.

Jervis, Robert. "Realism, Game Theory, and Cooperation." *World Politics* 40 (1980): 317–349.

Joffe, Avril, David Kaplan, Raphale Kaplinsky, and David Lewis. "Meeting the Global Challenge: A Framework for Industrial Revival in South Africa." In *South Africa and the World Economy in the 1990s,* ed. Pauline Baker, Alex Boraine, and Warren Krafchik, 91–126. Washington, D.C.: Brookings Institution, 1993.

Jones, Stuart, and Andre Muller. *The South African Economy, 1910–90.* New York: St. Martin's Press, 1992.

Jourdan, Paul. "Spatial Development Initiatives (SDIs)—The Official View." *Development Southern Africa* 15 (1998): 117–126.

Kahert, F., P. Richards, E. Stoutjesdijk, and P. Thomopoulos. *Economic Integration among Developing Countries.* Paris: Development Centre of the OECD, 1969.

Kahler, Miles. "Institutional Choice in International Monetary Affairs: Bretton Woods and its Competitors." Paper presented at the Annual Meeting of the American Political Science Association, Boston, Mass., September 2–6, 1998.

———. *International Institutions and the Political Economy of Integration.* Washington D.C.: The Brookings Institution, 1995.

Kahn, Brian. "An Overview of Exchange Rate Policy in South Africa." In *South Africa and the World Economy in the 1990s,* ed. Pauline Baker, Alex Boraine, and Warren Krafchik, 137–147. Washington, D.C.: Brookings Institution, 1993.

———. "South African Exchange Rate Policy, 1979–1991." Research Paper no. 7. Centre for the Study of the South African Economy and International Finance, London School of Economics, June 1992.

Kalenga, Paul. "Regional Trade Integration in Southern Africa: Critical Policy Issues." Working Paper no. 00/42. Development Policy Research Unit, University of Cape Town, Cape Town, South Africa, September 2000.

Kalula, Evance. "Labour Perspectives in Regional Interdependence." In *Prospects for Progress: Critical Choices for Southern Africa,* ed. Minnie Venter, 108–115. Cape Town: Longman, 1994.

Kalyalya, Denny Hamachila. "Regional Economic Integration in Southern Africa: An Evaluation of SADCC's Impact on Trade." Ph.D. diss., University of Massachusetts, 1993.

Kang, C. S. Eliot. "Regulating Inward Foreign Direct Investment." *International Organization* 51 (1997): 301–333.

Kapstein, Ethan. *Governing the Global Economy.* Cambridge, Mass.: Harvard University Press, 1994.

Katzen, Leo. "The Employment Problem in Post-Apartheid South Africa." In *Sustainable Development for a Democratic South Africa,* ed. Ken Cole, 50–57. New York: St. Martin's Press, 1994.

Keet, Dot. "Labour Issues in Southern Africa: Critical Choices for Trade Unions." In *Prospects for Progress: Critical Choices for Southern Africa,* ed. Minnie Venter, 116–130. Cape Town: Longman, 1994.

Kell, Sue, and Troy Dyer, "Economic Integration in Southern Africa." In *The Uncertain Promise of Southern Africa,* ed. York Bradshaw and Stephen Ndegwa, 363–393. Bloomington: Indiana University Press, 2000.

Keohane, Robert O. *After Hegemony: Cooperation and Discord in the World Political Economy.* Princeton, N.J.: Princeton University Press, 1984.

———. "Institutionalist Theory, Realist Challenge." In *Neorealism and Neoliberalism: The Contemporary Debate,* ed. David Baldwin, 269–300. New York: Columbia University Press, 1992.

———. "International Institutions: Two Approaches." *International Studies Quarterly* 32 (1988): 378–396.

———. "International Interdependence and Integration." In *International Politics,* ed. Fred Greenstein and Nelson Polsby, 363–414. Reading, Mass.: Addison-Wesley Publishing Company, 1975.

———. "Multilateralism: An Agenda for Research." *International Journal* 45 (1990): 731–764.

———. "Problematic Lucidity: Stephen Krasner's 'State Power and the Structure of International Trade.'" *World Politics* 50 (1997): 150–170.

———. "Transgovernmental Relations and International Organizations." *World Politics* 27 (1974): 39–63.

———, and Stanley Hoffman. "Institutional Change in Europe in the 1990s." In *The New European Community: Decision Making and Institutional Change,* ed. Robert Keohane and Stanley Hoffman, 1–40. Boulder, Colo.: Westview Press, 1991.

———, and Helen V. Milner, eds. *Internationalization and Domestic Politics.* New York: Cambridge University Press, 1996.

———, and Joseph Nye. "Power and Interdependence Revisited." *International Organization* 41 (1987): 725–753.

Khadiagala, Gilbert M. "The Front Line States, Regional Interstate Relations and Institution Building in Southern Africa." In *Toward Peace and Security in Southern Africa,* ed. Harvey Glickman, 131–162. Philadelphia: Gordon and Breach Science Publishers, 1990.

———. "Regional Dimensions of Sanctions." In *How Sanctions Work: Lessons from South Africa,* ed. Neta C. Crawford and Audie Klotz, 247–263. New York: St. Martin's Press, 1999.

———. "Southern Africa's Transitions: Prospects for Regional Security." In *South Africa: The Political Economy of Transformation,* ed. Stephen John Stedman, 167–180. Boulder, Colo.: Lynne Rienner, 1994.

Khama, Sir Seretse. "Introduction." In *Southern Africa toward Economic Liberation,* ed. Amon J. Nsekela, vii–xix. London: Rex Collins, 1981.

Koelble, Thomas A. *The Global Economy and Democracy in South Africa.* New Brunswick, N.J.: Rutgers University Press, 1998.

Kohler, Volkmar. "Prospects for European Cooperation with South Africa." South Africa Institute for International Affairs, Johannesburg, August 11, 1993.

Kornegay, Francis, and Chris Landsberg. "*Phapama iAfrika!* The African Renaissance and Corporate South Africa." *Africa Security Review* 7 (1998): 3–17.

Krasner, Stephen. "Approaches to the State: Alternative Conceptions and Historical Dynamics." *Comparative Politics* 16 (1984): 223–246.

———. "Global Communications and National Power: Life on the Pareto Frontier." *World Politics* 34 (1991): 336–366.

Kratochwil, Friedrich. "Regimes, Interpretation and the 'Science' of Politics." *Millennium* 17 (1988): 263–284.

———. *Rules, Norms, and Decisions: On the Conditions of Practical and Legal Reasoning in International and Domestic Affairs.* New York: Cambridge University Press, 1989.

———. "State Power and the Structure of International Trade." *World Politics* 28 (1976): 317–348.

————, and John Ruggie. "International Organization: The State of the Art on the Art of the State." *International Organization* 40 (1986): 753–775.

Kritzinger-van Niekerk, Lolette, ed. *Towards Strengthening Multisectoral Linkages in SADC*. Midrand: Development Bank of Southern Africa, March 1997.

Krueger, Anne. *Exchange Rate Determination*. New York: Cambridge University Press, 1983.

Kumar, Umesh. "Uruguay Round and the Southern African Customs Union." Paper presented at the Workshop on Reconstituting and Democratising the Southern African Customs Union, Gaborone, Botswana, March 6–8, 1994.

Lachman, Desmond, and Kenneth Bercuson. "Economic Policies for a New South Africa." Occasional Paper 91. International Monetary Fund, Washington, D.C., January 1992.

Lakatos, Imre. *The Methodology of Scientific Research Programmes: Philosophical Papers.* Vol. 1. New York: Cambridge: University Press, 1978.

Lake, David, and Patrick Morgan. "The New Regionalism in Security Affairs." In *Regional Orders: Building Security in a New World,* ed. David Lake and Patrick Morgan, 3–19. University Park: Pennsylvania State University Press, 1997.

Lall, Sanjaya. "What Will Make South Africa Internationally Competitive?" In *South Africa and the World Economy in the 1990s,* ed. Pauline Baker, Alex Boraine, and Warren Krafchik, 50–70. Washington, D.C.: Brookings Institution, 1993.

Lancaster, Carol. "Economic Regionalism in Sub-Sahara Africa." Unpublished paper, 1990. In author's possession.

Landell-Mills, P. M. "The 1969 Southern African Customs Union Agreement." *Journal of Modern African Studies* 9 (1971): 263–281.

Langhammer, Rolf J. "The Developing Countries and Regionalism." *Journal of Common Market Studies* 31 (1993): 211–231.

————. "Regional Integration and Cooperation in Africa: A History of Disappointment." *Intereconomics* no. 9 (1977): 257–262.

Lawrence, Robert. *Regionalism, Multilateralism, and Deeper Integration.* Washington, D.C.: The Brookings Institution, 1996.

Leblang, David. "Domestic Political Institutions and Exchange Rate Commitment in the Developing World." Paper presented at the Annual Meeting of the American Political Science Association Boston, Mass., September 2–6, 1998.

Lee, Margaret. "The European Union–South Africa Free Trade Agreement: In Whose Interest?" *Journal of Contemporary African Studies* 20 (2002): 81–106.

————. *SADCC: The Political Economy of Development in Southern Africa.* Nashville: Winston Derek Publishers, 1989.

Legro, Jeffrey. "Culture and Preferences in the International Two-Step." *American Political Science Review* 90 (1996): 118–137.

Legum, Colin. "Balance of Power in Southern Africa." In *The Uncertain Promise of Southern Africa,* ed. York W. Bradshaw and Stephen N. Ndegwa, 12–23. Bloomington: Indiana University Press, 2000.

————. *Vorster's Gamble for Africa: How the Search for Peace Failed.* London: Rex Collings, 1976.

Leistner, Erich. "Brussels Conference on Future Relations between the EC and Southern Africa." Draft, November 9, 1993.

————. "Designing the Framework for a Southern African Development Community." *Africa Insight* 22, no. 1 (1992): 4–13.

————. "Issues of Economic Integration in Southern Africa." Konrad-Adenauer Stiftung Occasional Papers 7. Johannesburg, September 1992.

————. "Migration of High-Level African Manpower to South Africa." *African Insight* 4 (1993): 219–224.

———. "South Africa a Member of the Lomé Convention?" *AI Bulletin* 32, no. 4 (1992): 1–3.

———, and Pieter Esterhuysen, eds. *South Africa in Southern Africa: Economic Interaction.* Pretoria: Africa Institute of South Africa, 1988.

Lenaghan, Patricia, and Xavier Philippe. "Contents and Influence of the Cotonou Agreement on the Trade and Development Cooperation Agreement." Paper presented at the launching conference of European Communities Studies Association in Southern Africa, 2000.

Levy, Brian. "How Can South African Manufacturing Efficiently Create Employment? An Analysis of the Impact of Trade and Industrial Policy." Southern Africa Department, World Bank, Washington, D.C., 1992.

Lewis, Stephen. *The Economics of Apartheid.* New York: Council on Foreign Relations, 1990.

Leys, Robert, and Arne Tostensen. "Regional Cooperation in Southern Africa: The Southern African Development Co-ordination Conference." *Review of African Political Economy* (January–April 1982), 52–71.

Libby, Ronald. *The Politics of Economic Power in Southern Africa.* Princeton, N.J.: Princeton University Press, 1987.

Lindberg, Leon, and Stuart Scheignold, eds. *Regional Integration: Theory and Research.* Cambridge, Mass.: Harvard University Press, 1971.

Lings, Kevin. "Export Incentives in South Africa." *Nedbank Guide to the Economy.* Johannesburg: Nedbank Economic Unit, November 1991.

Lipschitz, Leslie. "Review of the Debate on the Prospective Role of the IMF and World Bank in South Africa." In *South Africa and the World Economy in the 1990s,* ed. Pauline Baker, Alex Boraine, and Warren Krafchik, 212–215. Washington, D.C.: Brookings Institution, 1993.

Lipton, Merle. *Capitalism and Apartheid: South Africa, 1910–1986.* London: Wildwood House, 1989.

———, and Charles Simkins. "Introduction." In *State and Market in Post-Apartheid South Africa,* ed. Merle Lipton and Charles Simkins, 1–34. Boulder, Colo.: Westview Press, 1993.

Lizano, Eduardo. "Integration of Less Developed Areas and Areas of Different Levels of Development." In *Economic Integration Worldwide, Regional, Sectoral,* ed. Fritz Machlup, 274–284. New York: Macmillan Press, 1976.

Lodge, Tom. *Politics in South Africa: From Mandela to Mbeki.* Bloomington: Indiana University Press, 2002.

Lorenz, Detle. "Regional Economic Integration Opportunities, Obstacles and Options." Paper prepared for the Symposium on Regional Economic and National Development, Harare, Zimbabwe, May 1991.

Louw, Chris. "Manuel Warns of Apartheid Web." *Die Suid-Afrikaan,* October–November 1992, 2–22.

Maasdorp, Gavin. "Can Regional Integration Help Southern Africa?" In *Can South and Southern Africa Become Globally Competitive Economies?* ed. G. S. Maasdorp, 45–52. New York: St. Martin's Press, 1996.

———, ed. *Can South and Southern Africa Become Globally Competitive Economies?* New York: St. Martin's Press, 1996.

———. "A Changing Regional Role for SADCC?" *Harvard International Review* 12 (1989): 10–13.

———. "Economic Cooperation in Southern Africa: Prospects for Regional Cooperation." Conflict Studies 253. Research Institute for the Study of Conflict and Terrorism, London, 1992.

———. "A Vision for Economic Integration and Cooperation in Southern Africa." Paper prepared for the Department of Trade and Industry. Pretoria, March 1994.

———, and Alan Whiteside. "Project on Rethinking Economic Cooperation in Southern Africa." Paper prepared for the Regional Integration Conference. Harare,
Zimbabwe, 1992.

———, and Alan Whiteside. *Rethinking Economic Cooperation in Southern Africa: Trade
and Investment.* Johannesburg: Konrad-Adenauer Stiftung, 1993.

———, and Alan Whiteside. "South Africa—The Economy and Closer Regional Co-
operation." In *Symposium on Regional Economic Integration and National Development.*
Harare: Southern Africa Foundation for Economic Research and Konrad Adenauer
Foundation, 1991.

Macdonald, Michael, and Wilmot James. "The Hand on the Tiller: The Politics
of State and Class in South Africa." *Journal of Modern African Studies* 31 (1993):
387–405.

Macroeconomic Research Group (MERG). *Making Democracy Work: A Framework for
Macroeconomic Policy in South Africa: A Report to the Democratic Movement of South
Africa.* Bellville, South Africa: Centre for Development Studies, 1993.

Makoni, Simba. "Getting Down to Brass Tacks." *Southern African Economist* 4, no. 2
(April/May 1991): 11–13.

———. "SADCC's New Strategies." *Africa Report* 32 (1987): 30–33.

Malan, Theo. "The South African Black States' and Neighboring Black Africa's Re-
sponse to South Africa's Proposed Constellation of Southern African States." In
The Constellation of States, ed. Willie Breytenbach, 57–65. Johannesburg: South
Africa Foundation, 1980.

Mandaza, Ibbo, and Arne Tostensen. *Southern Africa in Search of a Common Future: From
Conference to a Community.* Gaborone, Botswana: Southern African Development
Community, 1994.

Mandela, Nelson. Address to the Opening of the 2nd Parliament, February 17, 1995.
PR Newswires Associates, Inc., February 21, 1995.

———. "South Africa's Future Foreign Policy." *Foreign Affairs* 72 (1993): 86–97.

Mansfield, Edward, and Helen Milner. "The New Wave of Regionalism." *International
Organization* 53 (1999): 589–622.

Manuel, Trevor. "Address to the SADC Annual Consultative Conference." Harare,
Zimbabwe, January 16–31, 1993. In author's possession.

Maphanyane, Emang Motlhabane. "SADCC—Future Challenges." In *Southern Africa
After Apartheid: Regional Integration and External Resources,* ed. Bertil Odén, 174–
181. Uppsala: Scandinavian Institute of African Studies, 1993.

Marais, Hein. *South Africa: Limits to Change: The Political Economy of Transition.* London:
Zed Books, 1998.

March, James, and Johan Olsen. "The New Institutionalism: Organizational Factors
in Political Life." *American Political Science Review* 78 (1984): 734–749.

Marchand, Marianne, Bøås Morten, and Timothy Shaw. "The Political Economy of
New Regionalisms." *Third World Quarterly* 20 (1999): 897–910.

Martin, Guy. "African Regional Cooperation and Integration: Achievements, Prob-
lems and Prospects." In *Twenty-First-Century Africa: Towards a New Vision of Self-
Sustainable Development,* ed. Ann Seidman and Frederick Anang, 69–99. Trenton,
N.J.: Africa World Press, 1992.

Martin, Lisa. "The Rational State Choice of Multilateralism." In *Multilateralism Matters: Theory and Praxis of an International Form,* ed. John G. Ruggie, 765–793. New
York: Columbia University Press, 1993.

Martin, William. "Region Formation under Crisis Conditions: South vs. Southern
Africa in the Interwar Period." *Journal of Southern African Studies* 16 (1990):
112–138.

Marx, Anthony W. *Lessons of Struggle: South African Internal Opposition, 1960–1990.* New York: Oxford University Press, 1992.

Mastanduno, Michael. "Do Relative Gains Matter? America's Response to Japanese Industrial Policy." In *Neorealism and Neoliberalism: The Contemporary Debate,* ed. David Baldwin, 250–268. New York: Columbia University Press, 1993.

Matsebula, Michael, and Vakashile Simelane. "Small Countries within Regional Integration." In *Can South and Southern Africa Become Globally Competitive Economies?* ed. Gavin Maasdorp, 53–60. New York: St. Martin's Press, 1996.

Mattli, Walter. *The Logic of Regional Integration: Europe and Beyond.* New York: Cambridge University Press, 1999.

Maxfield, Sylvia. *Governing Capital: International Finance and Mexican Politics.* Ithaca, N.Y.: Cornell University Press, 1990.

Mayer, Marina J. "Introduction and Overview." In *Towards Strengthening Multisectoral Linkages in SADC,* ed. Lolette Kritzinger-van Niekerk, 1–5. Midrand: Development Bank of Southern Africa, 1997.

———, and Rosalind Thomas. "Trade Integration in the Southern African Development Community: Prospects and Problems." Paper prepared for the Development Bank of Southern Africa, Midrand, 1997.

Mazzeo, D., ed. *African Regional Organizations.* New York: Cambridge University Press, 1984.

Mbeki, Thabo. "The Fatton Thesis: A Rejoinder." *Canadian Journal of African Studies* 18 (1984): 609–612.

———. "South Africa's International Relations—Today and Tomorrow." *South Africa International* 21 (1991): 231–235.

———. Speech to the South African Institute of International Affairs, Jan Smuts House. November 25, 1993. Author's notes.

McCarthy, Colin. "SACU and the Rand Zone." In *Regionalisation in Africa: Integration and Disintegration,* ed. Daniel C. Bach, 159–168. Bloomington: Indiana University Press, 1999.

———. "South Africa as a Cooperative Partner in Southern African Trade and Investment." Paper presented at the Regional Economic Integration Conference, Harare, Zimbabwe, December 3–4, 1992.

———. "Structural Development of South African Manufacturing Industry—A Policy Perspective." *The South African Journal of Economics* 56 (1988): 1–24.

McQueen, Matthew, and Christopher Stevens. "Trade Preferences and Lomé IV: Non-Traditional ACP Exports to the EC." *Development Policy Review* 7 (1989): 239–260.

Meth, Charles. "Capital Goods, 'Dependence' and Appropriate Technology." In *The Political Economy,* ed. N. Nattrass and E. Ardington, 292–312. Cape Town: Oxford University Press, 1990.

Meyer, Klaus, Saul Estrin, Suman Bhaumik, Stephen Gelb, Helb Handooussa, Maryse Louis, Subir Gokarn, Laveesh Bhandari, Nguyen Than Ha, and Nguyen Vo Hung. "Foreign Direct Investment in Emerging Markets: A Comparative Study in Egypt, India, South Africa and Vietnam." Paper presented at the 6th conference of the European Association of Comparative Economic Studies, Forli, Italy, June 2002.

Meyns, Peter. "The Southern African Development Coordination Conference (SADCC) and Regional Cooperation in Southern Africa." In *African Regional Organizations,* ed. Domenico Mazzeo, 198–224. New York: Cambridge University Press, 1984.

Midgley, D. C. "Co-operative Development of Water and Hydroelectric Potential." In *South Africa in Southern Africa: Economic Interaction,* ed. Erich Leistner and Pieter Esterhuysen, 158–176. Pretoria: Africa Institute of South Africa, 1988.

Mills, Greg. "Introduction." In *War and Peace in Southern Africa,* ed. Robert I. Rotberg and Greg Mills, 1–23. Washington, D.C.: Brookings Institution, 1998.

———. "South Africa's Foreign Policy: From Isolation to Respectability?" In *South Africa in Southern Africa: Reconfiguring the Region,* ed. David Simon, 72–88. Athens: Ohio University Press, 1998.

Milner, Helen. "International Theories of Cooperation among Nations: Strengths and Weaknesses." *World Politics* 44 (1992): 467–496.

Minney, Tom. "SADCC Dreams of the United States of Southern Africa." *Africa Investment Monitor,* February 25, 1991, 1.

Mistry, Magan. "The Trade Pattern of Southern Africa." *Nedbank Guide to the Economy* (Johannesburg: Nedbank Economic Unit, February 1992).

Mistry, Percy. "The Present Role of the World Bank in Africa." Edited version of lecture delivered at the Institute for African Alternatives, October 16, 1989, Johannesburg, South Africa.

———. "Regional Integration and Economic Development." In *The New Regionalism and the Future of Security and Development,* ed. Björn Hettne, András Inotai, and Osvaldo Sunkel, 26–49. New York: St. Martin's Press, 2000.

Mitrany, David. "Prospects of Integration: Federal or Functional?" *Journal of Common Market Studies* 4 (1965): 119–149.

———. *A Working Peace.* Chicago: Quadrangle Books, 1966.

Mittelman, James. *The Globalization Syndrome: Transformation and Resistance.* Princeton, N.J.: Princeton University Press, 2000.

———. "Rethinking the 'New Regionalism.'" *Global Governance* 2 (1996): 189–214.

Mkandawire, Thandika. "Dependence and Economic Cooperation: The Case of SADCC." *Zimbabwe Journal of Economics* 2 (1985): 1–10.

Mohr, P. J. "Fiscal Policy in South Africa." In *Leading Issues in South African Economics,* ed. Philip A. Black and Brian Dollery, 281–292. Johannesburg: Southern Book Publishers, 1989.

Moll, Terence. "Macroeconomic Policy in Turbulent Times." In *State and Market in Post-Apartheid South Africa,* ed. Merle Lipton and Charles Simkins, 235–270. Boulder, Colo.: Westview Press, 1993.

Moravcsik, Andrew. "The Future of European Integration Studies: Social Science of Social Theory." *Millennium* 28 (1999): 371–392.

———. "Negotiating the Single European Act." *International Organization* 45 (1991): 9–57.

———. "Taking Preferences Seriously: A Liberal Theory of International Politics." *International Organization* 51 (1997): 513–554.

Morna, Colleen Lowe. "SADCC's First Decade." *Africa Report* 35 (1990): 49–52.

Mugomba, Agrippah. "Regional Organizations and African Underdevelopment: The Collapse of the East African Community." *Journal of Modern African Studies* 16 (1978): 261–272.

Mulaisho, D. "SADCC: A New Approach to Integration." In *The Long-Term Perspective Study of Sub-Saharan Africa.* Vol. 4, *Proceedings of a Workshop on Regional Integration and Cooperation.* Washington, D.C.: The World Bank Press, 1990.

Muller, John, and Nico Cloete. "Social Scientists and Social Change in South Africa." *International Journal of Contemporary Sociology* 28 (1991): 171–192.

Mwase, N. "Regional Cooperation and Socialist Transformation in Southern Africa: Problems and Prospects." *Journal of African Studies* 13 (1980): 17–25.

Myrdal, Gunnar. *Economic Theory and Underdeveloped Regions.* London: Duckworth Press, 1957.

Mytelka, Lynn. "Regional Integration in the Third World: Some Internal Factors." In

International Dimensions of Regional Integration in the Third World: Proceedings of the 5th International Conference of the I.C.I. {Institute for International Cooperation}, 15–43. Ottawa: University of Ottawa Press, 1975.

NAMPO. "Maize Production in the Nineteen Nineties." The South African National Maize Producers' Organization (NAMPO), January 1993.

Nattrass, Nicoli. "Economic Power and Profits in Post-War Manufacturing." In *The Political Economy of South Africa,* ed. N. Nattrass and E. Ardington, 107–128. Cape Town: Oxford University Press, 1990.

———, and Jeremy Seekings. "Growth, Democracy, and Expectations in South Africa." In *Economic Globalization and Fiscal Policy,* ed. Iraj Abedian and Michael Biggs, 27–53. Cape Town: Oxford University Press, 1998.

———, and Jeremy Seekings. "Two Nations? Race and Economic Inequality in South Africa Today." *Daedalus* 130 (2001): 45–70.

Naude, Stef. "Evolving International Trade Policy in South Africa." South Africa Department of Trade and Industry, October 28, 1993.

Nel, Philip. "The Power of Ideas: 'Ambiguous Globalism' and South Africa's Foreign Policy." Paper presented at 19th World Congress of the International Political Science Association, Durban, South Africa, July 1, 2003.

Nkuhlu, Mfundo. "South Africa's Trade Policy with SADC and Africa." In *Trading on Development: South Africa's Trade and Development Relations with the European Union,* ed. Rachel Houghton, 78–85. Braamfontein, South Africa: Friedrich Ebert Stiftung, 1997.

———. "Southern Africa After Apartheid: Perspectives on Institutional Arrangements for Multi-Lateral Relations." Paper presented at the Workshop on the Correlation of Political Systems and Economic Development in Southern Africa, University of Fort Hare, Harare, Zimbabwe, November 1–2, 1993.

North, Douglas, and Barry Weingast. "Constitutions and Commitment: The Evolution of Institutions Governing Public Choice in Seventeenth Century England." *Journal of Economic History* 49 (1989): 803–832.

Nsekela, Amon J. *Southern Africa toward Economic Liberation.* London: Rex Collings, 1981.

Nye, Joseph, ed. *International Regionalism.* Boston: Little, Brown & Co., 1968.

Nzo, Alfred. "Address to SADCC." May 5–8, 1990. In author's possession.

Odell, John. *U.S. International Monetary Policy: Markets, Power and Ideas as Sources of Change.* Princeton, N.J.: Princeton University Press, 1982.

Odén, Bertil, ed. *Southern Africa After Apartheid: Regional Integration and External Resources.* Uppsala: Scandinavian Institute of African Studies, 1993.

———, and H. Othman, eds. *Regional Cooperation in Southern Africa: A Post-Apartheid Perspective.* Uppsala: The Scandinavian Institute of African Studies, 1989.

Ohlson, Thomas, and Stephen John Stedman. *The New Is Not Yet Born: Conflict Resolution in Southern Africa.* Washington, D.C.: The Brookings Institution, 1994.

Okolo, Julius Emeka. "Integrative and Cooperative Regionalism: The Economic Community of West African States." *International Organization* 39 (1985): 121–153.

Osborn, Edward. "Industrialization, Liberalization and Export Promotion." *Nedbank Quarterly Guide to the Economy.* Johannesburg, November 1992.

———. "An Organization for Southern African Co-operation." *Nedbank Quarterly Guide to the Economy* Johannesburg: Nedbank Economic Unit, February 1993.

———, and Kevin Lings. "Capital Intensity in the Manufacturing Sector." Paper presented at the EBM Research Conference, Vista University, Port Elizabeth, South Africa, November 30–December 1, 1992.

Østergaard, Tom. "Classical Models of Regional Integration—What Relevance for Southern Africa?" In *Southern Africa After Apartheid: Regional Integration and External Resources,* ed. Bertil Odén, 27–47. Uppsala: Scandinavian Institute of African Studies, 1993.

———. *SADCC beyond Transportation: The Challenge of Industrial Cooperation.* Uppsala: Scandinavian Institute of African Studies, 1989.

Ottaway, Marina. *South Africa: The Struggle for a New Order.* Washington, D.C.: The Brookings Institution, 1993.

Oye, Kenneth. "Explaining Cooperation under Anarchy: Hypotheses and Strategies." In *Cooperation under Anarchy,* ed. Kenneth Oye, 1–24. Princeton, N.J.: Princeton University Press, 1986.

Padayachee, Vishnu. "Development Implications for South Africa of Using IMF and World Bank Loans and Resources." In *South Africa and the World Economy in the 1990s,* ed. Pauline Baker, Alex Boraine, and Warren Krafchik, 184–203. Washington, D.C.: Brookings Institution, 1993.

Page, Sheila. "Some Questions for Industrial Research in SADC." Unpublished paper, June 1998.

———, and Christopher Stevens. "Trading with South Africa: The Policy Options for the EC." ODI Special Report, Overseas Development Institute, London, 1992.

Pagel, Chris Alexander. "Areas of Competitive Advantage in South African Manufacturing." MA Thesis, Rand Afrikaans University, November 1992.

Palmer, Norman. *The New Regionalism in Asia and the Pacific.* Toronto: Lexington Books, 1991.

Panitch, Leo. *Globalization and the State.* Mexico City: Universidad Nacional Autónoma de México, 1994.

Patel, Ebrahim. "New Institutions of Decision-Making." In *Engine of Development?* ed. Ebrahim Patel, 1–16. Kenwyn, South Africa: Juta, 1993.

Payne, Anthony. "The New Political Economy of Regional Studies." *Millennium* 27 (1998): 253–274.

———, and Andrew Gamble. "Introduction: The Political Economy of Regionalism and World Order." In *Regionalism and World Order,* ed. Anthony Payne and Andrew Gamble, 1–20. New York: St. Martin's Press, 1996.

Penaherra, Germanico Salgado. "Viable Integration and the Economic Co-operation Problems of the Developing World." Parts 1 and 2. *Journal of Common Market Studies* 19, no. 1 (1980): 65–76; no. 2 (1990): 175–188.

Petland, Charles. "Functionalism and Theories of Political Integration." In *Functionalism: Theory and Practice in International Relations,* ed. A. J. R. Groom and Paul Taylor. New York: Crane Russak & Co., 1975.

Pillay, Pundy. "Labour, Skills Shortages and Human Resource Development in Southern Africa: Issues and Prospects for Regional Integration." Paper presented at the Regional Economic Integration Conference, Harare, Zimbabwe, December 3–4, 1992.

Poku, Nana, and Maxi Schoeman. "Regional Integration in Southern Africa: A Cautionary Note." Paper presented at the 39th Convention of the International Studies Association, Washington, D.C., September 2–5, 1999.

Powell, Robert. "Absolute and Relative Gains in International Relations Theory." *American Political Science Review* 85 (1991): 1303–1331.

———. "The Neorealist-Neoliberal Debate." *International Organization* 48 (1994): 313–334.

Price, Robert. *The Apartheid State in Crisis: Political Transformation in South Africa.* New York: Oxford University Press, 1991.

———. "Majority Rule in South Africa: The Role of Global Pressure." In *Toward Peace and Security in Southern Africa,* ed. Harvey Glickman, 77–108. Philadelphia: Gordon and Breach Science Publishers, 1990.

Puchala, Donald. "Domestic Politics and Regional Harmonization in the European Communities." *World Politics* 27 (1974): 496–521.

Putnam, Robert. "Diplomacy and Domestic Politics: Logic of Two-Level Games." *International Organization* 32 (1978): 427–460.

Ramphele, Mamphela. "Citizenship Challenge for South Africa's Young Democracy." *Daedalus* 130 (2001): 1–18.

Ranger, T. O., ed. *Aspects of Central African History.* Evanston, Ill.: Northwestern University Press, 1968.

Ravenhill, John. "Collective Self-Reliance or Collective Self-Delusion: Is the Lagos Plan a Viable Alternative?" In *Africa in Economic Crisis,* ed. John Ravenhill, 85–107. New York: Columbia University Press, 1986.

———. "Overcoming Constraints to Regional Cooperation in Africa: Coordination Rather Than Integration?" In *The Long-Term Perspective Study of Sub-Saharan Africa, Background Papers.* Vol. 4, *Proceedings of a Workshop on Regional Integration and Cooperation,* 81–85. Washington D.C.: World Bank, 1991.

———. "Redrawing the Map of Africa?" In *The Precarious Balance: State and Society in Africa,* ed. Donald Rothchild and Naomi Chazan, 282–305. Boulder, Colo.: Westview Press, 1988.

———. "Regional Integration and Development in Africa: Lessons from the East African Community." *The Journal of Commonwealth and Comparative Politics* 17 (1978): 227–247.

———. "A Second Decade of Adjustment: Greater Complexity, Greater Uncertainty." In *Hemmed In: Response to Africa's Economic Decline,* 18–53. New York: Columbia University Press, 1993.

Ray, Edward John. "Changing Patterns of Protectionism: The Fall in Tariffs and the Rise in Non-Tariff Barriers." In *International Political Economy,* 3rd ed., ed. Jeffry A. Frieden and David Lake, 353–367. New York: St. Martin's Press, 1995.

Ray, Jayanta Kuma. "Focus on Issues." In *Regional Organizations: A Third World Perspective,* ed. Rama S. Melkote, 3–5. New Delhi: Sterling Publishers, 1990.

Reilly, Gavin. "Southern Africa: The Challenges of the 90s—Summary of Workshop and Keynote Address." The Institute of Directors, Zimbabwe Division, Harare, Zimbabwe, 1991.

Reno, William. *Warlord Politics and African States.* Boulder, Colo.: Lynne Rienner, 1998.

Republic of South Africa, Debates of the National Assembly, *Hansard No. 17, Third Session–1st Parliament, 5–7 November 1990.*

Rich, Paul, ed. *The Dynamics of Change in Southern Africa.* New York: Saint Martin's Press, 1994.

Robson, Peter. *Economic Integration in Africa.* Evanston, Ill.: Northwestern University Press, 1968.

———. "The New Regionalism and Developing Countries." *Journal of Common Market Studies* 31 (1993): 329–348.

———. "Regional Economic Cooperation among Developing Countries: Some Further Considerations." *World Development* 6 (1978): 771–779.

———. "Regional Integration and the Crisis in Sub-Saharan Africa." *Journal of Modern African Studies* 23 (1985): 603–622.

Rotberg, Robert. "Decision Making and the Military in South Africa." In *South Africa and Its Neighbors: Regional Security and Self-Interest,* ed. Robert Rotberg, Henry Bienen, Robert Legvold, and Gavin Maasdorp, 13–26. Lexington, Mass.: Lexington Books, 1985.

Ruggie, John. "International Responses to Technology." *International Organization* 29 (1975): 557–583.

———. "Political Structure and Change in the International Economic Order." In *The Antinomies of Interdependence,* ed. John Ruggie. New York: Columbia University Press, 1983.

Saasa, Oliver. "Economic Co-operation and Integration among Developing Countries: An Overview." In *Joining the Future: Economic Integration and Co-operation in Africa,* ed. Oliver Saasa, 7–26. Nairobi: Acts Press, 1991.

———. "SADCC Industrial Co-operation and Donor Support." In *Joining the Future: Economic Integration and Co-operation in Africa,* ed. Oliver Saasa, 59–82. Nairobi: Acts Press, 1991.

SADCC Secretariat. "Regional Integration in Southern Africa." Unpublished paper, Gaborone, Botswana, December 1993.

———. *SADCC: Towards Economic Integration.* Theme Document presented at SADCC Annual Consultative Conference, Maputo, South Africa, January 1992.

———. "Towards the Southern African Development Community: A Declaration by the Heads of State or Government of Southern African States." Gaborone, Botswana, 1992.

Sakamoto, Jorge. "Industrial Development and Integration of Underdeveloped Countries." *Journal of Common Market Studies* 12 (1969): 283–305.

Salama, Clara Mira, and Stephen Dearden. "The Cotonou Agreement." Discussion Paper no. 20, European Developmental Policy Study Group, Department of Economics, Manchester Metropolitan University, 2001. Available online at http://www.edpsg.org/Documents/Dp20.doc.

Sandbrook, Richard. *The Politics of African Economic Stagnation.* New York: Columbia University Press, 1986.

———. *The Politics of Africa's Economic Recovery.* New York: Cambridge University Press, 1993.

Sandholtz, Wayne. "Monetary Politics and Maastricht." *International Organization* 47 (1993): 1–41.

Scerri, M. "Research and Development in South African Manufacturing Industries." *South African Journal of Economics* 56 (1988): 111–123.

Schrire, Robert, ed. *Wealth or Poverty? Critical Choices for South Africa.* Cape Town: Oxford University Press, 1992.

Schulz, Michael, Fredrik Söderbaum, and Joakim Ojendal, eds. *Regionalization in a Globalizing World: A Comparative Perspective on Forms, Actors, and Processes.* London: Zed Books, 2001.

Seidman, Ann. "Towards Integrated Development in Southern Africa." *Development and Peace* 2 (1981): 67–97.

———, and Neva Magketla. *Outposts of Monopoly Capitalism.* London: Zed Press, 1980.

———, and Neva Seidman. *South Africa and U.S. Multinational Corporations.* Westport, Conn.: Lawrence Hill & Co., 1978.

Seleny, Anna. "Old Political Rationalities and New Democracies: Compromise and Confrontation in Hungary and Poland." *World Politics* 51 (July 1999): 484–519.

Sethi, S. Prakash, and Bharat Bhalla. "Strategic Economic Alliances: An Approach to Integrating the Economy of Post-Apartheid South Africa into Sub-Saharan Africa." *Development Southern Africa* 9 (1992): 331–345.

Shaw, Timothy M. "Africa in the Global Political Economy: Globalization, Regionalization, or Marginalization?" In *The New Regionalism and the Future of Security and Development,* ed. Björn Hettne, András Inotai, and Osvaldo Sunkel, 93–120. New York: St. Martin's Press, 2000.

Sidaway, James, and Richard Gibbs. "SADC, COMESA, SACU: Contradictory Formats for Regional Integration in Southern Africa: Reconfiguring the Region." In *South Africa in Southern Africa: Reconfiguring the Region,* ed. David Simon, 164–186. Athens: Ohio University Press, 1998.

Simon, David. "Regional Development—Environment Discourses, Policies and Practices in Post-Apartheid Southern Africa." Revised version of the paper presented at the International Geographical Union Congress, Durban, South Africa, August 4–7, 2002.

———, ed. *South Africa in Southern Africa: Reconfiguring the Region.* Athens: Ohio University Press, 1998.

Sisk, Timothy. *Democratization in South Africa: The Elusive Social Contract.* Princeton, N.J.: Princeton University Press, 1995.

Smit, P. "Regional Challenges Facing South Africa." *Southern African Forum Position Paper* 12 (1989): 6–11.

Söderbaum, Fredrik. "Institutional Aspects of the Maputo Development Corridor." Research report presented at the Regional Workshop, Development Policy Research Unit's Southern Africa Project, Windhoek, South Africa, September 28–29, 2000.

———. "The New Regionalism and the Quest for Development Cooperation and Integration in Southern Africa." Minor Field Study Series 73. Department of Economics at Lund University, Lund, Sweden, 1996.

———. "The New Regionalism in Southern Africa." *Politeia* 17 (1998): 75–94.

———. "The Role of the Regional Factor in West Africa." In *The New Regionalism and the Future of Security and Development,* ed. Björn Hettne, András Inotai, and Osvaldo Sunkel, 121–142. New York: St. Martin's Press, 2000.

———, and Ian Taylor, eds. *Kick-Starting Development? Reconstructing the Maputo Corridor in the Context of Globalisation.* London: Ashgate, 2003.

Solingen, Etel. *Regional Orders at Century's Dawn: Global and Domestic Influences on Grand Strategy.* Princeton, N.J.: Princeton University Press, 1998.

South Africa Chamber of Business (SACOB). "A Concept for the Development of a New Industrial Policy for South Africa." SACOB, Johannesburg, South Africa, May 30, 1991.

———. "The Formulation of a New Industrial Policy for South Africa: Discussion Document." SACOB, Johannesburg, South Africa, September 1993.

———. "South Africa's Options for Future Relations with Southern Africa and the European Community: Discussion Document." SACOB, Johannesburg, South Africa, October 19, 1992.

South African Consulate General. "Interdependence and Co-operation in Southern Africa." South African Briefing Paper no. 3/90, South African Consulate General, February 1990.

South African Government, Department of Foreign Affairs. "South African Foreign Policy Discussion Document." Department of Foreign Affairs, Pretoria, 1996.

———. "Statement on the Signature of the Cotonou Convention." June 22, 2000.

South African Reserve Bank. *The Reconstruction of the South African Economy: A Normative Model Approach.* Pretoria: SARB, March 1993.

Southall, Roger. "The South African Elections of 1994: The Remaking of a Dominant-Party State." *Journal of Modern African Studies* 32 (1994): 629–655.

Southern African Development Community (SADC). "Management of Regional Cooperation." Unpublished paper, SADC, Gaborone, Botswana, January 1994.

———. "Southern Africa: A Framework and Strategy for Building the Community." SADC, Harare, Zimbabwe, January 27–29, 1993.

Stadler, Alf. *The Political Economy of Modern South Africa.* London: Croom Helm, 1987.

Stals, Chris. "South African Exchange Rate Policy: A Reserve Bank Perspective." In

South Africa and the World Economy in the 1990s, ed. Pauline Baker, Alex Boraine, and Warren Krafchik, 148–150. Washington, D.C.: Brookings Institution, 1993.

Standish, B., and D. Galloway. "Exports, Efficiency and Capital in South African Manufacturing." *Journal for Studies in Economics and Econometrics* 15 (1991): 11–30.

Stedman, Stephen John, ed. *South Africa: The Political Economy of Transformation.* Boulder, Colo.: Lynne Rienner, 1994.

Stein, Arthur. "Coordination and Collaboration: Regimes in an Anarchic World." In *Neorealism and Neoliberalism,* ed. David Baldwin. New York: Columbia University Press, 1993.

———. *Why Nations Cooperate: Circumstance and Choice in International Relations,* 29–59. Ithaca, N.Y.: Cornell University Press, 1990.

Stein, Howard. "Deindustrialization, Adjustment, the World Bank and the IMF in Africa." *World Development* 20 (1992): 83–95.

Stein, Janice Gross, and Louis Pauly, eds. *Choosing to Co-operate: How States Avoid Loss.* Baltimore: Johns Hopkins University Press, 1993.

Stevens, Christopher. "Global Trends and Implications for Southern Africa." Paper presented at a Workshop on Reconstituting and Democratising the Southern African Customs Union, Gaborone, Botswana, March 6–8, 1994.

———, Jane Kennan, and Richard Ketley. "EC Trade Preferences and Post-Apartheid South Africa." *International Affairs* 69 (1993): 89–109.

Stoneman, Colin, and Carol Thompson. "Southern Africa After Apartheid." Economic Briefing Paper no. 4, United Nations, December 1991.

Swatuk, Larry. "Power and Water: The Coming Order in Southern Africa." In *The New Regionalism and the Future of Security and Development,* ed. Björn Hettne, András Inotai, and Osvaldo Sunkel, 210–247. New York: St. Martin's Press, 2000.

Synge, Richard. "SADC Tackles Donor Doubts." *Africa Recovery* 7, no. 1 (June 1993): 10.

Taylor, Ian. "Globalization and Regionalization in Africa: Reactions to Attempts at Neo-Liberal Regionalism." *Review of International Political Economy* 10 (2003): 310–330.

———. *Stuck in Middle GEAR: South Africa's Post-Apartheid Foreign Relations.* Westport, Conn.: Praeger, 2001.

Thede, Nancy. "Introduction: Post-Apartheid in Southern Africa—An Era of Change?" In *A Post-Apartheid Southern Africa,* ed. Nancy Thede and Pierre Beaudet, 1–30. New York: St. Martin's Press, 1993.

Thomas, Rosalind. "A South African Perspective on the SADC Trade and Development Protocol." Development Bank of Southern Africa, Midrand, South Africa, 1997.

———. "A South African Perspective on the SADC Trade and Development Protocol." Paper prepared for the Friedrich Ebert Stiftung Institute, Johannesburg, April 1997.

———. "The WTO and Trade Cooperation between the ACP and the EU: Assessing the Options." European Center for Development Policy Management Working Paper no. 16. Brussels, 1997.

Thompson, Carol. "African Initiatives for Development: The Practice of Regional Economic Cooperation in Southern Africa." *Journal of International Affairs* 46 (1992): 125–144.

———. *Harvests under Fire: Regional Cooperation for Food Security in Southern Africa.* Atlantic Highlands, N.J.: Zed Books, 1991.

———. *Regional Economic Policy under Crisis Conditions: The Case of the Southern African Development Coordination Conference (SADCC).* Uppsala: Scandinavian Institute of African Studies, 1986.

Tjonneland, Elling Njal. "Pax Pretoriana: The Fall of Apartheid and the Politics of Regional Destabilization." Discussion Paper 2. Scandinavian Institute of African Studies, Uppsala, 1989.

Tostensen, Arne. "What Role for SADC(C) in the Post-Apartheid Era?" In *Southern Africa After Apartheid: Regional Integration and External Resources,* ed. Bertil Odén, 147–173. Uppsala: The Scandinavian Institute of African Studies, 1993.

Tow, William. *Subregional Security Cooperation in the Third World.* Boulder, Colo.: Lynne Rienner, 1990.

Tsie, Balefi. "States and Markets in the Southern African Development Community (SADC): Beyond the Neo-Liberal Paradigm." *Journal of Southern African Studies* 22 (1996): 75–98.

UNCTAD Secretariat. "Trade Expansion and Economic Integration among Developing Countries." In *Economic Integration and Third World Development,* ed. Pradip Ghosh, 159–176. Westport, Conn.: Greenwood Press, 1984.

United Nations Economic and Social Council, "Which Way Economic Integration in Southern Africa? A Review of the Studies Carried Out by the World Bank/IMF/EU and the African Development Bank." Paper presented at the African Regional Workshop on Regional Integration, Cape Town, South Africa, March 24, 1994.

United Nations Industrial Development Organization. "Industrial Co-operation through the Southern African Development Co-ordination Conference (SADCC)." UNIDO document UNIDO/IS.570, October 15, 1985.

Vaitsos, Constantine. "Crisis in Regional Economic Cooperation (Integration) among Developing Countries: A Survey." *World Development* 6 (1978): 719–769.

Vale, Colin. "South Africa on a Derelict Continent." Occasional Paper no. 6. South African Institute of International Affairs, Johannesburg, 1982.

Vale, Peter C. J. *Security and Politics in South Africa: The Regional Dimension.* Boulder, Colo.: Lynne Rienner, 2003.

———. "Some Thoughts on the Political Economy of Control." In *The Constellation of States,* ed. Willie Breytenbach, 28–30. Johannesburg: South Africa Foundation, 1980.

———, Larry Swatuk, and Bertil Odén, eds. *Theory, Change and Southern Africa's Future* Basingstoke: Palgrave, 2001.

van Nieuwkerk, Anthoni. "Foreign Policy-Making in South Africa: Exploring Context, Actors, and Processes." Paper presented at 19th World Congress of the International Political Science Association, Durban, South Africa, July 1, 2003.

———. *Transitional Politics in South Africa: From Confrontation to Democracy?* Johannesburg: The South African Institute of International Affairs, 1992.

———, and Gary van Staden, eds. *Southern Africa at the Crossroads: Prospects for the Political Economy of the Region.* Johannesburg: South Africa Institute for International Affairs, 1991.

van Staden, Gary, and Malcolm Stewart. "Financial Markets and the Availability of Credit Facilities." In *Prospects for Progress: Critical Choices for Southern Africa,* ed. Minnie Venter, 84–97. Cape Town: Longman, 1994.

Van Zyl, Johan. "Southern Africa: Towards Closer Economic Co-operation in the 1990s—A Discussion Paper." Unpublished paper, Development Bank of Southern Africa, Midrand, South Africa, November 1990.

Vansina, Jan. *Paths in the Rainforests: Toward a History of Political Tradition in Equatorial Africa.* Madison: University of Wisconsin Press, 1990.

Venter, Minnie, ed. *Prospects for Progress: Critical Choices for Southern Africa.* Cape Town: Longman, 1994.

Verrier, Antony. *The Road to Zimbabwe.* London: Jonathan Cape, 1986.

von Holdt, Karl. "The LRA Agreement: 'Worker Victory' or 'Miserable Compromise'?" *SA Labour Bulletin* 19 (1995): 16–26.

Vorster, Paul J. "Interdependence of States in Southern Africa." *Southern African Forum Position Paper* 12 (1989): 1–8.

Wallace, William. *The Transformation of Western Europe.* London: Royal Institute of International Affairs, 1990.

Walters, Jon. "Renegotiating Dependency: The Case of the Southern African Customs Union." *Journal of Common Market Studies* 28 (1989): 29–53.

Waltz, Kenneth N. "Reflections on *Theory of International Politics:* A Response to My Critics." In *Neorealism and Its Critics,* ed. Robert O. Keohane, 322–346. New York: Columbia University Press, 1986.

Wangwe, S. W. "A Comparative Analysis of the PTA and SADCC Approaches to Regional Economic Integration." In *The Long-Term Perspective Study of Sub-Saharan Africa.* Vol. 4, *Proceedings of a Workshop on Regional Integration and Cooperation.* Washington, D.C.: The World Bank, 1990.

Webb, Michael. "International Economic Structures, Government Interests, and International Coordination of Macroeconomic Adjustment Policies." *International Organization* 45 (1991): 309–342.

Weber, Steven. "The European Bank for Reconstruction and Development." *International Organization* 48 (1994): 1–39.

Weimer, Bernard. "The Southern African Development Coordination Conference (SADCC), with Specific Reference to South Africa." Stiftung Wissenshaf und Politik (SWP), December 1990.

Weisfelder, Richard. "The Southern African Development Coordination Conference (SADCC)." *South Africa International* 13 (1982): 74–95.

Wendt, Alexander. "Anarchy Is What States Make of It." *International Organization* 46 (1992): 391–427.

Wheatcroft, Geoffrey. *The Landlords: The Exploits and Exploitation of South Africa's Mining Magnates.* New York: Atheneum, 1986.

Whiteside, Alan. *Industrialization in Southern Africa: Policies and Results.* London: Friedrich Ebert Stiftung, 1987.

Williams, Paul, and Ian Taylor. "Neoliberalism and the Political Economy of the 'New' South Africa." *New Political Economy* 5 (2000): 21–40.

Wionczek, Migule. "Can the Broken Humpty-Dumpty Be Put Together Again and by Whom? Comments on the Vaitsos Survey." *World Development* 6 (1978): 779–782.

———. "Regionalism for Viable Economic Integration." In *International Regionalism: Readings,* ed. Joseph Nye, 287–303. Boston: Little, Brown and Company, 1979.

World Bank. *Accelerated Development in Sub-Saharan Africa: An Agenda for Action.* New York: Oxford University Press, 1982.

———. "Cross-Border Initiative in Eastern and Southern Africa: Regional Integration by Emergence." *Findings* 166 (September 2000). Available online at http://www.worldbank.org/afr/findings/english/find166.htm.

———. "An Economic Perspective on South Africa." Southern Africa Department, The World Bank, Washington, D.C., May 1993.

———. *Global Economic Prospects and the Developing Countries, 1995.* Washington, D.C.: World Bank, 1995.

———. "Intra-Regional Trade in Sub-Saharan Africa." Economics and Finance Division, Technical Division, Africa Region, World Bank, Washington, D.C., 1991.

———. *Prior Review Contracts Approved by the World Bank in FY 93 by Country of Sup-*

plier. Operations Policy Department, Procurement Policy and Coordination Unit, World Bank, Washington, D.C., January 1994.

———. *Prior Review Contracts Approved by the World Bank in FY 94 by Country of Supplier.* Operations Policy Department, Procurement Policy and Coordination Unit, World Bank, Washington, D.C., September 1994.

———, the African Development Bank, the International Monetary Fund, and the Commission of the European Communities. "Concept Paper: Initiative to Facilitate Cross-Border Private Investment, Trade and Payments in Eastern and Southern Africa and the Indian Ocean." June 24, 1993.

Worrall, Denis. "The Republic of South Africa and Detente." Edited version of an address to a meeting of the Institute of International Affairs, Salisbury, June 24, 1974.

Yarbrough, Beth, and Robert Yarbrough. *Cooperation and Governance among Nations.* Ithaca, N.Y.: Cornell University Press, 1970.

Young, Oran. "International Regimes: Problems of Concept Formation." *World Politics* 20 (1980): 331–356.

———. "Political Discontinuities in the International System." *World Politics* 20 (1968): 369–392.

Zysman, John. *Governments, Markets, and Growth: Financial Systems and the Politics of Industrial Change.* Ithaca, N.Y.: Cornell University Press, 1983.

Newspapers and Magazines

Business Times (Johannesburg)
The Citizen (Johannesburg)
The Economist (London)
Economist Intelligence Unit, South African Country Profile 1992–1993
Financial Mail (Johannesburg)
Financial Times (London)
The New York Times
SA Labour Bulletin
Southern Africa Political and Economic Monthly
Southern African Economist
The Sowetan
The Star (Johannesburg)
The Weekly Mail (Johannesburg)

Interviews

South Africa and Botswana, 1993–1994

Bryan Bench, Coordinator of International Relations, Development Bank of Southern Africa, Midrand, February 14, 1994.

Ronnie Bethlehem, Johannesburg Consolidated Investment, Johannesburg economist, January 25, 1994.

Dr. Booysen, political analyst, Northern Transvaal Chamber of Industries, Pretoria, February 10, 1994.

David Brink, Chief Executive, Sankorp Limited, member of National Economic Council, Business Forum, Sandton, February 3, 1994.

Dave Brown, Managing Director, Stanbic Bank, Botswana Unlimited, Gaborone, March 23, 1994.

John Cambell, Council for Political Affairs, U.S. Embassy, Pretoria, February 2, 1994.

John Chigweedire, Zimbabwean Trade Representative to South Africa, Johannesburg, February 15, 1994.

J. Michael Cleverley, Counselor for Economic Affairs, U.S. Embassy, February 2, 1994.

P. J. Geringer, Assistant Director, South Africa Department of Transportation, Pretoria, March 8, 1994.

Pete Gloster, Assistant General Manager, GM Exchange Control, South African Reserve Bank, Pretoria, November 23, 1993.

C. T. Hattingh, South Africa Department of Trade and Industry, Pretoria, February 28, 1994.

Ernie Heath, Director, South African Tourism Board, Pretoria, February 28, 1994.

Andre Heydenrayh, Business Manager (Africa), Spoornot, Johannesburg, November 22, 1993.

Derik Hudson, consultant, Gaborone, March 22, 1994.

P. E. Immelman, Director, Africa Multilateral Department, Department of Foreign Affairs, Pretoria, November 8, 1993.

Adam Jacobs, Senior Economist, Amalgamated Banks of South Africa, Johannesburg, November 15, 1993.

Paul Jourdan, Department of Economic Planning, ANC, Johannesburg, November 3, 1993.

Judy Konz, executive, ESKOM, Sandton, February 1, 1994.

Chris Kotzé, economist, Industrial Development Corporation, Sandton, April 18, 1994.

N. M. Krige, Deputy Director-General, South African Department of Water Affairs, Pretoria, February 28, 1994.

Desmond Krogh, advisor (member of NEF), South African Reserve Bank, Pretoria, April 20, 1993.

Erich Leistner, former director, Africa Institute, Pretoria, November 8, 1993.

Herman Lemmer, Deputy Chief Executive, Road Freight Association, Johannesburg, March 7, 1994.

Elias Links, Chief Director, International Finance, South Africa Department of Finance, Pretoria, March 3, 1994.

Berénice Lue, Executive Vice President, Marketing and Business Development, CSIR, Pretoria, March 16, 1994.

Gavin Maasdorp, Professor of Economics, Natal University, Durban, October 27, 1993.

Michael McDonald, Head of Economic Division, Steel and Engineering Industries, Federation of South Africa, Johannesburg, March 15, 1994.

Theo Malan, Central Economic Advisory Service, Pretoria, March 18, 1994.

Alister Morphet, Head, Africa Division, First Merchant Bank, Johannesburg, March 1, 1994.

L. B. Monyake, Deputy Executive Secretary, Southern African Development Community, Gaborone, May 23, 1993.

Stef Naude, former director-general, Department of Trade and Industry, Pretoria, South Africa, April 26, 1994.

Ted Osborne, Economist, Economist Unit, Nedbank, Johannesburg, February 25, 1994.

Joseph Poolman, Executive Director, Afrikaanse Handelsinstituut, Pretoria, April 20, 1994.

Beth Robertson, Portfolio Manager, International Trade, South African Chamber of Business, Johannesburg, February 14, 1993.

Paul Runge, Senior Manager, Trade and Development, South African Foreign Trade Organisation, Sandton, February 2, 1994.

Joseph Sala, First Secretary, U.S. Embassy, Pretoria, February 2, 1994.

Herbie Schultz, International Relations Department, Amalgamated Banks of South Africa Bank, Johannesburg, November 15, 1993.

Smit, J. J., Deputy Director-General, South Africa Department of Transportation, Pretoria, March 8, 1994.

Rosalind Thomas, DBSA, Midland, November 12, 1993.

Max Tlakula, First Vice President and Acting Director, National African Chamber of Commerce, Johannesburg, March 2, 1994.

Ben Turok, Director, Institute for African Alternatives, Johannesburg, February 22, 1994.

Jackie Walters, Professor (transportation), Rand Afrikaans University, Johannesburg, October 18, 1993.

Pierre Voges, Assistant Director, International Economic Affairs, South Africa Department of Foreign Affairs, Pretoria, February 2, 1994.

Charles White, Manager African Operations, Standard Bank, Johannesburg, March 7, 1994.

Hein Wiese, Manager, Economic Department, Industrial Development Corporation, Sandton, April 10, 1994.

Len Van Zyl, Chief Executive, South African Foreign Trade Organisation, Sandton, December 14, 1993.

South Africa, 1998

Talitha Bertelsmann, European Union Fellow, South African Institute for International Affairs, Standard Bank, Johannesburg, August 3, 1998.

Eric Broekhuysen, Director, Department of Foreign Affairs, Africa Regional Development, Pretoria, August 6, 1998.

Rashad Cassim, Director, Trade and Industrial Policy Secretariat, Johannesburg, August 3, 1998.

Robert Davies, Member of Parliament, Cape Town, August 13, 1998.

Lolette Kritzinger-van Niekerk, Policy Analyst/Economist, Southern Africa Business Unit, Development Bank of Southern Africa, Midrand, August 4, 1998.

Marina Mayer, South Africa Department of Trade and Industry, August 6, 1998.

Michael McDonald, Head, Economic Division, Steel and Engineering Industries, Federation of South Africa, Johannesburg, August 7, 1998.

Shan Ramburuth, National Economic Development and Labour Council, Trade and Industry Chamber, Johannesburg, August 5, 1998.

Bess Robertson, Personal Assistant to the Director General, South Africa Chamber of Business, Johannesburg, August 19, 1998.

Max Sisulu, Chief Whip Majority Party (ANC), Member of Parliament, Cape Town, August 13, 1998.

Rosalind Thomas, Legal Advisor/Policy Analyst, Development Bank of Southern Africa, Johannesburg, August 4, 1998.

Ben Turok, Member of Parliament, Cape Town, August 13, 1998.

Neil Van Heerden, Executive Director, South Africa Foundation, former South African ambassador to the EU, Johannesburg, August 20, 1998.

Brussels, 1999

Jean Claude Boidin, Head of Unit, Southern Africa II and Task Force South Africa, European Commission, May 12, 1999.

Elisa Links, South African Ambassador to the EU, May 11, 1999.

Zedekia Ngavirue, Namibian Ambassador to the EU, May 13, 1999.

South Africa and Mozambique, 2002

Ivete Arao, Project Coordinator, MOZAL Community Development Trust, Maputo, May 22, 2002.

Alfred Guiamba, Secretary General, National Union of Metal and Energy Workers, Maputo, May 24, 2002.

Gerhard Kuhn, Economist, Industrial Development Corporation, Sandton, May 20, 2002.

Jaco Kriek, Executive Vice President, Projects Division, Industrial Development Corporation, Sandton, May 20, 2002.

Antonio Libombo, Director, Mozambique Ports and Railways, Maputo, May 23, 2002.

Alcido Mausse, Manager, MOZAL Community Development Trust, Maputo, May 22, 2002.

Antonio Macamo, Investment Promotion Center, Maputo, May 22, 2002.

Alfredo Namitete, Governor of Maputo Province, Maputo, May 23, 2002.

Ken Shirley, Operations Director, Maputo Port Development Company, Maputo, May 23, 2002.

Peter Wilshaw, General Manager, Mozal Aluminium Smelter, Maputo, May 22, 2002.

Index

James J. Hentz is Associate Professor of International Studies at the Virginia Military Institute. He is co-editor (with Morten Boas) of *New and Critical Security and Regionalism: Beyond the Nation State.* He was Visiting Fulbright Scholar at the Miklós Zrínyi National Defense University, Budapest, in the spring of 2003.